Going Public

Going Public

Feminism and the Shifting Boundaries of the Private Sphere

Edited by
Joan W. Scott and Debra Keates

UNIVERSITY OF ILLINOIS PRESS
URBANA AND CHAMPAIGN

Manufactured in the United States of America
1 2 3 4 5 C P 5 4 3 2 1

∞ This book is printed on acid-free paper.

Library of Congress Cataloging-in-Publication Data
Going public : feminism and the shifting boundaries
of the private sphere / edited by Joan W. Scott and Debra Keates.
p. cm.
Includes bibliographical references and index.
ISBN 0-252-02964-X (cl. : alk. paper)
ISBN 0-252-07209-X (pbk. : alk.paper)
1. Feminist theory. 2. Women in public life. 3. Privacy. 4. Sex role.
5. Women—Social conditions—Cross-cultural studies.
I. Scott, Joan Wallach. II. Keates, Debra.
HQ1190G64 2004
305.42'01—dc22 2004012106

CONTENTS

PART 4. DISPLACEMENTS OF THE PRIVATE/PUBLIC OPPOSITION

PREFACE

THIS BOOK OFFERS a group of essays aimed at rethinking the public/private distinction as it has been used by feminists in academic and political work. The categories of public and private are fundamental not only to Western liberal democracy (and thus to feminism's critique of it) but also to global human rights movements in the twentieth and twenty-first centuries. Interrogating these categories is thus a project with far-reaching implications.

The essays that follow provide a critical look at the operations of public and private. They do not contain an alternative set of firm definitions nor a single theoretical model. Instead, there are a series of unusual "takes" on the problem from different disciplines, different countries, and different theoretical perspectives. In their diversity and unexpected approaches the essays serve to unsettle received opinion and provoke new discussion. They rewrite the history of public/private—its operations and effects—as a more complicated story than is usually told. They offer critiques of and substitutes for standard disciplinary treatments and pose difficult questions about the nature and direction of social change. How does non-normative experience translate into resistance? What happens when different normative systems clash? Is public/private an ever-moving boundary and in force no matter what its different meanings? Can we develop new analytic concepts that would, instead of redrawing the boundary once again, dissolve it entirely? These are the kinds of questions the essays raise.

Historical Context

Since the inception of second wave feminism in the West scholars have been concerned with the boundaries that separate the public and private spheres, asking how it came to be that the private sphere—associated with family and emotional intimacy—was generally considered to be the domain of women, whereas the public sphere—associated with politics and rational activity—was a quintessentially masculine field. During the 1970s and 1980s feminists gave the public/private distinction a historical genealogy associated with the rise of capitalism and its attendant bourgeois ideologies, and they argued that it had outlived its capacity to regulate gendered divisions of labor. Because much of the scholarship had shown how closely tied state policy was to the creation and maintenance of the public/private distinction, feminists called for new policies to implement greater equality between women and men.

But the articulation of new policies was not as easy in practice as in theory. And the relation between public and private became the occasion for intense debate and reevaluation within feminist circles. One major area of contention involved the role of the state in relation to women's activities. Did women's sexual and reproductive activities belong to the private realm, or were they also to be considered as, in part, public functions? And which activities fell into which category?

Although feminists argued that the right of privacy and the right to some self-determination in matters of fertility meant the state should not regulate access to abortion or reproductive technologies, they also claimed that women were entitled to state protection for securing paid maternity leaves and the provision of welfare support. And they could not agree on the grounds for demanding state protection. Were women entitled to extraordinary consideration as the bearers and rearers of children, or was pregnancy better treated as if it were a disability, "a passing indisposition" like gout or a cold? If feminists granted the importance of the state in securing the rights of citizenship and preventing discriminatory educational and employment practices, did they want to concede that the state's jurisdiction extended to the regulation of population, sexuality, and marriage? And was state regulation of the private sphere an inevitable consequence of state guarantees of political rights? Was this a risk worth taking? No single consensus emerged on these questions.

In making explicitly political arguments in order to campaign for rights and entitlements, feminists faced the difficult question of how best to represent the interests of women and analyze the structural problem of sexual difference. They found themselves in a paradoxical situation of claiming both that women ought to be treated as men's equals and that sexual difference ought to be taken into account in any consideration of what equality might mean. Thus the question emerged of how far it was desirable or possible to level the differences between the sexes in the representation of feminist aims within the political sphere.

Psychologists and psychoanalysts, too, weighed in on such issues as equal pay, maternity leave, reproductive freedom, and family organization. Opinions ranged from those which held that changes in social practices (more women working, more fathers sharing child care) might gradually affect the development of gendered subjectivity, to those who insisted on the primacy of sexual difference for the formation of gendered identities. In one approach the public had determining effects on the private. In others the private was the ground on which social policy should be built (sexual subjectivity was taken to be relatively independent of and prior to social roles; girls' distinctive intellectual capacities and requirements needed to be appreciated by teachers; women "preferred" less competitive jobs than men). Here again, nothing that could be considered a feminist consensus was achieved. Indeed, not only were there internal differences within national feminist movements but there were also important national differences based at least in part on the existence (or not) of state welfare provisions.

The discussion of public and private was further complicated in the 1990s by the intensification of international and comparative feminism, a process accelerated by a series of United Nations conferences on women that began in 1975 in Mexico City and culminated at Beijing in 1995. At these conferences, delegates from outside the West offered ways of thinking about the relationships of public and private, and those between women and the state, that took local political, social, and cultural circumstances into account. It became clear that there was no transparent boundary between the public and the private. Indeed, "public" and "private" had different meanings in different national and cultural contexts. If Western feminists had challenged the public/private distinction by historicizing it, these conferences further destabilized it by demonstrating its vast cultural diversity.

At the same time, however, the international women's conferences themselves were contributing to the process of redrafting the public/private boundaries on a transnational scale as part of the process of globalization (a process that involved diffusing new technologies, reorganizing economic structures, revaluing national sovereignty, disseminating liberal notions of rights, and creating vast networks of implementation and resistance). The idea of rights, once understood as pertaining to the political realm (citizenship and freedom of expression, religion, and association), now also became associated with autonomy; reproduction ("the right of all women to control all aspects of their health, in particular their own fertility"); marital equality ("equal rights, opportunities and access to resources, equal sharing of responsibilities for the family by men and women, and a harmonious partnership between them are critical to their well-being and that of their families as well as to the consolidation of democracy"); and elimination of domestic violence ("prevent and eliminate all forms of violence against women and girls." All quotations in this paragraph are from the final Program of Action of the 1995 Beijing Conference.

The declaration that "women's rights are human rights" offered a universal standard that local women's groups would use, it was hoped, to demand change. It was also a standard that blurred boundaries between the public and the private because states were expected to protect women's rights on matters such as fertility and domestic violence, yet no right of privacy was invoked. From one perspective there is no longer a private realm at all. The 1970s' feminist slogan "the personal is the political," once a radical critique of the public/private, political/domestic divides, now legitimates the law. From another perspective, the terms of the private have only shifted. What has been the history of public/private discourses? How have they changed? In what ways and with what effects? The essays in this collection address those issues.

The Essays

The essays in this volume were originally prepared for a conference held at the Rockefeller Foundation Conference Center in Bellagio, Italy, in December 2000. The conference was interdisciplinary and international, in line with Rockefeller Foundation requirements and also because we wanted to think about public/private from as many perspectives as we could. The point was not to produce an exercise in comparative social science but to have materials that would permit collective theorizing. As is usually the case at such meetings, we had intense discussions of the theoretical implications of the papers but reached no consensus. There were, however, a set of recurring themes in our deliberations, and we have used these to organize the presentation of the essays in this volume.

An echo of the conference is evident in this book in the many references each author makes to others. In rewriting their conference papers, they engaged with (grappling, challenging, confirming) the ideas put forward by colleagues. This conversation links the disparate topics in unusual and surprising ways. In addition, Denise Riley's prologue offers an ironic comment on all that follows. Her plea for "the right to be lonely" not only confounds distinctions of public/private, insider/outsider, social/personal but also gives us pause about the grounds to which we so easily resort as we seek alternatives to them.

Despite their differences (of topic, focus, analytic position, and tone) the essays share a common assumption—that public/private has multiple and complex meanings that are not limited to gender narrowly conceived. Thus, Part 1 deals with the different ways in which public attribution constructs seemingly "private" identities, those of race, sex, and sexuality. Wendy Brown contrasts the "racialization" of Jews and the "sexualization" of (Christian) women in European liberal political theory concerned with national consolidation. As a result of their different characterizations (Jews as a race, women as "the sex"), attempts to enfranchise these two excluded groups within the field of universal citizenship took two different forms: toleration for Jews and emancipation for women. Afsaneh Najmabadi and Rosalind Morris deal with how resistance to Europeanization at different moments in the histories of Iran and Thailand set national standards of appropriate sexual behavior (defining what is morally acceptable, what is corrupt, what is excessive, and what is foreign). Melissa Wright examines the ways in which male factory managers legitimize their control of the laboring bodies of women workers in terms of the management of "waste." In the process, the intimate activities and functions considered most immune to employer and IMF oversight (dating, sexual liaisons, menstruation, and even love) become regulated by the employment contract.

If the essays in Part 1 detail the myriad ways in which the public constructs the private, those in Part 2 ask whether "private" practices can exist without some form of public recognition and whether they can arise and continue to exist independently of such recognition. Judith Butler examines this problem from every conceivable angle and explores the limits imposed on radical sexual politics by rendering them in normative terms (reducing new forms of kinship to "the family" or homosexual alliances to "marriage"). Zakia Pathak and Joan Scott deal with the mutability of normativity (in India and France) as it is expressed and contested in law. Pathak argues that although law constructs subjects, it does not do so in a linear or predictable fashion. Indeed, when law courts must address the enigmatic sexual behavior of women, in some cases the "women begin to perceive new possibilities of freedom and equality." Rayna Rapp and Faye Ginsburg address the ways in which "wounds in kinship and narrative practice" brought about by living with disabled children have "reshaped the habitus of daily life" and reconceived the meanings of kinship beyond the biological family. For them, changes in lived experience, when collectively recognized, have the power to alter normative rules. Rogaia Abusharaf stresses the tensions between customary practice (female genital circumcision) and modernizing regimes, offering a cautionary note about the impact of "non-indigenous conceptualizations of rights" on the "relational force" of local custom. Here the question is not about internal exceptions to prevailing rules but about conflict between two normative systems, African custom and international human rights.

Part 3 addresses the ways in which scholars study and evaluate change. It takes up some of the analytic figures used to understand conceptual arguments and their depiction of changed realities in places that have experienced profound economic and political transition. The object of Eric Fassin's investigation is the operations of social scientific definition. He focuses on the case of sociological and anthropological intervention in the French debates about family reform in the 1990s. Susan Gal analyzes the public/private distinction as a "communicative phenomenon," a complex and contradictory logic in everyday usage that has been rendered as a dichotomy by social analysts. Through what she calls "fractal analysis" she seeks to restore the many and shifting levels of meaning that have been mistaken for a single distinction, a mistake she believes may lead to the inability of social scientists to analyze different political situations (in her case, postcommunist Eastern Europe). Like Gal, Peggy Watson is interested in finding an intellectual paradigm that will give feminists a better way of thinking about public/private in the formerly communist countries of Eastern Europe. She not only insists on the different status and position of women in Western and Eastern Europe but also puts her analysis in the context of changing political ideologies. In addition, she offers a new metaphor—"curved space"—for thinking about gender and civil society. Also like Gal, Gail Hershatter explores the impact of shifting definitions—this time those made by the Chinese communist leadership about women's productive and domestic labor—on the lives of women whose work was rendered invisible by changed official perspectives. Returning to some of the themes in Part 2, Hershatter documents the power of state ideology to set the terms of social practice and the toll that nonrecognition of women's activity in the domestic realm takes on individual lives.

Part 4 presents alternatives to the public/private distinction. Ellen Rooney offers, in an innovative move, the semiprivate room as a metaphor that refuses the either/or of the binary opposition public/private. A term taken from "everyday life," the semiprivate "figures neither an inside, nor an outside, but the conscious practice of drawing boundaries in a field neither the private nor the public can anticipate or guarantee." Miglena Nikolchina provides ironic counterpoint to Rooney's optimism in a retrospective and fantastical account of the seminar—an institution of resistance to the communist regime in Bulgaria that was at once inside and outside the system. An example of the power of refiguration to reform both paradigm and structure, the seminar, she argues, helped bring about the demise of a totalitarian regime "by theory." The changes did not endure—they never do. The dream of permanent, liberatory transformation can never be finally fulfilled. The work of critical thinking, as exemplified in Nikolchina's essay as well as in this book as a whole, goes on.

The editors are grateful to The Rockefeller Foundation, especially Susan Garfield, and to the staff of the Rockefeller Foundation's Bellagio Study and Conference Center, Gianna Celli and Laura Podio in particular. The Hans Sigrist Foundation of the University of Bern, Switzerland, also provided critical support. Closer to home, we wish to thank Deborah Koehler and Nancy Cotterman for making both conference and book possible.

ACKNOWLEDGMENTS

Prologue: Denise Riley, "The Right to Be Lonely," was originally published in *differences: A Journal of Feminist Cultural Studies* 13 (Spring 2002): 1–13. © 2002 Brown University and *differences: A Journal of Feminist Cultural Studies*. All rights reserved. Used with permission.

Chapter 3: Rosalind C. Morris, "Failures of Domestication: Speculations on Globality, Economy, and the Sex of Excess in Thailand," was originally published in *differences: A Journal of Feminist Cultural Studies* 13 (Spring 2002): 45–76. © 2002 Brown University and *differences: A Journal of Feminist Cultural Studies*. All rights reserved. Used with permission.

Chapter 7: Rayna Rapp and Faye Ginsburg, "Enabling Disability: Rewriting Kinship, Reimagining Citizenship," was originally published in *Public Culture* 13, no. 3 (2001): 533–56. © 2001 Duke University Press. All rights reserved. Used by permission of the publisher.

Chapter 8: Rogaia Mustafa Abusharaf, "Virtuous Cuts: Female Genital Circumcision in an African Ontology," was originally published in *differences: A Journal of Feminist Cultural Studies* 12, no. 1 (2001): 112–40. © 2001 Duke University Press. All rights reserved. Used by permission of the publisher.

Chapter 9: Joan W. Scott, "Feminist Family Politics," was originally published in *French Politics, Culture and Society* 17 (Summer–Fall 1999): 20–30.

Chapter 10: Eric Fassin, "Usages of Science and Science of Usages: On Homoparental Families," was originally published in *L'Homme: Revue Française d'Anthropologie* 154–55 (April–Sept. 2000): 391–408, in a special issue entitled "Question de parenté."

Chapter 11: Susan Gal, "A Semiotics of the Public/Private Distinction," was originally published in *differences: A Journal of Feminist Cultural Studies* 13 (Spring 2002): 77–95. © 2002 Brown University and *differences: A Journal of Feminist Cultural Studies.* All rights reserved. Used with permission.

Chapter 12: Peggy Watson, "Rethinking Transition: Globalism, Gender, and Class," was originally published in *International Feminist Journal of Politics,* vol. 2, no. 2. <http://www.tandf.co.uk>.

Chapter 13: Gail Hershatter, "Making the Visible Invisible: The Fate of 'the Private in Revolutionary China,'" was originally published in *Wu sheng zhi sheng* (Voices amid silence), vol. 1: *Jindai Zhongguo de funü yu guojia, 1600–1950* (Women and the nation in modern China, 1600–1950), ed. Lu Fang-Shang (Taipei: Institute of Modern History, Academica Sinica, 2003), 257–81. Reprinted by permission.

Chapter 14: Ellen Rooney, "A Semiprivate Room," was originally published in *differences: A Journal of Feminist Cultural Studies* 13 (Spring 2002): 128–56. © 2002 Brown University and *differences: A Journal of Feminist Cultural Studies.* All rights reserved. Used with permission.

Chapter 15: Miglena Nikolchina, "The Seminar: *Mode d'emploi,* Impure Spaces in the Light of Late Totalitarianism," was originally published in *differences: A Journal of Feminist Cultural Studies* 13 (Spring 2002): 96–127. © 2002 Brown University and *differences: A Journal of Feminist Cultural Studies.* All rights reserved. Used with permission.

Going Public

Prologue: The Right to Be Lonely

DENISE RILEY

HOW SINGLE IS SINGLE? Is the numeral One the founding start of a series or an atom? There could be two broad tactics in the movements toward new family forms—to cope with the furious miseries of social exclusion by the gesture of nominating absolutely everyone as a legitimate family (and could a family of one also be ushered into this all-embracing kinship?) while an opposing gesture might declare that, really, no one constitutes a family, but no one should want to anyway.

In the teeth of the former tendency to incorporate more and more contenders into the realm of the familial (with which "the social" is increasingly and fatally taken to be coterminous), I offer instead the willful principle of The Right to Be Lonely. As oxymoronic as many another claim to rights, my theatrical slogan will be embellished with remarks about the immediately emotional metaphoricity—a metaphoricity not separable from but sunk in social realism—of all talk about societal "exclusion" and "inclusion," about outsiders and insiders. "The right to be lonely" is both a consoling defense that will not work and a parody. (This slogan is not, of course, intended to advocate "having one's own space" as a gleaming lifestyle in the name of some repellent and impossible "autonomy." Nor do I proffer it as any romanticization of loneliness—which must, if episodically or without acknowledgement, be everyone's common fate.) Still, this "right to be lonely" may serve to interrogate the diction of belonging. For do we unequivocally *want* this social inclusion? Certainly, we may want to speak for equality, but in doing so to steer clear of its now usual accompaniment of a treacly talk of belonging, spiritual recognition, community. Can it be avoided? Probably not. Does any rhetorical "we" (like the use I make of it now) rely on it? Yes.

But the impulse to inclusion also runs a circuit of envy in all agitation about who and what is in and who and what is not.

With such jealousy, any drive for greater social inclusion is as driven as any society gossip column—while one unhappy byproduct of striving for enlarged acceptability is to push the resulting residue of everyone else further into the backwoods of an unspeakable deviancy. This, ironically, is concomitant to promoting new family forms. No one is to blame for it. It is pragmatically necessary to fight for what is sometimes termed the "legitimation" of unorthodox lives. Yet this may be best done in the bitter knowledge that, in the process, new hierarchies of social acceptability are being generated.

Then what are the emotional limits to this thing called legitimation or recognition? If, for instance, you cannot have certain rights on the death of your lover, where that person is of the same sex as you, you might indeed be passionately concerned to gain legal recognition for your liaison. Yet if you are a long-established mistress or the male lover of a married man, you, too, are standardly excluded so as not to increase the distress of the wife and children. Is this not a social exclusion that you would find painfully acceptable? We also suffer greatly from the deaths of our friends, to whom we can have no state-sanctioned recognition. Our sorrow is sharpened by whatever form of neglect it happens to have at hand to feed it, but only in some circumstances do we interpret official nonrecognition as a cruel social exclusion. For this ambiguous state of affairs we might also reproach our wavering discourse of "public" and "private" itself, a language that also, unevenly, speaks to us. Language is hot and language is historical.[1] It drags along or cajoles lives. There is an emotive topography in that spatial conceptualization of "inclusion" and "exclusion" itself. It is this linguistic emotionality that suffuses all political philosophies of who is in and who is left out.

Concepts are often constructed in a language that is quietly figurative.[2] In the frequent spatiality of conceptual thought, a fundamental metaphoricity of place and depth is embedded (as in those words "residual," "fundamental," "embedded"). But is such an observation merely a rebirth of old fevers of the excessively literalized etymological radicalism that gripped many wild nineteenth-century linguists?[3] One soon becomes unsure of whether the "layers" of thought's organization are to be considered figurative or not—while to depict these topographies would demand a historian of extraordinary balance.[4] Then, if the names of the structures of thought are themselves metaphorical, is not the very idea of there being any "structure" to thought itself also figurative? Yet if so, what would constitute the nonfigurative here? Such doubts typically rise through the muffled half-silences of dead metaphor.[5]

Because one cannot extract oneself from it, this blurs the edges between what counts as metaphor and what as literal to that point of fascination where the seemingly literal has its presumption of nonmetaphoricity abruptly drained out of it. There is an area, almost unnameable, where metaphorical description bleeds into the nonmetaphorical. Or there is a lonely hour, which never quite arrives, of the nonmetaphoricity of language. Concepts, often figurative, are mapped onto each other, working in tandem "within the unity of the verbally constituted consciousness" as Volosinov put it (9–24). Yet what if the very concepts that ground this overlapped consciousness, those of an external world and an internal world, begin themselves to ring strangely in our ears? What if all this interiority and its opposing exteriority are also themselves metaphorical? And then the ensuing question relentlessly becomes, Metaphorical to what?

So we lurch on already unsteady ground when we scrutinize the public/private distinction and its relative, the social/personal, since from one angle these are particular and mutable historical and sociological renditions of the fundamental and vexed outer/inner division. There is a long history of worry about the volatile meanings of "the social" itself, which is arguably periodically sexed. Donzelot's comment here is exemplary—"How did we pass from a usage of 'the social' understood as the problem of poverty, the problem of others, to its current definition in terms of a general solidarity and the production of a life-style: what enabled it to be made into a showcase of development, whose defense comes before all else, something to be offered to the world at whatever cost?" (xxvii).

One answer turns on how the self is imagined to be distributed—whether it is torn and reallocated as aspects of the social or is kept as one thing set over and against the social. If we hold that the conception of social space is itself metaphorical, as there is not literally a great exterior that stands massively against our separate interiorities, it may be somewhat easier to disentangle that problem of the self's "passage" outward and across into the social, since one could claim instead to be already social. Then the puzzle of passing between these realms, of transferring between them, need not arise, with all its attendant apparatus of the dialectic of social outer and psychological inner.[6] For we are outside from the start.[7]

That resolution *tout court,* though, may be too breezy. Convictions of our interiority well up again, constantly. Perhaps that founding spatiality in thought, beyond which it seems impossible to reach, is partly based on our embodied senses, according to which, for instance, words do rise inwardly to pass outward through our lips.[8] Yet, especially if we take the thought of the body and what lies beyond its skin as founding perception, there is no commensurate equivalence of outer and inner, and as Bachelard warns, "It must be noted that the two terms 'outside' and 'inside' pose problems of metaphysical anthropology that are not symmetrical" (215). Then doesn't the usual inner/outer or private/public bifurcation have an element of fantasy in its symmetry—a fantasied regularity? If we then transpose the misleading neatness of these broad figurative pairings to a local variant, the couple of the social and the presocial seems romantically misconceived in its division. There is an unspeakable outside, an imagined asocial space,[9] where something howls beyond the edges, prowls in anguish around the dark perimeter encircling the glowing campfire of the family.

If, gripped by this image, we merely enlarge the scope of the family circle and see off a few truly recalcitrant hyenas to the outer blackness, then we have glossed over some interesting difficulties. There is a strong argument for rejecting this imagined lure of the thought of the wild outside versus the regulated familial inside. It is the lure of the tame that may best render strange the familiar.[10] Against the tidily paired antitheses are quite other conceptualizations that run right across them, whether from the side of the feminisms that have insisted on the imbrication of the political with the personal or from other traditions that have emphasized the enunciative weight of public language to work within the sites of intimacy,[11] whether as creator of the subject or as a rude encroachment. "Things have come to a pretty pass when religion is allowed to invade the sphere of private life," Lord Melbourne remarked on hearing an evangelical sermon (Russell 182).

Exteriority set against interiority surfaces, too, in questions of where the truth of the self is better located; here, the standard private/public opposition cannot begin to hold because language goes with us into the house. We are shaped in speech so as to make nonsense of any of the usual contrasts of domain. Language is already waiting in the house, too. And "the private" is neither the play of liberating anarchic abandon nor captured by a social control that stalks each bedroom. Rather, there are constantly regenerated, audibly argued accounts as to what counts as and what constitutes this private. If, as so many ways of thinking have intimated, there is a truth of ambivalence, then there are mutual instabilities of inner and outer, an innocent *ekstasis* of language, a propulsion of the unconscious from the outside, and an uneven mutability of public and private.[12]

All this is in contrast to the supposition that the public/social is a potentially generous ground for future harmony, or conversely that the social remains a realm of sheer coercion.[13] It is true that the concept of ambivalence cannot be readily translated into a good. And if from the side of optimism, "man is half-open being" (Bachelard 222), there is also a great deal of slamming shut to be heard. It isn't, though, helpful to retreat to the certainties of what I decide is closed to me, to suppose that I am condemned to try to insinuate my small way into some swollen place of the social that has shut me out. Spatial metaphor's ready linguistic affect may imply that I am the private and enfeebled inner while the vast outside of the social is the terrain of my coming emancipation. But then I cannot wait around too long for my inclusion there, since whatever is social has, like me, only a limited lease on life, is eroded by the brute passage of time. However, if ideas of temporality supplement the achronology of topographical metaphor, then such changes can be understood less devastatingly, as in Hegel's writings on the family as the natural form of ethical life, which passes in its division into civil society. At one point he meditates on the fact that as children grow up, "separated from their source—a separation in which the source dries up" (174), so their parents naturally fall away from their joint incarnation in their offspring and, altered by time, are disaggregated into their separate lives again. This is why Hegel's family, despite its thesis of eventual regeneration in disintegration, is tersely annotated by J. N. Findlay thus: "It is concerned with individuality raised out of the unrest and change of life into the universality of death, i.e., the Family exists to promote the cult of the dead" (552).[14] Indeed, death as our common prospect—rather than any pulsating communality of life—may be more darkly viewed as what truly underlies all visions of "social cohesion," as with John Donne's: "No man is an island, entire of its self. Every man is a piece of the continent, a part of the main: if a clod of earth be washed away by the sea, Europe is the less as well as if a promontory were; . . . any man's death diminishes me, because I am involved in mankind: And therefore never send to know for whom the bell tolls. It tolls for thee."[15]

This celebrated quotation flashes from collectivity straight to its justification as private death. Its sociality is that of our common steady journey from swaddling clothes to winding-sheet. I am diminished by any dying that in its bleakly democratic guarantee might as well be, and some day assuredly will be, my own. This communality of death as shared fate returns me forcefully to myself, since *timor mortis conturbat me.* Fearful apprehension of death disquiets me—it disturbs *me,* no longer us. It drives us into our terminally atomized selves; as particles we regain our singularity, our subjection to judgment, and our hope of resurrection.

Then the urgency of *timor mortis* may sharpen envy's hurry to attain incorporation in the social mass before my death. There are others I must win through to, now.[16] Here this question again becomes pressing: "But who are these others who form the outside in relation to this inside which we believe ourselves to be?" (Lacoue-Labarthe and Nancy 191). I am not inside anything. I'm not outside it either. Yet the public/private distinction, which has such solid realities in its effects, tends in its topographical conceptualization to underwrite the affective metaphoricity of inner and outer. This cuts many ways. I look on from outside at something "social" I want to penetrate, as if its secrets are withheld from me. Or, as if inexorably caught inside, I gaze dreamily outward. I may long to break out of my private cell and into the buoyant air of the wide world yet may also long to diminish this public space by cracking its secrets to ensure that it withholds nothing from my prying. I need the outside to fulfill its promise of largesse to me, I need to master it as my territory. So I cut it down to size, and its promises, viewed close up, may offer me only disappointment and intensify my persistent drive to compel it to reveal yet more of its receding interiority.

Whichever way the movement across the imagined membrane that separates the inner and the outer, it is envious and full of pathos. In such discursive spatiality there is, immediately, an affective topography of being excluded: You are where I myself would prefer to be; that is what I would like to have. "So that is marriage, Lily thought, a man and a woman looking at a girl throwing a ball" (Woolf 114). In this neatest of sentences, which holds so many pairs of eyes, we glimpse in a flash the meditative watcher who herself looks on at a couple who are conjoined as such through their contemplation of the child playing.

And perhaps just such a "looking on" might constitute more or less everyone's relation to the family, irrespective of whether they actually inhabit one. Suppose that the ideal of a proper familial life resists me, is something that I feel that others have, yet I lack. Even if I can offer some reasonable approximation to it, I do not have it in the same way that I imagine others having theirs. Not only because I may have failed to quite amass the correct ingredients (maybe I lack a father here, a cousin there, am rather short of ancestors) but because that thing, the Family, will, in its terrible iconicity, exceed my capture of it. This is all quite irrespective of the actual configurations of people I live with; the family may be something that, by definition, everyone else but me is felt to have. The commandment in the King James Bible, "Thou shalt not covet thy neighbor's house, thou shalt not covet thy neighbor's wife nor his manservant nor his maidservant, nor his ox, nor his ass, nor any thing that is thy neighbor's" (Exod. 20:17), isn't so much an instance of bathos in its intermingling of a consumerism of desire with a consumerism of household chattels as of the homogenizing logic of envy. Envy is a great maker of lists. It is sharply indifferent, as the commandment recognizes, to any hierarchies among goods because it reduces everything alike to that which cannot be enjoyed by me—while it is itself greatly energized by the entire diction of public or private boundaries.

That diction changes under our noses, often unforeseeably. Speaking now, and sheepishly, in the first person as a serial single parent,[17] I found consolation in the arrival in the 1990s social policy vocabulary of a new entity, the "single-parent *family*," with its formally depathologizing noun—as if this had at last let me detach myself from pressing my nose flat against the glass of the familial shop window and be ushered inside, tolerated now as nothing more noxious than a variation on a norm rather than as it had been—as an antagonistic thing, a failure in the light of the one true family form. Nevertheless, this liberalized talk in some quarters of British life was accompanied by wider kinds of denigration, repathologizing measures, and a welfare regime that is the least generous in Western Europe to single parents, even as their numbers increase.[18]

But beyond this, I am also suspicious of my happy relief in my newfound capacity to count as a family.[19] What is the longing to be a family *too* (beyond the wish to be recognized as a social unit that is treated in law and in culture accordingly), a longing that is not merely practical but resembles a search for some anchorage to secure us to a wider community? Why do "we all" want that—if indeed "we" do?[20] To be socially recognized also means to be tabulated, monitored, and regulated. As the psychoanalyst Moustafa Safouan remarked apropos recent liberalizing changes in French family law: "The more they ask for liberty, the more they ask for laws."[21]

This surface paradox is also all too comprehensible, and liberty has sound reasons for looking to its own policemen. It will also be patrolled by checks it does not entirely care for.[22] For example, any "stable" couple, irrespective of the sexes of those who constitute it, may well be judged more desirable parents than any single parent if the financial respectability of a joint household is opposed to the assumption of transient entanglements for the single mother and her lesser capacity to earn,[23] offering her only the faintest of prospects of achieving what the paterfamilias Gomez Addams calls "the indescribable joy of having children, and of paying someone else to raise them."[24] If the present expansion of the definition of a family is largely benign as it frays the stiff bonds of the old order, there's also the fact that any increased liberalization of speech, of law, and of culture—without an increased liberalization in the distribution of economic resources—will generate new inequalities of its own. An enlarged societal realm expanded by recently recognized familial ties pushes back the margins to swell and puff up the sphere of the social until only the thinnest fringe of an unutterably dreadful asociality skirts it.

Then is every utopia to be encircled by a dystopia? No doubt. It shouldn't surprise us to find that liberalizing moves also produce fresh forms of the socially inadmissible. Then demands for family equality and nondiscrimination should, ideally, be voiced without being couched in a rhetoric of competing virtue, higher claim. Yet such a rhetoric may well prove strategically indispensable; if only one could avoid believing that such strategies are anything more—or equally importantly, anything less—than strategical.

The "traditional" family's demise is coinciding with a furious intensification of its variants. It is as if one must count as a family in order to count at all, while the numbers of those living alone, across Western Europe at least, rise sharply. Yet as households of single people grow, the admission of even occasional loneliness remains taboo, while to be without visible social ties is inexcusable. Such common solitariness may be willed and preferred by its bearer, or may barely be tolerated, enforced; yet a taint of vice always clouds it. (In 1757 Diderot sent Rousseau his play *The Natural Son,* whence umbrage was taken: "In reading it, Rousseau came upon Constance's words 'Only the wicked man lives alone' and was instantly convinced that the remark was aimed at himself" [Furbank 151]).[25] And does to live alone render a woman not only wicked but also de-sexed? Need everyone be descriptively drawn into the meshes of the social, especially women, as if they owned a naturally greater emotional extensionality, had more tentacles, if you like? "The right to be lonely" could also suggest the hope of being alone yet understood as also social even within one's solitariness.

Solitude, as a pretty noun often religiously linked to creativity's desiderata, may be acknowledged to be necessary; *this* admission is anodyne. But there's a stronger solitude that refuses to be understood as merely presocial and that rejects the benevolent will to make everything, and it too, familial.[26] This solitude groans at the prospect of being tenderly ushered into the domain of the new social. Its bearers are in no constellation but tolerate being units of one, are maybe childless, parentless, without siblings, unattached, unmarried, widowed, not communitarian—are transiently or even (they can't know) permanently single and are not in a panic. They simply find themselves alone. The question, How single is single? could ask, How might such singleness neither be considered pathological nor be swept up, in an ostentatious depathologizing, into a compulsive sociability?[27] The figure of the Solitary might yet be retrieved, and in terms other than her failure to attain to the family. Might a properly recognized state of singleness (to wrench the notion of "recognition" away from its usual oppressively gregarious tone) recast that desolate and resentment-prone metaphoricity of social exclusion—might it also somewhat allay the burden, or at least the embarrassed self-reproach, of those who may find themselves living in solitude at the very same time as they live within the family?

NOTES

1. Behind this simple assertion lie generations of debate: "The word is a direct expression of the historical nature of human consciousness," as elaborated by L. S. Vygotsky (249–56).

2. Writing from the perspective of linguistic pragmatics, Mark Turner suggests the example of the metaphor of "intellectual progress" as embodying a virtually literal sense of direction (63).

3. These, including Wolfson and Brisset, are discussed extensively and helpfully by Gérard Genette and Jean-Jacques Lecercle.

4. Michel Foucault (1:117) raises this possibility in his interview "Polemics, Politics, and Problematizations": "For a long time, I have been trying to see if it would be possible to describe the history of thought as distinct both from the history of ideas (by which I mean the analyses of systems of representation) and from the history of mentalities (by which I mean the analysis of attitudes and types of action." Edward Casey's *The Fate of Place* gives an encyclopedic description of metaphors of space within thought yet does not dwell on the nature of this metaphoricity.

5. Likewise, the metaphor of "I see" or "I grasp" for "I understand," where a systematic series of metaphors of visualizing or apprehension stand for comprehension, supports Eve Sweetser's contention that metaphoricity migrates from the outside to the inside. "Thus we could say that 'This fact blocks us from reaching that conclusion.' This is another manifestation of the same broader mapping of external selves onto internal selves, and the forces and barriers of our external world onto those of our internal world" (66).

6. The whole idea of a fraught transition from an emphatic innerness causes unhappiness in itself, according to Michel Henry (302).

7. See Merleau-Ponty's meditations here, especially, "Nothing determines me from outside, not because nothing acts upon me, but, on the contrary, because I am from the start outside myself and open to the world" (456).

8. Must the brain inevitably grasp its surrounding world as patterns of depths and surfaces? See the persuasive and highly readable neurological accounts in Antonio Damasio's study.

9. See the elaborations in Foucault (2:147).

10. A strict etiquette (certainly more bourgeois than the bourgeois) for the conduct of affairs, as part of an ethics of the unethical, might prove less damaging than the usual opposition of the romantic versus the familial, which only sets this antagonistic pair in stone and makes everyone unhappy.

11. Enunciation has a long history as a concept. See, for instance, Todorov's *L'énonciation.* In aspects of Foucault's work, especially in Deleuze and Guattari (75–110), "bodies" are whatever thing or condition that can act or be acted on, and "enunciations" are any incorporeal but effective transforming statements that act on and through them.

12. Like the idea of the "fold of the self" that Gilles Deleuze discusses apropos Foucault in *Foucault* (94–123), or Philippe Lacoue-Labarthe and Jean-Luc Nancy: "For the affect, if it is, is only that: the affection of an inside by the outside, therefore the division of the two and their reciprocal penetration. Ambivalence is thus the affect itself, that is to say, the oscillation of what one could call an excision occurring as an

incision (which would be completely different from a castration), the incisive excision out of which arises a subject (or at least its project). And consequently—since this subject departs itself as well—an object" (198).

13. "Metaphysics has always thought sociality as either a positive election, a reciprocal esteem of subjects, or as the coercion of a pure force" (Lacoue-Labarthe and Nancy 207).

14. By his mention of this standing of the family as the cult of the dead in his "Analysis of the Text," J. N. Findlay no doubt intended a scholarly observation, not the acerbic aside we might imagine (Hegel 552).

15. The English poet and cleric, in his (unpaginated) *Devotions* of 1624.

16. "Others" is the inordinate measure of an outside that affects from within, of an inside that affects itself on the outside—or of an alterity that increases with its sameness, a sameness that grows with its affectivity. Affect, which is to say ambivalence, puts us at the heart of a sociality, of an "unsociable sociality" as Kant's phrase would have it. At the heart, we will say, of a dis-sociation (Lacoue-Labarthe and Nancy 191).

17. Adorno warns against the authoritarian impulse lurking behind any utterance of the form "speaking as a something-or other, I." "Transcendent critique sympathizes with authority in its very form, even before expressing any content: there is a moment of content to the form itself. The expression 'as a . . . , I,' in which one can insert any orientation, from dialectical materialism to Protestantism, is symptomatic of that" (194).

18. See Jane Lewis's study. Also, Carolyn Wright and Gill Jagger criticize the frequent use of data that obscures the specific states of single-parent families and ask how much newer and more refined definitions have entered into recent sociology (180).

19. As with ancient forms. Up to the seventeenth century, the family was a word for the social association within a household, not a blood-tie. See Raymond Williams (131).

20. Why are the bonds of friendship not quite enough to count, although many testify that these are more enduring than the bonds of marriage? It is as if the stronger affinities are felt to run downward through time to our descendants, not laterally.

21. This comment was made to me in the course of a conversation.

22. New reproductive technologies have massive implications; private arrangements, such as for surrogacy in all its forms, will tend to outpace and bypass legal regulation because of their sheer speed of technical development, while childbearing may become more and more a matter of "economic feasibility."

23. A competition between forms of "social deviance" to see which can attain greater respectability? Alarmed debates in the House of Lords in London have asked whether the implication of the proclaimed advantage for any child in having two parents, not just one, was that two "stable" homosexual parents might be just as good as two heterosexual parents (thus also opening the very strong possibility that two homosexual parents might well be judged superior to one single mother).

24. A line spoken by Raul Julia in the movie *Addams Family Values 2.*

25. I am much indebted to Susan Clarke for this reference.

26. Not that this is painless, since it is the fate of the newer performers to need to be seen to be doing it not simply as well but better than the older, as women have long

observed of their migrations into traditionally male work. The anomalous family must mimic the virtues supposedly enacted within the nuclear family, and outshine it.

27. Yet the impulse to attain warmth for the excluded, to respond to that call, is not to be scorned. My memory is strong of my own relief when I found by the late 1990s that we could constitute a "single-parent family" (my children, being of another generation, had never doubted it) because the language of family structures had altered so radically through the three decades I had been living them.

Works Cited

Addams Family Values 2. Screenplay by Paul Rudnick. Dir. Barry Sonnenfeld. Paramount, 1993.

Adorno, Theodor. *Hegel: Three Studies.* Trans. Shierry Weber Nicholsen. Cambridge: MIT Press, 1993.

Bachelard, Gaston. *The Poetics of Space.* Trans. Maria Jolas. Boston: Beacon Press, 1969.

Casey, Edward. *The Fate of Place: A Philosophical History.* Los Angeles: University of California Press, 1997.

Damasio, Antonio. *The Feeling of What Happens: Body and Emotion in the Making of Consciousness.* London: Heinemann, 1999.

Deleuze, Gilles. *Foucault.* Trans. Seán Hand. London: Athlone, 1988.

Deleuze, Gilles, and Félix Guattari. *A Thousand Plateaus.* Trans. Brian Massumi. London: Athlone, 1990.

Donzelot, Jacques. Preface. *The Policing of Families.* Trans. Robert Hurley. Baltimore: Johns Hopkins University Press, 1997.

Findlay, J. N. "Analysis of the Text." In *Phenomenology of the Spirit,* by G. W. F. Hegel, 495–591. Trans. A. V. Miller. New York: Oxford University Press, 1977.

Foucault, Michel. *Ethics: Subjectivity and Truth.* Vol. 1 of *The Essential Works.* Ed. Paul Rabinow. Trans. Robert Hurley et al. London: Allen Lane, 1997.

———. "The Thought of the Outside." In *Aesthetics, Method, and Epistemology.* Vol. 2 of *The Essential Works.* Ed. James D. Faubion, 147–70. Trans. Robert Hurley et al. New York: New Press, 1998.

Furbank, P. N. *Diderot: A Critical Biography.* New York: Secker and Warburg: 1992.

Genette, Gérard. *Mimologies.* Trans. Thais E. Morgan. Lincoln: University of Nebraska Press, 1995.

Hegel, G. W. F. *Phenomenology of Spirit.* Trans. A. V. Miller. New York: Oxford University Press, 1977.

Henry, Michel. *The Genealogy of Psychoanalysis.* Trans. Douglas Brick. Stanford: Stanford University Press, 1993.

Lacoue-Labarthe, Philippe, and Jean-Luc Nancy. "The Unconscious Is Destructured Like an Affect." *Stanford Literature Review* 6 (Fall 1989): 191–209.

Lecercle, Jean-Jacques. *The Violence of Language.* London: Routledge, 1990.

Lewis, Jane, ed. *Lone Mothers in European Welfare Regimes.* London: Kingsley, 1997.

Merleau-Ponty, Maurice. *Phenomenology of Perception.* Trans. Colin Smith. London: Routledge, 1978.

Russell, G. W. E. *Collections and Recollections, by One Who Has Kept a Diary.* London: n.p., 1898.

Sweetser, Eve. *From Etymology to Pragmatics; Metaphorical and Cultural Aspects of Semantic Structure.* New York: Cambridge University Press, 1990.
Todorov, Tsvetan. *L'énonciation.* Paris: Didier Larousse, 1970.
Turner, Mark. "Figure." In *Figurative Language and Thought.* Ed. N. Katz et al., 44–87. New York: Oxford University Press, 1998.
Volosinov, V. N. "Multiaccentuality and the Sign." In *Marxism and the Philosophy of Language.* Trans. L. Matejka and I. R. Titunik. Cambridge: Harvard University Press, 1986.
Vygotsky, L. S. *Thought and Language.* Ed. and trans. Eugenia Haufmann and Gertrude Vakar. Cambridge: MIT Press, 1962.
Williams, Raymond. *Keywords.* London: Fontana, 1981.
Woolf, Virginia. *To the Lighthouse.* London: Hogarth Press, 1927.
Wright, Carolyn, and Gill Jagger, eds. *Changing Family Values.* London: Routledge, 1999.

PART 1

Deconstructing Public versus Private: Sexuality in the Discourses of Nation and Political Economy

1 Tolerance and Equality: "The Jewish Question" and "the Woman Question"

WENDY BROWN

Tolerance is intolerant and demands assimilation.

—Herman Broch

The very being, or legal existence of the woman is suspended during the marriage, or at least is incorporated and consolidated into that of the husband.

—Sir William Blackstone

WHY IS THE CONDITION OF WOMEN, or relations between the sexes, so rarely framed in terms of a discourse of tolerance? Why did "the Woman Question" in the eighteenth and nineteenth centuries not emerge as a question of tolerance? Certainly, there are occasions when gender inclusion engages this discourse—when, for example, women seek access to ostentatiously male homosocial venues such as exclusive social clubs, military schools, and sports teams or their locker rooms. But equality, not tolerance, is our conventional rubric for speaking about gender desegregation and gender equity. Moreover, although women's "difference," whether identified as sexual, reproductive, or affective, may be an object of tolerance in workplaces, space missions, or combat zones, it is not women as such who are said to be tolerated in these instances but rather their *difference* that becomes a matter for practical accommodation through separate facilities or special arrangements related to pregnancy or the demands of early maternity. Why? Why is it that minority religions, minority ethnicities or races, and minority sexualities are all now treated as subjects for tolerance but women are not? Is the key in the word *minority?* That is, does tolerance always signify a majoritarian response to an outlying or minoritarian element in its midst? Is it the case that majorities can never be subjects for tolerance?

I think proportionalist demographic analyses provide the least interesting answer to this riddle, so in what follows I will explore other paths. We begin with a different take on the question, Why was "the Jewish Question" often framed as a matter of tolerance in eighteenth- and nineteenth-century Europe while the Woman Question, from the beginning, emerged through the language of subordination and equality? (A more contemporary version would be, Why was the 1984 Democratic vice-presidential candidacy of Geraldine Ferraro heralded as a victory for feminist equity struggles while sixteen years later political pundits cast the nomination of an orthodox Jew, Joseph Lieberman, to that position as a "triumph of tolerance"?)

It is insufficient to respond that Jews were historically ostracized while women were straightforwardly subordinated by law and by individual men, or that Jews were a religious group while women were excluded on the basis of their bodies. Such responses may open the question but certainly do not answer it. Whatever the difference in the mechanisms and putative bases of disenfranchisement, both exclusions were justified by an imagined difference from the figure of universal man at the heart of the emerging European constitutional political orders. And both exclusions provoked a common desire and goal: political membership; political and civil rights; and access to public institutions, education, and a range of vocations. The goal in a word—indeed, in the word most often used in the nineteenth century—was emancipation.

Why then did one emancipation movement remain within the rubric of tolerance and conditional inclusion while the other took shape as a project of political equality? How and why did emancipation efforts fork in this way, and what light does this historical phenomenon shed on the metamorphosing relationship of equality and tolerance in liberalism? More precisely, what transformation of the relationship between equality and tolerance in nineteenth-century liberalism can be discerned in the particular politicization of identity entailed in these respective emancipation efforts and their divergences? In liberal discourse, equality presumes sameness whereas tolerance is employed to manage difference. So why did "sex difference" become thinkable and politicizable through the terms of sameness while Jewishness did not?

The answers to these questions will be found in the imbrication of several different discourses in the nineteenth century, those constructing gender and Jewishness respectively on the one hand and those organizing the terms of liberal tolerance, equality, and emancipation on the other. Scrutiny of the way the discursive construction of Jewishness framed the politicization of the Jewish Question will enable us to see how the discourse of tolerance shifted its object from conscience and belief to racialized identity and soul, all the while appearing to broker religious difference. Moreover, scrutiny of the discursive construction of gender that made possible certain arguments about women's equality and foreclosed others, all the while retaining a strong notion of sex difference, will illuminate important features of nineteenth-century liberal notions of emancipation and equality.

The Jews

In considering the relationship of the formation of the Jewish Question to the discursive construction of Jews in the nineteenth century, and in connecting this formation and this construction to the establishment of Jews as subjects of tolerance, we will focus initially on postrevolutionary France. That may seem paradoxical at first blush, given that France, from 1791 until the Dreyfus Affair at the turn of the century, understood itself to have preempted the Jewish Question raging elsewhere on the Continent with straightforward emancipation and enfranchisement. In fact, as students of this period know well, the picture is more complex. Moreover, precisely because "emancipation" was the standard for the civic and political inclusion of Jews across Europe in the nineteenth century, France stands as a kind of paradigm, or even parable, of modernity in the story it harbors of Jewish emancipation, assimilation, and tolerance.[1]

In December 1789 the French National Assembly conducted an intense debate on the question of Jewish emancipation. The debate turned upon the question of whether Jews were Frenchmen, and, if not, whether they could become citizens in a newly born regime in which the republic and its members were held to be mutually constitutive (Vital 42). In the context of a general consensus in favor of secularizing the state and diminishing the public force of religion, no one in the Assembly argued straightforwardly for tolerance of practicing Jews—that argument would have implied a hegemonic and public religion at odds with the pervasive antireligious sentiment of the time. There was, however, heated argument about whether Jews constituted a nation apart, and, if so, whether such a constitution inherently debarred Jews from membership in the Republic. For those such as Abbe Maury, who insisted that the very term *Jew* "denotes a nation," it followed that Jews should be protected but not enfranchised—they could not simultaneously belong to two nations (Vital 44). But for those who understood the Revolution itself as encompassing the project of French nation-building, the clear task was to dismantle rather than honor the remnants of Jewish nationhood. As Count Stanislaw de Clermont-Tonnerre, the lead speaker on behalf of Jewish emancipation in the December 1789 Assembly session, put the case, "As a nation the Jews must be denied everything, as individuals they must be granted everything; their judges can no longer be recognized; their recourse must be to our own exclusively; legal protection for the doubtful laws by which Jewish corporate existence is maintained must end; they cannot be allowed to create a political body or a separate order within the state; it is necessary that they be citizens individually" (Vital 44).

Entwining Hobbes and Foucault in a single sentence, Clermont-Tonnerre specified requirements for carving the new citizen-subject out of the old corporate body: individuation, adherence to general rules and to a single legal and social norm, and undivided state authority. Even as the Assembly spurned conventional tolerance arguments, Clermont-Tonnerre made clear the tacit toleration deal undergirding emancipation, one that submits the tolerated subject to state administration at the very moment of emancipation and enfranchisement. His formulation precisely expressed the twin processes of individuation and privatization of subnational filliations and beliefs entailed in belonging to the new universal state, processes that required, in a phrase, the Protestantization of Jews. To be compatible with membership in the French republic, Jews had to be individuated, denationalized, and decorporatized as Jews. To cohabit with Frenchness, Jewishness could no longer consist in belonging to a distinct community bound by religious law, ritualized practices, and generational continuity but rather would consist at most in privately held and conducted beliefs.

In the 1789 debate the French Assembly stalemated on the question of rights for Jews. Two years later, however, when debating the issue of Jews inhabiting the eastern provinces, the Assembly voted to rescind all decrees, prohibitions, and privileges relating to Jews (Vital 48). Without resolving the question of whether Jews were French, of whether they constituted a nation apart, Jews were formally enfranchised as citizens. If the question of Jewish Frenchness could not be easily settled, the matter of incorporating outlying elements of the population into the state was pressing. According to Salo Baron, "Jewish emancipation was as much a historic necessity for the modern state as it was for the Jews" (57).

Jews were but one node in the "untidy complex of estates, guilds, classes and corporations, all quite loosely supervised from above, if at all, none totally devoid of autonomy and the capacity to go its own way," an untidiness and attendant subnational freedom and autonomy that had to be overcome for the consolidation of state power (Vital 50). Thus, the formulation of and the answer to the Jewish Question, was framed more by *raison d'état* than by political principle or considerations of Jewish welfare, although the latter sometimes figured importantly in the justification and legitimization of emancipation.[2] Put another way, retrospectively, the stumbling, stuttering approach to Jewish emancipation during the French Revolution is explainable according to the cross tides of immediate concern with membership criteria in building republican France and the longer-term process of consolidating state sovereignty. The Revolution's incorporation of Jews appears inevitable as the logical extension of principles of universal equality and liberty but is fundamentally consistent with the tendency of all European states, starting in the late eighteenth century, to centralize, rationalize, and regularize their power and reach. The anomalous status of Jews in Europe during the medieval and early modern periods—"in" but not "of" various European nations—had to be resolved. To that end, Jews had to be brought within the ambit and orbit of the state, a process that involved incorporation into a nation increasingly defined through abstract, universal citizenship.

To be brought into the nation, however, Jews had to be made to fit, and for that they needed to be transformed, cleaned up, and normalized, even as they were still marked as Jews. The triple forces of recognition, remaking, and marking, emancipation, assimilation, and subjection, and/or decorporatization as Jews, incorporation as nation-state citizens, and identification as different characterize the relation of the state to Jews in nineteenth-century Europe and compose the tacit regime of tolerance governing Jewish emancipation.

What did it mean for French Jews to become citizens? Insofar as citizenship in republican France was not a formal category extended to an individual with rights but rather involved membership in the Republic, identification with the state, and participation in French national culture, the process of making Jews citizens meant making them French. That meant modulating any distinctively Jewish sense of community and fealty along with distinctively Jewish public practices and habits. Becoming part of the French nation in this deep sociological way supplied yet another impetus for severing attachment to the dispersed Jewish nation, and it was ideologically framed by an Enlightenment modernizing rationalism as well. Assimilation, the thinking went, would make Jews more modern, more European, and more free. Shedding archaic and tribal Jewish practices and beliefs in favor of becoming French signified all three insofar as the French nation stood for all three. Emblematic in this regard is the nineteenth-century assimilationist Jewish historiography that cast the Revolution of 1789 as the "modern Passover," the second flight from Egypt (Marrus 91–92). In that historical metanarrative the Revolution that emancipated French Jews conferred a hallowed place in Jewish history upon the French nation. In so doing it established France as a nation especially worthy of Jewish attachment and loyalty.[3]

As assimilation proceeded over the course of the nineteenth century, what kept Jews from disappearing? The question pertains not only to Jews who abandoned religious belief but also to those who, in accord with the formulation of tolerance that the Reformation delivered, persisted in some semblance of religious practice as a private activity.[4] How could Jewish law and ritual practice, rabbinical authority, belief, and attachment to the Jewish nation decline or vanish altogether without taking the Jew with it? "Judaism . . . is not a religion: it is a race," declared Tourasse in 1895, encapsulating the half-century-long process by which a definition of Jews as a physiological *race* came to supplant a definition of Jews rooted in common language, beliefs, practices, and, above all, nationhood (Marrus 15).

Because, according to nineteenth-century race discourse, race was inscribed in every element of the body and soul, mind and sexuality, temperament and ability, it could endure after the constituent elements of nation-elements that had to be *performed*—and were not (discursively inscribed) attributes—had been reduced or eliminated (Gilman 175–80). Race allowed (or required) a Jew to be a Jew no matter how fully assimilated, no matter how secular. By marking Jewishness as a set of physically distinguishable attributes—skin color and health along with specified characteristics of the nose, genitals, and feet—and at the same time casting it as that which saturated every aspect of the being of the Jew, race sustained Jewishness through the process of assimilation as definitions of Jewishness rooted in nationhood or religious belief could not.

Racialization also produced a new subject of tolerance in Christian culture. Defined neither by belief nor filliation, the racialized Jew became highly individuated as well as physiologically, intellectually, and emotionally saturated by Jewishness. This new Jewish subject in turn became a critical site for, first, a new semiotics of tolerance in which otherness was carried on and in the racialized body; second, a new administrative subject of tolerance in which the racialized body, rather than practices, beliefs, or filiation, would be decisive or at least in which bodily being was presumed to carry the morphological code for all else such that difference was ontologized, hence cast as permanent; and, third, new and ambiguous sources for the conferral of tolerance dispersed through civil society rather than concentrated in the state and the Church.[5]

The racialization of Jews during the nineteenth century was produced by discourses ranging from anthropological and biological to philological and literary. All were built on the nineteenth-century zeal, both scholarly and popular, for typology, classification, and measurement and drew for evidence on everything from brain size and survival capacity to the origins of languages and language groups. The developing body of racial theory was not internally coherent or systematic, nor was it radically distinct from cultural theory and historical claims. Biological theories were mixed with historical analyses of oppression to explain how, for example, Jews had survived despite oppression and persecution, how certain physical atrophies in the Jewish body might have resulted from oppression, or why Jews came to look more like their gentile brethren in certain European nations than in others—indeed, why Jews across Europe varied so much in their appearances.[6]

What these notably unsystematic and unscientific theories provided to Jews, gentiles, leftists, liberals, and anti-Semites alike was a means of establishing the enduring fact of Jewishness independent of belief or ritual. Particularly in the context of French Catholicism but also in a more general context of tolerance discourse concerned with Protestant sects, the racialization of Jews circumvented the difficulties in submitting Jewishness to a construal of religion as a belief community. Rather, treating Jewishness as a racial formation meant that Jewish belief and the Jewish nation could fade while Jews lived. Neither God nor Torah nor Jewish corporate community nor ritual practices were relevant to the identification of Jewishness once race had taken hold. Defined racially, Jewishness was something one carried individually, everywhere, and always. Again, this meant tolerance would change the definition and circumscription of its object. Jews might still be thought of as a group, but the structure of affinity rendering them such was race rather than the nation. It was a matter of putatively objective traits rather than subjective attachment or matters of consciousness but traits carried individually, thus constituting Jews as individuals incorporable by the nation-state rather than as a community of believers potentially alien to or within the nation. Yet racialization also established the Jewish difference as permanent, deep, and impossible to overcome. Even after dismantling Jewish nationhood and enfranchising Jews, racialization constituted Jews as a permanent difference within the imaginary of a homogeneous nation-state.

Despite the anti-Semitic uses to which it could be (and was) put, nineteenth-century European Jews generally took up the discourse of racialization with equanimity and even zeal (Marrus 111–12). However awkwardly, this discourse allowed Jews to retain and comprehend a Jewish identity that established a modicum of community and connection across generations even as they assimilated; it guaranteed that Jewishness itself would not perish through assimilation.[7] Nor did accounts of Jews as a racial type run in a purely pejorative direction. From it Jews and non-Jews alike inferred Jewish superiority as well as inferiority. In the context of French nationalism, the racial discourse offered the peculiar potential for establishing a certain affinity between Jewishness and Frenchness in which superior moral characteristics attributed to each were understood as carrying the potential for mutual enrichment as Jews assimilated and intermarried.

If both Jews and the French, as racial types, were figured as sharing a bourgeois orientation toward family, work, money, and the future, and if both the Revolution of 1789 and ancient Israel were figured as historical episodes expressing a collective aspiration to liberty, equality, and fraternity, then not only were the French and the Jews each an elect people but they were also compatible elects. That line of thinking produced yet another argument for assimilation that had utility for the French bourgeoisie as well as for Jews. It conceived the Jewish blood coursing through France as strengthening French society and improving the overall stock of a nation already at the forefront of world history. According to one historian, by the time of the Dreyfus Affair at the turn of the century that theoretical association of the messianic projects of Judaism and modern France had become the official doctrine of the French Jewish community, challenged by none (Marrus 114, 120).

Assimilation, of course, came with various kinds of subtle tolls that reveal important features of the governmentality of tolerance. As bourgeois French Jews devoted themselves to becoming French and identifying with Frenchness, not only was their connection to and identification with Jews in other lands necessarily attenuated but they also had to moderate their responses to domestic anti-Semitism if they were not to seem excessively Jewish rather than French. To move from the margins to the mainstream of French society, French Judaism became increasingly politically and socially conservative during the second half of the nineteenth century. In particular, assimilated French Jews drew back sharply from the new Jewish immigrants fleeing the East European and Russian pogroms. These newcomers were an embarrassment—too poor, too unmannered, and above all, too Jewish (Marrus 158–62).

Thus, the process of trying to become French while racially marked as other involved disavowing not only Jewish belief, practice, or the nation but also disidentifying with one's most victimized brethren and politically radical brethren as well as abandoning political enmity (e.g., toward Russia) where it was not shared by the French state. Altogether, the price of tolerance was considerable: compromise of religious and political belief, repudiation of other Jews, and fealty to a state that did not return it.

To this point the term *tolerance* has been used in two different senses to analyze Jewish emancipation in the nineteenth century. First, there is the tolerance held out to Jews in exchange for assimilation, a tolerance administered simultaneously by the state and by Jews themselves. This practice was not named tolerance in France, that is, it was not framed as the orientation of the state or the Church toward a minoritized religion by a dominant religion. Rather, it was a project oriented toward producing a unified nation, a homogenous and manageable citizenry, and aimed as well at ending the clash of nations represented by the Jewish presence in France. Not named as tolerance but tolerance it was, as Clermont-Tonnerre made clear in delineating its strenuous conditions: disaggregation of the Jewish nation, decorporatization of Jews, attachment of Jews to the French nation, making Jews into modern French republicans, and dissociation of French Jews from Jews elsewhere. The binding force of the Jewish nation was replaced by the regulating discourses of racialization on one side and Frenchness on the other. Tolerance of assimilating Jews was administered through the normative powers of these mutually constitutive discourses. Nor was the effect of these powers slight. Assimilated French Jews became politically moderate, religiously closeted, and disinclined to affiliate with radical and/or Jewish causes. Yet Jews, as a racially marked and often racially disparaged people, lived in fear of vulnerability to tides of anti-Semitism (such as that inciting and buoying the Dreyfus Affair), a fear that is itself a sign of the regulatory work of tolerance even if this work is increasingly located in civil society rather than Church or state.

These anti-Semitic tides evoke a second sense of tolerance that brings us closer to the histories of Jews in other European nations. These histories were not always structured by early formal emancipation or liberal republicanism but did share the managed assimilation and racialization of the French case. Whether ghettoized or educated, heavily regulated or simply forced to adopt Christian surnames, serve in the military, and conduct business in German, the various approaches to Jews across Europe in the nineteenth century converged in construing them as a distinctive people who nevertheless had to be fitted into consolidating and centralizing nation-states. Thus they had to be reformed as well as tolerated. Tolerance in this sense involved a state and civil administrative practice toward a people who had to be incorporated into the nation but whose racial distinctiveness limited participation in an emerging universalistic formulation of man. Moreover, because Jewishness was racialized, and because racialization implicated every aspect of being (body, gait, sexuality, gesture, soul, mental capacity, and disposition), the object of tolerance was discursively relocated from belief to *ontoi.* Indeed, belief itself was now both distinct from yet also derivable from the ontics of race, a distinguishability and derivability that is critical in formulating subjects of tolerance today.

Women

Alongside the distinctive requirements of state consolidation and distinctive discourses of racialization configuring Jewish emancipation, certain parallel forces configured the emancipation of women in the nineteenth century. Of course, no historically prior subnational or transnational community of women had to be broken apart to produce women as citizen-subjects, nor did women pose the explicit governance problem that Jewish communities did. Women were, however, emerging from submersion in the corporate world of kinship to claim entitlements as individuals at the same time as the emerging discourses of science, medicine, social work, pedagogy, and sexology were individuating them as subjects. The new discourses of gender that were developing and circulating bound women exhaustively to sexed being, much as racialization came to define Jews. If Jewishness was racialized as Jews were emancipated, and if that racialization was deployed in part to mark the limits of emancipation, it is also true that sexual difference, amid debates about women's emancipation, was being drawn more radically and inscribed on the body more deeply than in earlier centuries.

As Thomas Laquer tells the story, being female in the ancien régime was a status related to activity and venue. Through the new biological, anthropological, literary, medical, and psychological discourses it was reconfigured as a matter of human sexual nature. Like race, this sexed nature was held to saturate the being.[8] Thus, writing in 1803, anthropologist Jacques-Louis Moreau insisted not merely upon the distinctiveness of the sexes but argued that "they are different in every conceivable aspect of body and soul, in every physical and moral aspect."[9] Or, in the words of a mid-nineteenth-century physician, "All parts of her body present the same differences: all express woman; the brow, the nose, the eyes, the mouth, the ears, the chin, the cheeks, If we shift our view to the inside, and with the help of the scalpel, lay bare the organs, the tissues, the fibers, we encounter everywhere . . . the same difference."[10]

Discourses about sex difference are hardly the only forces organizing gender and reconstituting the meaning of women during this century. The decline of feudal and petty bourgeois economies and the full onslaught of industrial capitalism wrought enormous changes in the sexual divisions of labor inside and outside the family and in the sexed ownership of trades and means of local production. The sexual division of labor, especially the heterosexually based economic partnerships of agricultural economies, gave way to an order in which women's and men's laboring hands were often—but not always or completely—interchangeable. In that order, women lost control of trades such as dairy and brewing that had heretofore secured them small beachheads of economic and social power. Laquer argues that the new sexual dimorphism emerges in response to "politics . . . the endless new struggles for power and position in the enormously enlarged public sphere of the eighteenth and particularly the postrevolutionary nineteenth centuries," but surely of equal if not greater importance is the breakdown of an ideologically naturalized sexual division of labor in many domains along with the severely reduced productivity of the household, in the transition from agrarian to industrial economies. Sexed bodily being is articulated as decisive at the very historical moment when practical activity and venue become less so (152). As household production decreases, as proletarianization amasses women in the factory, and as a growing class of bourgeois women are increasingly shorn of any productive economic function at all, incitements for demanding women's emancipation are stoked alongside new discourses of female sexual difference that repel those demands.

In sum, the extraordinary capacity of capital to "batter down Chinese Walls," in Marx's phrase, included a powerful capacity to erase gendered social distinctions and transform gendered social spaces heretofore reproduced by sexual divisions of labor in agricultural economies. But in place of these modalities of making and organizing gender arose a pervasively sexed body that produced a new foundation for subordination rooted in putative difference. Its meanings would be interminably debated for their implications about women's candidacy for political and social equality. As with the racialization of Jews, there are first-wave feminists who embrace the radical saturation of women by their sex and there are others who try to parse and contain it. None wholly reject it.

Equality and Tolerance

To return to the original question, How did the Woman Question and the Jewish Question take shape within a common rubric of emancipation and at the same time split into respective projects of equality and tolerance? Nineteenth-century European nations faced the problem of fitting two historically subordinated or excluded groups, Jews and (Christian) women, into an emerging universalist humanist rhetoric and liberal political ideology within which human sameness—underspecified but fraught with tacit norms—is taken to be the basis of equality. The discourses of subordination and exclusion producing Jewishness and gender are themselves in transition, and these discourses are an effect of and contribute to formulation of the problem of political membership for Jews and women. That is, the emerging racialization of Jews and the relentless gendering of sexed beings not only frame debates about emancipation but also are configured by those debates.

Before the emergence of the Jewish Question and the Woman Question, and before the political discourses of equality and the social discourses of racialization and gender configuring these questions, Jews and women were cast not simply as different from Christian men but as bearing a difference in status and social location that sharply distinguished them from Christian men and their privileges. Jews were a nation outside the nation; women were subsumed in the household, as it were, underneath the nation. But as new formulations of abstract citizenship, and new discourses of race and gender toward eligibility for that citizenship, carry each, difference is not retained but relocated from status and location to ontology. There were parallels in the construction of difference for each, especially in the extent to which difference was understood to saturate the respective bodies, minds, and souls of Jews and women, that is, to exhaustively define their respective identities, subjectivity, and potential public personae. But parallel is not identical. Counterintuitively perhaps, European feminist emancipation movements were able to cast women's difference as potentially less saturating of women's existence than Jewish emancipation movements could achieve for Jewishness.

Mary Wollstonecraft in the late eighteenth century and John Stuart Mill in the late nineteenth, for example, both base arguments for women's equality on the exploitation of a strong Cartesian split between body and mind (although neither maintains this split fully or consistently). "There is no sex in souls," Wollstonecraft proclaims and from that premise develops her insistence that women are, first and foremost, human beings not sexed beings (42, 51). Because "virtue has no sex" and the highest virtue is the rational use of the mental faculties, then as Poulain de la Barre, following Descartes, declared in 1673, "Mind has no sex."[11] In Wollstonecraft's analysis, if women and men share the same moral nature, then they ought to share the same moral status and rights. The fact that most women "act as creatures of sensation and feeling rather than as rational beings" is the consequence of a faulty education that makes women "plumed and feathered birds" rather than morally upright beings (33, 34, 39).[12]

Women and men both have the capacity for "educated understanding," and that capacity includes worldly knowledge and knowledge of God's scheme to direct and temper the passions. Wollstonecraft toys with the idea that the two sexes may have different amounts of such understanding as a consequence of differences in strength, but they have the same kind. Virtue is androgynous because mind and soul are (39, 51). Liberty and education, which together produce autonomous reasoning capacity, are the mothers of virtue and therefore must be equally available to women and men. In short, when engaged in mental deliberation and other practices of moral virtue, women are not women at all but simply reasoning beings. But what of the sex difference from which Wollstonecraft abstracts in order to make that argument? Where does it live, and what are the implications of its designated habitat for women's civic and political equality? I will return to that matter shortly.

John Stuart Mill makes remarkably little reference to women's bodies in *On Liberty; with The Subjection of Women* save for the terrible degradation he imagines women to suffer when they must have sex with men (husbands) they do not like or respect.[13] Mill's argument for women's freedom is pinned entirely on their intellectual potential even as he argues that their institutionalized subordination originated historically from physical weakness. What allows him to work both sides of the argument about women's bodies (weaker) and their minds (potentially equal) is not only Cartesian metaphysics but also a progressivist insistence that the age of bodies and physicality as determinants of merit and place is finished; it is as past as the age of blind adherence to custom, tradition, and rule by despotic monarchs (134). What makes women's subordination a historical relic, and hence wholly illegitimate, is its basis in physical difference at a time when other social and political practices—from abolition of slavery to repudiation of social rank as a criteria for rights or suffrage—signify popular and political rejection of stratification by physical difference or circumstances of birth (136–37). In the current age, according to Mill, what brokers legitimate distinction is mind, talent, capacity, and ambition—all set loose in an open field of competition. This age, too, knows the supreme importance to the individual and the species of choosing one's own life course and governors.[14]

Taken together, Mill and Wollstonecraft argue for a feminine subjectivity that is at once androgynous and different. It is androgynous in the rational, civic, and public order of things where mind alone matters and saturated with its sex difference in the private realm, where bodies, temperaments, emotional bearing, and "instinct" are thought to prevail. Neither rejects the sexualization of gender prevalent in the age. Rather, each contests only the totalizing reach of this sexualization and draws on Enlightenment rationalism and a certain Cartesian and bourgeois splitting of the modern subject to argue for the androgyny of public sphere existence. Indeed, the reassurance both Wollstonecraft and Mill offer to those potentially alarmed by the specter of emancipated women lies in confirming women's heterosexual and maternal identity in the domestic sphere, an identity treated as natural even if not exhaustive of women's existence. Although both Wollstonecraft and Mill advance the possibility that women ought to be able to choose whether to marry, neither can tarry long with the figure of the unmarried woman; both return incessantly to the assumption of women's married and maternal state. Moreover, both spill a great deal of ink on the ways that improvements in woman's education and liberty will improve wifely and maternal capacities. She will be more enlightened, less shrewish, more straightforward, less conniving, and a better model for her children, less of an embarrassment to them. All of these advantages, however, are to one side of the central point that women will not cease to be wives and mothers by virtue of emancipation. Through division of mind and body, and virtue and daily existence upon which each premises their arguments, women can be women in private and humans in public.

Of course, the counterargument to Mill's and Wollstonecraft's position, ubiquitous in the age and against which both are working, is that the sexual or reproductive functions of women's bodies fully saturate women's nature. That is exactly what the strong version of the new sex difference discourse establishes. At the extreme is Rousseau's contention that every element of woman's existence is conditioned by her sexuality—from her inherent lack of authenticity and *amour de soi-meme* to the natural strategic deployment of her sexuality to capture, hold, and even domestically govern men.[15] Similarly, Hegel's reduction of women to creatures of pure immanence is rooted in their reproductive capacities, and his argument that women are ethically fulfilled in families pertains to what he characterizes as their natural passivity in love, the unique capacity to both lose and achieve individuality in and through a male subject (114–15, 263–64).

For both Hegel and Rousseau, not just women's activities and proper venue but their minds and virtue differ radically from those of men. Indeed, what otherwise diverse late-eighteenth- and nineteenth-century antifeminist arguments carry in common is the notion that woman's nature, and the activities and entitlements appropriate to it, is fully determined by sexual difference, that women are fully saturated by this difference.[16] This is precisely the saturation that Enlightenment feminists resist. As Joan W. Scott recounts in her study of nineteenth-century French feminists, "They argued that there was neither a logical nor an empirical connection between the sex of one's body and one's ability to engage in politics, that sexual difference was not an indicator of social, intellectual, or political capacity" (x).

Nineteenth-century Europe, then, debated the Woman Question from a roughly common and strikingly new ontology of gender, one in which elaborate sex difference was taken to be a fact whereas the reach and significance of that difference was contested, particularly from a Cartesian perspective that permits the separability of mind and body, a separability that, like abstract rights and liberties, was difficult to elaborate for men while refusing to women. But it is not only Cartesianism that permits splitting the androgynous mind from the otherwise wholly sexed being, and it is not only the abstract character of liberal personhood that creates a wedge for feminism in the new formulation of citizenship. Rather, if the sex difference always recurs to the body in some way, that seemingly obstinate fact makes possible a humanist feminism in a liberal idiom that disunifies the female subject and abstracts from the body to make claims for women's equality. This disunification operates by literally splitting female ontology, parceling it out for different social spaces in which different activities and duties occur. Thus, the feminism of Wollstonecraft and Mill privatizes the sexed female body—leaving it to individual men, as it were—and abstracts from women's embodied existence to make claims on behalf of their capacity for public life, a capacity that makes women eligible for education, rights, and, above all, citizenship.

These moves to divide and abstract the subject from its embodied dwelling are typical of the age and by no means unique to the order of gender. The divided subject born with modernity and intensified by liberal ideological and capitalist political-economic ordering—particular/universal, subjective/objective, private/public, civic/political, religious/secular, bourgeois/*citoyen*—can be gathered under a universalizing political rubric such as "equality, liberty, fraternity" yet subsist in a civic and economic structure ordered by inequality, constraint, and individualism. The subject represented as free, equal, and solidaristic in state and legal discourse is abstracted from its concrete existence where it is limited, socially stratified, atomized, and alienated.

In short, the dominant figure of the age is the figure of man to which Wollstonecraft and Mill make recourse for their arguments about woman-man split in activities and consciousness and man abstracted from everyday embodied existence as represented by the state. If citizenship and rights are premised upon this abstract, disembodied figure of man, women's enfranchisement can also be claimed on that basis. If man has no body in public but only exists abstractly, discursively, through mediated voicing and representation, then woman need not have a body in public either, and the sexualization of gender ceases to be an impediment to public-sphere equality claims. That which is understood to make women women need not accompany them into public life, where we are all disembodied abstractions and split from private, economic, or civil existence. Women's difference is not, according to this kind of feminism, a public difference.[17]

But why is the same argument not made on behalf of Jews? What is the casting of the "Jewish difference" that permits the slide from "emancipation" to tolerance—with the latter's implications of a permanent, insoluble, difference—rather than equality? If modern citizenship is premised on man as man, not as he actually lives and works but as a potentially divisible and abstract being, why cannot Jews be split off from or abstracted from their Judaism to become rights-bearing citizens with the same relative conceptual ease exhibited by late-eighteenth- and nineteenth-century feminism? There were, of course, those (e.g., the leftist Hegelian Bruno Bauer, Marx's famous foil in "On the Jewish Question") who argued that Jews could be dealt with in precisely this fashion. From that perspective, racialization of Jews was no more determining than sexualization of women. Jews could be and were enfranchised on the condition of assimilation, on the condition that they shed identifying and constitutive Jewish practices—or at least on the condition that those practices became completely private.

It is already telling that there is a qualifier here, that emancipation was tacitly or expressly dependent upon assimilation, which is to say upon the transformation of Jews. Such a move was never made in debates about the Woman Question. Although at times cajoled to "ascend to reason," women were not asked to give up anything in order to become candidates for emancipation. Indeed, what could women be pressed to surrender in order to become more acceptable members of the nation, more like men, and gain proximity to, if not inclusion within, the universal? Any effort to de-sex women would be seen as making them monstrous, exactly what antifeminists accused feminism of doing. Thus, emancipation has different meaning for Jews and for women. Even with emancipation, the tolerance "deal" was already in place for Jews in a way it was not for women, where a different set of social powers sustained difference and their subordination through it.

For nonassimilated Jews, arguments against enfranchisement emerging from mid-nineteenth-century German debates on the question can be divided into three parts. First, the Jew has fealty to another (higher) god and another (higher) legal order that preempts their fealty to the Christian or secular state. Second, the Jew lives a "partial" (Jewish) life and does not conceive of himself as part of universal humanity but rather as belonging to the Jewish portion of humanity, hence does not participate in the universality the modern state is held to embody. Third, the Jewish religion cannot easily be rendered a purely private affair. Sabbath and holiday requirements as well as public worship and prayer contour the daily civic lives of Jews and thus prevent Judaism from the eligibility for tolerance, available to Protestant sects, in which religion can be rendered a purely individual and private order of belief. Judaism as a practice combined with Jewishness as a racial difference together cancel the possibility of containing the Jewishness of the Jew in the private sphere. To the extent that Jewishness and Judaism saturate the being and daily practices of the Jew and subtend the Jew through community, law, and/or ethnic affiliation, they leak into the domain where the abstract and universal equality, liberty, and community of man are held to reign.[18]

But if these are the arguments against emancipating or enfranchising nonassimilated Jews, arguments that all amount to refusing incorporation of a nation within a nation, how is it that assimilated Jews could be offered forms of "emancipation" that nonetheless left them vulnerable to anti-Semitic state and civil practices, signaling that emancipation opened onto a regulatory regime of tolerance rather than equality? To be sure, the regime of tolerance was a different creature from that administered by the seventeenth- and eighteenth-century Edicts of Tolerance in Austria and elsewhere. It had begun migration from the state to the social as the site of emanation, and it also was beginning to attach to individuals rather than subnational groups. But tolerance rather than equality it was, as became clear in ensuing episodes of state and civic "intolerance" in which Jews could lose privileges and be stripped of rights, (re)ghettoized, exiled, or exterminated.

What is the relationship between this vulnerability, experienced by Jews as subjects of tolerance but not by women as subjects of equality, and the respective nineteenth-century discourses of racialization and sexualization? How does each discourse position its subjects with respect to the emerging state discourses of universality that organize and confer citizenship? One way to address these questions is through consideration of Foucault's discussion in *The Order of Things* of the epistemic shift between early and high modernism. In the former, Foucault argues, the truth of an object or relation is based on manifest or visible signs. In the latter (the period under consideration), it comes to be rooted in the presumption of a generally invisible organic structure of things (chapter 7). If Foucault is right about the high modern episteme, only in the nineteenth century does it become possible to argue that the female body, for all its putative visible difference, does not carry the complete code for women's nature and capacities, or, more precisely, that the visibly sexed body is not the hermeneutic key to the mind or soul of women. Rather, feminists argue, the body is precisely that which must be seen past or seen through for women's soul and mental capacities to be grasped, just as antifeminists argued that gendering the female sex, determined by its reproductive function, was carried in every dimension of this being.

No one in the feminist debates argued directly from bodily appearances to soul and mind. Rather, appearances were as likely to belie as express a comprehensive ontology. If it could be rhetorically established that souls and minds were ungendered, then the question of women's bodies could be rendered largely irrelevant to public sphere feminist aims. Racialization, however, was another story. If, in racialized discourse, blood was the index of Jews, soul was their essence, and a people apart was their historical origin, then racialization is already a discourse, working from the inside (organic structure) outward (appearances) and from history (hidden) to present (manifest). In accord with what Foucault insists is the dominant episteme of the age, racialization is achieved genealogically and metaphorically rather than deduced directly from visible codes even as it also produces and interprets these visible codes. As Gustave LeBon formulated the racialization thesis at the end of the nineteenth century, "The life of each people, its institutions, its beliefs, and its arts, are only the visible traces of its invisible soul" (Marrus 14). In the nineteenth-century episteme, abstracting from bodily appearance to arrive at an ungendered mind or soul is a possibility; abstracting from blood and soul to arrive at the nature of a being is an oxymoron.

The sustained marking of Jews as racially distinctive even as they were emancipated was critical to the contradictory state imperative of simultaneously incorporating and regulating Jews, an imperative that Foucault identifies more broadly as the twin modern forces of "totalization and individuation" but the contradictory nature of which he rarely considers (Foucault, "Omnes," 225–28; Foucault, *Discipline,* 231–56). Racialization facilitated the coexistence of pressure to assimilate on the one hand and, on the other, marking Jews as objects of surveillance to ensure conformity with the terms of their emancipation. For Patchen Markell, "Such a surveillance requires that Jews be recognizable. The imperative of emancipation becomes, paradoxically, that *the state must see at all times that each Jew has ceased to be Jewish*" (146, emphasis in the original). In Markell's view, incorporation of an alien element in its Christian midst required a peculiar form of state recognition in which Jewishness never ceased to be identified and never ceased to be targeted for reduction or erasure. This form of recognition is paradoxically achieved by the assimilated Jewish embrace of a racialization discourse and refusal of solidarity with Eastern Jewry, figured as a lower, less cultured, and less modern form of life.

The difference between discourses of racialization and sexualization is not limited to the ways in which Jewishness and femininity are inscribed on and in individual bodies. Each discourse also posits distinctive forms of association (or lack of it) among those bodies. While racialization, in contrast with nationhood, potentially renders Jews in the image of sovereign individuals and hence as subjects ripe for nation-state incorporation, even decorporatized Jews remain available to a conception as a solidaristic people. If the decorporatization entailed in the pressures to assimilate, and required for the first order of formal emancipation and toleration, met its limit in the racialization of Jews, this racialization also links them naturally to one another and conjures their natural association.

The gendered sexualization of women, by contrast, casts them as individual complements of or opposites to individual men—if women are essentially similar, that does not imply their political or social relatedness, intra-group affinity, or solidarity. To the contrary, gendered sexualization establishes women's natural place in the heterosexual family as opposites or complements to individual men. It produces them as different from men but not as a solidaristic people or nation.

Both aspects of modern subject formation—that which ontologizes certain kinds of marked subjects and that which specifies the relation of marked subjects to other similarly marked subjects—remind us that the discourse of abstract universal citizenship was cross-cut during nation-state consolidation with other subject-producing discourses that facilitated classification and regulation of citizens who deviated from the Christian, bourgeois, white, heterosexual norm at the heart of these orders. Incorporation of the historically excluded through a discourse of abstract citizenship, a process that threatened to erase the subnormative status of the excluded, incited intensified forms of marking and regulation to reinscribe that status. Tolerance, coined originally to incorporate while regulating differences in belief, was an available vehicle for this incorporation. It simultaneously permitted individual and group regulation. It facilitated, that is, marking a difference through which the incorporation and individuation required for regulation could be sustained.

As tolerance begins to attach to identity rather than belief, which it does in the figure of Jews, it responds to the moment in liberalism when individualism combined with abstract citizenship falters as a principle of demarcation, when equality-as-sameness falters as a justice principle, and when the depoliticization of difference is either incompletely achievable or incompletely desirable on the part of either the subject or state. Tolerance emerges at this point as a supplement to equality rather than an extension of it. As a supplement, it is variously a substitute, an alternative, and, above all, that which finesses the incompleteness of equality—making equality true when it cannot do so on its own terms. Political and civic tolerance, then, emerges when a group difference that poses a challenge to the definition or binding features of the whole must be incorporated and sustained as a difference: regulated, managed, and controlled. Women, in their dispersal and in the sexualization of their identity, do not represent such a threat. They are not perceived as a group, nor does their manifest difference threaten to disappear. But Jews, in their association and in the racialization of their identity, do pose such a problem. Tolerance is the mantle cast over their emancipation to contain it.

One account, then, of the emergence of a discourse of equality for (Christian) women, and tolerance for Jews, reveals tolerance to be the sign of a discursively established, obstinate, and pervasive difference that cannot be assimilated in public life without disturbing the norms at the heart of that life. It signals a difference that cannot be abstracted from, and forms the basis for, community—whether imagined or literalized, minimal or substantial—apart from the nation-state. There is not just the question of a lingering Jewish nation conjured by the continued presence of unassimilated Jews in cities as well as the countryside. White supremacy combined with Christian hegemony in Euro-Atlantic states meant that even assimilated Jews would not be fully abstracted from their difference to participate in a universal order, whereas (Christian) women could be. In a bodiless public saturated with Christian norms (Christian) women can achieve a formal legal equality, whereas Jews, even when enfranchised and accorded rights, are still tolerated (or not) in their difference. Tolerance marks inassimilability to a hypostasized universal, and Jewishness—as a nation or a race—is figured as such unassimilability.

We cannot, however, be completely satisfied with this formulation. On the one hand, it overstates the assimilability of women into a humanist universalism, especially into the public and economic life of modern constitutional orders. We know that deep anxieties about sexual difference persist in these domains and that sexual difference is often far more of a barrier than religion—than even religious orthodoxy, ethnicity, or race—to participation in normatively masculine regimes. On the other hand, this argument understates what assimilation and racialization make possible by way of privatizing or eliminating Jewish practice and belief and detaching individual Jews from communities of Jews. Even if it was not completely successful, the project of detaching Jews from a transnational identity and fealty and producing them as European citizen subjects should have largely neutered political concern with Jewish difference. All that should have been left was scattered social prejudice, so I want to stir different ground.

If, according to Blackstone and Kant, women are naturally "concluded by their husbands," if husband and wife are "one person in the law," what makes women so incorporable, so available to being concluded or represented by individual men?[19] There would appear to be only two possibilities: similitude or natural subordination within an ontological hierarchy. Woman cannot be incorporated by man, cannot be represented by him as a true opposite but only as that which is either similar or naturally subordinate to him. If Laquer is right about the eighteenth-century shift from a one-sex to a two-sex model of gender, then we are not dealing with similitude. The similitude asserted even by feminists in this period pertains only to the realm of mind, virtue, and abstract citizenship. The argument is not that women are the same as men *tout court* but that rationality, virtue, and citizenship have no sex and are not embodied. Thus, woman's difference—as body, maternity, sexuality, subject, and sign of the household—remains outside the language and purview of equality, and thereby it remains a candidate for naturalization and for subordination.

Female difference within a presumed heterosexual sexual order is incorporable by men to the extent it is cast as a difference of inherent subjection, exactly the casting that Blackstone's and Kant's remarks imply. Moreover, within a heterosexual matrix, individual women can be claimed, "concluded," or represented by individual men. Their alterity within liberalism can in this way be secured at the same time it is politically resolved.[20] By contrast, the Jewish difference, however saturated with signs of inferiority within a Christian hegemonic order, cannot be assimilated or managed counterintuitively. It remains more unruly precisely because it directly mediates men's relations with one another, notwithstanding Judaism's matrilineal descent structure. It first appeared that racialization was a more powerfully determining discourse than sexualization in establishing limits to nation-state incorporation. It would now, however, seem that sexualization functions as a more relentlessly subordinating discourse and is therefore precisely what permits women's enfranchisement as political equals without risk of substantive equality and, more important, without risk of a challenge to the masculinist, heterosexual, and Christian norms at the heart of the putative universality of the state.

Another way to see this point involves turning slightly from the public/private axis as the vehicle of subordination and focusing on the sexual division of labor that formal emancipation leaves intact. As critics of liberal feminism have often pointed out, when women are made candidates for political equality a heterosocial division of labor and association is by no means called into question. Indeed, both Wollstonecraft and Mill anxiously reassured readers that legal gender neutrality—women's acquisition of economic, civil, and political rights—is not a ticket to gender integration in most substantive domains of life. With legal equality, social and economic sex segregation persists and so literally domesticates the effects of women's enfranchisement as citizens. An official policy of complete religious neutrality and racial equality, however, does promise and promote such integration and attendant ramifications. Once Jewish men are fully enfranchised and full bearers of rights, the "Jewish difference" lives on institutionally only in an epiphenomenal fashion.

There is potentially no limit to the political, social, and economic domains that Jews and gentiles will cohabit even as informal enclaves for each may persist—from commercial enterprises to neighborhoods, country clubs, and academic departments. Thus, the language of tolerance, which always signals the undesirable proximity of the other in the midst of the same, emerges as indexical of the capacity for mixing and the perceived threat to a social norm portended by such mixing. If the language of tolerance is invoked for women only when they are knocking at the doors of extreme male homosocial venues, to the extent that women mostly stay in their sexually assigned places and to the extent that the feminine body is heterosexually appropriated and privatized, the need for tolerance is not triggered.[21] Women's formal political equality is neither the sign nor the vehicle of their integration. To the contrary, that equality is founded in a presumption of difference organized by a heterosexual division of labor and underpinned by a heterosexual familial structure, all of which attenuate the need for tolerance and at the same time underscore the difference between formal and substantive equality.

What that means is familiar from several decades of feminist theorizing about effort to obtain gender equality in a liberal political frame. Precisely because this effort abstracts from women's condition and activities in the private realm (the condition and activities that implicate women's sexuality and women's designation through maternity) and reifies the subject, woman, rather than apprehends discourses constituting that subject, women's social equality within liberalism always remains incomplete. A subjection is presupposed and institutionalized that turns upon women's hypostasized heterosexual difference privatized and unemancipated and licenses everything from marital rape to the feminization of poverty to an inegalitarian sexual division of labor in both the family and the market. It is because and insofar that a sexual-social division of labor devolving on their bodies subordinates women that they can be rendered equals in the public. The capacity to split their existence in this fashion makes them candidates for equality rather than tolerance. More precisely, attainment of political equality does not require the supplement of tolerance for male superordination to be maintained.

The rhetoric of tolerance would seem to function, then, as one diagnostic key for relations of subordination in liberalism. It is invoked to redress histories of subordination or exclusion where a more thoroughgoing equality is immediately at stake and where maintenance of an abjected or subjected other is neither possible through a mechanism such as privatization of this subordination nor through its sustained institutionalization in the economy. Tolerance is invoked in liberal orders when a hegemonic norm cannot colonize or incorporate its other with ease, when that norm maintains or regroups strength through a new order of marginalization and regulation rather than through incorporation and direct relations of subordination.

Popular political discourse now treats heterosexual women as candidates for equality, whereas lesbians are candidates for tolerance. The subordinating difference of the former is secured by a heterosexual social and familial order while the latter cannot be. More generally, while gender-conceived heterosexually is not a subject for tolerance, gender detached from a heterosexual matrix—not only gay but also transgendered and transsexual bodies—immediately convenes the discourse of tolerance, confirming that it is the heterosexual family, the family-economy relation, and the sexual division of labor that secures an order of gender in which male superordination is achieved by means other than an expressly normative discourse excluding or abjecting women. In this regard, invocation of tolerance functions as a critical index of the limited reach of liberal equality claims. Practices of tolerance are tacit acknowledgments that the other remains politically outside a norm of citizenship, that the other remains politically other, and that it has not been fully incorporated by a liberal discourse of equality and cannot be managed through a division of labor suffused with the terms of its subordination.

This is not to argue that identity crafted from race, sexuality, ethnicity, Judaism, and Islam is crafted from material that inherently makes them eligible for tolerance. It is not to argue, *pace* Nancy Fraser, that these are primarily normative orders of subordination, producing claims for recognition while gender and class are materially organized powers and eligible for redistribution claims. To the contrary, assignation of one order of power to norms and the other to materiality is symptomatic of the discursive mystification of certain forms of inequality reinforced by tolerance discourse and the powers of subordination in tolerance discourse. Tolerance appears as a discourse of pure normativity, of pure recognition and its limits. What this appearance hides is inequality and regulation (achieved through the governmentality of tolerance dispersed in society) rather than the normative marginalization organizing its subjects. Norms of gender subordination can be entrenched through the privatization of one critical aspect—the laboring, sexualized, reproductive often-but-not-always heterosexual feminine body. The fashion in which the gendered body can be split and domesticated is mirrored for a homosexual, Jewish, or other racialized body only through the practice of passing. Are women in the public sphere passing in liberal democratic orders of justice?

If tolerance discourse is triggered when subordination at the site of a difference cannot be maintained through privatization of that difference, it would seem that gender subordination could be almost completely privatized. The Jewish difference figured as masculine and racialized, however, could not be. If tolerance discourse is triggered when a historical practice of social exclusion is to be sustained while its subordinating effects are somewhat attenuated, a social-familial division of labor allows male superordination to be sustained amid a discourse of formal equality. But there is no parallel institutional instantiation for white and Christian superordination. If tolerance discourse is triggered when incorporation of a given subcommunity threatens the unity and homogeneity, as well as the formal and informal norms, of the nation, sex difference construed heterosexually did not figure such subcommunity or such a threat, whereas Jews as a nation, and Jews as a race, did. If tolerance discourse is triggered when a marked group is simultaneously incorporated by the nation, yet is at the same time denoted as other in order not to disturb a governing norm, than such a discourse is not needed for a group whose incorporation does not erase the visible sign of difference.

But if tolerance entails privatization of a difference that matters, a privatization that always threatens to leak into the public, why isn't that women's situation? Privatization of a difference is not equivalent to subordination through difference in the private sphere. The former is an expressly political and discursive achievement, whereas the latter can occur inarticulately and independent of the law and independent of other discourses of governmentality. Women do not need to be tolerated because the discourse of their difference remains the site and vehicle of subordination achieved through division of labor working across and articulating a set of public/private distinctions.

Both Jews and women, formally emancipated in nineteenth- and twentieth-century Europe, gain political equality without fully shedding the stigma of their difference. For Jews, emancipation is accompanied by the governmentality of tolerance, because once the legal strictures are removed the discursive construction of the Jewish difference ceases to be systematically subordinating as a state or economic operation, but that loss constitutes a threat to a critical Euro-Atlantic nation-state norm. Tolerance in this regard iterates differences whose significance may be fading, but in so doing it veils its role in activating those differences and hence its work of subordination.

The veiling is enhanced by dispersion of the rationality of tolerance, its steady governmentalization over the nineteenth and twentieth centuries, a dispersion in which tolerance comes to emanate from a growing range of civil sites—schools and police forces to neighborhood associations and individuals—and targets ever more objects—from sexual minorities to Muslims—while appearing nothing more than a simple and benign strategy of peaceful social cohabitation.

NOTES

1. Jacob Katz argues that however different the national stories of Jewish emancipation across Western and Central Europe—Germany, Hungary, Austria, France, Holland, and England—"Jewish emancipation, in its wider sense, occurred more or less simultaneously. It can also be said to have followed a similar, if not identical course" (3). He observes further that "the story of Jewish emancipation in any of the Western European countries could be told separately but not for each country in isolation. For there is a reciprocal influence here that cannot be ignored. The example and teaching of German reformers like Moses Mendelssohn had their effect on French Jews; and the political advances gained by French Jews through the French Revolution had their impact on German Jewry" (3–4).

2. One instance of the change in political orientation toward Jews is the difference in both tenor and aim between two Viennese policies separated by less than twenty years. Empress Maria Theresa's Judenordnung of 1764 was hostile and punitive, whereas Emperor Joseph II's Toleranzpatent of 1782 was rational, benevolent, and administrative. Neither policy made Jews citizens, both aimed to reform Jewish practice and behavior in order that Jews could be tolerated, but the Toleranzpatent took up the task of reform in the style of an administrative and regulatory state rather than an antagonistic one.

3. As the French historian Theodore Reinach has formulated the historico-ontological effect of Jewish emancipation, "The Jews, since they have ceased to be treated as pariahs, must identify themselves, in heart and in fact, with the nations which have accepted them, renounce the practices, the aspirations, the peculiarities of costume or language which tended to isolate them from their fellow citizens, in a word cease to be a dispersed nation, and henceforth be considered only a religious denomination." *Histoire des israelites depuis la ruine de leur indépendance nationale jusqu'à nos jours,* 5th ed. (Paris: Hachette, 1914), cited in Marrus 94.

4. The Protestant character of religious tolerance in the West, in which religion is cast as a private matter of individual conscience and belief, is a poor fit for Jews as members of a *Volk* (nation). Patchen Markell underscores this ill-fit in his reading of the Prussian emancipation Edict of 1812. The Edict, Markell notes, refers to Jews as "persons of the Jewish faith," a gesture that discursively severs them from the Jewish nation and portrays them instead as "individual subscribers to a religious creed, akin to Lutheranism or Catholicism" (136).

5. Foucault makes a convincing case that nineteenth-century discourses of sexuality produced, in parallel fashion, a subject exhaustively defined by desires marked

as perverse: "The nineteenth-century homosexual became a personage . . . a type of life, a life form, and a morphology. . . . Nothing that went into his total composition was unaffected by his sexuality. It was everywhere present in him: at the root of all his actions because it was their insidious and indefinitely active principle. . . . It was consubstantial with him, less as a habitual sin than as a singular nature. The sodomite [of old] had been a temporary aberration; the homosexual was now a species" (*History of Sexuality* 1:43). There was significant intercourse, even interconstitutiveness, between the emerging discourses of racialization and sexualization; the racialization of Jews had a substantial sexual component.

6. As Sander Gilman notes, much of the racial theory marking Jews as "black" in nineteenth-century Germany and Austria was rooted in speculations about Jewish interbreeding with Africans during the period of the Alexandrian exile, thus constituting Jews as a mongrel rather than pure race and producing mongrelization as an explanation for Jewish inferiority. Gilman adds that Jews were regarded as having inherently endogamous kinship practices that resulted in impurity from the beginning. The mongrelization (as opposed to healthy mixing) of Jewishness did not make it any less categorizable (or reviled) as a race (174).

7. One can only wonder how much guilt associated with assimilation was relieved by embrace of the racialization thesis.

8. These emerging discourses of racialization and gender were not entirely distinct although they tend to be treated as such in the literature. Laquer, in *Making Sex,* discusses the sexualization of gender largely without reference to race, whereas Gilman tends to treat even the sexualized racialization of Jews without reference to the discourses of gender upon which Laquer draws. There is sad irony in this compartmentalized scholarship, for as even the popular imagination knows, the nineteenth-century racialization of Jews and Africans (and that of "Orientals," too) was markedly sexual, achieving its subordinating effects through feminization (in the case of Jews) or animalization (in the case of Africans) of both the sex drive and sexual morphology of male members of the "race."

9. Jacques-Louis Moreau, *Histoire naturelle de la femme,* vol. 1 (Paris: L. Duprat, 1803), cited in Laquer (5).

10. J. L. Brachet, *Traite de l'hysterie* (Paris, 1847), cited in Laquer (5).

11. Poulain de la Barre, cited in Schiebinger (1).

12. If what currently ruins women is an education that neglects or deforms their rational capacities, what ruins men in the existing sexual order of things? Here, Wollstonecraft draws on the Enlightenment conviction that illegitimate rank corrupts. Men born to high station rather than earning it is the toxic stuff of the ancien régime. Thus, privilege by birth, something men in male-dominant regimes everywhere possess, must be eliminated not just for the sake of an egalitarian ideal but to promote social virtues ranging from authenticity to industriousness. For Wollstonecraft, that is particularly important in the family, where virtue is nourished in the young (44–45, 146–50).

13. "However brutal a tyrant she may unfortunately be chained to—though she may know that he hates her, though it may be his daily pleasure to torture her, and though she may feel it impossible not to loathe him—he can claim from her and enforce the lowest degradation of a human being, that of being made the instrument of an animal function contrary to her own inclinations" (148).

14. Of course, to an even greater degree than Wollstonecraft, Mill flirts with the notion that women may have a group inferiority in certain areas. He even entertains the possibility of a mental difference related to their sex, but those differences are never expressly tied to the sexual or reproductive dimensions of the female body (175–88).

15. Rousseau's position was echoed a century later in British moral psychology. In his manifesto against educating women like men, Herbert Cowell declared, "Physiologists are . . . agreed that there is sex in mind as well as in body, and that the mental qualities of the sexes correlate their physical differences." "Sex in Mind and Education: A Commentary," *Blackwood's Edinburgh Magazine* 115 (1874): n.p., republished in Rowold (82).

16. Other strategies for legitimating women's foreclosure from political, intellectual, or economic life, however, rely less directly on the sexual or reproductive body and more on another kind of heterosexual functionalism that harken to the status-based arguments for gender subordination preceding what Laquer describes as sexualization of the gendered body commencing in the late eighteenth century.

17. This formulation of public equality on the back of privatized difference, of course, composes many of feminism's internal tensions and stumbling blocks over the next two centuries.

18. Indeed, this was precisely the worry voiced initially about vice-presidential candidate Lieberman's fitness for the job. Could he come to work, could he wage a war, on the Jewish sabbath or holy days? Was he too much of a Jew to be a universal representative of the people?

19. For a fuller discussion of this, see Sir William Blackstone, *Blackstone's Commentaries on the Laws of England,* cited in Pateman (77); see also Kant (139).

20. Such securing and resolution was beautifully exhibited in the pressure exerted on the wife of Bill Clinton by his advisors, after he lost his reelection bid for governor of Arkansas in 1980, to take his name. In 1981, after five years of marriage, she bid adieu to Hillary Rodham and became Mrs. Clinton.

21. Even now one hears the language of tolerance applied to women only when men are characterizing disruption to an avowed pleasure produced by the reigning masculinism in a particular venue. In such characterizations, the *equality* of men and women is rarely at issue, and men who might not want women in their social clubs might well consider them as equals. Rather, what is at stake is an alleged gender-based *affinity.*

Works Cited

Baron, Salo. "Newer Approaches to Jewish Emancipation." *Diogenes,* no. 29 (Spring 1960): 56–81.

Foucault, Michel. *Discipline and Punish: The Birth of the Prison.* Trans. Alan Sheridan. New York: Vintage Books, 1979.

———. *History of Sexuality.* Vol. 1, *An Introduction.* Trans. Robert Hurley. New York: Random House, 1978.

———. "Omnes et Singulatim: Towards a Criticism of Political Reason." *The Tanner Lectures on Human Values.* Vol. 2. Ed. Sterling McMurrin, 223–54. Salt Lake City: University of Utah Press, 1981.

———. *The Order of Things: An Archaeology of the Human Sciences.* New York: Random House, 1973.

Fraser, Nancy. "Recognition and Redistribution." *Justice Interruptus: Critical Reflections on the "Postsocialist" Condition.* New York: Routledge, 1997.

Gilman, Sander. *The Jew's Body.* New York: Routledge, 1991.

Hegel, G. W. F. *Philosophy of Right.* Trans. T. M. Knox. New York: Oxford University Press, 1962.

Kant, Immanuel. *The Metaphysics of Morals.* In *Political Writings.* Ed. H. S. Reiss, 131–75. New York: Cambridge University Press, 1970.

Katz, Jacob. *Out of the Ghetto: The Social Background of Jewish Emancipation, 1770–1870.* Cambridge: Harvard University Press, 1973.

Laquer, Thomas. *Making Sex: Body and Gender from the Greeks to Freud.* Cambridge: Harvard University Press, 1990.

Markell, Patchen. *Bound by Recognition.* Princeton: Princeton University Press, 2003.

Marrus, Michael R. *The Politics of Assimilation: The French Jewish Community at the Time of the Dreyfus Affair.* New York: Oxford University Press, 1971.

Mill, John Stuart. *On Liberty; with The Subjection of Women; and Chapters on Socialism.* Ed. Stefan Collini. New York: Cambridge University Press, 1989.

Pateman, Carole. "Women and Consent." In *The Disorder of Women*, 71–89. Stanford: Stanford University Press, 1989.

Rousseau, Jean-Jacques. *Emile.* Trans. Allan Bloom. New York: Basic Books, 1979.

Rowold, Katherina, ed. *Gender and Science: Late Nineteenth-Century Debates on the Female Mind and Body.* Bristol: Thoemmes Press, 1996.

Schiebinger, Londa. *The Mind Has No Sex: Women in the Origins of Modern Science.* Cambridge: Harvard University Press, 1989.

Scott, Joan W. *Only Paradoxes to Offer: French Feminists and the Rights of Man.* Cambridge: Harvard University Press, 1998.

Vital, David. *A People Apart: A Political History of the Jews in Europe 1789–1939.* New York: Oxford University Press, 1999.

Wollstonecraft, Mary. *A Vindication of the Rights of Woman.* Ed. Carol H. Poston. 2d ed. New York: W. W. Norton, 1988.

2 Gender and the Sexual Politics of Public Visibility in Iranian Modernity

AFSANEH NAJMABADI

FEMINIST CRITIQUE OF IRANIAN MODERNITY has been focused on the disciplinary work of a figure of female excess—in the 1960s termed the "Westoxicated woman"—for production of modern womanhood. This focus has worked as a "screen memory" for another figure of excess, the *fukuli* (bow-tied man) and *farangima'ab* (man mindlessly mimicking European ways).[1] A farangima'ab, however, was a figure of double displacement, double mimickery. Not only was he a displacement of European man but he was also a displacement of the figure of *amradnuma* (an adult man mimicking an *amrad,* a young male object of desire for adult men).

Beginning in the initial months of the Islamic Republic of Iran in 1979, for example, a great deal of popular energy was directed against what were perceived as cultural markers of the old regime. As part of this "cultural purification," as it was called, women's veils and men's beards, statements of Islamic belonging and political protest in the later years of Pahlavi rule, became recommended (for beards) and compulsory (for veils) visible markers of state-sponsored masculinity and femininity.

Although much has been written about women's veils, little has been said about beards. Men were also strongly pressured to not wear neckties. Often considered a symbol of Europeanization, the necktie had its own chain of associations, through the bow tie, connecting it with the figure of the fukuli. Moreover, since the 1979 Iranian revolution the issue of veiling and unveiling, compulsory or consensual for women in Islamicate societies and communities, has taken center stage in international discussions of the status of women in these societies. The veil, hypervisibile, has come to serve as a sign for more than gender. It has come to be read for "the state of modernity."

This hypervisibility, the multiple services the veil has come to render, by continuing the prior work of making woman stand as a privileged marker of modernity, has compounded, although unsuccessfully, further erasure of the other excess figure of Iranian modernity—the beard.

In a troubling sense the feminist critique of modernity has complemented its burden of birth—a disavowal of male homoeroticism. It has provided yet another way of forgetting the troublesome figure of amrad, which Iranian modernity has been keen to place in premodern times (by transporting particular sexualities to times forever past) or in a transcendental domain. Yet this haunting figure threatens to come back in the form of young women in urban Iran dressing and living as young men, a reminder that studies of gender and sexuality cannot be divided and demarcated into separate domains and objects (Butler).

The figure of Westoxicated woman, focus of a cultural critique of prerevolutionary Iran, was one of double displacement but of a different kind: a European woman onto an Iranian figure (Tavakoli-Targhi, "Imagining Western Women"). The figure was also a displacement of the "sex troubles" of Iranian modernity, woman had come to act as a masquerade for an amrad. Feminism's "burden of birth," its insistent disavowal of male homoeroticism, has made this connection impossible to recognize. It is vital, however, for these associations to be re-made if Iranian feminism is to retain its critical edge, especially because current Iranian culture wars have become explicitly rearticulated around a concept of cultural imperialism and the West that is focused on "moral corruption, sexual excess, and homosexuality."[2]

Modernity's Excess

During the early decades of the twentieth century there were two figures of excess. In the text of a women's journal in 1915, for instance, women and men who flouted rules of decent behavior in public were described as articulating the excesses of urban transformations.[3] The female figure was critiqued for abrogating "the verse on *hijab*," for refusing modesty, enjoying showing off in public, and wanting to have fun with men. The man, marked "with his bow tie and flower perfume," was described as "having consumed some alcohol, with a cane, vane and drunk" and popping up next to a woman everywhere.

The fukuli remained a stock figure of critical satire throughout the 1940s. By the 1970s, however, the Westoxicated woman became the dominant, if not sole, figure of modernity's excesses. What does the disappearance of the fukuli say about gender and the sexual politics of public visibility in twentieth-century Iran? The fukuli, an over-Europeanized man, was compounded trouble. He transgressed the rules of gender proprietorship by attempting to socialize with kin-unaffiliated women (and in public), yet he was also a figure of abjection through his affiliation with an amradnuma. This compound structure allowed public critique of this figure to avoid "sexuality trouble" and remain at the level of "inauthenticity"—mimicking the European—even if abject affiliation with an amradnuma, along with attempts at denial and erasure, continued to inform the vehemence of the cultural critique. To understand the work of the fukuli as modernity's excess, and his erasure in current critique, one needs to consider the nineteenth-century's enormous transformations of gender and sexuality in Iran.

Men, Amrads, Amradnumas, and Women

Qajar Iran (1785–1925) began with notions of beauty that were largely gender-undifferentiated. Beautiful men and women were depicted as having very similar facial and bodily features. In written sources the same adjectives were used to describe male and female beauty.

The gender-undifferentiated figures of male and female beauty corresponded to the two figures of pleasure—in addition to wine—promised to Muslim male believers in the heavenly afterlife. Allegorical gardens of Persian poetry and painting are populated by *huri* (beautiful, eternally young, and virgin females) and more commonly and frequently by *ghilman* (beautiful young and beardless men), who often doubled as *saqi* (cup-bearer) (Meisami). Most commonly in current writings the figure of a young, beardless man, amrad, is referred to as "boy," and *amradparasti* (loving amrads) is rendered as "boy-love." I refuse that naming because of the close affiliation of "boy" with contemporary notions of pedophilia and the notion of "boy" as child.

In premodern and early modern male homoerotic Persian culture an amrad was more commonly a young male who in contemporary terms would be considered an adolescent teenager or even in his early twenties so long as he did not have a fully visible beard.[4] The face considered the most beautiful was that of a *nawkhatt* (an adolescent who had the first trace of a mustache before the full growth of facial hair), a process that could take a number of years. At the same time, however, that sign of beauty heralded the beginning of the end of his status as an object of desire for adult men and his own movement into adult malehood. It signaled the beginning of his loss as a beloved.

The growth of a full beard marked adult manhood. Books of etiquette and moral behavior contained severe edicts against men shaving their beards and were (are) related to this critical passage from a state in which it was acceptable to be an object of desire of adult men to a state in which that desire would constitute unmanliness. A beard was not so much a marker of man from woman as the modern naming of beardless men as effeminate would imply. The common naming of beardless amrads as effeminate indicates the current depth of heteronormalization. "Amrad" and other words used for adolescent beardless men are not derivative from words that connote femaleness. Adult men who chose to shave their beards were termed "amradnuma," which meant nothing like *zan'numa* (looking like a woman).

Edicts against shaving one's beard would thus express the cultural fear that young men might continue to be interested in remaining objects of desire rather than becoming individuals who themselves desired. An adult man who shaved his beard, an act taken as a declaration of desire to be desired by other men, would be linked to *'ubnah,* considered in medical discourse as an illness (Nathan; Rosenthal). *Birish* (beardless) men and "naked" (unveiled) women were visual spectacles of European society for Iranian men who traveled there. They were alternatively inscribed as icons of the ungodliness and corruption of Europeans or as the ghilman and huri, making Europe paradise on earth.

Nineteenth-Century Transformations of Beauty, Love, and Sexuality

Highly gender-differentiated portrayals of beauty appeared by the end of the nineteenth century. Royal portraits of late-nineteenth-century Qajar, for instance, do not show the slim waistes and facial features associated with the beautiful male bodies of earlier decades. Similarly, female figures became more individualized and distinct in facial and body features. In a closely connected development, depictions of male beauty completely disappeared, along with those of male-male loving couples.

A first reading of the transformation would indicate that although male homoeroticism in earlier times was an openly celebrated theme, Qajar Iran marked a radical change in sexual mores and erotic sensibilities toward heteronormalization of love and beauty. The process of heteronormalization in nineteenth-century Iran, however, was more complex than the presence or absence of male homoeroticism. What marks these transformations is male homoeroticism masquarading as heteroeroticism and disavowal of homoeroticism in a way that produced the social space for such a masquerade.

The processes took place in two distinct sites of cultural interaction. First, European men (and women later in the nineteenth century) traveled to Iran and published accounts of those trips. Second, Iranian men traveled to Europe. The nineteenth century marked the intensification of these interactions as well as an important increase in circulation of travelogs as printed texts.

By the early nineteenth century Iranian men had become acutely and increasingly aware that Europeans considered older man–younger man love and sexual practices to be very prevalent in Iran and also considered them as vices. This theme goes back to at least the seventeenth century. European accounts often linked same-sex practices with young male dancers who were sometimes, in European eyes, cross-dressed as female. On occasion the accounts, especially those by travelers familiar with Chardin's late-seventeenth-century work, were linked to women's seclusion.[5] William Ouseley (1767–1842), who accompanied his brother, Ambassador Gore Ouseley, to the court of Qajar in 1810–12, reported on a dance staged in Tabriz in June 1812 as part of a variety of entertainments for his benefit:

> After the usual refreshments of coffee and *kaleans,* a dance was exhibited, the performer being a birish or beardless boy of fifteen or sixteen years, wearing the complete dress of a woman and imitating, with most disgusting effeminacy, the looks and attitudes of the dancing girls; sometimes turning round on one spot for several minutes to the sound of a *kemáncheh* or Persian violin, or moving slowly along the floor with much ungraceful distortion or dislocation with the musick. . . . Another boy, disguised likewise as a woman, then stood up to dance. (3: 402, 1: 190)

Beardlessness began to be associated with effeminacy at this point. In addition to the young male dancers, William Ouseley also described many images of young, beardless men—often wall-inserted paintings paired with similar female faces—as effeminate (3: 125, 3: 156). Although European men read beardless Iranian male faces as effeminate, Iranian men read beardless European males as ghilman (or amrad).[6]

Perhaps the best-known, most influential writing about the social habits of Iranians in Iran during the early decades of the nineteenth century were those of James Morier. Iranians were hurt or angered by his portrayals, not only in travelogs but also the many works of fiction, in particular *Hajji Baba,* inspired by his travels. Among the disputed attributes were Morier's various references to what he called "this rascally beggarly b-gg-rly country."[7] About Crown Prince 'Abbas Mirza, he noted with approval in his journal entry for June 19, 1812, "[A strict Muslim, particularly with regard to wine, he is] equally temperate in the indulgences of the harem & strictly punishes that horrid offense against nature of which I have mentioned some abominable instances in the government of his effeminate, vicious brother of Shiraz" (Johnston 176).

European reports on Iranians' sexual mores, in particular the issue of male homosexual practices, continued throughout the nineteenth century and into the twentieth. Could that repetition have pressured Iranian men in contact with Europeans to dissimulate and disavow male same-sex practices? Could this pressure have contributed to the process of heteronormalization of male sexuality in Qajar Iran? Some Iranian men who traveled to and wrote about Europe used strong language to disavow European perceptions. As Mirza Fattah Khan Garmrudi, traveling through Europe in 1838, observed:

> With all this corruption and the unseemly state [in Europe that he had been so far describing and documenting], they write books condemning and moralizing people of Iran. In particular, Fraser has insinuated and exaggerated a great deal. For instance: that Iranian people [men] are greatly inclined toward young beautiful boys and some commit evil acts with them. Yes, in all nations of the world, some deeply ignorant people, overcome by spirit of lasciviousness and satanic temptations, commit some unacceptable practices. But the people of Europe who are known for all kinds of ill reputes, and especially for this evil act, who have houses of young men [*amradkhanah*], similar to houses of prostitution [*qahbah'khanah*], who go to these places all the time, pay money and commit this evil act—it is totally unfair that they, who are known to engage in this evil practice, would tell off people of Iran and attribute this practice to us and write about it in books. (962)

This anxiety over European judgment of Iranian sexual mores and practices remained a preoccupation throughout the nineteenth century. Moments of disavowal were not just related to particular sexual practices. The anger over Morier's, Fraser's, and other Europeans' readings of Iranian social and sexual mores began to reconfigure structures of desire by introducing a demarcation line by which we now distinguish homosociality from homosexuality. Iranians began to find themselves "explaining" to European visitors that at least some practices that could be read as homosexuality—for example, men holding hands, embracing, and kissing in public—were not so. Europeans were misreading homosociality for homosexuality.

Disavowal of homosexuality out of homosociality—a cultural work by no means in some distance past but that still continues—set two seemingly contradictory, yet enabling, dynamics in motion.[8] It marked homosociality as empty of homosexuality, thus making homosexuality "homeless" and endangered because it was denied. Yet by insisting on that exclusion it also provided homosexuality a homosocial home in which to masquerade.

Before this cultural interaction, the delineation between the two categories was meaningless. Were practices such as *siqah-'i khwaharkhwandigi* (vow of sisterhood) celebrations of the homosocial bonds of women's close friendships, or did they involve same-sex practices? The question is unanswerable, not so much because lesbians have been erased from history or archives do not exist but because it arises from a structure of desire, naming and categorizing it, that does not pertain to the period in which a demarcation between homosociality and homosexuality had been formed. The naming of homosociality as distinct from homosexuality assumes a particular structure of desire. Did "the sisters" engage in bodily acts that we now name as lesbian? Perhaps they did. Did they desire, name, or perceive their vow in any way close to what the later dynamic of naming through disavowal effected in structure of sexuality? Most likely not. Formation of homosexuality through denial and disavowal became its condition of possibility and reproducibility. The denial of any overlap between the now-delineated domains of homosociality and homosexuality paradoxically provided a shelter, a masqueraded home, for homosexuality. We can continue to hold each other's hand in public, that is, because we have declared doing so as a sign of homosociality empty of homosexuality.

Denial and disavowal was only one response to coming under European gaze.[9] Dissimulation and "cross-representation" was another. In the visual field, for instance, female figures of beauty came to stand for denial of the maleness of a beloved; at the same time, they provided shelter for him.[10] As "another gaze" entered the scene of desire, as if an intruder had walked onto a private chamber, the scene of homoerotic desire had to be covered, masqueraded, for Iranian men who interacted with Europeans. The female-male "loving couple" (figure 1) in this context served as a masquerade of desire. European viewers could read the male-female couple as a scene of heteroeroticism, while male Iranian viewers could maintain that young male beauty would continue to stand as such for their *shahid* (witness to divine beauty).

One marker of Iranian modernity became the transformation of homoeroticism into masqueraded hetero-eros.[11] As Europeans came to identify Iran for and by its homosocial and homosexual practices, Iranian modernity came to identify itself with, and simultaneously disavow, that abject position.

Figure 1. *Embracing Lovers,* attributed to Muhammad Sadiq, Shiraz, ca. 1770–80. (Collection of Eskandar Aryeh)

Masquerading could not but affect homoeroticism itself. The disappearance of ghilman and repeated appearance of female figures performed the same cultural labor: the heteronormalization of desire, at least in its public visual presentation and appearance. Although sharing common features with hur, the ghilman had been a distinct figure of desire as an object and a figure for narcissistic identification. The screening of the ghilman by the hur now made both positions of desire feminized. To desire to be desired by a man became positions that only women could occupy. Homosexual desire became derivative, a substitute for heterosexual desire. The triumphant modernist proclamation was that homoerotic practices were what men did in the old days, when women were not available due to gender segregation.

The disappearance of the ghilman strongly consolidated the feminization of beauty as well. The only representations of human beauty that emerged by the end of the nineteenth century were those of young women, a process facilitated by the increased possibility and acceptability of women coming into public view during the same period.

European(ized) Man as Cultural Masquerade of Amrad(numa)

If representations of young men as heterosexual lovers of young women provided a gender masquerade for male homoeroticism, there was yet a second figure—a cultural masquerade—located in the other site for the enormous transformation of sexuality in the nineteenth century. Iranian men who visited Europe described young European men as ghilman in their travelogs, paradisic male figures who would act for the comfort of the shahid, the witnesses to the young male beauty which served as the object of sufi gaze. Visual representations of Europe, which often took the form of allegorical encounters between Europe and Iran through renarrativization of a sufi tale, that of Shaykh San'an, depicted such figures.

As Tavakoli-Targhi has argued persuasively, the nineteenth-century travelers' naming of European women as huri echoed the Qur'anic and other Islamic classical descriptions of the pleasures of paradise. It was not, however, only huri whom these early travelers saw; they also saw ghilman. When Qajar men of religion tried to arouse Muslim Iranian men to fight a holy war and expel infidel intruders (Tzarist Russia) in northwestern Iran by reminding them of their desire to become martyrs and go to paradise, where "the hur had decorated the paradise and the ghilman were standing to serve you" (Qa'im'maqami 19), Iranian men argued that huri and ghilman could be seen without martyrdom in the earthly paradise of Europe.

Mirza Abu al-Hasan Khan Shirazi, one of the earliest nineteenth-century Iranian travelers to Europe, visited London's St. James Park in December 1809 and described the sight of young men and women strolling there:

> In the park we saw some 100,000 men and women parading themselves on foot and on horseback. Elsewhere pretty girls *and handsome youth* were admiring the gardens: although it was winter, the verdure of the park rivaled the Bagh-i Eram, the Garden of Eden. . . .
>
> Indeed, it is a vast and delightful pleasure-ground—as exhilarating as a draught of wine. If a sorrowing soul traverse these heavenly fields, his head is crowned with flowers of joy. . . . In the gardens and on the paths, beauteous women shine like the sun and rouse the envy of the stars; and the houris [and ghilman in Persian, missing from English translation] of paradise blush with shame to look upon the rose-cheeked beauties of the earth below. In absolute amazement, I said to Sir Gore Ouseley:
>
> *If there be paradise on earth*
> *It is this, oh! it is this!* (Shirazi 143–44, emphasis in the original)[12]

Whereas in previous readings the repeated reporting of males and females socializing in public had been read as a spectacle of heterosociality, reading heterosexuality as the privileged desire that informed the cultural reportage of the Iranian male travelers to Europe allowed a cultural sensibility that perceived both male and female beauties as the objects of desire for the male viewer/reporter to recede into oblivion. Contrast the description of a reception at the house of the British consul in Beirut, Rizaquli Mirza, on his way to England, described the consul's wife as "moon of England" who sat on his one side. On the other sat a young man. "I did not know if I should look at the lady or pay attention to the youth. I was devastated from one side and wondrous about the other. I would enlighten my eye with the light of the lady for a while and then give my heart's attention to the young man" (Rizaquli 271).

Repetitious reportings of "handsome young men and beautiful young women" were in the first instance not accounts of public heterosociality—sighting and reciting some wondrously unfamiliar cultural practice that constituted the difference between us and them. Rather, an earlier event to this cultural production was a different wondrous moment—a paradisic fantasy of desire for wine and male and female beauty come real. I am not suggesting that the other cultural meaning was absent but that the spectacle of heterosociality, and emergence of a desire for it in Iranian society, may have been enabled by earlier scenes of paradisic (and once homo- and heterosexual) desire.

Many nineteenth-century travelog accounts of Europe depicted it as paradise through the story of Shaykh San'an (Tavakoli-Targhi, "Nigaran-i" 29–35). An important shift takes place in these recollections. No longer a tale narrating *nazar* (the sufi practice of gazing), love, abjection, redemption, and eventual unity with the divine, Shaykh San'an's nineteenth-century renditions told of a journey to paradise. It was a spectacle of forbidden pleasures-become-available and instigated by the cultural memory of paradisic forbidden pleasures-become-allowable.

Even more than in written travelogs, visual texts of the period (paintings, pen boxes, vases, and book illustrations), often produced and incited by oral and written descriptions of early "eyewitnesses," depicted Europe as paradise through the story of Shaykh San'an. Pre-Qajar illustrations of the story focused on two of its scenes: the scene of nazar (the shaykh first sights the Christian maiden and gazes at her) and the spectacle of abjection (the shaykh tends swine). Nineteenth-century visual representations privileged the scene of the shaykh receiving the fateful cup of wine from the young woman and drinking it (figure 2).

The old man's mouth receiving wine from a cup in the hand of a Christian woman forms the visual focus of the painting. To one side are often disciples, young and old, of the shaykh who accompanied him on his journey to Rum/Europe. It is an-all male group ranging in age from the very young (also objects of homoerotic desire within the sufi community) to the very elderly, signifying the relevant homosocial group that constituted the world of Shaykh San'an. On the other side of the image the Christian maiden is flanked by a mixed group of women and men. I have argued elsewhere that this group signified the heterosociality of European society. It is a marker of cultural difference between "us" and "them" (Najmabadi, "Reading for Gender").

This reading marks the male and female group as a spectacle of heterosociality that early Iranian travelers, in a mirror "mis-reading" of Europeans in Iran, often viewed as heterosexuality, thus reporting Europe to be a land of rampant public heterosexual display. To understand transformations of sexuality as well as gender it is critical to re-read the scene as representing the ghilman and the hur. As a whole, it centers on the critical cup of wine, which presents a spectacle of paradise where pleasures forbidden the male believer on earth—in particular the pleasure of young men, wine, and huri—are abundantly available.

Figure 2. *Shaykh San'an and the Christian Girl,* artist unknown. Iran, ca. 1830. (Private collection)

The Iranian cultural distinction between "them" and "us" was not only centered on the issue of "their" women being naked and "ours" being covered, as Tavakoli-Targhi has powerfully argued and amply documented ("Imagining" and "Nigaran-i"). It was also focused on "their" men's beardlessness and "ours" being full-bearded. A full beard was considered a sign of male adulthood; beardlessness marked a man as an amrad or amradnuma. As Morier had satirized, Iranian men were shocked by the lack of beards on European men. Mir ʿAbd al-Latif Shushtari, whose work in 1801 provided one of the earliest references for later Persophone writers on Europe, noted that European "men shave their beard and mustache, and braid their hair" (295). Mirza Salih Shirazi marked to the day (the "last day of July") in 1816 his own conflicted adoption of the English habit of shaving his beard as a way of fitting into the culture, a sacrifice that would make his effort to study in England possible (178–80). Even Nasir al-Din Shah (1848–96) continued to note meticulously the state of the beards and mustaches of the European men whom he met on his first visit in 1873 (88, 224, 231, 239).

Visual representations of the wine-drinking episode from Shaykh Sanʿan's story included "bare-breasted" European women and beardless men. The bearded man at the center of these depictions symbolized every Iranian adult man, drinking wine from the hand of one of the hur. At a certain level the simultaneous presence of hur and ghilman in the representation of Europe as paradise signaled an important cultural shift. Although the promised rewards of paradise included young creatures of both sexes, in another genre—Persian love poetry composed by male poets—the beloved was almost always male. *Maʿshuq* (beloved) and shahid are decidedly male, even though the grammatical gender neutrality of the Persian language has made it possible for later modernist literary critics to deny or neutralize that fact.

In contrast to this tradition of male beloved, the actual embodiment of female hur in the persons of European women seems to have shifted that gender configuration. The females it produced were subjects of love lyrics—a shift that was critical to the eventual feminization of the beloved. As Tavakoli-Targhi has observed, one change crafted through the travelog as a literary genre was the emergence of an individualized specific figure for the beloved ("Nigaran-i" 35–36). But the process of individualization included a sex change that transformed a male beloved into a female beloved. Although Mirza Abu Talib Khan has at least one lyric for a young man—a young English captain he named "heavenly youth"—the majority of love lyrics he and other travelers composed were for young European women.[13]

How, then, did the shift from male beloved to female beloved take place, even as travelers "witnessed" both hur and ghilman in the European paradise? How was a sense of pleasure, which saw both handsome young men and beautiful young women as objects of desire, reeducated and disciplined into heteronormativity by the end of the nineteenth century, transforming male-male love from natural, even divine, to unnatural and abominable?

That Mirza Abu Talib Khan's lyrics were largely composed for particular women and only exceptionally in praise of individual men may provide a clue. Male Iranian travelers noted both male and female beauties in their reports, but it was European women who courted them, surrounded them at parties, conversed and flirted with them, invited them persistently to dance, and took them to plays, operas, and other entertainments.[14] It was a cultural interpellation that reeducated their senses and sensualities. European women hailed Iranian men as if the latter shared the emerging heteronormativity of European public culture, and the men seem to have responded with minimal haggling.[15] In fact, later travelers anticipated being reeducated. When in Damascus on his way to England, Rizaquli Mirza asked the British general consul to provide him with a manual on how to behave in Europe. The handbook included sections on how to behave with women (222–23). Some found themselves in unimagined circumstances. Farhad Mirza, accompanied by family members, including his wife, on the journey to Mecca in 1875, was hosted by the governor of Baku and found himself boarding the same carriage as his wife upon departure from Baku. "I would have never imagined in Tehran," he wrote, "that one could sit in the same carriage with one's wife or sister and go to pay a visit to a shrine or go to Tajrish [a northern suburb of Tehran used for strolling] in public, facing relatives and strangers" (Mu'tamid al-Dawlah 41).

Being surrounded and saturated by unrelated female company in public ceremonies was a new cultural experience, a very intense one about which these men reported at great length and in minute detail. Instead of the homosocial male spaces they had experienced all their adult lives, their daily encounters in Europe were over and over heterosocial—and not only in ballrooms and at dances. Streets and parks, royal audiences, schools and workplaces, boats, trains, railroad stations and ports were all public spaces populated by men and "uncovered" women. Heterosocial European cultural practices, in other words, proved to be heteronormalizing of Iranian men's sensibilities.

The spectacle of seeing handsome young men and beautiful young women dancing together was at once the culturally familiar paradisic phantasm of huri and ghilman and an unfamiliar spectacle of public heterosociality. The phantasmic familiarity of the former familiarized the unfamiliarity of the latter. The voyeuristic pleasure generated by the former worked to transform the unfamiliar heterosocial spectacle from one of *hayrat* (a wondrous sight) to one of admiration—a social good—and finally to something desired. The desirous sight of hur and ghilman became productive of a desire for heterosociality. Seeing a young, beardless Englishman was for one moment a sight of the paradisic ghilman, yet at the next moment the same young man was the husband of an English huri or an officer of the Royal Court.

For someone accustomed to seeing men in and as public, encountering men and women together in public was a profound transformation of gender and sexual meaning. It began a major heteronormalization of sensibilities, a process that was never fully "accomplished" at either gender or sexual level. What in part worked against it were continued social practices at home: female and male homosociality, spousal relations, and child-rearing.[16] In Europe, Iranian men were not only courted by women but were also interrogated about "their women," their marital arrangements, and even their sex lives. During such conversations they began to imagine alternative gender relations and sexual orientations. If only Iranian women were more like European ones, then perhaps gender relations and sexualities could be reconfigured (Tavakoli-Targhi, "Nigaran-i").

It took a century for things to change. By the end of the nineteenth century, male travelers continued to report seeing beautiful women but no longer recorded seeing ghilman and shahids. (In fact, they rarely referred to European women as huris. By then, the women had become realized, defantasized from earlier paradisic creatures.)[17] Correspondingly, gender-differentiated notions of beauty became consolidated. Late-nineteenth-century men were no longer represented as being as slim-waisted as their forefathers, nor were male-male love couples being portrayed by the turn of the twentieth century.

While the male beloved disappeared from modernist male literary and visual representations, and sufi love was rendered transcendental, homosexual desire was transformed from natural to unnatural and abominable and was seen to result from the undesirable social practice of women's seclusion and gender segregation.

Normative Heterosexuality and Its Effects

The heteronormalization of sexuality did not, of course, mean elimination of homoeroticism or same-sex practices, hard as Iranian modernists (secular or Islamist) may have been trying through denial, disavowal, legal sanction, and social approbation.[18] What was heteronormalizing about the transformation was the simultaneous production of heterosexuality as natural and same-sex desire as derivative, forced on the natural as a consequence of unfortunate social arrangement of sex segregation. In other words, one critical distinction between the process of heteronormalization in Iran and that in Western Europe, as proposed by Foucault, is that no notion of the homosexual as a type emerged in Iran as a dominant discourse.[19]

The dominant, although not sole, notion of sexuality has continued to remain centered on acts as being distinct from inherent forms of desire. Despite the emergence of strong moral repugnance against homoeroticism as celebrated in classical Persian literature, along with the denial and transcendentalization of such love, the concept of homoerotic desire or homosexuality as a distinct type of sexuality has not become culturally hegemonic in Iran. The modernist project of compulsory heterosocialization and expectation that homosexual practices would disappear once women became "available" to men and were treated fairly could have produced pressure toward "typing" men and women who "still" engaged in same-sex practices as a-normal, if not abnormal, and stricken with some sort of "illness."[20] Yet that does not seem to have become a hegemonic or dominant view. It works against consolidation of generalized homophobia that emerged with production of "homosexual as a species." Sexual acts between men continue to be seen as what men do before settling into heterosexual, procreative sex with wives (or even as they do so, as long as they perform their reproductive obligations) rather than as what marks them as a particular human type.[21]

The initial impulse to employ masquerading moves as resistance against the European gaze may also have been enabling against internal threats. Iranian modernity began to cast homosexuality as an unnatural vice and a form of moral corruption—especially when threats took the form of violent punishments, as in the early years of the establishment of Islamic Republic of Iran and the continuing menacing terror of its penal code.[22]

Unveiling: A Modernist Veil

That modernist efforts to heteronormalize Iranian society have not focused on the production of the homosexual as a type has had significant repercussions on yet another level. Having decided that male same-sex practices were caused by gender segregation—more particularly, the veiling of women—male-male sexual practices, much like the veil and linked with it, became a sign of national backwardness in modernist discourse. Modernist drives at gender desegregation, with unveiling as its central element, worked as veiled campaigns to eradicate same-sex practices and "unnatural sexualities." What was sought was a double miracle: to overcome the backwardness of women (e.g., transform them into companionate wives, educated mothers, and useful citizens) and make same-sex practices, especially among men, socially redundant.

If the social regime of Qajar Iran was one of compulsory homosociality combined with procreative heterosexuality that left the structure of sexual desire indeterminate, then Iranian modernity insisted on a regime of compulsory heterosociality that was to underwrite normative heterosexuality.[23] From that perspective the issue of unveiling (and, more generally, emergence of a modern dress code) became somewhat more complicated than a plan aimed at modernizing women or producing uniformed citizens.

The continued focus of current analysis of the issues of the veil and women's emancipation as the centrally contested projects of Iranian modernity misses, overlooks, or covers up the productive work of modernist moves for heteronormalization of Iranian society. It has become a "screen memory" of Iranian history, filtering the other achievement of the nation's modernity—the erasure of ghilman from the national imagination. The modernist normative gender moves were public performances of normative sexuality; they had to navigate anxieties of modern sexualities.

If women and men had to be refashioned to become modern citizens, their publicly visible appearance and outfits had to stop looking alike and, more urgently, like those other figures to be forgotten, the amrad and the amradnuma. In order to appear more European, men had to abandon their *'abas* (long and enveloping outer garments) and wear suits, ties, and hats. The hair question posed a particular challenge. To look European, a man was to shave his beard, but that made him look perilously like an amradnuma. Impressive manly mustaches, a popular fashion, could help deflect that affiliation but only to some extent, as many popular satires of the fukuli reminded. It was one more reason for trying to banish ghilman and amrad from Iran's cultural imagination and for the current drive among many Islamists to grow a full beard. Despite denial, disavowal, and transcendentalization, not to mention suppression and punishment, the figure of ghilman has remained ever-present, a threat to modern normative masculinity.

Where the pressure to typologize sexuality seems to have produced a long-lasting effect is in the transformation of the notion of *bachchahbazi* (literally, playing with children) and with it of the Iranian concept of *bachchah* (child). "Bachchah," in combinations such as *ghulambachchah* (young male slaves), *tarsabachchah* (young male Christian), and *kafirbachchah* (young male infidel) as well as the general term *bachchahbazi* (fooling around with/

loving young male adolescents) once connoted older man–younger man sexual practices, with the word *bachchah* meaning something much closer to the contemporary meaning of "teenager." Once older man–younger man sexual practices were considered an unnatural vice, however "bachchah" was transformed to what now would be "child," and the sexual practices became "pederasty."

Any discussion of such a charged topic immediately raises the specter of a defense of pederasty. My point, however, is to draw attention to the fact that the processes that named older man–younger man sexual practices as "pederasty" and transformed bachchah into "a child" blocked any possibility of these practices acquiring a modern equivalent in Iranian society. Older man–younger woman sexual practices—as many marriages in Qajar Iran were, and thus in a modernist sense were also bachchahbazi—could be recast into modern marriages in which man and woman were to be closer in age. No modern equivalent was imagined desirable for sexual practices involving older and younger men. Although marriages that involve an older man with a much younger woman (in the same age range as a young man) may be considered unwise, they are not banned or considered immoral.[24] Their acceptance demands approbation of similar same-sex practices and denying socially sanctioned possibilities for the latter.

From the start then, the modernist project of female emancipation—centered on the desirability of heterosocialization, unveiling women and encouraging them to socialize with men, and transforming marriage from a sexual contract to a romantic one—was premised on (and productive of) the disavowal of male homoeroticism. It was also pushed for eradication of same-sex practices among males.

The project of women's emancipation involved a "heterosocial promise" inviting women to remove themselves from from female bonds and join modern men in the effort to give birth—jointly— to a new nation. Men were to be "civilized"—modernized—by socializing with women. Heterosocializing practices would perform regulatory and disciplinary work for refashioning modern masculinities.[25] Women haggled over the terms of men's heterosocial promise. They demanded that men desexualize *their* homosociality. To have a loving, companianate wife, the idea went, was to stop fooling around with young men and boys. Bibi Khanum Astarabadi's *Vices of Men* (1894) considered *amradbazi* (older man–younger man sexual liaisons) to be not only one of the main vices of men but also, more significantly, a vice that disrupted companionate marital relationship (49, 61–63, 80–81).

It was not a symmetrical process. Whereas all female homosociality was deemed unmodern, unscientific, ignorant, and superstitious, and "female homosexuality" was an absent term from this discourse, women's critique of male homosociality was centered exclusively on homosexuality. Nonsexual sociality among males, in fact, was perceived as co-terminus with public life and patriotic virtue, a model of citizen bonding and a domain not to be disavowed but opened to female presence by accepting women as capable of similar asexual bonding with men as citizens. They, as masculinized women, could partake in politicized male homosociality of modern citizenship. Women, however, called for male homosexuality to be abandoned as a condition for reform of family and marriage.

In a sense, modernist optimism that homoeroticism was a consequence of gender segregation and thus in due time would disappear, combined with a masqueraded recasting of homoeroticism and same-sex practices, made more open homophobia unnecessary. In women's writings the disavowal concerned cultural practices in men's sexual lives should companionate romantic marriage replace marriage as a sexual procreative contract. It was demanded that men give up a variety of culturally sanctioned sexual practices—such as sex with other (younger) men and boys, temporary marriage, and illicit sex with prostitutes and house servants—should women commit themselves to the new deal. In that sense the modernist project of women's emancipation is marked by a disavowal of male homosexuality.

Yet the disavowal may have been inevitable. The same process that made it possible for women to occupy the position of beloved made that position a masquerade for amrad. Women's call for men to disavow same-sex practices as a price for a heterosocializing/sexualizing modernity could be seen as a move to rid themselves from that double occupancy. The move would further mark over-Europeanized men as masculine (although of questionable masculinity) figures of modernity's excess.

A number of twentieth-century transformations, central among them the compulsory unveiling campaign of 1936 through 1941, made the over-Europeanized woman (in the 1960s termed "Westoxicated") a figure of privileged excess. Yet the figure of the fukuli was never very far from the scene. Firaydun Huvayda, Iran's prime minister for much of the final decades of Muhammad Riza Shah's reign and who was executed in 1979, was rumored to be a Baha'i and a homosexual. Whether he was or not, the two designations indicated Iranian modernity's alterity and excess.[26] He was thought to be politically impotent and passive with respect to the shah and a passive homosexual as well. His marriage was considered a ruse, and his sex life, a barely concealed topic of satire and social gossip, was joked about. The fact that Huvayda wore an orchid on his coat pocket and was always meticulously shaven and immaculate linked him with the figure of fukuli, a mimic man, always suspected of being an amradnuma.[27]

The centrality of the Westoxicated woman to current historiographies of Iranian modernity has allowed the fukuli to be forgotten. The post-1979 concentration on a critique of cultural construction of gender in forming Iranian modernity, and the price many women have paid for that project in their daily lives, have in a sense come to continue "remembering woman to forget the amrad." That Iranian feminism was shaped within a discursive terrain that demanded disavowal of male homoeroticism and same-sex practices puts it in a place of political and cultural responsibility to take account of its disavowal and screening work.

The current focus has let the other figure of excess in Iranian modernity off the hook, but other transformations of post-1979 Iran have continued to haunt the present. Iranians will not be let alone without facing what they have constituted as gender and the sexual excess of modernity. Current anxieties continue to emphasize the imbrications of gender and sexuality. Scores of female teenagers have discovered that transdressing helps them cope with difficulties of everyday life.[28] The alarm with which the phenomenon is being reported in the Iranian press does not arise out of concern for the hazard that the young women may face on urban streets. Transdressed young females recall—despite the cultural work that has been done to forget it—the nineteenth-century figure of an amrad—or in this case an amradnuma with a difference.

Reintegration of the issues of sexuality and gender, bringing to bear on each other how modern masculinity and femininity were intimately constructed within the same historical project as modern sexualities, is called for by the contingency of how the terms have, so far, defined each other. The problem has been that since the mid-nineteenth century the visiblity of one axis, gender focused on the veiling and unveiling of women, has worked to screen off the axis of sexuality. The process of heterosexualization as a masquerade for homosexuality has reinforced the screening, and thus my proposition is a rather hazardous one. Under conditions that the safest existence may be a masquerade, perhaps screening issues of sexuality by gender is not such a bad thing after all. Yet if we are to accept that a "youth crisis," the euphemism for adult panic over the sexual and gender experimentations of young Iranians, is gripping Iran, it may be the case that such issues are no longer able to remain screened.

NOTES

This essay is based on three chapters of my book *Women with Mustaches and Men without Beards: Gender and Sexual Anxieties of Iranian Modernity.*

1. My attention to the analytical productivity of the concept of excess was drawn through the work of my colleague Ann Pellegrini.

2. This marking of "danger" as centered on "moral looseness and homosexuality" is not limited to dominant Islamist discourse. It is a ground shared with oppositional discourse, inside and outside the country. *Homan,* a journal published by Iranian gay and lesbian communities in Europe and the United States, has kept up a courageous critical engagment with the exilic opposition.

3. "It Must Be Said, Even If No One Listens!" *Shukufah,* Sept. 7, 1915, 2–3.

4. Some figures of beloved young men reported in literary and historical chronicles were, as Yarshater has argued, accomplished warriors and soldiers or known for other valued skills (see Yarshater; de Bruijn).

5. On Chardin's observations and judgment on the prevalence of male homosexuality and unfavorable conditions for women in Safavi Iran, see Ferrier, *Journey to Persia* (22, 118, 176; see also Ferrier, "Women in Safavid Iran").

6. Europeans were anxious about Iranians' reading of their mores, just as Iranians were about the Europeans. In particular, they were aware of the meaning of beardlessness for adult male Iranians. Morier, in *Hajji Baba of Ispahan in England,* uses the Hajji as a ventriloquist to express some of those anxieties: "I must not omit to mention here, that, out of compliment to us, he [the Englishman accompanying them in their journey to London—persumably Morier himself if one takes the journey of Mirza Abu al-Hasan Shirazi to London in 1809 and 1810 and the latter's travelog of that journey as the event and text that inspired this book, as most commentators have concurred (Johnston)] permitted his beard to grow, and thus cleared up the question whether Franks ever could have beards? All those who visited our country looked as if they had been prepared for offices in our harems; but now that we were positive they possessed the seeds of a beard within the soil of their face, we were angry that they did themselves and their country such little justice in our eyes" (Morier 1: 50–51; see also 1: 88 and 1: 104–5).

That Morier was quite aware of the many meanings of beardlessness for Iranians is also evident from another episode at a social gathering: "I perceived a strange looking *birish,* or 'no beard,' [*note:* Youths, particularly effeminate-looking youths, are so called.] his clothes pasted tighter to his body than those of any other man present, as if he were in the deepest wo; his head flattened at the top, and curled out behind; his neck stiff, and in his deportment full of nothing but himself. . . . 'Who can that personage be?' said I to my [English] companion; 'in our country we should soon teach his mincing feet better manners, and he should limp for something.'

"'That sort of person now-a-days we call an exquisite, a dandy; formerly he would have been called a 'd——d buck,' so much does fashion even change our forms of speech'" (2: 9–10).

7. Morier to his brother, David, June 1, 1811, quoted by Johnston (168); the deletions are in Johnston and, presumably, in the original letter.

8. See Morris (71) for a discussion of a somewhat similar dynamic in Thailand.

9. Discussing transformations of sexualities in modern Thailand, Rosalind Morris has similarly observed, "Reformations in the sexual domain are at least partly the result of transnational gazes and of the discourses that Orientalizing and self-Orientalizing desire produces" (53–54).

10. The masquerading may have some similarities to one in eighteenth-century Urdu literature: "Avoiding the ambiguous *Gazal-e muzakkar* of Persian, i.e., the lyric in which a male lover seemingly addressed another male, the Urdu poets of South India . . . adopted the Indian tradition of having a female address a male" (Naim 121). Carla Petievich is at work on a manuscript and translation of this genre of poetry from Urdu to English.

11. Although I have concentrated on male homoeroticism, similar transformations can be traced for female same-sex desire. The nineteenth century, for example, openly celebrated the prevalent practice of "vow of sisterhood," which seems to have given way to spatial masquerades such as rooming in the same house or heteronormative screens such as two women marrying the same man. I concentrate on male homoeroticism for two reasons. First, the modernist project, which is the topic of my book (*Women with Mustaches*), historically was developed by the political and cultural elite of Iran, an all-male brotherhood until at least the closing decade of the nineteenth century, when a modernist project by women began to emerge. The second reason is that as far as female homoeroticism is concerned, most of my sources relate to masquerading practices rather than discourses and representations. Masquerading desire was not just a one-time event that happened in some historical past. It has become the dominant form of homoeroticism in Iran. Further discussion of female homoeroticism would imply discussing transformations that have very direct contemporary manifestations. It would also amount to outing those practices, which, for obvious reasons, I am reluctant to do in contemporary Iran.

12. I have used the partial English translation of this text, *A Persian at the Court of King George, 1809–10: The Journal of Mirza Abul Hassan Khan*, tr. Margaret Morris Cloake (London: Barrie and Jenjins, 1988), 78. A slightly different version of the passage is quoted in Tavakoli-Targhi, "Nigaran-i zan-i Farang" (25), to which I have added "and ghilman." I am indebted to Tavakoli-Targhi for including many passages deleted in the printed versions from a manuscript to which he has had access.

13. Mirza Abu Talib Kahn (94–95). For the "heavenly youth," he wrote:

> And that youth with heavenly features / for whose shining face ghilman would serve as a slave.
> His stature as a cypress, his face like a rose garden / like fresh basil, his trace of a mustache [nawkhatt] shines green." (95)

14. A description of some of these interactions appears in Tavakoli-Targhi, "Nigaran-i." For Mirza Abu al-Hasan Khan's socializing and popularity among English women in London, see Johnston (131–33); for an account of experiences of Rizaquli Mirza and his brothers, see Fraser.

15. Iranian men were quite conscious and proud of their heterosocial performance. They repeatedly noted, for example, whether they accepted dances with women. Sarabi reported that a M. Kulman (Coleman?), chair of Chamber of Commerce (*ra'is al-tujjar*) of Lille, France, had joked that he was relieved that the Iranian ambassador, Amin al-Dawlah (1856–57), was departing Lille for Paris. Even though they enjoyed

his company immensely, they were anxious that his prolonged stay would make their wives cold to them because the women seemed to converse with no one but al-Dawlah (Sarabi, 281–82). In Morier's satire of Mirza Abu al-Hasan Khan's London visit he observed, "We had now been several months in England, and little by little began to adopt many of the customs of the infidels. When two of us walked together, instead of holding each other's hands as in our own country, we proceeded arm in arm: moreover, we made no scruple occasionally to be seen in a similar predicament with a woman" (2: 27). It could, of course, have been Morier's embarrassed wish that Iranian men would stop holding hands in public.

The homoerotic possibilities of some heterosocial occasions, especially masked balls, did not escape the Iranians' attention. Sarabi, in his description of a *boeuf gras* carnival in Paris, noted, "Some men dress as women, and some women as men; in the midst of this cross-dressing, all intercourse [*suhbat*, which in Persian carries the double meaning it has in English] is possible and any joking, flirtation, and fooling around acceptable" (214).

16. For a brief discussion of these issues, see Najmabadi "Reading 'Wiles of Women.'"

17. See, for instance, Hamadani. Traveling in 1884, he consistently speaks of beautiful ladies (*khanumha*) and women (*zanha*). See also Sahhafbashi, traveling in 1897, whose report is thoroughly written in a realist mode rather than as a phantasm of paradise.

18. Modern Islamist attitudes toward homoeroticism are informed by denial, disavowal, sanction, and approbation. The line of differentiation concerns where homoeroticism and the same-sex practices of the Iranian past or present are translocated once disavowed from the modern or Islamic. Secular modernist thought has located what was turned into "the vice" in the domain of Arabo-Islamic backwardness, but contemporary Islamists locate it in the domain of Western-secular corruption. Yet that is no less a modern argument. "Vice" they both agree it is. The Islamic Republic of Iran is set on eradicating homosexuality, especially male same-sex practices, in the name of eradicating the Western cultural and moral corruption that has seeped into Iranian Islamic culture, all the while depending on a concept of homosexuality more akin to the West European, late-nineteenth-century concept of deviance than to its own classical heritage. I am grateful to Negar Mottahedeh for pointing this out.

19. I do not suggest that this is a peculiarly Iranian phenomenon. Nor am I willing to generalize these trends to all Islamicate cultures. Historically, specific studies for other places are needed to make a comparative study possible (Ghoussoub and Sinclair-Webb, eds.); Lagrange's essay is particularly pertinent to my argument.

20. Although premodern Islamic medical and legal treatises categorized *'ubnah* as illness, the concept of homosexuality as illness became inclusive of both desire and act in the modernist redefinition and covered both partners to the act and the desire.

21. Yet one should ask whether the notion that male-male sexual acts are what men do before they settle into procreative sexuality with wives (or what women do when not satisfied with their husbands' performance) is not an idea that defers recognition of homosexuality as an erotic preference. Is it not yet another way of denial and disavowal of homosexuality? After all, we are assured, that all men will eventually become practicing (if not believing) heterosexuals. Is it not a cultural

move to make homosexuality a "readable text," a containable, at least temporally, phenomenon? Instead of marginalizing by considering homosexual men a minority of peculiar, queer disposition, all men, but only for a marginal period of their lives, engage in same-sex practices. Modernist heterosocialization disrupts this temporal marginalization work and has had to craft new marginalizing moves, among which are the effeminization of homosexuals, the attempt to render them into "types" to which medical and psychological categorization is appropriate, and the attribution of their desire to the cultural disruptions of the West.

22. These are not gender-symmetric processes. Although legal punishments against female same-sex practices are lighter than those for men, women come under harsher scrutiny than men. Their intense friendships, unless given the formal cover of vow of sisterhood (and even then) or becoming co-wives to one man, are often more suspect than men's intimate and long-lasting intense friendships. Women continue to carry the load of being "objects of traffic among men" (Rubin) and thus subject to the "protection" of fathers, brothers, and husbands, as well as the nation, in a way that is not the case with men.

23. The Islamic Republic has been trying to reinstitute compulsory homosociality while preserving the modernist normative heterosexuality.

24. In the second half of the twentieth century there were several legislative attempts to set a minimum age for the marriage of young girls. All such legislation can be suspended if a state-certified doctor testifies that the girl is physically mature enough to marry even if under the minimum age. The issue of minimum age is evoked in relation to perceived physical and psychological health of the girl, not in relation immorality as it is invariably with an older man/younger man union.

25. Kandiyoti concludes that "underlying reformers' and polemicists' writings on the modern family, monogamy, and educated mothers and housewives . . . is a new regulatory discourse on sexuality that attempts to institutionalize monogamous heterosexuality as the normative ideal" (284).

26. For the Babi as the figure haunting historiographies of Iranian modernity, see Mottahedeh.

27. See Milani for a biography.

28. Although first viewed as an alarming phenomenon in the context of runaway girls, continued press reports (and cinematic production) about transdressed young women seem to indicate a wider social practice. Articles are in *Zanan* 58 (Dec. 1999): 6–13; *Huquq-i zanan* 13 (Jan.–Feb. 2000): 12–17, 64–65; *Zanan* 61 (March 2000): 27; and *Iran Times*, June 29, 2001, 11.

Works Cited

Astarabadi, Bibi Khanum. *Ma'ayib al-rijal* [Vices of Men]. Ed. Afsaneh Najmabadi. New York: Nigarish va nigarish-i zan, 1992.

Butler, Judith. "Against Proper Objects." *differences: A Journal of Feminist Cultural Studies* 6, nos. 2–3 (1994): 1–26.

de Bruijn, J. T. P. "Beloved." In *Encyclopaedia Iranica.* Ed. Ehsan Yarshater, 128–29. Boston: Routledge and Kegan Paul, 1982.

Ferrier, Ronald W. Ed. and trans. *A Journey to Persia: Jean Chardin's Portrait of a Seventeenth-century Empire.* London: I. B. Tauris, 1996.

———. "Women in Safavid Iran: The Evidence of European Travelers." In *Women in the Medieval Islamic World: Power, Patronage, and Piety.* Ed. Gavin R. G. Hambly, 383–406. New York: St. Martin's Press, 1998.

Fraser, James Baillie. *Narrative of the Residence of the Persian Princes in London in 1835 and 1836.* 2 vols. London: Richard Bentley, 1838.

Garmrudi, Mirza Fattah Khan. *Safarnamah.* Ed. Fath al-Din Fattahi. N.p., 1969.

Ghoussoub, Mai, and Emma Sinclair-Webb, eds. *Imagined Masculinities: Male Identity and Culture in the Modern Middle East.* London: Saqi Books, 2000.

Hamadani, Mirza Muhammad ʻAlikhan Farid al-Mulk. *Khatirat-i Farid.* Ed. Masʻud Farid. Tehran: Zavvar, 1975.

Johnston, Henry McKenzie. *Ottoman and Persian Odysseys: James Morier, Creator of Hajji Baba of Ispahan, and His Brothers.* London: British Academic Press, 1998.

Kandiyoti, Deniz. "Some Awkward Questions on Women and Modernity in Turkey." In *Remaking Women: Feminism and Modernity in the Middle East.* Ed. Lila Abu-Lughod, 270–87. Princeton: Princeton University Press, 1998.

Lagrange, Frédéric. "Male Homosexuality in Modern Arabic Literature." In *Imagined Masculinities: Male Identity and Culture in the Modern Middle East.* Ed. Mai Ghoussoub and Emma Sinclair-Webb, 169–98. London: Saqi Books, 2000.

Meisami, Julie Scott. "Allegorical Gardens in the Persian Poetic Tradition: Nezami, Rumi, Hafez." *International Journal of Middle Eastern Studies* 17 (May 1985): 229–60.

Milani, Abbas. *The Persian Sphinx.* Washington, D.C.: Mage Publishers, 2000.

Mirza Abu Talib Khan Lakhinaw'i Isfahani. *Masir-i Talibi.* Tehran: Sazman-i intisharat va amuzish-i inqilab-i Islami, 1984.

Mirza Salih Shirazi. *Guzarish-i safar.* Ed. Humayun Shahidi. Tehran: Rah-i naw, 1983.

Morier, James. *Adventures of Hajji Baba of Ispahan in England.* 2 vols. New York: J.and J. Harper, 1828.

Morris, Rosalind C. "Educating Desire: Thailand, Transnationalism, and Transgression." *Social Text* 52–53 (Autumn–Winter 1997): 53–79.

Mottahedeh, Negar. "Representing the Unpresentable: Historical Images from the Qajars to the Islamic Republic of Iran." Ph.D. diss., University of Minnesota, 1998.

Muʻtamid al-Dawlah, Farhad Mirza. *Safarnamah.* Ed. Ismaʻil Navvab Safa. Tehran: Zavvar, 1987.

Naim, C. M. "The Theme of Homosexual (Pederastic) Love in Pre-Modern Urdu Poetry." In *Studies in the Urdu Gazal and Prose Fiction.* Ed. Muhammad Umar Memon, 120–42. Madison: South Asian Studies, University of Wisconsin Press, 1979.

Najmabadi, Afsaneh. "Reading for Gender Through Qajar Art." In *Royal Persian Paintings: The Qajar Epoch, 1785–1925.* Ed. Layla S. Diba and Maryam Ekhtiar, 76–89. Brooklyn: Brooklyn Museum of Art in association with I. B. Tauris of London, 1998.

———. "Reading 'Wiles of Women' Stories as Fictions of Masculinity." In *Imagined Masculinities: Male Identity and Culture in the Modern Middle East.* Ed. Mai Ghoussoub and Emma Sinclair-Webb, 147–68. London: Saqi Books, 2000.

———. *Women with Mustaches and Men without Beards: Gender and Sexual Anxieties of Iranian Modernity.* Berkeley: University of California Press, in press.

Nasir al-Din Shah Qajar. *Safarnamah.* Tehran: Sazman-i intisharat-i andishah, 1964.

Nathan, Bassem. "Medieval Arabic Medical Views on Male Homosexuality." *Journal of Homosexuality* 26, no. 4 (1994): 37–39.

Ouseley, William. *Travels in Various Countries of the East; More Particularly Persia.* 3 vols. London: Rodwell and Martin, 1819–23.

Qa'im'maqami, Jahangir. *Jahadiyah.* Ed. Mirza Buzurg Qa'im'maqam Farahani. Tehran: Intisharat-i farhang-i Iran'zamin, 1980.

Rizaquli Mirza. *Safarnamah.* Edited by Asghar Farmanfarma'i Qajar. Tehran: Asatir, 1982.

Rosenthal, Franz. "Ar-Razi on the Hidden Illness." *Bulletin of the History of Medicine* 52 (1978): 45–60.

Rubin, Gail. "The Traffic in Women." In *Toward an Anthropology of Women.* Ed. Rayna Rapp, 157–210. New York: Monthly Review Press, 1975.

Sahhafbashi, Ibrahim. *Safarnamah-i Ibrahim Sahhafbashi.* Ed. Muhammad Mushiri. Tehran: Shirkat-i mu'allifan va mutarjiman-i Iran, 1978.

Sarabi, Husayn. *Makhzan al-vaqayi': Safarnamah-i Farrukh Khan Amin al-Dawlah.* Ed. Karim Isfahani and Qudrat'allah Rawshani. Tehran: Asatir, 1982.

Shirazi, Mirza Abu al-Hasan Khan. *Hayrat'namah.* Ed. Hasan Mursil'vand. Tehran: Rasa, 1986.

Shushtari, Mir 'Abd al-Latif. *Tuhfat al-'alam va zayl al-tuhfah.* Ed. Samad Muvahhid. Tehran: Tahuri, 1984.

Tavakoli-Targhi, Mohamad. "Imagining Western Women: Occidentalism and Euro-eroticism." *Radical America* 24, no. 3 (1990): 73–87.

———. "Nigaran-i zan-i Farang." *Nimeye Digar* 2, no. 3 (1997): 3–71.

Yarshater, Ehsan. "The Theme of Wine-Drinking and the Concept of the Beloved in Early Persian Poetry." *Studia Islamica* 13 (1961): 43–53.

3

Failures of Domestication: Speculations on Globality, Economy, and the Sex of Excess in Thailand

ROSALIND C. MORRIS

WHAT ARE WE TO MAKE OF the fact that, at the close of the twentieth century, the most pervasive discourse of political discontent was written in the idiom of corruption, and that of social crisis in the idiom of contagion? If there was a specter haunting the Euro-Americanized world[1] as the new millennium arrived, it was no longer communism (as Marx and Engels had prophesied a century and a half before) nor, it seemed, the mutual annihilation of geopolitical superpowers (as cold warriors had feared only fifty years earlier). Instead, the century of war, which was also the century of the nation-state's apotheosis, ended in the shadow of new and newly mobile forms of social and economic violence. From within the dominant discourses of the West, these forms of violence were construed not as symptoms of a contest between alternative laws and orders, much less opposition, but rather as modes of criminality, as departures from or failures to recognize a law and an order that had its normative center in the late capitalist West. The violence of the new moment was therefore of a peculiarly doubled nature; it was violence against the sovereignty of local subjects and it was violence against an internationalized regime that increasingly claimed exclusive sovereignty for itself. Such doubleness concealed what it presumed, namely, that the goal of all historical development had itself become both unified and singular: an abstractly homogenized global space subject to one economic law in which the presumption of equality would allow for the exercise of differential authority. Francis Fukuyama's euphoric proclamations of conservative victory assumed nearly axiomatic status even among those who were seeking destinations other than the terminus of history. Some of the most powerful indices of this transformation can be found in the shifting lexicons of political-economic commentary. In this context, it is important to note that wherever the language of corruption and contagion came to dominate political discourse, it construed inequality and economic crisis in terms of failure. Indeed, in the millennial moment, "failure" came to displace "class" and "structural contradiction" as the orienting term of debate. Like "corruption" or "contagion," failure suggests the existence of a normative ideal that can be recognized and in relation to which acts can be adjudicated. But insofar as economic failure is typically read as the *function* of corruption and also as the *origin* of contagion, it suggests something else, namely that certain kinds of mobility and categorical instability are risks for neoliberalism. In 1997, when currency speculation and the collapse of the banking sector in Thailand were followed by currency devaluation and the rapid, sequential implosion of several Southeast Asian economies, a pattern of analysis emerged that quickly became paradigmatic. The more that capital and the theories of its operation become delocalized, the more that local regimes are held accountable for their place within the global organization of capital. Under such circumstances, the chains of events by which economic crisis is said to spread in a region tend to be explained through recourse to a rhetoric of contagion; catastrophe is said to spread from one site to another, usually because of improper mechanisms ensuring the boundaries of the "local-as-nation." When the local regulatory apparatus fails to ensure that economic crisis is contained in and by the nationstate, it is invariably accused of being weak, and this weakness is said to permit a certain leakage, a movement of failure from one place to another. Moreover, it seems to propel that movement, to lie at its origin. The point to be noted here is that failure, like lack, signifies very differently than does "absence." Indeed, it doesn't signify so much as it seems to call for signification. To this extent, the economy that is failed seems to become the origin of a movement by which value is lost elsewhere; it calls for its own movement, the improbable movement of a lack.

The structure of this movement, whereby a certain failure and a lack in one place becomes uncontainable and then incites a similar failure and lack elsewhere, might be described as promiscuous in the sense that it entails transience and indiscriminateness, which is to say an indifference to borders. But the specifically sexual implications of this designation (as promiscuous) should not be overlooked. Indeed, in what follows I shall trace precisely this kind of sexed and sexualized imagery; but for now, we can note that, here, in the case of regional economic phenomena, the attribution of causality and the attempt to represent historical process entail and evoke gestures of metaphoricity that link them to other domains and that posit a compulsive (contagious) force at the point of first manifestation. Thus, for example, as Thailand was the nation in which economic crisis first appeared in Southeast Asia, it was also recognized as the origin not only of the crisis but of its tendency to spread. The linkage between firstness, manifestness, and propulsion across boundaries is significant, for it reveals a certain logic of visibility that underscores and links many of the terms of contemporary political-economic analysis. These terms are familiar by now: corruption, contagion, terrorism, civil warfare, militia violence, etc. There are others, of course, but these ones are symptomatic. And while it is not my intention to explore each of them here, one notes that they are all characterized by a reliance on secrecy, on the production of interstitial zones in the midst of, but distinct from, the nation-state and the forms of alliance that constitute multinational bodies. They point to forms of resistance that no longer even fantasize their exteriority to the systems they might undermine. And, even more than this, they suggest a transformation in notions of foreignness such that the foreign is no longer that which is spatially distant but is, rather, that which is already within—as a potentiality.

If the violences to which such terms point constitute a limit to the Habermasian statement of modernity's ideal as total communicative transparency and total publicity, they also rely on forms of mass mediation that transmit the knowledge and the existence of secrets. The corrupt politician is powerful to the extent that he can be known as corrupt without, at the same time, being subject to the law. The terrorist is powerful to the extent that he is generally known in a spectral form (as the agent of a possible future violence) without, at the same time, being locatable. Civil warfare is awful because the foreignness of the opponent contradicts the appearance of shared identity and incites suspicion in relation to one's own. And so forth. Each of these terms, but perhaps especially corruption, betrays an anxiety about the reformation of social logics, about the dissipating power of spatialized metaphors of opposition, including that of public and private. And each belies a sense that the force operating in any of these domains is radically transformed in the moment of its disclosure. As shall become apparent, *the moment of such a force "becoming visible" is the moment of its movement elsewhere, and hence of its extension.* Like Poe's purloined letter, these terms and the practices to which they attempt to refer derive power from the fact that visibility and invisibility turn on each other. And if visibility and transparency are not reducible to each other, neither are visibility and opacity mutually exclusive terms. But there is another, more historical dimension to this logic. Whenever "disclosure" fails to mitigate violence or inhibit the trajectory of contagion, an excess is posited beyond or behind apparent surfaces. This is why occult phenomena seem to erupt so frequently in the midst of rationalizing discourses and despite expanding procedures of oversight and accountability. This is why suspicion haunts every confession. And this is why the specter of the specter won't disappear from economic theory. More important for my purposes here is the fact that the positing of an excess beyond vision, of a secret whose force cannot be eliminated through disclosure but that nonetheless seems to beg revelation, is one of the ways by which sex and economy become linked at the structural level. And this is especially true in the discourse of corruption.

More generally than any of the other terms mentioned above, corruption designates the traversal, collapse, or mutual contamination of oppositional categories. To the extent that these categories are often sexed, its circulation is also the circulation of a discourse about sexual difference. Indeed, as often as not, and especially in the case of Thailand to which I shall now turn, corruption names categorical failure in the mode of sexualized excess. This is why it so frequently finds its ideal figure in the prostitute and vice versa. This is why a politician can be said to prostitute himself or his party for power, dissimulating and conflating his private interests with those of the public in order to obtain for private use that which belongs in the public domain. A prostitute, by contrast, is said to corrupt herself and, occasionally, the nation by selling that which is not supposed to be sold and, in many postcolonial cases, by mimicking domesticity in order to introduce a calculating economic logic into the heart of what would have been (according to bourgeois ideals, at least) the private sphere. Prostitution and corruption are thought to interrupt what is presumed to be the proper state of modern polities; they undermine or transgress a particular ordering of the social world according to which the private and the public, the singular and the general, the gift and the exchange are kept separate and made the conditions of each other's meaningfulness. Moreover, they name sets of practices in which money is made the instrument of a contagion that moves along the paths of desire. It is not incidental that these discourses are mapped onto a sexual politics that assigns to women and other feminized beings the values of the private and the radically singular and that locates them in an ideal space of domesticity from which their history is constantly read as a departure.

In the pages that follow, I attempt to trace the figuration of corruption in and by prostitution and the implications of this figuration for an analysis of new political-economic relations dominated by the goals of democracy and civil society. I am interested in exploring these questions vis-à-vis Thailand because of the centrality given it by discussions of global economic crisis at the end of the nineties and because, in the global imagination of corruption and prostitution, it occupies a historically privileged place. These discussions and attributions have ramified within Thailand as well, such that political reform is imagined as the mitigation of corruption through the institution of transparency or the totalization of the public sphere. At the same time, economic reform is imagined as that which would be marked by the demise of prostitution or the end of a need to subject the private (the incalculable) to the public (the realm of all calculability). There is a profound contradiction here, but the contradiction itself alerts us to the force of (mis)translation in Thai history.

Two Tales of Sex and the City

In Thai, politics and the discourse of politics are designated by the term *kaan muang,* or the "business of the polis." It carries with it the stigma of the urban but also the shimmering aura of the metropolitan. To the extent that urbanity itself is described by rural people, it is invariably linked to prostitution; indeed, the city is deemed the proper place of prostitution. If there are thousands of brothels in and amid the rice fields of the Central Plains or along winding mountain roads and transnational highways, it nonetheless remains the case that most Thais imagine prostitution as that kind of corruption which thrives amid the confusion of pleasures that anonymous urban existence and a plethora of commodities incite. It is no wonder, then, that today in Thailand and in the conversations that people have about Thailand from afar it seems that there are always (at least) two discourses of failure circulating at any given time: prostitution and corruption. Both discourses carry within themselves, and perhaps cover over, differences that, were they named, would refer us to the particular worlds of women and children, boys and men, local economies and global traffic, patriarchal complicities and feminist solidarities.

We can and should speak of a multiplicity of "prostitutions" ranging from slavery to indentured labor to relatively free transactions of pleasure and money. Similarly, we can speak of a range of "corruptions" extending from private exchanges of immediate violence to Mafia-style politics, to theft at the level of the state, to institutional relations of both illegitimate and legitimated nondisclosure. Here, however, I want to attend to the more generalized discourses, the ideological reifications by which global relations and sociohistorical difference are figured. What does it mean when a politician, or a nation, is accused of whoring itself to foreignness, or when a young woman is accused of corrupting her nation?

Let us then consider these two stories circulating in gossip and in the press about Thailand, the stories about prostitution and the stories about corruption. Often, the latter is written in the idiom of the former, especially when "corruption," a word that has not yet been lexicalized in Thai, is seen to emanate from a relationship with foreigners.[2] Sometimes, too, the former is written in the idiom of the latter, as when foreigners read the history of Thailand's trade and economic policy as a kind of promiscuity in which the recognition of the national proper fails to produce either a sense of Thai economic domesticity or an understanding of the foreign as something that is itself spatialized. This is what lay at the heart of English anxieties about Thailand's (then Siam's) refusal to consider China a foreign trading partner during the nineteenth century, when Chinese junk trade was exempt from the tariffs that afflicted English merchants. For the Siamese of the 1800s, who paid annual tribute to China and who had not yet undertaken that cartographic project by which national sovereignty becomes a matter of territorial integrity, English demands seemed ludicrous. Foreignness could not then be reduced to a calculus of spatial distance, and national integrity was secured rather than threatened by the recognition of China's imperial authority. Of course the English wanted favored trading partner status, but that would mean nothing if China went untaxed. For them, Siamese relations with China were improper, and the intimacy between Siam and England's chief competitor in textile manufacture could only seem excessive to them because it was inadequately concerned with the policing of domesticity's boundaries.

The second story mirrors and reiterates the first in several important respects but is more overtly concerned with the problem of appearances. One version of the first story, and that most fondly reproduced in foreign popular and scholarly media, invariably poses the questions of where the limits of prostitution are to be drawn in Thailand and whether these limits should encompass relations between (foreign) men and (Thai) women that mimic the relations of concubinage which defined earlier colonial regimes in other parts of Southeast Asia.[3] These are the relations in which foreign men and Thai women agree to a long-term performance of domestic intimacy, for which performance the foreign man agrees to provide money and support while the Thai woman agrees to provide pleasure, nurturance, and translational abilities. This form of prostitution, one of many in Thailand, is traceable to the period of the Vietnam War, when the U.S. military used Thailand as a rest and relaxation base and the attendant infusion of U.S. currency led to a dislocation of the previously dominant economy of prostitution, which had been oriented mainly to Thai men.[4] In commonly recited narratives, the women who cater to foreigners are said to do so because they desire, in excess, the commodities that are associated with foreign power. Not incidentally, these are commodities of appearance: cosmetics, fashion, and the experiences of a lifestyle heretofore unavailable to them. It is the desire for these commodities, say the moralizing critics of Thai prostitution, that leads rural women to move to Bangkok or Chiang Mai—for the pleasure of things.[5] In these stories (which *must* be distinguished from the accounts of child prostitution, sexual slavery, and overtly coerced forms of sexual exchange), the woman is said to follow the path of money but also to function as the medium of communication for her "man." The woman translates, gives the foreign man access to the local world, renders him competent both in terms of his masculinity and in terms of his foreignness. The woman is linked to both language and money through her sexuality, and as both instrument and object of desire's movement she is the enigma behind those innumerable articles and queries that wonder about the "true" affect and intentionality of the woman who, in the end and after all else, is said to "sell herself."[6] Does she love the man? Is she voluntarily participating in this relationship? Is it possible for her to do so? What constitutes the limits of voluntarism in this economy? And, most pointed of all from a Thai perspective, what kind of local woman is always translating in the service of the foreign?

The attribution of commodity desire to the local woman renders her as one who has departed from home, from authentic Thainess (*khwaam pen thai*), even before she moves to the city. Few narratives have been more powerful in the literature of the last thirty years than that which laments the loss of authentic Thainess, and it is this loss that the stories of prostitution invariably metaphorize. Lest "home"—which, in Thailand, is usually coded as the rural—be imagined as the origin of a desire for foreignness, however, the prostitute (who, as male or female, is always feminized) must also be the one who was out of place even there. Ironically, her exteriority to Thainess takes the form of an overinvestment in appearances. She mistakes them for reality and acts accordingly. Thus, for example, most stories about prostitution feature a young woman who wrongly believes she has fallen in love with a dubious recruiter (usually a visitor from the city) when, in fact, she has merely discovered the appearance of love in the experience of physical desire.

The woman's "sin"—against Thainess and against the Theravada Buddhism with which it is seen as coterminous in nationalist discourse—is that she does not know that appearances are simultaneously unreal and potentially effective. Having allowed them to assume more force than they ought to possess, the rural woman becomes a sign for that desire to become other, the name of which is promiscuity. This is why rural women who move to the city, for whatever reason, are so frequently cast under a suspicious light in the news media and in the gossip of rural working class and urban middle-class women. For every progressive statement by a feminist in Thailand, a thousand more remarks condemn the women of Patpong and *kamphaendin*[7] to despicable status and render them the origins of a transformation through which Thailand has lost itself in the mad pursuit of the other. This contempt for prostitution was not always so pervasive, and the history of this moralizing reveals much about a more general process through which commodity logics have been naturalized, which is to say obscured, in Thailand. Today, prostitution is both the most talked about relation to foreignness and the most denied actuality of contemporary life. It is not uncommon for police personnel to deny the existence of brothels or to remark the illegality of prostitution even as government policies have sought to limit activities such as overt AIDS education for tourists that would inhibit sex tourism.

In the end, it would not be inaccurate to say that the anxiety over prostitution is mainly an anxiety over appearances. But it would be wrong if the anxiety over appearances were construed as a desire for appearances to reflect or disclose—indeed to exfoliate—an inner truth, a private reality. To the contrary, I want to suggest that the anxiety over appearances that manifests itself in the fetishistic discourses about Thai prostitution is a function of the mistranslation of seemingly similar, but profoundly different, concerns in the West. This tension between two anxieties, and the two epistemologies underlying them, has to do with the very different significatory demands that have historically been made upon appearances in Thailand and in the largely Protestant cultures of Western capitalism. Whereas the latter have assumed and demanded a relationship of transparency between inner truth and outward appearance, between value and its sign, and whereas the ideology of Protestant capitalism has claimed an ethics of sincerity as the ground for an economy of abstract valuation, the cultural logics that were historically dominant in Thailand permitted appearances and truths to be radically disjunct.[8] Indeed, insofar as the production of appearances (*kaan sang phaap*) was and is said to be necessary, it is because there is no assumption of a systematic—culturally natural—process by which truth will necessarily disclose itself. Here, proper behavior requires no attitude other than respect for display of correct form. No "order of things" can be assumed from the signs that meet the eye in Thailand. In this context, the recently emergent discourse of prostitution *as a discourse of "insincerity"* marks a historical transformation in the regimes of the visible within which both sexual and economic activity occur in Thailand as well as in the global sphere that functions as the extension of Western political-economic rationality. The Western "john" now reads the performance of domesticity in "Thai-farang" relations as one of only two possibilities: as the real and true display of "love" *or* as the intentional dissimulation (the real falsification) of a contrary truth. This contrary truth is an economic one in that the woman may be desiring money. According to the prevailing notion of companionate relation in the West, love and money are the terms of mutually exclusive processes: gift and exchange. That which is given must be given fully, without reserve and with no thought of return. To love, then, means that materials received are also of the order of the gift. A circuitry of gestures and objects thereby binds individuals in the fiction of a freedom, which they surrender to each other. But if the domestic relation is one of appearances only, then love will be superceded by exchange and the traffic in things will be just that: a traffic in things and a war of competing aspirations. The problem for the john is that it is hard to tell which is which, and, more important, it is not clear that the two exclude each other. Thai prostitutes often proclaim the desire for love and the need for exchange in a single breath. But to the extent that the john is invested in the performance of domesticity, in the rituals of intimacy and the public display of companionship, he is vulnerable to the possibility that a devotion to the appearance of domesticity will be a devotion to appearances and not the testament of love. Banal but not insignificant, his anxious perception crystalizes the history of a widely pervasive mistranslation by which visibility is assumed to entail transparency even as its ritualization allows for the continued separation of truth from appearance. Such mistranslations have a long and complex genealogy in the history of Thailand's relationships to the West but were intensified by the emergence of a pseudocolonial relation between the United States and Thailand during the 1970s (so often misrepresented as the invention of prostitution) and the transformation of prostitution since then. Before examining that history more closely, however, let us consider for a moment the transposition of a discourse of promiscuity and sexual excess into the domain of the political, where it now displaces a more critical engagement with the social and economic effects of what we now term "globalization." As stated earlier, stories about prostitution and corruption are often stories about each other.

To Give or Not to Give: The Corruptions of Economy

Consider, for example, the fact that in the last months of 2000 the democratically elected government of Chuan Leekpai[9] was often accused of that kind of prostitution said to have emerged during the Vietnam era. In the months preceding the call for elections (which took place on January 6, 2001),

Chuan's government became the object of nearly daily attacks, all of which suggested that it had merely mimicked a relationship of familiarity with the IMF and the United States in the absence of any substantive intimacy or reciprocity. Chuan, the technocratic apologist for liberalization, was said by many to have been duped by virtue of his overinvestment in the promise of Western styles of economic reform. The accusations of "madly following the foreigner" (*taamkon farang*) and of not knowing the difference between a real intimacy and its mere appearance seem to be accusations of desiring only money and the appearance of equality. But desiring money is not the problem here. Nor is appearance, for that is all one ever has in a (Thai Theravada Buddhist) world that disavows ontology. The problem is the exchange and a mistaken belief that there is an equivalence between truth and appearance. Because Chuan was said not to have known the difference, he was also said to have betrayed Thailand and Thainess. Here, Thainess is the knowledge that appearances are always autonomous and that the difference between truth and appearance is what saves one from the fetishism to which the rest of the world has made its premature obeisance.

It is no wonder then that among the twenty-two parties vying for election, the most successful challenger to Chuan's Democrats was a party called Thai Rak Thai (Thai Love Thai). The name verily trumpets an authenticity that Chuan's Prachatipat Party was said to have squandered. That Thai Rak Thai was most famous for the promise of its leader, Thaksin Shinawatra, to pay electors millions of baht from his private coffer suggests that corruption is not necessarily construed in all acts of political gift giving and influence peddling. That Thaksin was later forced to convert his promise of a gift into a promise of a loan, however, suggests that there were limits to which even he had to subject his otherwise flagrant disregard for international political protocols. The promise—of a gift or a loan (which, without interest, is still a gift of sorts)—nonetheless suggests that, in Thailand, good (or bad) intentions may inform any number of gestures. However, these intentions will not necessarily be legible in a retrospective reading that presumes the transparency of intent and effect. Here, as in the case of a prostitution that mimes domestic relations, there are no guaranteed mechanisms for knowing the truth of the matter. The one who presumes a transparency between appearance and truth is liable to be duped by a false intention, or worse, a bad intention masquerading as authenticity, as in the case of the IMF and the World Bank or the United States. Or so said the candidates for Thai Rak Thai. Perhaps it is no wonder, then, that even when Thaksin was found guilty of concealing his wealth by a national anticorruption commission (in August 2001) he managed to escape conviction on charges that he had intentionally deceived the public and the law. He was found guilty of nondisclosure but not of dissimulation. Prior to the elections, however, as the baht fell and the country scrambled to implement fiscal restructuring policies that would save it from the utter abjection that had befallen Indonesia and the Philippines, Thailand was increasingly left out of the promised circle of free trade favors. Trade barriers, investor flight, and the fact that wages and currencies had fallen even more radically in other Southeast Asian nations, making them more attractive for offshore manufacturing, led to a 60 percent decline in exports from Thailand to the United States. Because the export industry is a feminized one, female factory workers have endured an inordinate burden of suffering in the post-crisis era, and job losses for them far surpassed those in many other sectors.

After nearly a half-century of devoted alliance and military support for the U.S., the recent cooling of Thai-U.S. trade relations can only be perceived on the ground in Thailand as the disavowal of a relation that had promised money for political, and especially anticommunist, loyalty. At the turn of the century, in opposition to IMF policies and U.S. bullying, Thai government spokespeople joined other Asian leaders in calling for stronger regional ties, lauding Malaysia's repudiation of the global economy's gatekeepers and longing for similar courage themselves. Yet having accepted billions of dollars in loans, Thailand and other nations were hard-pressed to maintain their autonomy. Mostly, they simply regretted their fall from favored trading partner status. The IMF merely turned the criticism of betrayal back on Thailand, accusing the latter of moral failure both in the extension of credit to unworthy persons and corporations (i.e., overvaluation of assets) and in failure to disclose the extent of that practice. Such failure, say the critics, generated excess in the system, which is to say the appearance of value beyond what could be actualized in exchange, beyond even what could be speculated. The cure for this infectious state of affairs, argued the IMF and most neoliberal economists, would be found in the establishment of standards for transparency and in the demand for regular disclosure.

Despite a sense of betrayal, many Thais were quick to endorse this perspective, and the discourses of transparency within which excess is repudiated are beginning to find their spokespeople. Since the beginning of the 1990s a series of governmentally sanctioned but relatively autonomous institutions have been charged with the responsibility for monitoring the activities of politicians and for bringing charges of corruption against those whose acts are said to be "excessive." The forms of this excess include the acquisition of more wealth than can be accounted for, called "unusual wealth," vote buying, and the unlawful dissemination of monetary or other favors to corporations and persons who have not transparently competed for the same. In their unprecedented long-term study of corruption and democracy in Thailand, Pasuk Phongpaichit and Sungsidh Piriyarangsan have noted that there are two general patterns of corruption in Thailand. In the first, money is leaked out of the center to secure support for those in power. This leakage is estimated to account for about twenty to forty percent of national revenues (Pasuk and Sungsidh 53). The second kind of corruption sees the movement of money upward, into the hands of police and military officials as well as mafiosi, in a colossal kind of protectionism (57–130). Although Pasuk and Sungsidh see the same patterns of corruption in Thailand since the 1950s, they are clear that the situation has improved since the time of the U.S.-backed regime of General Sarit, who accumulated personal wealth at a rate of 42 percent of the national budget (52). At the conclusion of their provocative account, however, the two authors are confronted with a problem that every advocate of Western-style democratic reforms in Thailand must address, namely that, historically, there has been no categorical means of distinguishing the culturally sanctioned, and even mandated, performance of giving generously (*kaan sin nam jai*) from "corruption," which is to say excessive giving in return for favors.

Like all forms of gifting, sin nam jai is a logically impossible necessity in most of Thailand. It is a gift that must be given freely and compassionately (*hia duai khwaam saneha*), without anticipation of a return. It must also be received without interest or "prior expectation." The ideal of this gift is the alms given to monks, but everything from the feeding of strangers to the support for poor people demanded of godfathers (*jao pho*) is subject to this imperative, which flirts endlessly with its own violation. Insofar as it recognizes itself as a gift, the gift is annulled, of course (Derrida). And what prevents the gift from being named to and by itself is the exclusion of calculation. Sin nam jai is not worked out contractually, even though it often follows a path that resembles that of exchange. As Pasuk and Sungsidh remark, citing a local member of parliament, services may be reciprocated with a gift, but the fact that the gift may range from 100 baht to 500 baht, depending on the pleasure of the giver, means that the "payment" is merely an appreciation, and not a calculation of abstract value, based on the putative and anterior truth of labor time (170). Freedom to give is privileged here, and the violence of that privilege is rarely lost on those who perform services; but, contrary to the institution's ideal, this does not mean that they do not manipulate the giver or anticipate the gift. Even so, it is less the "time of the gift" than the fact of abstraction that determines the possibility of an act being construed as corruption. This is because gifts in an economic regime that disavows them constantly appear to be mere exchange. Read backward, the gift can be asked to disclose a desire for something other than itself. It can be read as a bribe, as a threat, as humiliation, as compensation. Transparency, then, is the discourse that threatens to metamorphose all acts of giving into a bad intentionality. Perhaps this is why, in the aftermath of the Chuan government's spectacular failure to facilitate economic recovery, a certain suspicion of transparency's discourse has arisen, and with that suspicion have come calls for a return to Thai ways of doing politics and Thai ways of nurturing the people. Despite the efforts by reformists to suggest that this putative return is nothing but the revalorization of corruption, this nostalgic drive is what permitted the Thai Rak Thai Party to enjoy such enormous popular support. Often flying in the face of advice from those mainly foreign-educated advocates of reform, the Thai Rak Thai Party now finds itself supported both by people on the rural periphery and those in the metropolitan centers who see only betrayal in the aftermath of Thailand's commitment to the putatively modern politics of sincerity and the economic and moral modernity that they are supposed to support. Poor farmers and impoverished businesspeople alike now argue that when one believes that acts are the transparent disclosure of intentions, and when this disclosure is itself theatricalized, everyone is vulnerable to the (bad) intentionality of the most powerful party. Dissimulation is possible there in a way that it is not possible in a context where surface appearance and inner truth bear no obvious relationship to each other. The one who might have retained the sovereign power of refusal—the recipient of the gift—is here destined to suffer the ignominious fate of the naïf. And, of course, this is the fate both of the rural girl lured into prostitution and of the politician who madly followed the foreigner, believing that time was not an issue and that the future would merely project what the present desired. This is why Chuan could be construed as a whore to the foreign, even as the foreigner stands outraged by the fact that everything is not what it seemed to be in Thailand.

It is both telling and ironic that this sensation of naïveté is precisely how moderate intellectuals and reformers now feel vis-à-vis Thai Rak Thai, as Thaksin, forced to adopt a certain rhetoric of sincerity following his electoral victory, has been both convicted of nondisclosure of assets and saved from the graver charge of intentional dissimulation and hence of eviction from political life.[10] To the extent that Thaksin adopted this rhetoric, claiming he had not known of the many billions of baht in shares transferred to his wife, son, and private staff, and to the extent that he could use ignorance as a defense, it was because a small group of Western-oriented reformers accepted this rhetoric and its logic as the ground for assessing his gestures.[11] To the extent that his popularity survived—and the petitions in his favor bearing millions of signatures suggest that his popularity did indeed survive—it is because he is believed to have acted as a good Thai politician should. Indeed, the ranking judge on the supreme court, which upheld the National Counter-Corruption Commission's finding, accused Thaksin of precisely this "sin": of acting like an old-style politician, one who exerts his power secretly through gifts and who thereby conceals his ambition in the form of generosity.[12]

Technologies of Sincerity and Discernment: A History of Failure

The two stories of sex and the city might be rewritten as the flip sides of each other. In the one story, prostitution's story, that which is not supposed to be sold (pleasure and love, the real affect of a private heart) is transacted in the domain of money, which is to say a public sphere that is itself nested within an international structure of monetary relation. When prostitution in Thailand first became visible following the elimination of debt bondage (1905) and the first appearance of a street trade, it was the publicness of the trade that made the connection between desire and money sayable. What is at stake in the recent transformations wrought by the U.S. military presence in Thailand is the fact that the new public trade appears in the mode of domesticity. And this mimesis of domesticity in the space of the market leads inexorably to questions about what is real, which in this context is that (love, desire, pleasure) which ought to remain beyond the abstracting power of the generalized commodity form. In the second story, corruption's story, the economy is wrongly subjected to the private sphere and to interpersonal relations that exceed money's capacity to perform rationally by permitting the calculation of equivalence. In both cases there is an obtrusion of the private into the public, one in which the linkage of money and desire threatens the undoing of that disinterested law on which the Kantian political and its neoliberal forms rest. How did this come to pass? To begin, in both prostitution and corruption there is a disjuncture between the "scene" and the "seen," between what could be acknowledged and what is recognized. Everyone in Thailand knows what is happening despite police denials of prostitution's existence and government ministers' claims to having forgotten their assets in Swiss banks. But in Thailand, seeing does not always require recognition (one can turn a blind eye). It is this disjuncture between what is visible and what is acknowledged, between what is seen and what is recognized as part of the scene, that so often leads outsiders (from "johns" to investors) to accuse Thailand of betrayal and to claim that they, rather than Thais, are the victims of dissimulation. Things are not what they seem, or so say the pundits of disappointment.

What is being dissimulated? American and World Bank pundits accuse Thailand of transforming banking into a personal affair by acting without regard to truth and granting credit in the absence of collateral.[13] The public domain, and civil society in particular, relies on its differentiation from the private, so the confusion here is tantamount to a repudiation of liberalism's political structure. There was nothing there but the appearance of civil society, say the critics, and a whole world of investors was duped into believing otherwise, just as Western "johns" can mistakenly believe they have married for love rather than money. More important, they say, this practice of dissimulation by which private structures determine and infuse the political was undertaken in the interest of producing other appearances. They say Thailand acted like something it was not (a modernizing tiger), attiring itself in the clothing of Western capitalism even as it performed the script of an older, Asiatic gift economy. Banks lent to friends, gave credit to those whose authority they respected, and recognized the demands of those whom history and familial ties had privileged. If Thailand had displayed its "true Asian identity," by which is meant a tendency to pursue business in terms of filial obligation rather than rational assessments of value, to play by the rules of "face" (*naa*) rather than transparency (*khwaam prongsai*), the international business community would have known not to invest there. But its simultaneous imitation of sincerity and foreign things, and its desire for Western power, incited failures throughout the region and the world. And more. Thailand, it is often said, infected other economies with the effects of nontransparency, with an Asianness it pretended not to inhabit. As if a global script of *M. Butterfly* was being performed with the IMF as the unsuspecting lover, Thailand is accused of dissimulation—for not being what it appears to be and for not admitting that there is something other behind the facade.

What ought to have been behind the facade? In Western contexts, Protestant and neo-Kantian politics claim to demand truth, affective authenticity, singular intentionality—even when these are not forthcoming. What ought to be behind the public? Privacy: the originary domain of truth, affective authenticity, singular intentionality. I have been arguing that the history in which Thai reformists have come to echo these foreign demands is the history within which prostitution has come to signify a promiscuous relation to foreignness and in which Thailand has come to represent a kind of excess vis-à-vis the performance of national domesticity. It is, moreover, the history within which the logic of transparency has begun its ascent, a history of strange convergences and incomplete translations in the domain of the visible. Insofar as it is a history of failures, it is a history of Thailand's choice not to comply with the global economy's demands on third world economies, namely that they perform and signify a domesticity that is both antecedent and structurally prior to the globality of a transnational, neoliberal mode of capital. Let us then consider that doubled history within which the failure to be local and the failure to recognize the binary relation between domesticity and publicity became mutually representative.

Histories of Mimesis: Love's Labor Lost

It is not incidental that the first problematization of prostitution for and by self-consciously Siamese nationals occurred during King Chulalongkorn's reign (1868–1910). A public discourse about prostitution emerged at the end of the nineteenth century when slavery was abolished. Because slavery had provided the majority of brothels with their labor, the prohibition on the enslavement of anyone born after the ascension of King Chulalongkorn meant that brothels, like other economic institutions, had to seek wage laborers (Suwadee 139). Advance-payment contracts emerged to fill the gap left by slavery, temporizing its logics but nonetheless installing what has been interpreted by many Thai scholars as a "modified form of slavery" (Suwadee 172–73). In fact, Jit Poumisak, the Marxist scholar and hero of the communist movement in Thailand, argued that the "nature of prostitution in the saktina age and the capitalist age was [*sic*] identical, i.e., many women who could no longer endure conditions of hunger and suffering had to sell their bodies" (134).[14] He notes that prior to the nineteenth century, the concern of legislation directed at the matter was not with prostitution per se but with miscegenation. And he cites an eighteenth-century edict prohibiting secret sexual relations between what we might now call ethnically Southeast Asian individuals (Thai, Mon, and Lao) and Indians, French, English, or Kula persons (quoted in Jit 134). Jit heaps scorn on the degree to which this edict preserved access to prostitutes for Thai men: "This meant that it was perfectly all right for prostitutes to have sexual intercourse with Thais who, because they were Buddhists, were not heathens violating the principles of the Religion" (134). And he observes just how much surplus value was extracted from the legitimate form of a labor that could, under the new edict, be punished by death if clients were of the wrong national group. Taxes on prostitution were estimated at this time to provide the king's government with 50,000 baht per year.

A hundred years later, following the fall of Ayutthaya and the establishment of the Chakkri dynasty in Bangkok, prostitution again became the subject of regulation, and, as before, the debate about it concerned both the monetary value and the publicness—or the secrecy—of the relations concerned. These latter two terms were old, but they provided the currency of a new discourse of the public sphere that was emerging at century's end along with the other phenomena of modernity: technological infrastructures, bureaucratic rationalization, a rule of law, and so on. "Prostitution" became central to that discourse for a number of reasons, the most prominent being the apparent disjuncture between Chulalongkorn's abolition of slavery and the emergence of indentured labor at the brothels. Prince Naresvorait, who was the minister of local government in 1895, was especially vexed by this contradiction and with the king's permission—but not his blessing—established a special court to bring charges and hear cases against brothel owners who had deceived women (Suwadee 184–87). In the first year of its operation, 122 cases were processed by the court.

In 1912, however, the minister of local government expressed a more utilitarian interest in prostitution. In a dispute over competing claims for land that had been inadvertently promised to both a school and a brothel, the minister remarked to the king that "the prostitution business is increasingly fruitful. No other government income is comparable to it" (cited in Suwadee 190). The king agreed, but in the end the space was given over to a university that would later bear his name. Prostitution had come to promise such lucre by virtue of the "Prevention of Contagious Diseases Act" passed in 1908. The act required brothel owners and prostitutes to be licensed on a three-month basis and made the licenses subject to medical examination. Although the director of the police department noted no medical exams that first year, the revenue from license sales doubled following the act, from 20,000 to 39,540 baht (Suwadee 189). One cannot help but observe that the revenue was less than that reaped a century earlier. This is perhaps a function of the procedures for estimation. What is less questionable is that by the end of the nineteenth century foreignness was less an attribute of the men who would use prostitutes and more a property of the women themselves. In fact, fewer than half of the women registered in 1908 were Thai. The majority, it turns out, were Chinese.[15] The alterity of the prostitutes would be variously imagined over the century, eventually splitting between that of the national margin, typically Northern Thailand, and that of the radical other, typically Burma or Laos. In the meantime, it would mark that space in which the masculinized public sphere of the nation would open—and close—to the possibility of women's economic autonomy.

Beginning at century's end, one finds evidence of a growing anxiety in the popular press about public sex, cast mainly in the idiom of public hygiene. It was at this time that the term for "evil woman," *ying khon chua*, was given a synonym in "woman who transmits contagious diseases (*ying sanchonrok*)." Much overlooked today by critics who claim that prostitution has always constituted the "unspeakable" of Thailand's public discourse, women's magazines and daily newspapers were full of columns addressed to the subject of women who worked in public spaces rather than brothels to attract their customers.[16]

Perhaps the most prolific writer on this subject was Thianwan, whose editorials in the journal *Satrithai* (Thai Woman) provided sympathetic explanations of prostitutes as victims of sexual double standards and coercive seduction.[17]

An exemplary instance of those editorials runs as follows: "Any woman who has turned to an evil way of life has done so as a result of her being so badly abused by her man. She is, therefore, devoid of love for any man, and as long as she needs to struggle to survive, her body will do whatever her luck and fate direct her to do" (quoted in Suwadee 218). The same journal also made women the chaperones of public hygiene and the agents of national morality. It was, indeed, because they held women responsible for the proper upbringing of children that they could read the descent into evil as such an enormous social loss. Thus the political liberalism of intellectuals like Thianwan was matched by the cultural conservatism of an emergent aristocratic movement led by the new King Rama VI, also known as Vajiravudh (r. 1910–25), and later by Luang Wichit Watthakan. Vajiravudh himself saw prostitution as a dissipating force and blamed it on foreign men despite the fact that the prostitutes themselves were increasingly non-Tai.[18] Accordingly, the defense of prostitutes was aligned with the move to make a newly heteronormativized masculinity the pillar of a new kind of nationalism, oriented around the "Nation, Religion, and Monarchy."[19] Such masculinity would be valorized in new anthems, regulated in cultural mandates that controlled everything from attire to properly gendered comportment, and dramatized in plays and pageants that Wichit penned for the radio and the royal tour. Both urban and national, this masculinity would have as its counterpart a feminized tradition.[20]

Historians now agree that it was Wichit's genius to promote national culture (*watthanatham thai*) by encouraging affiliation with "local tradition" (*praphaenii pheun baan*). This he did by making local tradition a matter of historical representation. So, local festivals, literature, and forms of appearance were staged as the expression of a tradition that was then represented as the origin of a nation which both transcended and encompassed it. Locality emerged here as the retrospective value of a movement that needed both to claim representativeness at the village level—thanks to the creation of a constitutional government in 1932—and sustain the integration of numerous linguistic and regional histories.[21] We need not itemize the forms within which that movement took place, but it is significant that every effort to produce a space of Thainess that was also the space of modernity seemed to be haunted by the figure of prostitution and the traces of an authenticity that it had both betrayed and represented in the form of loss.

So it is that the opening scene of K. Surangkhanang's effusively romantic novel about a prostitute, entitled *Ying khon chua* [Evil Woman, translated into English as *The Prostitute*], has two men meet in a train and discuss people they have known. Through a sequence of metonymic associations the conversation moves to a mutual friend named Wit and is overrun by the tale of a prostitute who has fallen in love with him after having been seduced and coerced into the trade from her up-country village. The novel enacts that strange logic by which prostitution enters discursive space accidentally through a series of fateful encounters. And it transfers an instability in the causal chain of represented events to the prostitute herself. In the case of Rheun, the young woman protagonist of the novel, rural innocence is irreparably brutalized by the experience of modernity, which for her takes the form of rape, betrayal, and sexual servitude but also intense intimacy with another woman at the brothel. Her innocence damns her to lose what she ought to have protected, and she is redeemed only in the moment that she accepts responsibility for the naïveté that transforms itself into an excess of sexual knowledge. "Who was to blame, except herself, for being so foolish?" (Surangkhanang 63). This rendering of naïveté as the source of sin is, as already stated, an accusation of conflating appearances with truth. But if the anxiety of authenticity during the century's early decades revolved around the actual foreignness of the woman herself, the years of anticommunist warfare and near civil war would make prostitution a sign for the desirous relation to the foreign (in the form of either Chinese and Vietnamese communism or American capitalism). Ironically, this transformation was associated with a competing anxiety that the seeming domesticity of sexual relations between Thai women and foreign men (domestic relations that were nonetheless being paid for) may have been concealing an *absence* of desire. The even greater threat was that too much desire and a lack of desire might have the same appearance. To the extent that prostitution during the Vietnam War mimicked domesticity, it became the site of an anxiety about a lost capacity to discern the difference between private truth and public performance. The risk for the Westerner seeking domesticity in a foreign place was therefore the possibility of becoming like the prostitute: a naïf, one who believes in truth and who wrongly assumes that appearances will reveal it.

Against Representation

The one who follows money and translates locality into foreignness will almost always be accused of prostitution. But what about the one who says that the local is already, always already foreign? What if it is this very recognition that gives the local its particular contours? Such a response can be discerned in Thai history. As Marx argued, the commodity is a form that exists only at the boundaries of communities in the mode of translation. An internal difference is the very source of its power to move, across space, in time. It is because there are different commodities that one trades, but it is because commodities are internally differentiated by a coexistent use and exchange value that they can be used to trade. Indeed, it was against the idiomatics of blood, and even of language, that Marx argued for translation as the metaphor and analytic device par excellence in the analysis of commodities (*Grundrisse* 162–63). Commodities and generalized commodity economies, in Marx's analysis, cannot be local. They are *essentially* translocal, foreign to and at the core. Consequently, there can be no truly domestic economy, but merely spaces delimited for the distribution of wealth. Needless to say, national economies survive precisely to the extent that they can occlude or repress this fact, and the global economy achieves its status *as* global only by positing locality as both logically and temporally anterior to itself. Any attempt to overturn this axiom, any performance of an alternative reading, must be experienced as perverse. Thailand is, in this sense, a perverse place. Renowned as a nation of rip-offs, superficial appearance, and cultural promiscuity, it is nonetheless the only nation in Southeast Asia not to have been colonized, and its refusal fully to serve the global economy as the foreign site of domestic production is one of the extraordinary facts of modern history. The episode that is most frequently said to stand at the origin of Thailand's insertion into the globalizing political economy occurred in 1855, with the signing of a treaty by Sir John Bowring and then King Rama IV, or Mongkut (r. 1855–68). The treaty was signed to displace a prior treaty that had been negotiated with Rama III, and it had been demanded by English merchants, especially those in the manufacturing sectors of the Midlands who felt they had not been given adequate access to Thai markets. Bowring negotiated this new treaty with a king much more predisposed to speak with foreigners than had been his predecessor. However, when Bowring arrived in the service of English merchant capital, this same king was in the midst of a scandal arising from rumors (emanating from the Singaporean press) that he was unfairly restricting the movement of English and American missionaries in Thailand. Most irksome to the king, the rumors were accompanied by a disparaging discourse that identified him and, by extension, his nation as morally corrupt. Printed stories describing the impasse in *The Straights Times* cited numerous wives and concubines as evidence of a depravity and sexual excess that, the anonymous authors said, proved him constitutionally incapable of the work of government.

The backdrop of scandal and inflamed monarchical egos was a mere diversion for Bowring, however. It was less the putative sexual excess of the king (highly dubious, given the king's forty years as a monk) and his compatriots than the incapacity to delimit the boundaries of the local that stood at the center of Bowring's treaty-making efforts. The English merchants wanted free access to Siam's markets. But more than this, they wanted the Chinese junk trade construed as foreign. That is to say, they believed a Siamese failure to distinguish between foreign and local trade lay at the heart of their own incapacity to compete. They wanted tariffs on commodities being brought into Siam on Chinese junks (agricultural goods, paper products, silks), and they wanted them removed on British commodities. The differentiating factor (that which would separate Siamese policy toward English and Chinese trade), they insisted, must be the legal document, the negotiated decision to relinquish the prerogative of differential tariffs not simply the failure to differentiate. That is to say, the English demanded that a spatially delimitable national identity be deemed natural, part of the order of things. Law, and especially trade law, was to be the means of its heroic transcendence and the sign of political relation entered "at will." Law, unnatural relation between men, would be the instrument for nature's violent restructuring and the means through which England would insert itself between Siam and China. In the end, England could only fantasize the former for her own—as concubine and consumer, as domesticated other rather than favored trading partner.

The Bowring Treaty reversed the protocol and structure of previous agreements (which had commenced with the Siamese king and made him the grammatical subject of the treaty), making Queen Victoria rather than her Asian counterpart the author of the pact. However, the universal force ascribed to law by the English found little correspondence among the Siamese, for whom a thoroughgoing legal reform and the establishment of constitutional documents would have to wait another fifty years. Moreover, despite English demands, the entity called Siam did not yet exist in any way that would permit the English treaty to be enforced. Innumerable conflicts would ensue as local princes in the *muangs* of the North would try to negotiate their own relations with English merchants (especially teak merchants), much to the consternation of the English government, which thought it had already resolved the issue and which perceived these conflicts as efforts to double-bill on the part of Siam. Though Bangkok claimed the fealty of these princes, they were not territorially subject to central government. Indeed, as Thongchai Winichakul has so elegantly demonstrated in *Siam Mapped*, there was no abstractly spatialized geo-body over which the king could be said to reign or exercise authority. There were only people and classes of people, city-states in far-flung regions that pledged loyalty to Siam but not necessarily to the exclusion of loyalties owed to other states and their monarchs. There was, in other words, monarchical power but no domain.

One might say, in a Heideggerian vein, that the English were demanding not only the formation of a national and nationalized political economy under the authority of a single (local) administrative entity but they were also summoning the establishment of a national "worldview." That is to say, they were demanding that the Siamese accede to that technologized perspective which renders the world as that thing of which one can "get the picture." Not merely a disciplining Panoptic oversight, nor a subjectless Archimedean perspective, this "worldview" works by assuming an imminence in the object world. It instrumentalizes that world and, with a certain aggressivity, abstracts from it a value solely *for* the subject. In this context, it is surely not incidental that the majority of gifts exchanged between Victoria, Bowring, and Rama IV as part of their long diplomatic flirtation were scientific toys and instruments of industrial technology: cameras, photographs, telescopes, sewing machines, printing presses, and so on. Initially curiosities in Thailand, these objects quickly found interested consumers and, more important, technically adept reproducers. Ultimately, these objects produced and then rooted themselves in a new epistemological context. The positing of an imminence in the world, of a productivity whose future realization would be the function of technology, went hand in hand with this new orientation. Among its many manifestations were new discourses of geography, new practices of cartography, and a reimagination of the state apparatus as a spatially structured one (with right- and left-hand ministers acquiring responsibility of North and South, respectively). These are abundantly evident in the nationalist poetics of Luang Wichit Wathakan and in the new fetishisms of the nation that accused prostitutes of dissipating the national essence. They were also visible in the laborious legislation of etiquette—especially that promulgated during midcentury by the government of General Phibul Sonkhram—that asked

Thais to act and especially dress like Westerners so as to appear "modern." Yet not everything was translated. Although Thongchai has discerned in the birth of Siamese discourses of geography a new episteme, he attributes this emergence to a false correspondence between Siamese commitments to astrology and Western commitments to astronomy. The seeming translatability of these discourses, he says, permitted a slippage and a movement of one discourse across the horizon of another, thus inciting a transformation in Siamese thought even as (elite) Siamese thought seemed to be maintaining its autonomy and its epistemological authority. But if, in the end, Thai people became subject to the languages of space and place, if they ultimately acceded to a notion of the geo-body, not all discourses of identity were as easily translated. Ironically, however, the mistranslation of some discourses manifested itself in an excessive devotion to transliteration, to the appearance of perfect equivalence. This is especially true in the economic sphere.

Consider, for example, the case of the 1905 Holy Men's Revolts. In Northeastern Thailand (Isaan), resistance to new taxation and demands for payment in cash rather than kind came in the form of millenarian movements led by men said to have magical powers of insight.[22] These men prophesied an eschatological transformation in which the metaphors of the natural world would be actualized. Flowers named for fish would become fish. Those named for gold and precious stones would become gold and precious stones. Everything, said the Holy Men (*phu mii bun*), would be what it seemed to be. Equivalence would be dissolved into identity, and abstraction would be overcome.

One way to read the Holy Men's Revolts is to see them as a naïve misrecognition of commodity logics, an overliteralization of the translation promised by money (which turns one thing into another by virtue of exchange, which is to say mediation). The monarchy dismissed the promises of the phuu mii bun as mere rumor—language without substance or reference. His majesty's officers published warnings against the prophecies that had themselves been printed anonymously on a new printing apparatus. But many Northeasterners were prepared to bet their lives on the miracle of money. This is at least partly attributable to a deeply felt sense that appearances, in general, can have performative effect. Nor was that commitment completely antithetical to the new economy being cultivated by taxation and commodity aesthetics, for the investment in appearances was precisely what the new economy demanded. The problem this time was the failure of mediation and hence the failure of deferral. If words were things, if gold flowers really were gold, then money would be irrelevant. The monarchy wanted plants (albeit rice) to become something else (imports of cotton, for example) but only by virtue of their passage through money, for, in money, the difference between use and exchange value, and the possibility of extracting surplus value, resided. Moreover, in money the future of desire could be infinitely sustained. In the end, the holy men erred in believing too quickly and too thoroughly in the literal promises—one wants to say appearances—of the market and the magic of money. They believed that mediation was transubstantiation. The elite knew better, knew that the fantasies of money were only productive if they were recognized as such—as the anticipations of a future value that would only be guaranteed by others' similar fantasies in future value. For this wisdom, however, they would be as roundly punished, as were the holy men for their naïveté. The solicitation by and for commodity aesthetics during the early part of this century, a solicitation that generated in Thailand a thoroughgoing commitment to capitalism, has been repaid by accusations of crass materialism and a willingness to subject everything (including the private sphere of love) to the universalist claims of the commodity form. When, recently, the "plague" of economic failure saw the local currency devalued by up to 50 percent (in Thailand—more elsewhere), Thais were accused of not knowing the limits and of not playing by the rules—of investing too much in appearances and infecting the world with a desire that was more properly its own.

History Again: Toward a Conclusion

The Holy Men's Revolts occurred at precisely the same time as slavery was abolished, which is to say the same year that prostitution assumed its public form. This is the moment of the market's consolidation, the period in which money began to displace (or so it seemed) other forms of economic relation, especially the gifting practices of a tributary order organized as a series of concentric circles of power and difference. For the most part, however, few people remember these practices or the marvelous imaginings of magical wealth they promised and betrayed. Prostitution, on the other hand, has assumed iconic status in the imaging of modernity as a promiscuous relation to foreignness and as an idiom within which a retrospectively felt loss can be spoken: as the result of a failure to maintain the boundaries between what is private and what is public, what is domestic and what is foreign. It is also the idiom within which the overinvestment in appearances is linked to an improperly performed domesticity. Its function as discourse far exceeds its perceived significance within the national imaginary of Thailand, and its effects in the transnational imagination of Southeast Asian economies cannot be overestimated.

The history of the twentieth century, which is also the history of Thailand's entrenchment in the binary politics of globality and locality, has been haunted by the recurring specter of a woman whose desire for things is transformed by acts of duplicity so as to incite desire in another. The same story is told of sex tourists and currency speculators. But if, as stated earlier, the one who follows money and translates locality into foreignness will always be accused of prostitution, then, given the originarily translocal nature of all commodity relations, perhaps all third-world economies are doomed to accusations of exceeding their function and desiring too much. The Global South has been asked to be local in relation to the neoliberal global. Its economy is to be split between resource extraction, industrial manufacture, and service. Speculation and finance is reserved for the first world. When nations like Thailand become the sites of significant speculative economies, as occurred during the 1980s, they are said to have departed from their "homely" status and become too "canny" for their own good. When speculation overruns them, as happened in 1997, they are accused of not knowing their place, of having misrecognized the source of their own wealth, namely productive labor and the labor of sexual servitude. Now, when, in the wake of the 1997 crash of the Thai Stock Market and the subsequent devaluation of that nation's currency there emerged what many economic pundits described as a pan-Asian "plague" (sometimes called a "flu") of currency speculation and economic collapse, the figure of the prostitute came back. She seemed to float above the space that, only recently, had been recognized as the ground of a national proper whose boundaries could be maintained and whose integrity could be lost. She infected every discourse of loss, and the talk about infection could not but evoke her putative transmission of those sexual diseases whose policing had originally earned his majesty's government so much money. Many foreign journalists commenting on the crash managed to insinuate into their columns about banking and national economic policy some reference to prostitution and illicit foreign earnings. In a country where everything seems always to be for sale, say the pundits, one can never really know what is valued. Therefore one can never really know what is valuable. The lack of domesticity, one lamented by the English as a failure to differentiate between what is local and what is truly foreign, as well as between what is ineradicably foreign and what can be domesticated by law, is now read as the failure to maintain an authentically private domain where love and compassion and the possibility of a gift reside.

But a gift in the world of exchange and love for sale on the market? Corruption and prostitution, each metaphorizing the other, can only spell confusion for those who assume the ethics and representational logics of transparency. There is no technology adequate to the traversal of this epistemological chasm—except, perhaps, the discourse of transparency itself. In 1998 the uncannily named "Transparency International" opened its first branch office in Bangkok.[23] In 2000, following a lengthy investigation by the official National Counter-Corruption Commission, Thaksin Shinawatra was charged with corruption. Half a world away, a French man was found guilty in a Parisian court of raping an eleven-year-old Thai "prostitute" whose face he could not remember but who was nonetheless tracked down and flown from Hua Hin (thanks to international NGO money) to receive his bathetic tears of apology. Apology, the most extreme gesture of transparency, the promise of affect's total disclosure, was dubious compensation for the injuries suffered. Always belated, this gesture mocks the demand for authenticity and is rightly seen by many Thais as the least true of all gestures because it has the least performative effect. Precisely because he didn't have to apologize, Thaksin Shinawatra can now take on the improbable task of writing an article on honesty for the in-house magazine of the National Counter-Corruption Commission. His reconciliation with its leadership is the seal on a transformation by which he has taken for himself the task of "stamping out corruption." But it would be an error to assume that this transformation is anything but superficial, if by superficial we understand that it is an investment in the truth of appearances. Thaksin is doing what is asked of him, performing in the role of a politician whose image must satisfy the looks of both citizens and foreigners, whose image must speak of both homeliness and canniness. What his supporters and the eleven-year-old child, now grown, wanted is not sincerity, or not only sincerity, but compensation. And they want compensation calculated on the basis of future value. They want not to be called whores for the wanting, and they want not to be condemned for the belief that appearances are everything in the domain of appearances, even when they are nothing elsewhere.

NOTES

1. I use "Euro-Americanized" instead of "globalized" to underscore the fact that the globality of which we are now all a part is nonetheless centered, and that the flexibility of capital does not mitigate its tendency to return to sites in Europe and North America, where it sustains the claim of particular states upon international imagination and international regulatory institutions.

2. It is interesting to note in this context that many English terms concerning the new economy have been completely translated into Thai. *Khwaam prongsai*, meaning "transparency," is a case in point. "Corruption" retains its English form, however, signaling both a local ambivalence toward the category, which is read as something

irreducibly foreign, and a lack of homogeneity in the importation of economic discourse as such.

3. To my mind the most intelligent discussion of this history, albeit one confined to Indonesia, is to be found in James T. Siegal's *Fetish, Recognition, Revolution.*

4. The formal agreement between Thailand and the United States was signed in 1971. The "local" economy is nonetheless still dominant in terms of the numbers of participants, but as a source of earnings, prostitution associated with foreign men far exceeds the local "industry," even without calculating the additional earnings associated with sex tourism. In all analyses of prostitution in Thailand, one must remain aware that "prostitution" is not one. That economy ranges from the enslavement of minors to the relatively knowing participation of adult women. I do not mean to conflate them all here but wish merely to focus on that which is associated with current discussions of foreignness.

5. Locally, the stories in which parents are said to sell their children in order to repay debts constitute a small minority of the compensatory explanations intended to hold a more stringent criticism at bay.

6. Examples of this kind of anxious interrogation can be seen most explicitly in Dennis O'Rourke's film *The Good Woman of Bangkok* and the debates surrounding it. Berry et al., *The Filmmaker and the Prostitute;* Cohen, "Lovelorn Farangs."

7. Patpong is a district in Bangkok, off Silom Road, famous for its sex clubs and also for its market of brand-name rip-offs, both of which cater to foreigners. *Kamphaendin* is both a generic term for "mud wall," which constituted the boundary of ancient cities, and a designation of that area on the periphery of the city, and particularly Chiang Mai, where there are brothels serving foreigners.

8. It has been pointed out to me by Melissa Wright and Wendy Brown, among others, that the culture of "sincerity" is an ideological mystification and that Protestant capitalism thrives upon deceit as much as any other value. This may be the case, but the deceit rests upon the presumption that others will trust in the truth of appearances—and it is this generalized presumption that has been absent in Thai and perhaps other Southeast Asian contexts. I do not mean to imply that the demand for disclosure ever achieves a fully performative force; I do, however, mean to suggest that it circulates as a value that can be summoned and against which failure can be measured in the West.

9. Chuan Leekpai came to power following elections that were demanded by democracy protestors in 1992 following the usurpation of power by General Suchinda Kraphrayoon, a member of the junta that had staged a coup in February of 1991. Although Chuan was considered the moderate at the time, and the best alternative to either military strongmen or notoriously corrupt politicians like Chatichai Choonhaven (whose government Suchinda had ousted), he has since fallen into extreme disfavor thanks to the economy's continued stagnation and the belief that he has sacrificed Thailand to the IMF.

10. Thaksin was acquitted of the serious offense by a margin of eight to seven.

11. Thaksin's transfer of shares to his family and private staff was explained as a decision by which he had incurred enormous debt. His transfer of shares at the cost of 10 baht each, despite a market trading price of 160 baht, was thereby reframed not as a loan, which would have left him responsible for declaring the assets, but as the assumption of debt on his part and hence as a gift.

12. Prasert Nasakul, president of the Constitutional Court, was one of seven dissenting judges and especially vitriolic in his attack on Thaksin, who would have had to leave political life for a minimum of five years following conviction for intentional dissimulation. Yuwadee Tunyasiri, "Thaksin 'A Product of the Past.'"

13. As late as autumn 2000 the rate of nonperforming loans averaged across all banks exceeded 30 percent.

14. *Saktina* here refers to the "feudal" organization of labor in Ayutthaya and Siam. Although the applicability of the term *saktina* has been questioned, Jit, writing from an orthodox and somewhat derivative Marxian position, used the term with relatively little circumspection. For a more comprehensive history of this term and period, see Akin Rabibhadana, *The Organization of Thai Society in the Early Bangkok Period.*

15. The statistics for that year are as follows: of 2,500 prostitutes total, 950 were Thais, 1,441 Chinese, 58 Vietnamese, 40 Laotians, 1 was Mon, and several were of unknown ethnicity (Suwadee 189). It is possible that some of those women registered as Chinese were not actually Chinese. Because the clientele of the brothels was predominantly Chinese (male laborers from China were recruited in Thailand, but their wives were not permitted to join them), owners sometimes made their workers wear Chinese clothing and change their names. Regardless of the real ethnic identity of the women, the values of foreignness and prostitution were riveted to each other in the discourse of the time.

16. The spurious claim about such unspeakability has been made most recently and most forcefully by Bishop and Robinson who, in *Night Market,* manage to fuse the ideological discourse of a bourgeois elite in Thailand with the proprietary idiom of (Stephen) Tylerian postmodernism. See especially 195–217.

17. See especially the *Satrithai* issues of Mar. 22, 1925, May 10, 1926, Nov. 14, 1926, and Jan. 10, 1927.

18. Although Jit wrote of prostitutes in ethnic terms using the word *Thai,* it is more properly written as *Tai,* which designates a linguistic and ethnic category rather than a national one, as suggested by the aspirated "Thai."

19. It may be noted that the sexuality of those promoting these values was anything but straightforwardly heteronormative. However, the values being disseminated as the ground of nationalism were, I believe, both emphatically masculinist and heternormative.

20. The best accounts of Luang Wichit and this era of nationalism can be found in Scot Barmé's *Luang Wichit Wathakan and the Creation of a Thai Identity,* and Walter Vella's *Chaiyo! King Vajiravudh and the Development of Modern Thai Nationalism.*

21. I discuss this historical development of national culturalism in some detail; see *In the Place of Origins,* especially chapter 7.

22. On the Holy Men's Revolts, see Chatthip Nartsupha, "The Ideology of the 'Holy Men' Revolts"; Yoneo Ishii, "A Note on Buddhistic Millenarian Revolts in Northeastern Siam"; and Shigeharu Tanabe, "Ideological Practice in Peasant Rebellions."

23. Transparency International is an international NGO with the mandate of combating corruption and promoting civil society. The Bangkok office's Web-site can be viewed at <http://www.transparency.org>.

Works Cited

Akin Rabibhadana. *The Organization of Thai Society in the Early Bangkok Period.* Ithaca: Cornell University Press, 1969.

Barmé, Scot. *Luang Wichit Wathakan and the Creation of a Thai Identity.* Singapore: Institute of Southeast Asian Studies, 1993.

Berry, Chris, Annette Hamilton, Laleen Jayamanne, and Dennis O'Rourke, eds. *The Filmmaker and the Prostitute: Dennis O'Rourke's* The Good Woman of Bangkok. Sydney: Power Publications, 1997.

Bishop, Ryan, and Lillian S. Robinson. *Night Market: Sexual Cultures and the Thai Economic Miracle.* New York: Routledge, 1998.

Chatthip Nartsupha. "The Ideology of the 'Holy Men' Revolts in North East Thailand." In *History and Peasant Consciousness in South East Asia.* Ed. Andrew Turton and Shigeharu Tanabe, 111–34. Osaka: National Museum of Ethnology, 1984.

Cohen, Erik. "Lovelorn Farangs: The Correspondence between Foreign Men and Thai Girls." *Anthropological Quarterly* 59, no. 3 (1986): 115–27.

Derrida, Jacques. *Given Time: I. Counterfeit Money.* Trans. Peggy Kamuf. Chicago: University of Chicago Press, 1991.

Fukuyama, Francis. "The End of History?" *The National Interest* 16 (Summer 1989): 3–18.

The Good Woman of Bangkok. Dir. Dennis O'Rourke. Film Australia, 1992.

Heidegger, Martin. "The Art of the World Picture." In *The Question Concerning Technology and Other Essays.* Trans. William Lovitt, 115–54. New York: Harper and Row, 1977.

Ishii, Yoneo. "A Note on Buddhistic Millenarian Revolts in Northeastern Siam." *Journal of Southeast Asian Studies* 6, no. 2 (1997): 121–26.

Jit Poumisak. "The Real Face of Thai Feudalism Today." In *Thai Radical Discourse: The Real Face of Thai Feudalism Today.* Trans. Craig Reynolds. Ithaca: Cornell University Press, 1987.

Marx, Karl. *Grundrisse: Foundations of the Critique of Political Ecomony.* Trans. Martin Nicolaus. New York: Penguin, 1993.

Morris, Rosalind C. *In the Place of Origins: Modernity and Its Mediums in Northern Thailand.* Durham: Duke University Press, 2000.

Pasuk Phongpaichit, and Sungsidh Piriyarangsan. *Corruption and Democracy in Thailand.* Chiang Mai: Silkworm Books, 1994.

Siegal, James T. *Fetish, Recognition, Revolution.* Princeton: Princeton University Press, 1997.

Surangkhanang, K. *The Prostitute.* Trans. David Smyth. New York: Oxford University Press, 1994.

Suwadee Tanaprasitpatana. "Thai Society's Expectations of Women, 1851–1935." Ph.D. diss., University of Sydney, 1989.

Tanabe, Shigeharu. "Ideological Practice in Peasant Rebellions: Siam at the Turn of the Twentieth Century." In *History and Peasant Consciousness in South East Asia.* Ed. Andrew Turton and Shigeharu Tanabe, 75–110. Osaka: National Museum of Ethnology, 1984.

Thongchai Winichakul. *Siam Mapped: The History of the Geo-body of a Nation.* Honolulu: University of Hawaii Press, 1994.

Turton, Andrew, and Shigeharu Tanabe. *History and Peasant Consciousness in South East Asia.* Osaka: National Museum of Ethnology, 1984.

Vella, Walter. *Chaiyo! King Vajiravudh and the Development of Modern Thai Nationalism.* Honolulu: University of Hawaii Press, 1978.

Yuwadee Tunyasiri. "Thaksin 'A Product of the Past.'" *Bangkok Post,* Sept. 1, 2001. <http://scoop.bangkokpost.co.th/bkkpost/2001/september2001/bp20010901/news/01sep2001news16.html>.

4 The Private Parts of Public Value: The Regulation of Women Workers in China's Export-Processing Zones

MELISSA W. WRIGHT

EVERY DAY AROUND THE WORLD, women who work in the third-world factories of global firms face the idea that they are disposable.[1] This idea proliferates in the form of a story, told by factory managers in these facilities, that explains how the women represent a homogenous worker whose productive value inevitably depletes over time until she is worth no more than the value of her own replacement. Her devaluation, according to the terms of this story, derives not from the external circumstances that many women encounter—exhausting work schedules, repetitious labor, repetitive stress injuries, lack of day care, inadequate training, and low pay. Instead, these women are told that the source of their disposability lies within their bodies—specifically, within their reproductive cycles and sexual impulses. According to this story's narrators, the female workers eventually succumb to the pressures of their wombs, their sexual impulses, and their traditional family duties, whereupon they become a worker who requires replacement.

Yet, as the story goes, these wasting women are not worthless from the outset. They possess the traits of dexterity and attention to detail that have long been associated with "natural" femininity. Added to the supposed "docility" of third-world women who, as other well-known stories have it, are cowed by their oppressive traditional cultures, the "disposable woman" is a figure of capitalist dreams. She embodies the valuable traits of dexterity, patience, and docility as well as the sources of her own devaluation. Indeed, the story depicts devaluation as the result of a natural battle between internal forces of value and waste that inevitably renders female workers unsuitable for employment.[2]

In this essay I examine how the managers of a production facility in southern China, owned by a U.S. corporation, deploy this narrative of disposable women workers as part of their strategy to produce value in the facility. "Value" here refers to the production of valuable commodities and the managers' self-reproduction as valuable employees within the company's international division of labor. By examining what is at stake in their telling of this story of disposable workers we can see how the managers divert attention from corporate practices that lead to injury and illness and how contemporary corporations devise labor and production policies by means of a narrative that justifies disposing of thousands upon thousands of women as if they were little more than trash.

My argument draws principally from ethnography I conducted in 1993 and 1997 in a factory I call "Asia on the Water" (AOTW), a subsidiary of the multinational firm "On the Water" (OTW), based in Illinois. OTW manufactures motors, boats, and other water-sport equipment and has factories in the United States, Mexico, Brazil, Hong Kong, and China.[3] The branch facility of AOTW consists of two manufacturing operations, one in Dongguan in Guangdong Province and the other in Hong Kong. The administrative facilities are housed primarily in Hong Kong, and the top AOTW managers and engineers commute between Dongguan and Hong Kong regularly. Some supplemental material for this essay also comes from ethnography and the interviews I conducted in OTW's Mexican facilities located in Ciudad Juárez, Chihuahua.

This research reflects some of the challenges facing ethnographers of global capital and its principal agents, multinational firms. Because the multinational corporation represents a "multi-sited" field site, a domain located in many different places simultaneously, a researcher in this "field" must often conduct research in multiple political and cultural contexts, often across different linguistic domains as part of the same project. When, in 1993, I followed OTW's operations into China and Hong Kong, I found myself on unfamiliar terrain. I had never been either to Hong Kong or southern China, and I spoke neither Cantonese nor Mandarin. I relied on English-speaking informants, all managers and engineers who referred to themselves as "Hong Kong–Chinese" and presented the corporate environment to me. Over a three-month period (in two different years) I commuted to work with them, both in Hong Kong and in Dongguan, and I worked in their offices and on the factory floors. My presence alongside the several men who were my informants was regarded as a curiosity and also a favor to their American colleagues in Mexico, who had requested that they accommodate my presence.

In my study of AOTW, I focused on managers and engineers.[4] Three individuals—the general manager, the production manager, and the head engineer—provide the bulk of material for this essay. The general manager, Howard Li, is a second-generation Hong Kong–Chinese citizen whose family migrated from southern China. In 1993 he had worked in OTW for fifteen years, starting as an engineer and then working his way up the corporate ladder. He received a master's degree in mechanical engineering in Canada and had plans to send his daughter to college in the United States. The production manager, Harry Chen, also is a second-generation Hong Kong–Chinese citizen who started at AOTW as a line supervisor in 1984. He has a technical degree from a Hong Kong polytechnic. The head engineer, Stephen Chan, said his family has long lived in Hong Kong. He started his career at AOTW in 1990, when he and his family moved back from California. He had also worked for corporations in Tokyo.

Each informant expressed belief that because I was from the United States I would be critical of the labor practices in southern China. Yet each also expected that I would see their facility as a reasonable and decent workplace where there was, as Howard Li said, "nothing to hide." Although their different jobs and backgrounds informed this study in various ways, the three informants agreed with each other and with other colleagues whom I also interviewed that female workers on the line were, for a variety of reasons, disposable. My research at AOTW focused on how these managers and engineers tried to convince me of this disposability, which aspects of the women's work made them vulnerable, and what was at stake for them in making this depreciating condition believable.

I was not given direct access to the women workers. As a result, and unlike most other ethnographic studies on the southern Chinese manufacturing sector, my research does not explore the experiences of the young women and girls described by the discourses I present. My analysis is not about workers' work experiences, nor is it my intent to claim that workers are helpless against managerial machinations to work them as hard and as long as possible. Several scholars and journalists have found that many Chinese women experience an independence and renovated sense of their own worth as a result of employment beyond the family purview (Farley; Lee). There are also many studies of global manufacturing operations that demonstrate that even though women endure humiliating and oppressive managerial policies they nevertheless find creative and effective forms of subversion (Fernandez-Kelly; Ong; Salzinger). Instead, I focus on the managers: on their verbal explanations of what they believe, their actions and decisions, and my observations of them at work. As I accompanied them throughout their days I constantly focused on how and when the story of female disposability was told, how it developed as a believable description of "reality," and how practices based on this tale appeared rational and justified.

The Capital of Female Disposability

My interview in Dongguan revealed ways in which the AOTW managerial team deployed the story of female disposability, also described by other scholars. Their job—as managers of production and engineers of industrial manufacture—was to extract value from these workers before waste-creating elements that drive their disposability overcome them. This task is tricky. Workers are hired for the value their labor represents to the corporation. In the case of AOTW as with virtually every multinational firm in the electronics industry, managers hire women to work on the assembly line. The assumption is that women make the best electronic assemblers because of their famous "dexterity," "docility," "patience," "attentiveness," and "cheapness" (Elson and Pearson, eds.; Fernandez-Kelly).

At the time of my research, women workers at AOTW—who earned 11 cents per hour—represented one of the world's best bargains. A manager who dismisses a worker before her coveted qualities are fully exploited is considered inefficient and wasteful. AOTW, again like most electronic manufacturers, assumes a month-long start-up period for workers and does not expect electronic assemblers to reach full speed until after three months on the job. Employing a worker beyond her prime, however, opens the company to the risk of maintaining a labor force whose fingers have stiffened, whose eyes have blurred, and whose minds wander. Contemporary electronic assembly work around the world is typically organized cyclicly, and workers perform the same tasks within delimited timeframes. At AOTW, the cycle time for assembly work is twenty-six seconds, a period during which assemblers perform numerous tasks on as many as five hundred units a day.

People in this line of work commonly experience injuries from repetitive stress, such as carpal tunnel, tendonitis, shoulder and back pains, and eyestrain. Depression due to the lack of future opportunities and advanced training is also prevalent in less-productive labor forces. Moreover, assembly-line workers who have more tenure and experience are likely to organize grievance committees, subversive tactics, and work stoppages. Consequently, managers are challenged with devising a strategy for keeping women electronic assembly workers just long enough to extract value from their dexterity, attentiveness, and docility before injury, illness, and anger overcome them.

The trajectory of workers heading toward a state of waste is captured within the concept of "turnover," a mundane idea within the quotidian of capitalist workplaces, industrial and otherwise. Turnover includes two related dimensions, "corporate turnover" and "labor turnover." Corporate turnover refers to workers coming into and going out of particular jobs. The corporate turnover "rate" refers to the percentage of workers who have left particular jobs within a given period of time, and determination of "high" versus "low" turnover depends on calculation of whether a turnover rate inhibits or fosters the production of capitalist value.

According to my interviews in OTW, the optimal turnover rate in both the Mexican and Chinese facilities is an annual 7 percent, which guarantees a certain degree of flexibility in the labor supply. The corporate turnover rate is distinguished from another measurement of "labor turnover" that calculates the amount of time each individual employee remains with the corporation. The optimal level of labor turnover, according to my interviews and other research on multinational manufacturers, for assembly-line workers is two years. The optimal rate is much higher for "skilled" employees.[5] In other words, companies prefer to have, on average, a constant turnover rate of 7 percent every year across a spectrum of jobs and a constant labor turnover rate of two years among unskilled assembly workers, such that those who have more than two years' tenure represent a numerical minority.

The desire for a two-year labor turnover rate reveals the belief that unskilled workers operate on a trajectory of diminishing returns. At some point (in this case within two years) replacement of these workers is regarded as more valuable to the company than their continued employment. For managers, the challenge is to keep the two turnover rates in proper alignment so the two-year timeframe does not disrupt the 7 percent figure. In other words, management does not want workers leaving en masse every two years. Such a pattern of turnover would lead to total disruption of the labor process. Instead, management desires a steady rate of attrition so the 7 percent turnover derives from the departure of workers who have entered the period of diminishing returns.

The combined concept of turnover reveals the devastating logic of capitalist value production that captured Marx's attention and led to his proclamation that the more riches workers produce, the poorer they become.[6] He captured this logic within his description of workers as "variable capital," the kind whose value is distinct from the value they create through their labor. In short, by identifying workers as "variable capital" Marx exposes how the worker is socially produced as a subject whose labor (which is sold as a commodity) is evaluated separately from a laborer's own reproduction such that a difference in value exists between the laborer's worth and that of the labor produced. And this variation in value between the worker's value and the value of the worker's labor is the critical ingredient for creating capitalist profit. When the logic of worker as variable capital is extended, we can see that profit grows if workers are cheapened, whereas the value of their labor remains constant or increases. The greater variation between workers' value and the value of their labor, the greater the profit.

Within such logic the value of disposable workers is clear. Under capitalism, profit increases when the difference between the cost for reproducing workers and the marketed cost of their products expands, so workers whose labor circulates through the circuitry of production and consumption simultaneous to the depreciation in the cost of their reproduction represent a most valuable form of labor power. In short, the "disposable woman worker," her social worth located on a continuum of diminishing returns, is the most valuable kind of worker so long as her labor contributes to the making of commodities. Unlike other employees who might be valued for on-the-job experience, she loses value with experience. She does not, therefore, merit promotions, training that leads to advancement, timely raises, or other incentives designed to foster long-term loyalty. Nor does she deserve programs designed to minimize the risk of repetitive stress disorders and diminished vision. She is expected to wear out, fall apart, and become disillusioned with the job even as her labor circulates through the creation of commodities that simultaneously increase in value. The more wealth she produces the poorer she becomes.[7]

How that process unfolds within the particular context of any workplace, however, is not addressed by Marx's abstractions. As many feminist scholars have shown, what he identifies as the signature feature of capitalism—the labor theory of value within which the logic of variable capital plays out—does not have a signature mechanism for its materialization.[8] Instead, it unfolds through many conflicting negotiations over differentiated identities and their multiple meanings that snarl the smooth materialization of capitalism and reproduction of capitalist value. Required, therefore, for any study into the production of value is a theoretical toolset that investigates how negotiation of social differences contributes to the reproduction of capitalism as a system that materializes through social distinctions.

It is thus necessary to combine a poststructuralist interrogation into the production of subjects with Marx's insights into the reproduction of workers as variable capital (Joseph). These theoretical approaches demonstrate how the story of disposable third-world women—documented by others as a dominant discourse in global companies—is a form of technology for bringing this most valuable depreciating laborer into existence. The technology functions through the repetition of a plotline that describes the third-world woman worker's descent along the continuum of depreciation.[9] Although the story has achieved familiarity through repetition, I wish to help defamiliarize it so as to return to it something of the shock value that has been lost in its transition to a commonplace of global assembly processes. The fact that third-world women are unremarkably considered to represent a disposable labor force contributes to the ability of corporate managers to organize labor policies and production processes with this normative figure in mind.

At AOTW, "disposability" turns on a calculation that measures the worth of discrete bodily functions against each other—but only in the bodies of female workers. Although workers are hired according to the assumption that all women workers in third-world countries possess the valuable combination of docility, dexterity, and attentiveness, they are monitored according to the equally widespread assumption that their reproductive cycles and sexual desires will eventually turn their productivity into waste.

AOTW managers, like managers in other facilities of third-world manufacturers, believe it critical to monitor workers' reproductive organs, menstrual cycles, and sexual behavior on the theory that such monitoring is key to managing commodity production. By focusing on the detrimental effects of women's reproductive urges, AOTW managers generate a smokescreen for the attrition caused by illnesses and injuries derived from long overtime and draconian punishments for minor infractions. Moreover, they contribute to capitalist value accumulation by shielding the company from the scrutiny of local and international industry regulators. In effect, by turning attention to an internal wasting process, the story of disposable third-world women workers diverts attention from corporate labor policies that wear people down during the workday. What we see instead is a worker who needs to be turned inside out in order to evaluate the ratio of her worth, as a laborer, to the value of her labor. Based on this story and the working subject it produces, AOTW managers have devised numerous policies that function as speculums for opening the private parts of women's bodies to public scrutiny.

Asia on the Water

In 1993 Asia on the Water opened a factory in the municipality of Dongguan, a metropolitan area along the Pearl River Delta of Guangdong Province. During the 1990s, Dongguan was one of the fastest-growing export-processing enclaves in southern China ("The Comeback Kid"). By 1995, AOTW occupied several contiguous buildings and had expanded factory production from one to three product lines with a labor force of about seven hundred. Women between the ages of eighteen and twenty-four represented 70 percent of the labor force. All hourly employees lived and worked in the company's factory complex. AOTW's was one of many new factories in one of the city's industrial estates, and identical buildings, all housing workers' dormitories and work spaces under a single roof and owned by dozens of different companies, surrounded it on all sides. The company's top managers and engineers, who commuted weekly from Hong Kong, stayed in managerial quarters within the male workers' dormitories.

At the time of my study in 1993, the AOTW managers were concerned about the company's poor market performance in the previous two years. By 1997 that concern had turned to alarm over the corporate board's decision to downsize by selling off either the Mexican or the Asian facilities to a competitor. Howard Li explained that the decision came on the heels of a protracted internal battle between AOTW managers and the U.S.-American managers in Mexico (MOTW) over corporate resources and product lines. Li referred to this period as a "civil war" between the Chinese managers in Hong Kong and the U.S.-American (Anglo) managers in Mexico (Wright, "Asian Spies").

The American team had opposed the opening of the Dongguan facility and its subsequent expansion on the belief that the Chinese managers were not qualified—due to cultural limitations—to oversee the operation. When the AOTW operation did expand into Dongguan, the Chinese managers were subject to racial slurs and other forms of hostility by their American colleagues. "I was called an 'Asian spy,'" said Li, "and locked out of the office [in the U.S. corporate headquarters]."

The tension intensified during the company's financial crisis in the late 1990s. OTW had fallen into dire financial straits. Sales of its engines began to flag during the late 1980s, a decline that continued into the following decade. There was also erosion of the across-the-board market against Japanese competition. In addition, internal political upheaval within the firm had shaken investor confidence, and company stock lost about 40 percent of its value between 1995 and 1997 without subsequent recovery. In response to the financial crisis the corporate executive board decided that the company had to scale back production and seek subcontracting relationships with other firms. Either the Chinese or the Mexican operations would be sold to a competitor. That, in turn, meant a number of long-term American and Chinese employees would be laid off, left to their own devices for securing jobs with the new employer. As Howard Li said in 1997, "It is between us and Mexico."

A comparison between the Mexican and the Chinese facilities would determine the OTW executive board's decision about which to close. The Mexican facility had been in business for almost thirty years and manufactured components for the gasoline-powered engines assembled in Georgia and marketed in the United States and Europe. It produced the company's signature engine, the retail price of which generated more profit than the sale of twenty-five of the small electrical motors manufactured in AOTW. By contrast, the Chinese facility was still largely untested in 1997. Although it was on the edge of the world's potentially largest industrial labor force as well as its biggest retail market. Unlike its counterpart in Mexico, proven adept at manufacturing quality products, its labor process was plagued by high defect rates and erratic production scheduling. Chinese managers also had to pay ever-increasing bribes to local officials. Even with these problems there was a sense of urgency about getting into China and preparing for opening that market and the maturation of not only the largest but also one of the least-expensive labor markets in the world (Powell; Whelan).

The board informed both managerial teams that they would be compared on the basis of product quality and turnover rate. Product quality was measured in terms of the percentages of defective products for every batch manufactured. It was linked directly to turnover rates in several ways. For instance, high turnover rates—above 7 percent—meant workers were leaving prematurely before their "on-the-job training" had been fully used. New recruits did not perform as well, on average, as seasoned workers. As the Production Manager Harry Chen explained, "New girls have more problems. They make mistakes." Product defects, however could also emerge from turnover rates that were too low if workers were still employed "past their prime." Workers who suffered from illnesses and injuries, for instance, also made mistakes. As Howard Li put it, "This is not work they do for years. . . . You want fresh workers, with fresh eyes and fingers." Quality was considered to derive from monitoring a rate of turnover that constantly cycled fresh workers into the labor process.

The connection between turnover and product quality meant that the AOTW managerial team was even keener on demonstrating that they could manage the right amount of turnover as they competed for their jobs against the U.S.-American managers in Mexico. For Howard Li, the competition presented another opportunity to prove to his overseas bosses and colleagues that the Chinese people were qualified managers. "The Americans don't think we can do this here," he observed. "They think China is backwards. But China is changing very fast. And Chinese people work very hard. . . . If we fail here, then they will say 'I told you so.' And they would say that. I tell you the truth."

At stake was the ability of the Hong Kong–Chinese managers to counter the racism used against them for years within OTW. Toward that end, they relied on a strategy for monitoring their workers' reproductive cycles and sexual drives to help determine how to keep the workers just long enough. Their strategy was, in essence, a procedure for making use of the rhythm of the workers' reproductive drives to accommodate the company's timeframe for extracting value.

Managing Feminine Waste

The sexual segregation of the Dongguan facility reveals the centrality of sex difference to the organization of production and of labor. The facility consists of two buildings, known as Plants 1 and 2. Plant 1 houses the administrative offices and the supplies inventory, both male-dominated areas. On its upper three floors women assemble motors through various steps, including wire-splicing, electrical assembly, and final assembly. Across the street in Plant 2, male workers paint and package the motors for final shipping. Like most manufacturing facilities in the city's industrial estates, both buildings house worker dormitories. Female workers sleep in Plant 1, and male workers and managers in Plant 2.

This spatial segregation both reflected and facilitated a supervisory system organized around the notion that female workers require more surveillance than male employees. Howard Li said of his female labor force, "We have problems with quality in Plant 1. That is where we have our biggest problems." To emphasize his point he held up a partially assembled 1.5 horsepower motor, its unattached wires dangling as evidence of its uselessness. He replaced it on the shelf, next to several motors in similar shape. "Many problems. Too many," he said. Then, ensuring I understood how problems in the motors had to do with problems on the line, he directed my attention to a woman using pliers to twist two wires together before attaching a plastic cap. "This girl is good here, but there was one before her. She always thought about her boyfriend, always wanted to talk with him, so we told her to leave. We can't have workers like that and make a good product." "Sometimes," Harry Chen elaborated, "they hide in the stairs to meet their boyfriends. The other girls say, 'She's in the ladies room,' so the supervisor won't look for her. But she's really meeting her boyfriend outside. That's the kind of problem we have to watch."

By thus linking female sexuality to product defects the managers justified their obvious intensification of surveillance over female workers compared to the relatively lax supervision of the male employees in Plant 2. In female-dominated work areas of Plant 1, supervisors are omnipresent. Women are seated along long tables, forbidden from moving from their seats for any reason, including standing to stretch, without permission. To perform their work they reach into overhead bins for supplies, which they use to assemble some part of the motors they then pass on to a subsequent worker. Their mistakes are posted on overhead signs affixed to their stations. Talking, pausing, or any other activity than working on motor assembly is forbidden, and each worker is allotted fewer than thirty seconds per unit to perform her tasks. She repeats those tasks every thirty seconds over the course of an eight-to-ten-hour workday, six to seven days per week, depending on the scheduling and overtime required.

The men who work in Plant 2 and in the inventory sections of Plant 1 are supervised as teams rather than as individuals. They work in groups of three to five and are free to move around their work areas. Supervisors are seen walking through the male-dominated areas but do not stand over individual workers as they do over the women. Nor are the performances of male workers posted publicly.

Expectations for labor tenure also varied with the sex of the laborer. For instance, AOTW, like most companies in southern China, requires the signing of a two-year labor contract. If a worker leaves before the contract's termination for any reason, including justified dismissal, the worker forfeits a deposit (usually a month's wages), which is paid at the beginning of the job. At the end of the two-year period neither the employer nor the employee is obligated to renew the working relationship. According to Harry Chen, however, AOTW managers would like more male employees to return after the two-year period because "some of them are good and we can teach them technical work." In other words, some male workers are designated as having potential for career development. Women workers, however, receive no such attention. There are no women in positions above secretary or assembly operator, both entry-level, at AOTW, and managers prefer that women workers, once they complete their two-year contracts, seek employment elsewhere. Again, Harry Chen, explained, "We give them recommendation if they are good workers. Two years is enough time."

The dormitories are also supervised differently, according to the assumption that female residents require stricter surveillance than males. "We have rules," explained Howard Li, "the girls have to be in their rooms every night, by eight o'clock. It's not good for them to be out at night. They get into trouble." The "trouble" to which he refers is the kind caused by illicit female sexuality and prostitution. Li frequently mentioned the naiveté he associated with female workers, who were vulnerable, in his view, given their sheltered rural upbringing, to the temptations of fast money in the export-processing zone's booming sex trade.

The association between female assembly workers and prostitution proliferates also throughout the business press, which has dubbed Dongguan a "concubine village" (Landler; Zielbrauer) and blamed the migration of young female workers into southern export-processing zones for the resurgence of the "old vice" of prostitution in a "new" capitalist China. As the author of a *Business China* article in 2000 phrased it, there are many incentives "for women to move out of the factory dormitory and into another trade" ("New China, Old Vice," 7). To guard against such movement between trades, the AOTW managerial staff resorts to a common practice industrywide: locking female workers within the factory complex for six—sometimes seven—days per week (Chan). Those at AOTW were not allowed to leave Plant 1 except on Sundays and if they were not working overtime. Male residents, however, walked between Plants 1 and 2 regularly, which meant they crossed a street and often smoked cigarettes and talked to each other outside the factory gates. I never saw a woman standing outside.

The restrictions on female workers resonated with similar policies applied by other corporations in China's export-processing zones.[10] As sociologist Anita Chan has written, in some cases management imposes coercive regulations on workers, during and after working hours, that are unbelievably detailed: prohibitions on talking, even while eating; marked routes for walking within the factory-dormitory compound; bans on leaving the compound at any time without special permission; and prohibitions against getting pregnant, married, or even engaged (106).

Li and his colleagues enforced such regulations only in areas of the facility devoted to females. When I asked Harry Chen, for example, why there were fewer supervisors in the male-dominated areas of Plant 2, he replied, "These workers mind each other. Some are leaders and tell the others what to do." Indeed, male workers are not prohibited from talking to each or from moving around their work areas. They often confer while working rather than relying on supervisors to tell them what to do every thirty seconds, as is the case in the assembly rooms of Plant 1.

The managerial staff frequently justified strict rules governing women workers on the basis that women's sexuality and reproductive cycles directly affect production rates and quality. "Girls who think of boys all the time are not thinking about their work," Harry Chen said. His concerns over the sexual thoughts, in addition to the sexual deeds, of female workers reflect the prevailing view in AOTW that problems of high defect rates in production emerge not from lack of training but from reproductive drives and cycles internal to workers' bodies.[11] As Chen put it, "They tell you they will behave and do their work, but they think about boys and do not do their work." Stephen Chan described the "ticking" of a woman's "biological clock" as a source of worker distraction: "They hear that biological clock . . . and we tell them they still have time for a family, but first they can make some money and work here, and then they can have their families."

By locating the sources of product defects within the hormones, reproductive drives, and sexual thoughts of women workers, the AOTW managers devised the invasive procedures for controlling and limiting the problem. The policies were based on the idea that because the problems were found in hormones and reproductive cycles, these aspects of the female body had to be policed for signs of trouble. All female workers had to submit to pregnancy tests. "All companies do that," Howard Li explained. "We cannot keep pregnant workers here. That is against the rules." Stephen Chan told me, "We have these tests so the girls will know that if they do get pregnant, we will know. It is really a deterrent. We are like their parents, we know everything about them, and it is for their own good. They do their work and make their money to send back to their families."

On-site pregnancy tests were one among many means for monitoring the sexual organs and desires of women workers; in 1997 AOTW managers began requiring regular pelvic examinations as well. Howard Li explained that the policy was not developed as a corporate initiative that worked with the Chinese government's "one-child" policy. In the late 1970s the Chinese government designed a population policy—its fourth birth planning campaign.[12] The policy was organized around the concept of birth limitation, whereby a series of sanctions and rewards were devised to restrict couples to raising only one child (White). The directive, however, is not uniformly enforced across the country because it is regulated at the local level, by municipal and county governments. Enforcement is strictest in urban areas and those rural counties with zealous officials who use severe punitive measures such as destruction of violators' homes, steep fines, and forced sterilization (Pan).

According to Howard Li, the one-child policy created disruptions for the company because certain county governments, particularly in the provinces of Hubei and Hunan, demanded that female workers from their jurisdictions return each year so it could be determined whether they had experienced an "illegal" pregnancy. "This," said Li, "is very disruptive because we lose those workers for that time." The trips also presented difficulties for workers, who lost earnings and had to finance their own travel. "I talked with local people here," he said, "to do the evaluation." As a result, he arranged with local officials to allow the workers to remain in Dongguan for their examinations. In exchange, the female workers, all of them expected to undergo such evaluations, did not have to travel, the company would not lose its laborers, and the AOTW managers would receive all medical information.

I later learned that Howard Li's description of the Chinese government's one-child policy did not correspond to its usual application throughout China, which deals specifically with married women.[13] Because AOTW did not hire married women and actively encouraged married women to quit, the one-child policy that Li described is enforced almost solely on the unmarried women in his employment.[14] I was not allowed to discuss this policy with women workers, nor could I attend any of the evaluations, so I was never able to verify how this practice was organized and applied.

I am also perplexed by the virtual absence within the research record of any mention of corporate involvement in enforcement of the one-child policy. I find it hard to believe that AOTW, a relatively small factory system, would be the only company in China that has such policies. Nor did I ever entirely decide why Howard Li chose to speak of this particular issue to me. Our discussions of the one-child policy arose when I asked his views on the Chinese government's respect for human rights. Because I had seen nothing in the research record, it never occurred to me to ask whether AOTW was involved in enforcing the one-child policy. Rather, Li raised the issue as part of his explanation into how AOTW tries to protect workers from an uncaring government. "I know this looks bad to you," he said, "but it's the way things are done here. It is a different system here. This is not just AOTW policy. This is the Chinese government. . . . It is better for us to do it than the government. We care about these girls. The government does not." He often expressed belief that I would be alarmed over the treatment of workers, especially women workers, in China not only because of corporate policies but also due to the Chinese government's regulations over migration, fertility, and rural development.

Regardless of the discrepancies between Howard Li's explanations and the existing literature on the one-child policy and corporate involvement, his description reflects a bias within the Chinese labor code that calls for regulation of women's menstrual cycles as part of the labor process and for special treatment for women while they menstruate. In the mid-1980s, the Chinese government devised a set of regulations that imposed limits and rules organized explicitly around women's reproductive cycles (Woo 280–81). The female reproductive cycle was identified as consisting of menstruation, pregnancy, birthing, nursing, and menopause, each with its own set of rules governing the kind of work women can perform as they experience it. Women are granted, for example, paid maternity leave of ninety days and work breaks for pregnancy and nursing. They are also restricted from heavy lifting or working in cold environments while they menstruate.

The Chinese government organized these regulations with the aim of protecting women workers and providing them with standardized gynecological care, but recent enforcement of the rules has contributed to the idea that women's problems—such as problems of labor exploitation and harassment—are rooted in the intricacies of female biology (Woo 279). In other words, the regulations define the work cycles of women workers, including problems they experience in the labor process, in terms of their reproductive cycles.

The creation of work regulations structured explicitly around women's reproductive cycles reveals a long-standing view in Chinese labor regulation that women are weakened by their reproductive cycles, particularly during menstruation (Furth; Woo). The 1986 health care provisions, for example, established a menstruation card system for women workers. Although that practice certainly facilitates surveillance of pregnancies as part of the one-child policy, it is also organized around the idea that menstrual cycles must constantly be regulated as part of their work lives. Therefore, their private experiences of menstruation constitute a source of public knowledge for the organization of their labor as part of the production process.

The logic behind such practices does not mirror the typical Western view that menstruation is a "social contaminant" but instead that it leads to weakness and vulnerability to illness among workers (Frazier 193). Howard Li reflected that logic: "Females are more sensitive. They get sick." He confirmed he was referring to illness resulting from menstrual cycles, "They will not say anything to you, so you have to get the doctor to look at them, make sure they are all right."

Despite such expressions of concern for women's health, however, the AOTW managers did not implement the health regulations designed to protect women from strain and injury during menstruation and pregnancy. Indeed, as other researchers have found (Chan; Hsing; Woo), the labor regulations were largely ignored. There were no breaks for women during menstruation beyond the normal two bathroom breaks per nine-hour workday. And protections for maternity leave, nursing, and rests during pregnancy were moot issues; all pregnant women were dismissed, and children were not allowed on the premises. Yet surveillance of menstruation was still justified on the grounds that women needed to be protected from the illnesses and weaknesses stemming from their cycles.

Even though the company did not implement a monthly menstruation registration, the discourse of menstruation as a source of illness legitimated the requirement of biannual physical examinations that elicited information that extended beyond the gynecological health of the worker, beyond her status as pregnant or not, and beyond the possibility of cervical and uterine cancers. The information gathered during the forced examinations sought to determine if workers still had flexible fingers and sharp eyes after several months of assembly work, and that medical information was given directly to the AOTW managerial staff. "Sometimes," said Howard Li, "there is something wrong. We want to know."

When there was something "wrong" and a worker was diagnosed with an injury or illness that would prevent full job performance, the AOTW managers had, according to the terms of their labor contract, justifiable cause for dismissal.[15] The information did not affect the organization of production. Management could dismiss workers as a result of injury or illness, regardless of cause, and it was not responsible for rehabilitating or treating workers. No allowances were made for having ill or injured workers on the premises, nor were steps taken to avoid further injury or illness of workers as a result of information gleaned from the medical reports. Medical surveillance, in other words, was not designed to develop prognoses of illness or injury or to catch uterine or cervical cancers but rather to provide management with information about workers' ability to perform their jobs up to expectations. Therefore, the discourse of menstruation as a source of weakness and the legacy of labor codes in China organized around that view were pretexts for forcing women to submit to invasive medical surveillance in order to provide AOTW management with information about their suitability for employment.

Managers were not interested in regulating the menstrual cycles of their labor force as part of an effort to comply with labor regulations designed to protect workers' health. Rather, they were interested in monitoring the physical abilities of workers to perform repetitive work, up to speed, and to avoid any costs associated with maternity leave. The discourse of menstruation as constitutive of illness thus functioned as a handy mechanism for diverting attention from the wear and tear of the labor process and focusing instead on women's problems at work as products of their biology. AOTW managers used that discourse effectively to turn female workers inside out and declare that any problems found in their wrists, their eyes, their backs, and so forth stemmed from problems in their wombs that needed constant surveillance.[16] In this way the discourse of menstruation as linked to illness was instrumental to Howard Li's goals of employing only "fresh workers, with fresh eyes and fingers" by providing the information necessary to know when workers had been rendered disposable.[17]

Although longitudinal studies of repetitive stress disorders have not been conducted in China's export-processing zones, shorter-term studies and anecdotal evidence from studies conducted in export-processing factories reveal that workers report high rates of injuries from repetitive work (Chao; Eckholm; Lin). Nevertheless, the AOTW labor contract, which resembles the contracts of other export-processing companies in southern China, justifies dismissal of any worker who suffers an injury that impairs job performance (Hsing). The company is neither responsible for worker rehabilitation nor for implementing practices to avoid future injuries.

Meanwhile, those who pass their pregnancy tests, who sit still, who do not reveal sexual desire, who stay quiet, whose fingers remain dexterous, whose eyes keep their focus, and who preserve their docility are bound by contract to remain with AOTW for two years. If they leave before that time they forfeit their deposit and often encounter difficulties in finding jobs elsewhere (Chan; Hsing; Woo).

AOTW's managers were charged with aligning individual workers' effectiveness with the cyclical flows of the company's turnover rate. The labor pool from which this turnover is drawn is congruent with the population of female workers. As Harry Chen said, "The male workers stay for two years. Almost all of them." The 7 percent expected to leave, therefore, were from the pool of women workers. The two-year labor contract; forced medical examinations; justification of dismissal on the grounds of injury, illness, and pregnancy; restrictions against resting during the labor process; and lack of measures to guard against repetitive stress disorders all took root in the story of a woman who would eventually, no matter what the company did, lose her value as a worker.

Victory and Disposability

By the end of 1999 AOTW had defeated their American colleagues in the competition over corporate resources. When OTW's board sold the Mexican facility to a competitor and kept the factory in China, Howard Li declared that it was "only decision to make" for the "long run." He explained that his system for managing turnover had demonstrated to the board that AOTW could have a systematic labor process even when rural migrant women were its principal labor force. "They know we can do the work," he said. "China is catching up." As a result of the company's decision, two product lines in the Mexican operation were transferred to the AOTW facility. And, as Li put it, his team earned "more respect. They recognize we know what to do out here. At first they didn't believe that we could make it work, but now they do." He continued, "Things have improved here . . . it is much better. . . . The other problems are now in the past."

One year later, however, OTW dissolved as a company, and its stock was sold and removed from public exchange. In 2000 a former vice president and former general manager of the Mexican facility described the company's problems as many. "Quality problems really hurt us," he emphasized. "If word gets around that you're not putting out a good product, then you lose your market. Without a market, you can't keep your head above water." He added, "Quality is still a problem in China. It's a problem in Mexico, too, but it's a bigger problem in China." Then he said, "The best thing that happened to [the Mexican operation] is it got sold. Getting stuck with a losing company kills your career."

Evidently, OTW as a corporation had not resolved problems that beleaguered it since the 1980s. Its products were not competitive. The Chinese managers had proven their value to the corporation for producing and managing worker disposability but had not managed to put its workforce labor into circulation as value. Somehow the requisite equation for creating capitalist value did not congeal, and labor did not contribute to the ongoing exchange of things deemed useful. In fact, OTW's products had become largely regarded as useless things without quality, not worthy of investment and not worth reproducing. So the company was sold and its organization dismantled. Just like many of its workers, the company became disposable. It crumbled under the sign of its own destruction.

Was the Chinese managers' victory in defeating their counterparts in Mexico, however, a Pyrrhic one? Not at all. Their goal had been to prove their value to the firm, and they did so by proving they could do what the Mexican facility had never been able to achieve: manage the turnover of women employees. The value of their own social reproduction for the firm had been affirmed. Their identity as skillful managers emerged brilliantly in contrast to the workers they managed, who established common ground for comparing the Chinese managerial team to the Mexican one. Their identity is the commodity produced via the circulation of the women's labor. Through the managed circulation of disposable third-world women the Chinese managers stand out as rational subjects bringing China full steam ahead into the global economy ("China is catching up"). In that sense the managers are the products that emerge from a technological reproduction of third-world woman worker as waste-in-the-making. Through the repetition of this story and a widespread belief in its veracity, the disposable women workers at AOTW materialize, to borrow from Rey Chow, as the hinges that allow Chinese managers to realize themselves as "modern."

NOTES

1. I have chosen to use "third world" amid the other obvious choices of "developing countries/regions," "lesser developed countries/regions," or "undeveloped countries/regions." Each of these options reifies in slightly different but overlapping ways the "'first in Europe, then elsewhere' structure of global time," as Dipesh Chakrabarty has put it (7). My decision to use "third world" derives somewhat from its usage in the scholarship on "third world feminism," where the term is critically challenged and deployed (Grewal and Kaplan; Mohanty). Still, all such references reproduce, even in critical usage, the dichotomies they identify. But for a variety of reasons, including the tremendous economic disparities that contribute to the flourishing of export-processing zones in third-world regions, these terms are not fully avoidable.

2. Feminist scholars across disciplines have brought attention to these representations of female workers in assembly-line operations around the world (Elson and Pearson; Elson and Pearson, eds.; Lamphere; Ong).

3. All references to companies and employees are pseudonyms.

4. Within the company, and always in my presence, the AOTW managers and engineers referred to themselves by a combination of an English first name with their family surname. The general manager, whom I call "Howard Li," explained that his American colleagues were not comfortable with the Chinese names, so it was standard practice for all Chinese employees to choose an English first name to be used as their corporate identity. Indeed, their counterparts in Mexico knew the AOTW team only by these invented names. Because the names are the ones they used when talking with me, I have created pseudonyms similar to them here.

5. My references to skill are intended to mimic the managers' classification of "unskilled" and "skilled" tasks and people. Although I do not explore the intersection of this social difference with the valorization of male and female employees, the designation of skill, in addition to other significant identifiers such as age and regional affiliation, is integrated with such references. An in-depth discussion of how skill classifications contribute to the production of differentially valued social subjects appears in Elson and Pearson (eds.).

6. I refer to Marx's words, "The worker becomes all the poorer the more wealth he produces" (*Economic and Philosphic Manuscripts of 1844*, 71).

7. According to a 1988 translation, Marx said, "The worker becomes all the poorer the more wealth he produces" (ibid., 71).

8. Feminist critiques of Marx's abstractions and blind Marxian application of them are numerous (e.g., Lamphere; McDowell; Scott; Spivak, "Scattered Speculations").

9. My argument draws directly from Judith Butler's formulation in *Bodies That*

Matter: Discursive repetition is requisite, given the material instability of the subject and its intelligibility across a dynamic field of difference.

10. Hsing provides a detailed account of these sorts of practices.

11. Of course, such associations between women's reproductive cycles and organs and the concept of "social trouble" are not isolated to China or to the industrial sector. Such views have proliferated throughout the West and in numerous contexts (Bashford; Douglas; Grosz; Laquer; Tuana).

12. Margaret Woo discusses this latest population control campaign as part of a larger historical continuum in which control of women's reproductive cycles have formed the basis of social policy.

13. I thank Gail Hershatter for pointing out this discrepancy.

14. I have not seen evidence of this practice in other studies of export-processing companies in southern China. I have tried, but without luck, to contact Howard Li in order to discuss the discrepancies between his description of the one-child policy and the prevalence of corporate involvement in its enforcement.

15. The labor contract indicated that illness, injury, substandard work performance, and moral impurity are justifiable causes for dismissal.

16. This kind of medical surveillance is a form of body searching. Alice Kwan, a researcher at the Hong Kong Christian Industrial Committee that monitors labor conditions in southern China, reported in May 2000 that workers in some factories are subjected to body searches as a way to keep them from stealing ("Chinese Rights, U.S. Wrongs").

17. This discourse of menstruation as linked to weakness in the workplace contrasts with managerial attitudes regarding women's reproductive cycles in OTW's Mexican facilities as well as throughout other facilities in Mexico's export-processing zones. In OTW's Mexican factory, a discourse of female reproductive cycles as threatening male concentration and the organization of production more broadly justified the segregation of women workers, regarded as dangerous to male-dominated areas of the facility (Wright, "Maquiladora Mestizas"). Managers in the Mexican facility described the young female labor force as possessing dangerous sexuality that had a powerful and chaotic effect on production scheduling and the manufacture of quality products. This discourse, in effect, set up female Mexican assembly workers as dangerous to workplaces and therefore deserving the managerial policies that treated her as a hazard or something that needed to be contained (Wright, "Dialectics of Still Life").

In the maquiladora industry there is a widespread suspicion of the negative effects of women's reproductive cycles on the organization of work. Although most maquiladora factories, for example, require that women submit to a pregnancy test upon employment, some regulate workers' menstrual cycles by forcing women workers to show their soiled sanitary napkins to a company nurse or doctor on a monthly basis (Nathan; Wright, "Dialectics of Still Life"). According to a worker in a television manufacturer in Ciudad Juárez, her entire line had to march into the doctor's office one day after the supervisor announced that all women had to be checked out. "Even the señoras!" she exclaimed, by which she meant women who had already gone through menopause. The practice does not provide a sure way to guard against the employment of pregnant workers, but it does put women on notice that even their most intimate internal functions are under management's domain. It is a constant reminder that the panoptican of management is unavoidable.

Works Cited

Bashford, Alison. *Purity and Pollution: Gender, Embodiment and Victorian Medicine.* New York: St. Martin's Press, 1998.

Butler, Judith. *Bodies That Matter.* New York: Routledge, 1993.

Chakrabarty, Dipesh. *Provincializing Europe: Postcolonial Thought and Historical Difference.* Princeton: Princeton University Press, 2000.

Chan, Anita. "China's Troubled Workers." *Foreign Affairs* 76, no. 2 (1997): 104–17.

Chao, J. "Made in China." *Austin American-Statesman,* July 7, 2002, H1–H4.

"Chinese Rights, U.S. Wrongs: Interviews with Wei Jinghsheng and Alice Kwan." *Multinational Monitor* 21, no. 5 (2000): 19–23.

Chow, Rey. *Woman and Chinese Modernity: The Politics of Reading between West and East.* Minneapolis: University of Minnesota Press, 1991.

Douglas, Mary. *Purity and Danger an Analysis of the Concepts of Pollution and Taboo.* New York: Routledge, 1984.

Eckholm, E. "Workers' Rights Are Suffering China as Manufacturing Goes Capitalist." *New York Times,* Aug. 22, 2000, A8.

Elson, Diane, and Ruth Pearson. "Nimble Fingers Make Cheap Workers: An Analysis of Women's Employment in Third World Export Manufacturing." *Feminist Review* 8 (1981): 87–107.

———. Eds. *Women, Employment and Multinationals in Europe.* New York: Macmillan, 1989.

Farley, Maggie. "Hard Labor: Women at Work in China's Economy: First of Two Parts." *Los Angeles Times,* Nov. 22, 1998, A1.

Fernandez-Kelly, Maria P. *For We Are Sold, I and My People.* Albany: SUNY Press, 1983.

Frazier, Mark W. *The Making of the Chinese Industrial Workplace.* New York: Cambridge University Press, 2002.

Furth, Charlotte. "Blood, Body, and Gender: Medical Images of the Female Condition in China, 1600–1850." *Chinese Science* 7 (1986): 43–65.

Grewal, Inderpal, and Caren Kaplan. "Introduction: Transnational Feminist Practices and Questions of Postmodernity." In *Scattered Hegemonies.* Ed. Inderpal Grewal and Caren Kaplan, 1–33. Minneapolis: University of Minnesota Press, 2002.

Grosz, Elizabeth. *Space, Time and Perversion: Essays on the Politics of Bodies.* New York: Routledge, 1996.

Hershatter, Gail. *Dangerous Pleasures: Prostitution and Modernity in Twentieth-Century Shanghai.* Berkeley: University of California Press, 1997.

Hsing, You-tien. *Making Capitalism in China.* New York: Oxford University Press, 1998.

Joseph, Miranda. *Against the Romance of Community.* Minneapolis: University of Minnesota Press, 2002.

Laquer, Thomas. "Orgasm, Generation, and the Politics of Reproductive Biology." In *The Gender/Sexuality Reader.* Ed. Roger Lancaster and Micalea di Leonardo, 219–43. New York: Routledge, 1997.

Lamphere, Louise. *From Working Daughters to Working Mothers: Immigrant Women in a New England Industrial Community.* Ithaca: Cornell University Press, 1987.

Landler, Mark. "For Hong Kong Men, Mistresses on the Mainland." *New York Times,* Aug. 14, 2000, A4.

Lee, Ching Kwan. *Gender and the South China Miracle.* Berkeley: University of California Press, 1998.

Lin, Vivian. *Health, Women's Work, and Industrialization: Semi-Conductor Workers in Singapore and Malaysia.* New York: Garland Publishing, 1991.

Marx, Karl. *Economic and Philosophic Manuscripts of 1844.* Buffalo: Prometheus Books, 1988.

McDowell, Linda. *Capital Culture and Gender at Work in the City.* Oxford: Basil Blackwell, 1996.

Mohanty, Chandra. "Under Western Eyes: Feminist Scholarship and Colonial Discourses." In *Third World Women and the Politics of Feminism.* Ed. Chandra Mohanty, Anna Russo, and Lordes Torres, 51–80. Bloomington: Indiana University Press, 1991.

Nathan, Debbie. "Work, Sex and Danger in Ciudad Juárez" *NACLA Report on the Americas* 33, no. 3 (1999): 24–32.

"New China, Old Vice." *Business China* 26, no. 7 (2000): 6–7.

Ong, Aihwa. *Spirits of Resistance and Capitalist Discipline: Factory Women in Malaysia.* Albany: SUNY Press, 1987.

Pan, Philip P. "China's One-Child Policy Now a Double Standard." *Washington Post,* Aug. 20, 2002, A1.

Powell, R. et al. "Twenty-five Rising Stars." *Fortune,* May 14, 2001, 140ff.

Salzinger, Leslie. *Genders in Production.* Berkeley: University of California Press, 2002.

Scott, Joan W. *Gender and the Politics of History.* New York: Columbia University Press, 1999.

Spivak, Gayatri. "Scattered Speculations on the Question of Value." In *In Other Worlds: Essays in Cultural Politics,* 154–75. New York: Routledge, 1988.

Tuana, Nancy. *The Less Noble Sex: Scientific, Religious and Philiosophical Conceptions of Women's Nature.* Bloomington: Indiana University Press, 1993.

Whelan, C. "Emerging Markets That Live Up to the Name." *Fortune,* Dec 18, 2000, 184ff.

White, Tyrene. "The Origins of China's Birth Planning Policy." In *Engendering China: Women, Culture and the State.* Ed. Christina Gilmartin, Gail Hershatter, Lisa Rofel, and Tyrene White, 250–78. Cambridge: Harvard University Press, 1994.

Woo, Margaret Y. K. "Chinese Women Workers: The Delicate Balance between Protection and Equality." In *Engendering China: Women, Culture and the State.* Ed. Christina Gilmartin, Gail Hershatter, Lisa Rofel, and Tyrene White, 279–95. Cambridge: Harvard University Press, 1994.

Wright, Melissa W. "Asian Spies, American Motors and Speculations on the Space-Time of Value." *Environment and Planning* 33, no. 12 (2001): 2175–88.

———. "The Dialectics of Still Life: Murder, Women, and Maquiladoras." *Public Culture* 11 (1999): 453–74.

———. "Maquiladora Mestizas and a Feminist Border Politics: Revisiting Anzaldúa." *Hypatia: A Journal of Feminist Philosophy* 3, no. 3 (1998): 114–31.

Zielbrauer, Paul. "Officials' Trip to China Angers Flagging City." *New York Times,* Mar. 4, 2001, A32.

PART 2

State, Law, and Custom: Contests about the Recognition and Legitimation of New Forms of Kinship and Sexuality

5 Is Kinship Always Already Heterosexual?

JUDITH BUTLER

THE TOPIC OF GAY MARRIAGE is not the same as that of gay kinship, but it seems that the two become confounded in U.S. popular opinion when we hear not only that marriage is and ought to remain a heterosexual institution and bond but also that kinship does not work, or does not qualify as kinship, unless it assumes a recognizable family form. There are several ways to link these views. One way to claim that sexuality needs to be organized in the service of reproductive relations and that marriage, which gives legal status to the family form or rather is conceived as that which *should* secure the institution through conferring that legal status, should remain the fulcrum that keeps these institutions leveraging one another.

The challenges to this link are, of course, legion and take various forms domestically and internationally. On the one hand, there are various sociological ways of showing that a number of kinship relations exist and persist in the United States that do not conform to the nuclear family model and draw on biological and nonbiological relations, exceeding the reach of current juridical conceptions, functioning according to nonformalizable rules. If we understand kinship as a set of practices that institutes relationships of various kinds that negotiate the reproduction of life and the demands of death, then kinship practices will be those that emerge to address fundamental forms of human dependency, which may include birth, child-rearing, relations of emotional dependency and support, generational ties, illness, dying, and death (to name a few). Kinship is neither a fully autonomous sphere, proclaimed to be distinct from community and friendship—or the regulations of the state—through some definitional fiat, nor "over" or "dead" just because, as David Schneider has consequentially argued, it has lost the capacity to be formalized and tracked in the conventional ways that ethnologists in the past have attempted to do.[1]

In recent sociology's conceptions of kinship have become disjoined from the marriage assumption so that, for example, Carol Stack's now-classic study of urban African American kinship, *All Our Kin,* shows how kinship functions well through a network of women, some related through biological ties and some not. The enduring effect of the history of slavery on African American kinship relations has become the focus of new studies by Nathaniel Mackey and Fred Moten showing how dispossession of kin relations by slavery offers a continuing legacy of "wounded kinship" within African American life. If, as Saidiya Hartman maintains, "Slavery is the ghost in the machine of kinship," it is because African American kinship has been at once the site of intense state surveillance and pathologization, which leads to the double bind of being subject to normalizing pressures within the context of a continuing social and political delegitimation.[2] As a result, it is not possible to separate questions of kinship from property relations (and conceiving persons as property) and the fictions of "bloodline" as well as the national and racial interests by which these lines are sustained.

Kath Weston has supplied ethnographic descriptions of lesbian and gay nonmarital kinship relations that emerge outside heterosexually based family ties and only partially approximate the family form in some instances. Most recently, anthropologist Cai Hua has offered a dramatic refutation of the Lévi-Straussian view of kinship as the negotiation of a patrilineal line through marriage ties in his recent study of the Na of China, in which neither husbands nor fathers figure prominently in determinations of kinship.[3]

Marriage has also recently been separated from questions of kinship to the extent that gay marriage legislative proposals often exclude rights to adoption or reproductive technologies as one of the assumed entitlements of marriage. These have not only taken place in Germany and France but also in the United States. Successful "gay marriage" proposals do not always have direct impact on family law, especially when they seek as their primary aim to establish "symbolic recognition" for dyadic relations by the state.[4]

The petition for marriage rights seeks to solicit state recognition for nonheterosexual unions and so configures the state as withholding an entitlement that it really should distribute in a nondiscriminatory way, regardless of sexual orientation. That the state's offer might result in the intensification of normalization is not widely recognized as a problem within the mainstream lesbian and gay movement, typified by the Human Rights Campaign (Warner). The normalizing powers of the state are made especially clear, however, when we consider how continuing quandaries about kinship both condition and limit marriage debates. In some contexts the symbolic allocation of marriage, or marriagelike arrangements, is preferable to altering the requirements for kinship to secure individual or plural rights to bear or adopt children or, legally, to co-parent. Variations on kinship that depart from normative, dyadic, heterosexually based family forms secured through the marriage vow are figured not only as dangerous for the child but also as perilous to the putative natural and cultural laws said to sustain human intelligibility.

As background for this essay, it is probably important to know that the recent debates in France targeted certain U.S. views on the social construction and variability of gender relations as portending a perilous "Americanization" of kinship relations (*filiation*) in France.[5] In response, I seek to address this critique, outlined in the third section that follows, not as an effort to defend Americanization but to suggest that the kinship dilemmas of first-world nations often provide one another with allegories of their own worries about the disruptive effects of kinship variability on respective national projects. In turn, I query the French debate on kinship and marriage in order to show how the argument in favor of legal alliance can work in tandem with a state normalization of recognizable kinship relations, a condition that extends rights of contract while in no way disrupting the patrilineal assumptions of kinship or the project of the unified nation that it supports. I will also consider at least two dimensions of this contemporary predicament in which the state is sought for the recognition it might confer on same-sex couples and countered for the regulatory control on normative kinship that it continues to exercise.

The state is not the same state in each of these bids, for we ask for an intervention by the state in the one domain (marriage) only to suffer excessive regulation in another (kinship). Does the turn to marriage make it thus more difficult to argue in favor of the viability of alternative kinship arrangements and for the well-being of the child in any number of social forms? Moreover, what happens to the radical project of articulating and supporting the proliferation of sexual practices outside marriage and the obligations of kinship? Does the turn to the state signal the end of a radical sexual culture? Does such a prospect become eclipsed as we become increasingly preoccupied with landing the state's desire?

Gay Marriage: Desiring the State's Desire and the Eclipse of Sexuality

Gay marriage obviously draws upon profound and abiding investments not only in the heterosexual couple but also in the question of what forms of relationship ought to be legitimated by the state.[6] The crisis of legitimation can be considered from a number of perspectives, but let us consider for the moment the ambivalent gift that legitimation can become. To be legitimated by the state is to enter into the terms of legitimation offered there and find that one's public and recognizable sense of personhood is fundamentally dependent on the lexicon of that legitimation. Moreover, it follows that the delimitation of legitimation will take place only through an exclusion of a certain sort although not a patently dialectical one. The sphere of legitimate intimate alliance is established through producing and intensifying regions of illegitimacy.

There is, however, a more fundamental occlusion at work. We misunderstand the sexual field if we consider that the legitimate and the illegitimate appear to exhaust its immanent possibilities. There is, thus, outside the struggle between the legitimate and the illegitimate—which is one that has as its goal the conversion of the illegitimate into the legitimate—a field that is less thinkable and not figured in light of its ultimate convertibility into legitimacy. This field is outside the disjunction of illegitimate and legitimate. It is not yet thought of as a domain, a sphere, or a field; is not yet either legitimate or illegitimate; and has not yet been thought through in the explicit discourse of legitimacy. Indeed, this would be a sexual field that does not have legitimacy as its point of reference, its ultimate desire. The debate over gay marriage takes place through such a logic. The debate breaks down almost immediately into the question of whether marriage ought to be legitimately extended to homosexuals, which means that the sexual field is circumscribed in such a way that sexuality is already thought in terms of marriage and marriage is already thought as the purchase on legitimacy.

In the case of gay marriage or of affiliative legal alliances, we see how various sexual practices and relationships that fall outside the purview of the sanctifying law become illegible or, worse, untenable, and how new hierarchies emerge within public discourse. These hierarchies not only enforce the distinction between legitimate and illegitimate queer lives but also produce tacit distinctions among forms of illegitimacy. The stable pair who would marry if only they could are cast as currently illegitimate but eligible for future legitimacy, whereas the sexual agents who function outside the purview of the marriage bond and its recognized, if illegitimate, alternative form now constitute sexual possibilities that will never be eligible for a translation into legitimacy. These possibilities become increasingly disregarded within the sphere of politics as a consequence of the priority that the marriage debate has assumed. This is an illegitimacy whose temporal condition is to be foreclosed from any possible future transformation. It is not only *not yet* legitimate but also the irrecoverable and irreversible past of legitimacy—the never will be, the never was.

Here a certain normative crisis ensues. On the one hand, it is important to mark how the field of intelligible and speakable sexuality is circumscribed and thus see how options outside marriage are becoming foreclosed as unthinkable and also how the narrow debates over who (and what) will be included in the norm enforce the terms of thinkability. On the other hand, there is always the possibility of savoring the status of unthinkability, if it is a status, as the most critical, the most radical, and the most valuable. As the sexually unrepresentable, such sexual possibilities can figure the sublime within the contemporary field of sexuality, a site of pure resistance uncoopted by normativity.

But how does one think politics from such a site of unrepresentability? Moreover, how can one think politics without considering these sites of unrepresentability? One may wish for another lexicon altogether. The history of sexual progressivism surely recurs time and again to the possibility of a new language and the promise of a new mode of being. In light of this quandary, one might find oneself wanting to opt out of the whole story and operate somewhere that is neither legitimate nor illegitimate. But here is where the critical perspective, the one that operates at the limit of the intelligible, risks being regarded as apolitical.

Politics, as constituted through this discourse of intelligibility, demands that we take a stand for or against gay marriage. Critical reflection, however, which is surely part of any seriously normative political philosophy and practice, demands that we ask why and how this question defines what will and will not qualify as meaningful political discourse here. Why, under present conditions, does the very prospect of "becoming political" depend on our ability to operate within that discursively instituted binary and not to ask, and endeavor not to know, that the sexual field is forcibly constricted through accepting those terms?

This dynamic of force is rendered all the more forceful because it grounds the contemporary field of the political through the forcible exclusion of that sexual field from the political. And yet the operation of this force of exclusion is set outside the domain of contest, as if it were not part of power or an object for political reflection. Thus, to become political, to act and speak in ways that are recognizably political, is to rely on a foreclosure of the very political field that is not subject to political scrutiny. Without the critical perspective, we might say, politics relies fundamentally on an unknowingness—and depoliticization—of the relations of force by which its field of operation is instituted. Criticality is thus not a position per se, not a site or a place that might be located within an already delimitable field, although one must, in an obligatory catachresis, speak of sites, of fields and domains.

One critical function is to scrutinize the action of delimitation itself. By recommending that we become critical, that we risk criticality, in thinking about how the sexual field is constituted, I do not mean to suggest that we could or should occupy an atopical elsewhere, undelimited and radically free. The questioning of taken-for-granted conditions becomes possible on occasion, but one cannot do so through a thought experiment, an *epoché,* an act of will. One gets there, as it were, through suffering the dehiscence, the breakup, of the ground itself.

Even within the field of intelligible sexuality, the binaries that anchor its operations permit middle zones and hybrid formations, suggesting that the binary relation does not exhaust the field in question. Indeed, there are middle regions—hybrid regions of legitimacy and illegitimacy that have no clear names and where nomination falls into a crisis produced by the variable, sometimes violent, boundaries of legitimating practices that come into uneasy, sometimes conflictual, contact. These are not precisely places where one can choose to hang out, subject positions one might opt to occupy; these are nonplaces where one finds oneself in spite of oneself. These are nonplaces where recognition, including self-recognition, proves precarious if not elusive in spite of one's best efforts to be a subject in some recognizable sense. They are not sites of enunciation but shifts in the topography from which a questionably audible claim emerges, a claim of the not-yet-subject and the nearly recognizable.

That there are such regions, and that they are not precisely options, suggests that what troubles the distinction between legitimacy and illegitimacy are social practices—specifically, sexual practices—which do not appear immediately as coherent within the available lexicon of legitimation. These are sites of uncertain ontology, difficult nomination. The foreclosure of the possible takes place when someone, urgent to stake a political claim, naturalizes options that figure most legibly within the sexual field. Attending to this foreclosure as an act of politics, unwittingly performed time and again, offers the possibility for a different conception of politics, one that attends to its own foreclosures as an effect of conscious activism. Yet one must maintain a double edge in relation to this difficult terrain. Neither the violence of foreclosure that stabilizes the field of activism nor the path of critical paralysis entrenched at the level of fundamental reflection will suffice. It becomes increasingly important to maintain tension between a critical perspective on the topic of gay marriage and making a politically legible claim.

My point is not to suggest that one must remain critical rather than political in relation to gay marriage and kinship debates, as if such a distinction were finally possible or desirable, but that a politics which incorporates critical understanding is the only one that can maintain a claim to being self-reflective and nondogmatic. To be political does not just mean taking a single and enduring "stand." To say that one is for or against gay marriage, for example, is not always easy. It may be that one wants to secure the right for those who wish to make use of it, even though one does not want to do so personally. Or it may be that one wants to counter the homophobic discourses marshaled against gay marriage but does not want to be, therefore, in favor of it. Perhaps it is the case that one believes very strongly that marriage is best for lesbian and gay people and would like to install it as a future norm. Or perhaps it may be that one not only opposes gay marriage for oneself but also for everyone. Then the task at hand is to rework and revise the social organization of friendship, sexual contacts, and community to produce nonstate-centered forms of support and alliance. Marriage, given its historical weight, only becomes an "option" by extending itself as a norm (and thus foreclosing options), one that also extends property relations and renders social forms for sexuality more conservative.

For progressive sexual movement, even one that may want to produce marriage as an option for nonheterosexuals, the proposition that marriage should become the only way to sanction or legitimate sexuality is unacceptably conservative. Even if the question is not one of marriage but of augmenting domestic partnership arrangements as legal contracts, certain questions still follow. Why should it be that marriage or legal contracts become the basis on which health-care benefits, for instance, are allocated? Why shouldn't there be ways of organizing health-care entitlements such that everyone, regardless of marital status, has access to them? If one argues for marriage as a way of securing those entitlements, then does one not also affirm that entitlements as important as health care ought to remain allocated on the basis of marital status? What does that do to the community of the nonmarried, the single, the divorced, the uninterested, and the nonmonogamous, and how does the sexual field become reduced in legibility once marriage as a norm is extended?[7]

Regardless of one's view on gay marriage, there is clearly a demand upon those who work in sexuality studies to respond to many of the most homophobic arguments marshalled against gay marriage proposals. Many are not only fueled by homophobic sentiment but also often focus on fears about reproductive relations, whether they are natural or "artificial" and what happens to the child—the child, the poor child, martyred figure of an ostensibly selfish or dogged social progressivism. The debates on gay marriage and gay kinship, two issues that are often conflated, have become sites of intense displacement for other political fears about technology, new demographics, and the unity and transmissibility of the nation, fears that feminism, in its insistence on child care, has effectively opened kinship outside the family, opened it to strangers.

In debates in France on the "pacts of civil solidarity" (PaCS) that constitute an alternative marriage for any two individuals unrelated by blood, regardless of sexual orientation), passage of the bill finally depended on proscribing nonheterosexual couples' rights to adopt children and have access to reproductive technology. The same provision has been proposed and adopted in Germany as well.[8]

In both cases one can see that the child figures in the debate as a dense site for transfer and reproduction of culture, where "culture" carries implicit norms of racial purity and domination.[9] It may be possible to see the arguments in France that rail against the threat to "culture" posed by the prospect of legally allied gay people having children (and I suspend for the purposes of this discussion the question of what it means to "have" in this instance) as converging with debates on the issues of immigration, of what Europe is, and, implicitly and explicitly, of what is truly French.

What is truly French concerns the basis of that nation's culture, which becomes, through imperial logic, the basis of culture itself, its universal and invariable conditions. Debates center not only on the questions of what is culture, who should be admitted, and how should the subjects of culture be reproduced but also on the status of the state, in particular its power to confer or withdraw recognition for forms of sexual alliance. The argument against gay marriage is always, implicitly or explicitly, an argument about what the state should do, what it should provide. It is also about what kinds of intimate relations ought to be eligible for state legitimation.

What is this desire to keep the state from offering recognition to nonheterosexual partners, and what is the desire to compel the state to offer such recognition? At issue on both sides of the debate is not only the question of which relations of desire ought to be legitimated by the state but also who may desire the state. Who may, that is, desire the state's desire? The questions are even more complicated. Whose desire might qualify as a desire for state legitimation? Moreover, whose desire might qualify *as* the desire of the state? Who may desire the state, and whom may the state desire? Whose desire will be the state's desire?

Conversely, and this is just speculation (but perhaps academic work might be regarded as a social site for such speculation), it seems that what one is wanting when one wants "state recognition" for marriage, and what one is not wanting when one wants to limit the scope of that recognition for others, are complex wants. Fantasy becomes literalized by means of the state. Desire and sexuality are ratified, justified, known, publicly instated, and imagined as permanent and durable. At that very moment, desire and sexuality are dispossessed and displaced so that what one "is," and what one's relationship "is," are no longer private. Ironically, one might say that personal desire, through marriage, acquires a certain anonymity and interchangeability. It becomes publicly mediated and in that sense a kind of legitimated, public sex. More than that, marriage compels, at least logically, universal recognition. Everyone must let you enter the door of the hospital; everyone must honor your claim to grief; everyone will assume your natural rights to a child; and everyone will regard your relationship as elevated into eternity. In that way the desire for universal recognition is a desire to become universal, to become interchangeable in one's universality, to vacate the lonely particularity of the nonratified relation, and, perhaps above all, to gain place and sanctification in that imagined relation to the state.

Place and sanctification: these are surely powerful fantasies that acquire particular phantasmatic form when we consider the bid for gay marriage. The state can become the site for recirculating religious desires, for redemption, for belonging, and for eternity. And, we might well ask, what happens to sexuality when it runs through this particular circuit of fantasy? Is it alleviated of guilt, deviance, discontinuity, asociality, and spectrality? If that is the case, where, precisely, do these negativities go? Are they projected onto those who have not or will not enter this hallowed domain? Does the projection take the form of judging others morally, of enacting a social abjection and hence becoming the occasion to institute a new hierarchy of legitimate and illegitimate sexual arrangements?

The Poor Child and the Fate of the Nation

The proposal in France to institute civil unions (pacts of civil solidarity) as an alternative to marriage sought at once to sidestep marriage and secure legal ties. It ran up against a limit, however, when questions of reproduction and adoption surfaced. Indeed, in France concerns over reproduction work in tandem with concerns over the reproduction of an identifiably French culture. As suggested above, one can see a certain implicit identification of French culture with universalism, and that has consequences for the fantasy of the nation. For understanding this debate it is important to recognize how, in particular, the figure of the child of nonheterosexual parents becomes a cathected site for anxieties about cultural purity and cultural transmission. In the fracas over PaCS, the only way the proposal could pass was by denying rights of joint adoption to individuals within such relations. As Eric Fassin and others have argued, it is the alteration of rights of filiation that is most scandalous in the French context, not marriage itself. The life of the contract can be, within range, extended, but the rights of filiation cannot.

Among the cultural commentary that accompanied the decision to deny adoptive rights to openly gay people was that of Sylviane Agacinski, a well-known French philosopher who maintained that it goes against the "symbolic order" to let homosexuals form families ("Questions" 23). Whatever social forms these union are, they are not marriages, and they are not families. In her view they are not properly "social" at all but private. The struggle is, in part, one over words, over where and how they apply and about their plasticity and equivocity. But it is more specifically a struggle over whether certain practices of nomination maintain presuppositions about the limits of what is humanly recognizable.

The argument rests on a paradox, however, that would be hard to deny. If one does not want to recognize certain human relations as part of the humanly recognizable, then one has already recognized them and seeks to deny what it is one has already, in one way or another, understood. "Recognition" becomes an effort to deny what exists and hence the instrument for the refusal of recognition. In this way it becomes a way of shoring up a normative fantasy of the human over and against dissonant versions of itself. To defend the limits of what is recognizable against that which challenges it is to understand that the norms governing recognizability have already been challenged. In the United States we are used to hearing conservative and reactionary polemics against homosexuality as unnatural, but that is not precisely the discourse through which the French polemic proceeds. Agacinski, for instance, does not assume that the family takes a natural form. The state is constrained in recognizing marriage as heterosexual, in her view, not by nature or natural law but by something called "the symbolic order" (which corresponds to and ratifies a natural law). It is according to the dictates of this order that the state is obligated to refuse to recognize such relations.

I will lay out Agacinski's view not because she is the most vocal opponent to the transformations in kinship that gay marriage might imply but because some time ago a colleague sent me an editorial she had written in *Le Monde,* a missive that in some way demanded a response ("Contre l'effacement"). In her editorial, Agacinski identifies a certain American strain of queer and gender theory as the monstrous future for France were these transformations to occur. Without going into detail, an interpellation occurred on the front page of *Le Monde* in which my name figured as a sign of the coming monstrosity. Moreover, I am in a quandary because my views are used to caution against a monstrous future that will come to pass should lesbian and gay people be permitted to form state-ratified kinship arrangements. On one hand, there is a demand, in a way, to respond and rebut these allegations. On the other hand, it seems critical not to accept the terms in which one's opponent has framed the debate, a debate that, I fear, is no debate at all but a highly publicized polemic and fear-mongering.

The quandary is not mine alone. Will I, in opposing Agacinski, occupy a position in which I argue for state legitimation? Is that what I desire? It would be easy enough to argue that she is wrong, that the family forms in question are viable social forms, and that the current episteme of intelligibility might be usefully challenged and rearticulated in light of these social forms.[10] After all, her view matches and fortifies those that maintain that legitimate sexual relations take a heterosexual and state-sanctioned form and work to derealize viable and significant sexual alliances that fail to conform to that model.

Of course, there are consequences to this kind of derealization that go beyond hurting someone's feelings or causing offense to a group of people. It means that when you arrive at the hospital to see your lover, you may not. It means that when your lover falls into a coma, you may not assume certain executorial rights. It means that when your lover dies, you may not be able to be the one to receive the body. It means that when a child is left with a nonbiological parent, that parent may not be able to counter the claims of biological relatives in court, and you lose custody and even access. It means you may not be able to provide health-care benefits for one another.

These are all significant forms of disenfranchisement, made all the worse by the personal effacements that occur in daily life and invariably take a toll on a relationship. If you are not real, it can be hard to sustain yourselves over time. The sense of delegitimation can make it harder to sustain a bond, which is not real anyway, does not "exist," never had a chance to exist, and was never meant to exist. Here the absence of state legitimation can emerge within the psyche as a pervasive, if not fatal, sense of self-doubt. If you have lost the lover who was never recognized to be your lover, then did you really lose that person? Is this a loss and can it be publicly grieved? Surely this has become a pervasive problem in the queer community, given the losses from AIDS, the loss of lives and loves that are always in struggle to be recognized as such.

Yet to pursue state legitimation in order to repair these injuries brings a host of new problems if not new heartaches. Failure to secure state recognition for one's intimate arrangements can only be experienced as a form of derealization if the terms of state legitimation maintain hegemonic control over the norms of recognition—in other words, if the state monopolizes the resources of recognition. Are there not other ways of feeling possible, intelligible, and even real apart from the sphere of state recognition? And should there not be other ways? It makes sense that the lesbian and gay movement would turn to the state, given its recent history. The current drive for gay marriage is in some ways a response to AIDS, a shamed response in which a gay community seeks to disavow its so-called promiscuity, one in which gay people appear as healthy, normal, and capable of sustaining monogamous relations. That, of course, brings me back to a question posed poignantly by Michael Warner: Does the drive to become recognizable within existing norms of legitimacy require that we subscribe to a practice that delegitimates those sexual lives structured outside the bonds of marriage and the presumptions of monogamy? Is the queer community willing to make this disavowal, and with what social consequence? How is it that we give the power of recognition over to the state at the moment we insist we are unreal and illegitimate without it? Are there other resources by which we might become recognizable or mobilize to challenge the existing regimes within which the terms of recognizability take place?

The terrain of the dilemma is apparent. On the one hand, living without norms of recognition results in significant suffering and forms of disenfranchisement that confound distinctions among psychic, cultural, and material consequences. On the other hand, the demand to be recognized, a powerful political demand, can lead to new and invidious forms of social hierarchy, to a precipitous foreclosure of the sexual field, and to new ways of supporting and extending state power if it does not institute a critical challenge to the norms of recognition that state legitimation supplies and requires.

In making a bid to the state for recognition, we effectively restrict the domain of what will become recognizable as legitimate sexual arrangements, thus fortifying the state as the source for norms of recognition and eclipsing other possibilities within civil society and cultural life. To demand and receive recognition according to norms that legitimate marriage and delegitimate forms of sexual alliance outside marriage, or to norms articulated in a critical relation to marriage, is to displace the site of delegitimation from one part of the queer community to another, or rather to transform a collective delegitimation into a selective one. Such a practice is difficult, if not impossible, to reconcile with a radically democratic, sexually progressive movement. What would it mean to exclude from the field of potential legitimation those who are outside of marriage, those who live nonmonogamously, those who live alone, and those in whatever arrangements they are in that are not the marriage form?

And I would add a caveat here: We do not always know what we mean by "the state" when referring to the kind of "state legitimation" that occurs in marriage. The state is not a simple unity, and its parts and operations are not always coordinated. The state is not reducible to law, and power is not reducible to state power. It would be wrong to understand the state as operating with a single set of interests or to gauge its effects as if they were unilaterally successful. The state can also be worked and exploited; social policy, which involves the implementation of law in local instances, can often be the site where law is challenged, where it is thrown to a court to adjudicate, and where new kinship arrangements stand a chance of gaining legitimacy. Of course, certain propositions remain highly controversial—interracial adoption and adoption by single men, gay male couples, parties who are unmarried, and kinship structures in which there are more than two adults in play.

If there are reasons to worry about requesting state recognition for intimate alliances and so becoming part of an extension of state power into the socius, do those reasons outweigh ones for seeking recognition and entitlement through entering legal contract? Contracts work in different ways—and surely they work differently in U.S. and French contexts—to garner state authority and to subject the individuals who enter into them to regulatory control. But even if contracts in France are conceived as individual entitlements and therefore less tethered to state control, the form of individuation is thus sustained by state legitimation, even if, or precisely when, the state appears to be relatively withdrawn from the contractual process itself. In this way the norms of the state work differently in these disparate national contexts.

In the United States the norms of recognition supplied by the state not only often fail to describe or regulate existing social practice but also become the site of articulation for a fantasy of normativity, projecting and delineating an ideological account of kinship, for instance, precisely at the moment when it is undergoing social challenge and dissemination. Thus it seems that the appeal to the state is at once an appeal to a fantasy already institutionalized by the state and a leave-taking from existing social complexity in the hope of becoming "socially coherent" at last.

What this means as well is that there is a site to which we can turn, understood as the state, that will finally render us coherent, a turn that commits us to the fantasy of state power. As Jacqueline Rose persuasively argues, "If the state has meaning only 'partly as something existing,' if it rests on the belief of individuals that it 'exists or should exist,' then it starts to look uncannily like what psychoanalysis would call an 'as if' phenomenon" (8–9). Its regulations do not always seek to order what exists but to figure social life in certain imaginary ways. The incommensurability between state stipulation and existing social life means that the gap must be covered over for the state to continue to exercise authority and exemplify the kind of coherence it is expected to confer on subjects. As Rose reminds us, "It is because the state has become so alien and distant from the people it is meant to represent that, according to Engels, it has to rely, more and more desperately, on the sacredness and inviolability of its own laws" (10).

So there are at least two sides to this coin, and I do not mean to resolve this dilemma in favor of one or the other but to develop a critical practice that is mindful of both. Legitimation is double-edged. It is critical that, politically, we lay claim to intelligibility and recognizability. It is also important, politically, that we maintain a critical and transformative relation to the norms that govern what will and will not count as an intelligible and recognizable alliance and kinship. The latter would also involve a critical relation to the desire for legitimation. It is critical as well that we question the assumption that the state furnish these norms and that we come to think about what the state has become during these times, or how it has become a site for the articulation of a fantasy that seeks to deny or overturn what these times have brought.

To return to the French debate, it seems important to remember that the debate about laws is at once a debate about what kinds of sexual arrangements and forms of kinship can be admitted to exist or deemed possible and what the limits of imaginability might be. For many who opposed the PaCS or who, minimally, voiced skeptical views about it, the variability of legitimated sexual alliance called the status of culture into question. Immigration and gay parenting were figured as challenging the fundamentals of a culture that had already been transformed but sought to deny the transformation it had undergone (Raissiguier). To understand that, we have to consider how the term *culture* operates and how, in the French context, the term came to be invoked in these debates to designate not the culturally variable formations of human life but the universal conditions for human intelligibility.

Natural, Cultural, State Law

Although Agacinski is not a Lacanian—indeed, she is hardly a psychoanalyst—her commentary, which was prominent in the French debate, shares a certain anthropological belief with many followers of Jacques Lacan and other psychoanalytic practitioners in France and elsewhere.[11] Culture, according to this belief, requires that a man and a woman produce a child and that the child have this dual point of reference for initiation into the symbolic order, which consists of a set of rules that order and support our sense of reality and cultural intelligibility. Gay parenting, Agacinski writes, is both unnatural and a threat to culture in the sense that sexual difference, in her view irrefutably biological, gains significance in the cultural sphere as the foundation of life in procreation. "This foundation [of sexual difference] is generation; this is the difference between the paternal and maternal roles. There must be the masculine and the feminine to give 'life'" ("Questions" 23).

Over and against this life-giving heterosexuality at the foundation of culture is the specter of homosexual parenting, a practice that not only departs from nature and from culture but also centers on the dangerous and artificial fabrication of the human and is figured as a kind of violence or destruction. "It takes," Agacinski maintains, "a certain 'violence,' if one is homosexual, to want a child [Il faut une certaine "violence," quand on est homosexuel, pour vouloir un enfant] . . . I think that there is no absolute right to a child, since the right implies an increasingly artificial fabrication of children. In the interests of the child, one cannot efface its double origin" (23, my translation). The "double origin" is its invariable beginning with a man and woman. The man occupies the place of the father, and the woman occupies the place of the mother. "This mixed origin, which is natural," she adds, "is also a cultural and symbolic foundation" (23).

The argument that there must be a father and a mother as a double point of reference for the child's origin rests on a set of presumptions that resonate with the Lévi-Straussian position in *The Elementary Structures of Kinship* (1949). Although Agacinski is not a Lévi-Straussian, her framework nevertheless borrows from a set of structuralist premises about culture that have been revived and redeployed in the context of the present debate. My point is less to hold the views of Lévi-Strauss responsible for the terms of the debate than to ask what purpose the reanimation of these views serves within the contemporary political horizon, considering that within anthropology the Lévi-Straussian views promulgated during the late 1940s are generally considered surpassed, even as they are no longer owned in the same form by Lévi-Strauss himself.[12]

For Lévi-Strauss, the Oedipal drama is not to be construed as a developmental moment or phase. It consists instead of a prohibition at work in the inception of language that works at all times to facilitate transition from nature to culture for all emerging subjects. The bar that prohibits the sexual union with the mother is not arrived at in time but is there, in some sense, as a precondition of individuation, a presumption and support of cultural intelligibility. No subject emerges without this bar or prohibition as its condition, and no cultural intelligibility can be claimed without first passing through this founding structure. The mother is disallowed because she belongs to the father, so if the prohibition is fundamental and understood, then the father and the mother exist as logically necessary features of the prohibition. Psychoanalysis will explain that the father and the mother do not have to actually exist. They can be positions or imaginary figures, but they have to figure structurally in some manner. Agacinski's point is also ambiguous in this way, but she will insist that they must have existed and that the child must understand their existence as essential to his or her origin.

To understand how the prohibition becomes foundational to a conception of culture is to follow the way in which the Oedipal complex in Freud becomes recast as an inaugural structure of language and the subject in Lacan, something I cannot do in this context and probably have done too many times before (Butler, "Competing Universalities"). What I want to underscore is the use of Oedipus to establish a certain conception of culture that has rather narrow consequences for formations of gender and sexual arrangements and implicitly figures culture as a whole, a unity, one with a stake in reproducing itself and its singular wholeness through the reproduction of the child. When Agacinski argues, for instance, that there must be a father and a mother for every child to emerge in a nonpsychotic way, she appears at first not to be making the empirical point that a father and mother must be present and known through all phases of child-rearing. She means something more ideal—that there must at least be a psychic point of reference for mother and father and a narrative effort to recuperate the male and female parent, even if one or the other is never present and never known. But if that were guaranteed without the social arrangement of heterosexuality, she would have no reason to oppose lesbian and gay adoption. It would therefore appear that social arrangements support and maintain the symbolic structure even as the symbolic structure legitimates the social arrangement. Heterosexual coitus will be understood for her, regardless of the parent or parents who rear the child, as the origin of the child, and that origin will have symbolic importance.

The symbolic importance of the child's origin in heterosexuality is understood to be essential to culture for the following reason. If the child enters culture through the process of assuming a symbolic position, and if these symbolic positions are differentiated by virtue of Oedipalization, then the child presumably will become gendered on the occasion that he or she takes up a position in relation to parental positions that are prohibited as overt sexual objects. The boy will become a boy to the extent that he recognizes that he cannot have his mother, that he must find a substitute woman for her. The girl will become a girl to the extent that she recognizes that she cannot have her mother, substitutes for that loss through identification with the mother, and then recognizes she cannot have the father and substitutes a male object for him. According to this fairly rigid schematic of Oedipalization, gender is achieved through accomplishment of heterosexual desire. This structure, put forward much more rigidly here in an effort to reconstruct Agacinski's position than one would find in Freud (i.e., in either *The Three Essays on the Theory of Sexuality* or *The Ego and the Id*), is then deprived of its status as a developmental phase and asserted as the means by which an individuated subject within language is established. To become part of culture means to have passed through the gender differentiating mechanism of this taboo and accomplish both normative heterosexuality and discrete gender identity at once.

There are many reasons to reject this particular rendition of Oedipalization as the precondition of language and cultural intelligibility. There are also many versions of psychoanalysis that would reject this schema, allowing for various ways of rearticulating the Oedipal and limiting its function in relation to the pre-Oedipal. Moreover, some forms of structural anthropology sought to elevate the exchange of women into a precondition of culture and identify that mandate for exogamy with the incest taboo operating within the Oedipal drama. Other theories of culture have come to take its place and call that structuralist account into question. The failure of structuralism to take into account kinship systems that do not conform to its model was made clear by anthropologists such as David Schneider, Sylvia Yanagisako, Sarah Franklin, Clifford Geertz, and Marilyn Strathern. These theories emphasize different modes of exchange than those presumed by structuralism, and they also call into question the universality of structuralism's claims. Sociologists of kinship such as Judith Stacey and Carol Stack as well as Kath Weston, an anthropologist, have also underscored a variety of kin relations that work according to rules that are not always or only traceable to the incest taboo.

So why would the structuralist account of sexual difference, conceived according to the exchange of women, make a "comeback" in the context of the present debates in France? Why would various intellectuals, some of them feminist, proclaim that sexual difference is not only fundamental to culture but also to its transmissibility and that reproduction must remain the prerogative of heterosexual marriage and limits must be set on viable and recognizable forms of nonheterosexual parenting arrangements?

To understand the resurgence of a largely anachronistic structuralism in this context it is important to consider that the incest taboo functions in Lévi-Strauss not only to secure the exogamous reproduction of children but also to maintain a unity to the "clan" through compulsory exogamy as it is articulated through compulsory heterosexuality. The woman from elsewhere makes sure that the men from here will reproduce their own kind. She secures the reproduction of cultural identity in this way. The ambiguous "clan" designated a "primitive" group for Lévi-Strauss in 1949 but came to function ideologically for the cultural unity of the nation in 1999–2000 in the context of a Europe beset by opening borders and new immigrants. The incest taboo thus comes to function in tandem with a racialist project to reproduce culture and, in the French context, to reproduce the implicit identification of French culture with universality. It is a "law" that works in the service of the "as if," securing a fantasy of the nation that is already, irreversibly, under siege. In this sense the invocation of symbolic law defends against the threat to French cultural purity that has taken place, and is taking place, through new patterns of immigration, increased instances of miscegenation, and blurring national boundaries. Even in Lévi-Strauss, whose earlier theory of clan formation is redescribed in his short text *Race and History,* we see that the reproducibility of racial identity is linked to the reproduction of culture.[13]

Is there a link between the account of the reproduction of culture in Lévi-Strauss's early work and his later reflections on cultural identity and the reproduction of race? Is there a connection between these texts that might help us read the cultural link that takes place in France now between fears about immigration and desires to regulate nonheterosexual kinship? The incest taboo might be seen as working in conjunction with the taboo against miscegenation, especially in the contemporary French context, insofar as the defense of culture that takes place through mandating the family as heterosexual is simultaneously an extension of new forms of European racism. Something of this link is prefigured in Lévi-Strauss, which explains in part why his theory has been resurrected in the context of the present debate.

When Lévi-Strauss argues that the incest taboo is the basis of culture and that it mandates exogamy, or marriage outside the clan, is "the clan" being read in terms of race or more specifically in terms of a racial presupposition of culture that maintains purity through regulating transmissibility? Marriage must take place outside the clan. There must be exogamy. But there must also be a limit to exogamy. Marriage, that is, must be outside the clan but not outside a certain racial self-understanding or racial commonality. The incest taboo mandates exogamy, but the taboo against miscegenation limits the exogamy that the incest taboo mandates. Cornered, then, between compulsory heterosexuality and prohibited miscegenation, something called culture, saturated with the anxiety and identity of dominant European whiteness, reproduces itself in and as universality itself.

Of course, many other ways of contesting the Lévi-Straussian model have emerged in recent years, and its strange resurgence in the recent political debate will no doubt strike anthropologists as the spectral appearance of an anachronism. Arguments have been made, for instance, that other kinds of kinship arrangements are possible within a culture and that there are other ways of explaining the ordering practices that kinship sometimes exemplified. These debates, however, remain internal to a study of kinship that assumes its primary place within a culture and also assumes, for the most part, that a culture is a unitary and discrete totality. Pierre Clastres made that point polemically in the late 1980s in the French context, arguing that it is not possible to treat rules of kinship as supplying rules of intelligibility for any society and that culture is not a self-standing notion but must be regarded as fundamentally imbued by power relations that are not reducible to rules.[14]

But if we begin to understand that cultures are not self-standing entities or unities, that the exchanges among them, their modes of delimiting themselves in distinction, constitute their provisional ontology and are as a result fraught with power, then we are compelled to rethink the problem of exchange. It becomes no longer the gift of women, which assumes and produces the self-identity of the patrilineal clan, but a set of potentially unpredictable and contested practices of self-definition that are not reducible to a primary and culture-founding heterosexuality. Indeed, if one were to elaborate on this point, the task would be to take up David Schneider's suggestion that kinship is a kind of doing that does not reflect a prior structure but can only be understood as an enacted practice. That would help us, I believe, move away from the situation in which a hypostatized structure of relations lurks behind any actual social arrangement and permit us to consider how modes of patterned and performative doing bring kinship categories into operation and become the means by which they undergo transformation and displacement.

Hypostatized heterosexuality, construed by some to be symbolic rather than social and so to operate as a structure that founds the field of kinship itself—and informs social arrangements no matter how they appear, no matter what they do—has been the basis of the claim that kinship is always already heterosexual. According to its precept, those who enter kinship terms as nonheterosexual will only make sense if they assume the position of Mother or Father. The social variability of kinship has little or no efficacy in rewriting the founding and pervasive symbolic law. The postulate of a founding heterosexuality must also be read as part of the operation of power—and fantasy—such that we can begin to ask how the invocation of such a foundation works in building a certain fantasy of state and nation. The relations of exchange that constitute culture as a series of transactions or translations are not only or primarily sexual, but they do take sexuality as their issue when the question of cultural transmission and reproduction is at stake. And I do not mean to say that cultural reproduction takes place solely or exclusively or fundamentally through the child. I mean only to suggest that the figure of the child is but one eroticized site in the reproduction of culture, one that implicitly raises the questions of whether a sure transmission of culture will occur through heterosexual procreation, whether heterosexuality will transmit culture faithfully, and whether culture will be defined, in part, as the prerogative of heterosexuality.

To call the entire theoretical apparatus into question is not only to question the founding norms of heterosexuality but also to wonder whether "culture" can be talked about at all as a self-sufficient kind of field or terrain. Although I do it, manifesting or symptomatizing a struggle to work through this position in an act of public thinking, I am aware that I am using a term that no longer signifies in the way it once could. It is a placeholder for a past position, one I must use to make that position and its limits clear but one I also suspend in the using. The relation between heterosexuality and the unity and, implicitly, purity of culture is not a functional one. Although we may be tempted to say that heterosexuality secures the reproduction of culture and that patrilineality secures the reproduction of culture in the form of a whole that is reproducible in its identity through time, it is equally true that the conceit of a culture as a self-sustaining and self-replicating totality supports the naturalization of heterosexuality and that the entirety of the structuralist approach to sexual difference emblematizes this movement to secure heterosexuality through the thematics of culture.

Yet is there a way to break out of this circle whereby heterosexuality institutes monolithic culture and monolithic culture reinstitutes and renaturalizes heterosexuality? Efforts within anthropology since the 1980s no longer situate kinship as the basis of culture but conceive it as one cultural phenomenon complexly interlinked with other phenomena, cultural, social, political, and economic. Anthropologists Franklin and McKinnon write, for instance, that kinship has become linked to "the political formations of national and transnational identities, the economic movements of labor and capital, the cosmologies of religion, the hierarchies of race, gender, and species taxonomies, and the epistemologies of science, medicine, and technology" ("New Directions" 278).[15] As a result, they argue, the ethnographic study of kinship has changed such that it now "include[s] topics such as diasporic cultures, the dynamics of global political economy, or changes occurring in the contexts of biotechnology and biomedicine" (278). In the French debate, Eric Fassin observes that one must understand the invocation of the "symbolic order" that links marriage to filiation in a necessary and foundational way as a compensatory response to the historical breakup of marriage as a hegemonic institution, the name for which in French is *démariage* (same sex). In that sense, opposition to the PaCS is an effort to make the state sustain a certain fantasy of marriage and nation whose hegemony is already, irreversibly, challenged at the level of social practice.

Similarly, Franklin and McKinnon understand kinship to be a site where certain displacements are already at work, where anxieties about biotechnology and transnational migrations become focused and disavowed. That seems to be at work in Agacinski's position in at least two ways. First, her fear of the Americanization of sexual and gender relations in France attests to a desire to keep those relations organized in a specifically French form, and the appeal to the universality of the symbolic order is, of course, a trope of the French effort to identify its nationalist project with a universalist one. Second, her fear that lesbians and gay men will start to fabricate human beings, exaggerating the biotechnology of reproduction, suggests that these "unnatural" practices will eventuate in a wholesale social engineering of the human, linking, once again, homosexuality with the potential resurgence of fascism.

One might well wonder what technological forces at work within the global economy, or what consequences of the human genome project, raise such anxieties within contemporary cultural life. But it seems a displacement, if not a hallucination, to identify the source of this social threat (if it is a threat) with lesbians who excavate sperm from dry ice on a cold winter day in Iowa when one of them is ovulating. Franklin and McKinnon write that kinship is "no longer conceptualized as grounded in a singular and fixed idea of 'natural' relation, but is seen to be self-consciously assembled from a multiplicity of possible bits and pieces" ("New Directions" 276). It would seem critical, then, to understand the assembling operation they describe in light of the thesis that kinship is itself a kind of doing, a practice that enacts that assemblage of significations as it takes place.

Yet with such a definition in place, can kinship be definitively separated from other communal and affiliative practices? Kinship loses specificity as an object once it becomes characterized loosely as modes of enduring relationship. Obviously, not all kinship relations last, but whatever relations qualify for kinship enter into a norm or convention that has some durability, and that norm acquires durability through being reinstated time and again. Thus, a norm does not have to be static in order to last; in fact, it cannot be static if it is to last. These relations are prone to naturalization and disrupted repeatedly by the impossibility of settling the relation between nature and culture. Moreover, in their terms, kinship is one way for signifying the origin of culture. I would put it this way: The story of kinship, as we have it from Lévi-Strauss, is an allegory for the origin of culture and a symptom of the process of naturalization itself, one that takes place, brilliantly, insidiously, in the name of culture itself. Thus, debates about the distinction between nature and culture, heightened when the distinctions between animal, human, machine, hybrid, and cyborg remain unsettled, become figured at the site of kinship, for even a theory of kinship that is radically culturalist frames itself against a discredited "nature" and remains in a constitutive and definitional relation to that which it claims to transcend.

One can see how quickly kinship loses its specificity in terms of the global economy, for instance, when one considers the politics of international adoption and donor insemination. New "families," in which relations of filiation are not based on biology, are sometimes conditioned by innovations in biotechnology or international commodity relations and the trade in children. And now there is the question of control over genetic resources, conceived of as a new set of property relations to be negotiated by legislation and court decisions. Yet there are salutary consequences, as well, of the breakdown of the symbolic order, because kinship ties that bind persons to one another may well be no more or less than the intensification of community ties. They may or may not be based on enduring or exclusive sexual relations and may well consist of ex-lovers, non-lovers, friends, and community members. In that sense, then, the relations of kinship arrive at boundaries that call into question the distinguishability of kinship from community or call for a different conception of friendship. These constitute a breakdown of traditional kinship that not only displaces the central place of biological and sexual relations from its definition but also gives sexuality a separate domain from that of kinship. It allows for the durable tie to be thought outside the conjugal frame and opening kinship to a set of community ties that are irreducible to family.

Psychoanalytic Narrative, Normative Discourse, and Critique

Unfortunately, the important work in what might be called post-kinship studies in anthropology has not been matched by similarly innovative work in psychoanalysis, and the latter sometimes still relies on presumptive heterosexual kinship to theorize the sexual formation of the subject. Several anthropologists have not only opened the meaning and possible forms of kinship but also called into question whether kinship is always the defining moment of culture, but this opening has not been matched by an equally well-known body of scholarship within psychoanalysis, although there is some important work there, for example, in the work of Ken Corbett.

If we call into question the postulate by which Oedipalization, conceived in rigid terms, becomes the condition for culture, how do we return to psychoanalysis once this delinkage has taken place? If Oedipus is not the sine qua non of culture, that does not mean there is no place for Oedipus. It does mean that the complex that goes by that name may take a variety of cultural forms and will no longer be able to function as a normative condition of culture. Oedipus may or may not function universally, but even those who claim that it does would have to find out in what ways it figures and would not be able to maintain that it always figures in the same way. For it to be a universal—and I confess to being agnostic on this point—in no way confirms the thesis that it is the condition of culture. That latter thesis purports to know that it always functions in the same way, as a condition of culture. But if Oedipus is interpreted broadly, as a name for the triangularity of desire, then the salient question becomes, What forms does that triangularity take? Must it presume heterosexuality? And what happens when we begin to understand Oedipus outside the exchange of women and the presumption of heterosexual exchange?

Psychoanalysis does not need to be associated exclusively with the reactionary moment in which culture is understood to be based on an irrefutable heterosexuality. The discipline might pursue many questions in order to help understand the psychic life of those who live outside normative kinship or in some mix of normative and "non-." What fantasy of homosexual love, for example, does the child unconsciously adopt in gay families? How do children displaced from original families or born through implantation or donor insemination understand their origins? What cultural narratives are at their disposal, and what particular interpretations do they give to these conditions? Must the story the child tells, a story that will no doubt be subject to many retellings, about his or her origin conform to a single story about how the human comes into being? Or will we find the human emerging through narrative structures that are not reducible to one story, that of a capitalized Culture itself? How must we revise our understanding of the need for a narrative understanding of self that a child may have, which includes a consideration of how those narratives are revised and interrupted? And how do we begin to understand what forms of gender differentiation take place for the child when heterosexuality is not the presumption of Oedipalization?

This is the occasion not only for psychoanalysis to rethink its own uncritically accepted notions of culture but also for new kinship and sexual arrangements to compel a rethinking of culture. When the relations that bind are no longer traced to heterosexual procreation, the homology between nature and culture that philosophers such as Agacinski support tends to become undermined. They do not stay static in her own work, because if it is the symbolic order that mandates heterosexual origins, and the symbolic is understood to legitimate social relations, why would she worry about putatively illegitimate social relations? She assumes that the latter have the power to undermine the symbolic, suggesting that the symbolic does not precede the social and, finally, has no independence from it.

It seems clear that when psychoanalytic practitioners make public claims about the psychotic or dangerous status of gay families they are wielding public discourse in ways that need to be strongly countered. Lacanians do not have a monopoly on such claims. In an interview with Jacqueline Rose, the well-known Kleinian practitioner Hanna Segal reiterated her view that "homosexuality is an attack on the parental couple" (210), "a developmental arrest" (211), and expressed outrage over a situation in which two lesbians raise a boy (210). She added that she considers "the adult homosexual structure to be pathological."[16] When asked at a public presentation in October of 1998 whether she approved of two lesbians raising a boy, she answered flatly "no."

To respond directly to Segal, as many people have, and insist on the normalcy of lesbian and gay families is to accept that the debate should center on the distinction between normal and pathological—whether she is wrong to think of homosexuality, for instance, as pathological, or whether it ought rightly be said to be normal. But whether we seek entrance to the halls of normalcy or reverse the discourse to applaud our "pathology"—that is, as the only "sane" position within homophobic culture—we have not called the defining framework into question. Once we enter that framework, we are to some degree defined by its terms. We are as defined by those terms when we seek to establish ourselves within the boundaries of normality, as we are when we assume the impermeability of those boundaries and position ourselves as its permanent outside. After all, even Agacinski knows how to make use of the claim that lesbians and gays are "inherently" subversive when she claims that they should not be given the right to marry because homosexuality is, by definition, "outside institutions and fixed models" ("Questions" 24).

We may contend that double-edged thinking will only lead us to political paralysis, but consider the more serious consequences that follow from taking a single stand within such debates. If we engage the terms that these debates supply, then we ratify the frame at the moment in which we take our stand. And that signals a certain paralysis in the face of exercising power to change the terms by which such topics are rendered thinkable. A more radical social transformation is precisely at stake when we refuse, for instance, to allow kinship to become reducible to "family," or when we refuse to allow the field of sexuality to become gauged against the marriage form. As surely as rights to marriage, to adoption, and to reproductive technology ought to be secured for individuals and alliances outside the marriage frame, it would constitute a drastic curtailment of progressive sexual politics to allow marriage and family, even kinship, to mark the exclusive parameters within which sexual life is thought. That the sexual field has become foreclosed through such debates on whether we might marry or conceive or raise children makes clear that either answer, whether the "yes" or the "no," can work in the service of circumscribing reality in precipitous ways.

If we decide that these are the decisive issues and know which side we are on, then we have accepted an epistemological field structured by a fundamental loss, one which we can no longer name enough even to grieve. The life of sexuality, kinship, and community that becomes unthinkable within the terms of these norms constitutes the lost horizon of radical sexual politics, and we find our way "politically" in the wake of the ungrievable.

NOTES

1. An important analysis of how the approach to studying kinship has been fatally undermined by inappropriate assumptions about heterosexuality and the marriage bond brought to ethnographic description appears in Schneider, *A Critique* (see also Schneider, *American Kinship*). For a continuation of this critique, especially as it relates to the presuppositional status of the marriage bond in kinship systems, see John Borneman's critical review of contemporary feminist kinship studies in "Until Death Do Us Part."

2. Author conversation with Saidiya Hartman, spring 2001, University of California, Berkeley.

3. In a blurb for *A Society without Fathers or Husbands: The Na of China,* Lévi-Strauss notes that Cai Hua has discovered a society in which the role of fathers "is

denied or belittled," thus suggesting that the role may still be at work but disavowed by those who practice kinship there. That interpretation effectively diminishes the challenge of the text, which argues that kinship is organized along nonpaternal lines.

4. I gather that recent domestic partnership legislation in the United States, as in California, does offer explicit provisions for parental rights shared equally by the couple, although many proposals, such as the one in Vermont, explicitly seek to separate the recognition of domestic partnerships from rights of joint parenting.

5. For a full consideration of Franco-American cultural relations with respect to gender and sexuality, see the following work by Eric Fassin which, in many ways, has formed a background for my own views on this subject: "'Good Cop, Bad Cop': The American Model and Countermodel in French Liberal Rhetoric since the 1980s"; "'Good to Think': The American Reference in French Discourses of Immigration and Ethnicity"; "Le savant, l'expert et le politique: la famille des sociologues"; "Same Sex, Different Politics: Comparing and Contrasting 'Gay Marriage' Debates in France and the United States"; and "The Purloined Gender: American Feminism in a French Mirror."

6. In 1999 the state of California passed the Knight initiative, which mandated that marriage be a contract entered into exclusively by a man and a woman. It passed with 63 percent of the voting public in its favor.

7. Agacinski, "Questions." For an excellent rejoinder, see Feher, "Quelques réflexions sur 'Politiques des sexes.'"

8. In Germany, the "Eingetragene Lebenspartnerschaft" legislation that passed in August 2001 clearly stipulates that the two individuals entering into this alliance be gay and that the law obligates them to a long-term relationship of support and responsibility. The law thus obligates two individuals, understood to be gay, to an approximation of the social form of marriage. Whereas the French PaCS simply extend the right of contract to any two individuals who wish to enter into it in order to share or bequeath property, the German arrangement requires, in neo-Hegelian fashion, that the contract reflect a specific way of life, one recognizably marital and thereby worthy of recognition by the state. Deutscher Buundestag, 14 Wahlperiode, Drucksache 14/5627 (German Parliament, fourteenth election session, document 14/5627), March 20, 2001.

9. Lauren Berlant argues persuasively that "in the reactionary culture of imperiled privilege, the nation's value is figured not on behalf of an actually existing and laboring adult, but of a future American, both incipient and pre-historical: especially invested with this hope are the American fetus and the American child" (5).

10. This argument forms the center of my objection to Lacanian arguments against the viability of same-sex marriages and in favor of heteronormative family in *Antigone's Claim* (especially 6–73). For a further argument against Jacques-Alain Miller's and other forms of Lacanian skepticism toward same-sex unions, see my "Competing Universalities" in *Contingency, Hegemony, and Universality* 13–81.

11. The Lévi-Straussian position has been even more adamantly defended by Françoise Héritier. For her most vehement opposition to the PaCS, see "Entretien," where she remarks that "aucune société n'admet de parenté homosexuelle." See also *Masculin/féminin* and *L'exercice de la parenté.*

12. Lévi-Strauss made his own contribution to the debate, making clear that his

views of over fifty years ago do not coincide with his present positions and suggesting that the theory of exchange does not have to be tied to sexual difference but must always have a formal and specific expression. See Claude Lévi-Strauss, "Postface."

13. Lévi-Strauss, *Race et histoire,* 1–26.

14. Clastres, *Society against the State* and *Archeology of Violence.* For a consideration of anthropological approaches to kinship after Lévi-Strauss, see Carsten and Hugh-Jones, eds., *About the House: Lévi-Strauss and Beyond.*

15. See also Franklin and McKinnon, eds., *Relative Values.*

16. Segal remarks, "An analyst, worth his salt, knows about illness from the *inside.* He doesn't feel 'you are a pervert unlike me'—he feels: 'I know a bit how you came to that point, I've been there, am partly there still.' If he believes in God, he would say: 'there but for the grace of God go I.'" And then a bit later: "You could argue rightly that heterosexual relationships can be as, or more, perverse or narcissistic. But it's not inbuilt in them. Heterosexuality can be more or less narcissistic, it can be very disturbed or not so. In homosexuality it's inbuilt" (212).

Works Cited

Agacinski, Sylviane. "Contre l'effacement des sexes." *Le Monde,* Feb. 6, 1999, 1+.

———. "Questions autour de la filiation." Interview with Eric Lamien and Michel Feher. *Ex æquo* (July 1998): 2–24.

Berlant, Lauren. *The Queen of America Goes to Washington City: Essays on Sex and Citizenship.* Durham: Duke University Press, 1997.

Borneman, John. "Until Death Do Us Part: Marriage/Death in Anthropological Discourse." *American Ethnologist* 23, no. 2 (1996): 21–35.

Butler, Judith. *Antigone's Claim: Kinship between Life and Death.* The Wellek Library Lectures. New York: Columbia University Press, 2000.

———. "Competing Universalities." In Judith Butler, Ernesto Laclau, and Slavoj Žižek. *Contingency, Hegemony, and Universality: Contemporary Dialogues on the Left.* London: Verso, 2000.

Carsten, Janet, and Stephen Hugh-Jones, eds. *About the House: Lévi-Strauss and Beyond.* New York: Cambridge University Press, 1995.

Clastres, Pierre. *Archeology of Violence.* Trans. Jeanine Herman. New York: Semiotext, 1994.

———. *Society against the State: Essays in Political Anthropology.* Trans. Robert Hurley. New York: Zone, 1987.

Corbett, Ken. "Nontraditional Family Romance: Normative Logic, Family Reverie, and the Primal Scene." *Psychoanalytic Quarterly* 70, no. 3 (2001): 599–624.

Fassin, Eric. "'Good Cop, Bad Cop': Modèle et contre-modèle américains dans le discours libéral français depuis les années 1980." *Raisons Politiques* 1 (Feb. 2001): 77–87.

———. "'Good to Think': The American Reference in French Discourses of Immigration and Ethnicity." In *Multicultural Questions.* Ed. Christian Joppke and Steven Lukes, 22–41. London: Oxford University Press, 1999.

———. "The Purloined Gender: American Feminism in a French Mirror." *French Historical Studies* 22 (Winter 1999): 11–39.

———. "Le savant, l'expert et le politique: La famille des sociologues." *Genèses* 32 (1998): 15–69.
———. "Same Sex, Different Politics: Comparing and Contrasting 'Gay Marriage' Debates in France and the United States." Unpublished essay.
Feher, Michel. "Quelques réflexions sur 'politiques des sexes.'" *Ex æquo* (1998): 2–25.
Franklin, Sarah, and Susan McKinnon. "New Directions in Kinship Study: A Core Concept Revisited." *Current Anthropology* 41, no. 2 (2000): 275–78.
———, eds. *Relative Values: Reconfiguring Kinship Studies.* Durham: Duke University Press, 2001.
Héritier, Françoise. "Aucune société n'admet de parenté homosexuelle." Interview with Marianne Gomez. *La Croix.* (Nov. 1998): 16.
———. *L'Exercice de la parenté.* Paris: Gallimard, 1981.
———. *Masculin/Féminin: La pensée de la différence.* Paris: Odile Jacob, 1996.
Hua, Cai. *A Society without Fathers or Husbands: The Na of China.* Trans. Asti Hustvedt. New York: Zone, 2001.
Lévi-Strauss, Claude. "Postface." *L'Homme* 154–55 (April–Sept. 2000): 713–20. Special issue on "Question de parenté."
———. *Race et histoire.* Paris: Denoël, 1987.
———. *The Elementary Structures of Kinship.* Rev. ed. Trans. James Harle Bell, John Richard von Sturmer, and Rodney Needham. Ed. Rodney Needham. Boston: Beacon Press, 1969.
Mackey, Nathaniel. *Discrepant Engagement: Dissonance, Cross-Culturality, and Experimental Writing.* Tuscaloosa: University of Alabama Press, 2000.
Moten, Fred. *In the Break: The Aesthetics of the Black Radical Tradition.* Minneapolis: University of Minnesota Press, 2003.
Raissiguier, Catherine. "Bodily Metaphors, Material Exclusions: The Sexual and Racial Politics of Domestic Partnerships in France." In *Violence and the Body: Race, Gender, and the State.* Ed. Arturo Aldama, 94–112. Indiana: Indiana University Press, 2003.
Rose, Jacqueline. *States of Fantasy.* New York: Oxford University Press, 1996.
Schneider, David. *American Kinship: A Cultural Account.* 2d ed. Chicago: University of Chicago Press, 1980.
———. *A Critique of the Study of Kinship.* Ann Arbor: University of Michigan Press, 1984.
Segal, Hanna. "Hanna Segal interviewed by Jacqueline Rose." *Women: A Cultural Review* 1, no. 2 (1990): 19–214.
Stack, Carol. *All Our Kin: Strategies for Survival in a Black Community.* New York: Harper and Row, 1974.
Warner, Michael. *The Trouble with Normal: Sex, Politics, and the Ethics of Queer Life.* New York: Free Press, 1999.
Weston, Kath. *Families We Choose: Lesbians, Gays, Kinship.* New York: Columbia University Press, 1991.

6 De-casing Women: Dialogue and Difference in the Law

ZAKIA PATHAK

The Argument

This essay will be concerned with the engendering of the legal subject and subjectification of women in courts of modern law in India. The truths of family discourse that circulate in alternative judiciaries outside the state law courts infiltrate modern law through production of subjectivities that cannot be bounded. The tangling modern knowledge and discursive truths, that which can be publicly avowed and that which must be confined to the epistemological private, causes epistemological confusion that complicates classification of behavior and pronouncements of verdicts.

The encounter of modern knowledge and discursive truth in the criminal justice system can make or mar the fortunes of women before the law. In this essay, I will analyze three cases, two of which came up before the Supreme Court of India during the last decade of the twentieth century and one that was withdrawn, in which women who were involved in sexually transgressive behaviors or at various removes from the physical violence that marked them were impelled into criminal courts of law. I will attempt to identify epistemological encounters that marked the shifting boundaries of the private.

As sexuality emerges into the public domain of modern law, women begin to perceive new possibilities of freedom and equality. But they enter the public domain trailing the truths of the private, resulting in behavior that constitutes enigmas under the law. That behavior is accessible to understanding only as a differential relation to the truths and the true woman of family discourse. It demands recognition of agency and the multiple forms that feminist agency can take in India.

Modern Knowledge and Discursive Truth

"The rise in the importance of discourse has coincided with a falling-off of intellectual security in what we know and what it means to know—that is, a shift in epistemology" (Jaworski and Coupland, eds. 3). With the turn of the century, and more than fifty years after independence from colonial rule, the truth-claims of modern knowledge—the rational, the scientific, and the secular—are being interrogated by local knowledge emerging from the intimidating institutionalism and professionalism of the modern.[1] In the field of medicine, for example, indigenous forms of medicine like *ayurveda* are engaging in a critical relationship with the modern allopathic system. Pedagogical institutions now offer courses in "integrated medicine." In the field of architecture, *vastu shastra* (building on the premise that the building is a living body, that every element contains a dimensional code that speaks of the whole structure) is of interest. In the field of law—in which this essay proposes to gambol—adversarial judicial procedures inherited from the British legal system are being displaced by the conciliatory procedures of the family in setting up family courts by the state.

Alternative knowledge or discursive truth did not wither but were displaced onto the epistemological private. Because the private is culturally contingent its boundaries are shifting and porous; discursive truths seep into the courts of modern law. Discursive subjectivities throw up epistemological challenges that interrogate the boundedness of official knowledge. Case law in civil courts has always revealed the determining power of discursive truth in arriving at judicial verdicts. A judgment in a writ petition in the Karnataka High Court is an example. A terminally ill patient, kept alive by artificial means, sought release from suffering for himself and his family. The court, however, rejected his petition, describing him as "sentimental." Holding that such a death is suicide, the court pointed out that suicide is a sin "that will attract in the next life worse results there than in the one he is living" (Rao). The Hindu dharma of karma, or reincarnation, thus determined a legal verdict in a modern debate on euthanasia.

This essay differentiates modern knowledge and discourse without opposing them. Both are cognitive and yield different orders of truth. Knowledge is built by a process of defining boundaries among conceptual classes and labeling them and the relations between them. Discourse works by inference (Jaworski and Coupland, eds. 4); the etymological root of the word is *discurrere* (to run in several directions). Several texts construct a space of intertextuality that inferentially produces understanding. Discourse is a context of acts and statements in a cultural history that by inference determines the meaning of any specific statement or act. Knowledge deals with macro-level structures. Discourse focuses at the micro-level, where larger structures are lived and experienced. "Discourse analysis is a sort of forensic activity with a libertarian slant" (Jaworski and Coupland, eds. 6). It works to deconstruct meaning structures in both the public and the private and to expose the power relations that shape them. In showing how the pressure of broad social and institutional norms is brought to bear on the identity and classification of individuals, discourse analysis works in the interests of women and other disadvantaged populations in that it destabilizes taken-for-granted systematized meaning. Both modern knowledge and discourse are powerful and produce subjects in conflictual relations. Because the power of the modern state is behind it, modern knowledge is publicly privileged, institutionalized, and rendered pedagogical. Discourse becomes displaced onto the epistemological private.

A Genealogy for the Hindu Woman

Female nature, always presented a major problem in understanding, was contradictorily conceptualized as both libidinous and pure in the *Manav Dharmasastra* (Law of Manu), the most influential of the ancient texts, and is cited more often in other texts than any other *sastra* (scriptures). "Running after men like whores, by their fickle minds and natural lack of affection [women] are unfaithful to their husbands . . . a man should make the utmost effort to guard them. . . . A woman's mouth, a girl's breast, a child's prayer, the smoke of the sacrifice are always pure" (Doniger and Smith xxi).

The *Sankhyakarita,* a classical text of Indian philosophy of the fourth century A.D., divides women into three categories corresponding to the three traits of *prakriti* (nature): *sattwa* (goodness), *rajas* (passion), and *tamas* (darkness). "Sexuality well guarded by males is the best category while women seeking pleasure belong to the mediocre category, and totally licentious and independent women belong to the worst category. Further more they are bad mouthed and quarrelsome" (Natarajan 1400). It engenders the two basic principles, prakriti and *purush* (self or consciousness), in a dualism where each is dependent on the other but never fuse into one (1403).[2] Sankhya dualism greatly influenced pan-Indian culture and also Indian constructions of women (1398).

Not all ancient texts are preoccupied with libidinous female nature in the family. The *Arthasastra,* written during the period of the formation of brahamic ideology in the middle of the first millenium B.C., is concerned with managing female sexuality, which is differentially controlled, as it pertains to public order. Gail Omvedt stresses the need to read the *Arthasastra* alongside the more traditionally cited *Manav Dharmasastra* because it is more concerned with the state and its interests. Public order was to be maintained by a differentially permitted right of movement outside the home. The wives of professional dancers and wandering minstrels, for example, were to be permitted a freedom of movement withheld from other women, and brothels were regulated by the king—in some instances even run as a state enterprise. Omvedt concludes that, under the *Arthasastra* state, women were dominated by a state patriarchy rather than a family patriarchy.

Intradiscursive contradictions make problems of the prescriptive status of texts and their constructions of women. (But the marriage relation is always idealized; for a woman to serve her husband is equivalent to serving a guru.) With their bias for the textual, the British tended to elevate the scriptural texts to prescriptive status. Contemporary scholarship debates that status. In their introduction to the English translation of the *Manav Dharmasastra* the editors explain these contradictions as arising out of the need for unifying and consolidating existing modes of law that were often diverse and contradictory. Whereas Doniger thinks this attempt obsessive—"its goal is not applicability but totality" (xlvi)—Smith grants it coherence. Rajeev Dhavan appears to concur with the view that the text was never meant to serve as a rule book and suggest that it should be read as a discourse about women.[3] These texts have been cited in order to provide a genealogy for contemporary constructions of female nature. There is little attempt to reconcile the contradictions or motivation to question the truths of discourse. Those are taken as givens and produce varied understandings of behavior.

When discourses of female nature threaten the power of the rulers, however, the latter move to safeguard their interests. In the process, the boundaries of the private are breached. In colonial India, ceding jurisdiction in family and religious affairs to private authorities was aimed at achieving native consent for foreign rule. It was hoped that autonomy in the private sphere would compensate for loss of authority in the governance of the public sphere. But boundaries between the domains are always liable to be destabilized by behaviors that are open to different, sometimes contradictory, epistemological explanations. The behavior of women is a major site for the eruption of epistemological encounters. In the Islamic practice of the *kurh* for instance (Singha), when the native authority awarded the death sentence to a man, his wife sacrificed her life in his stead. Discursively, her honor was bound up in his, and the act was construed as being of her own free will.

This came to be unacceptable to the British, who perceived kurh as a rival mode of law and, under pressure from evangelical opinion back home, as being of dubious morality. Such practices had to be stopped from claiming authority under "the erroneous prejudices of superstition" (Singha ch. 3) The Islamic law was eventually amended to put such killing on the footing of murder, and male culpability was established.

Similarly, the rendering of female nature as iconic was a move by nationalists to preserve their power in the private sector. The British-inspired division of public and private colluded nicely with the need of the nationalists to do something about the "woman question." Claims of Western civilization to material superiority had to be acknowledged, but in the spiritual sphere the East was considered superior. What was necessary was to cultivate the material techniques of modern Western civilization while retaining and strengthening the distinctive spiritual essence of local culture. That completed formulation of the national project and, as ideological justification for the selective appropriation of Western modernity, it continues to hold sway (Chatterjee 238). Whether private or public, inner or outer, spiritual essence or material interests, home or world, women and men came to be placed on an axis where the first term was privileged. "Nationalism had . . . resolved the women question in complete accordance with its preferred goals" (Chatterjee 237).

Today, the Hindu right has need, in its push for power, of ancient texts to consolidate a constituency of Hindu women, but the right must also negotiate modern antagonism to its obnoxious construction of women. The doctrine of *hindutva* (what counts as being a Hindu) is motivated by the political need to homogenize Hindu women so as to provide the right with a "vote bank." But intradiscursive contradictions about women in the ancient texts militate against the right's endeavor to mold Hindus into one united nation of equals. Women and untouchables have the potential to splinter elections with their votes, and thus must be contained by positing Hinduness as a spiritual essence shared by all Hindus, "making the essential spiritual east superior to the essential material west" (Vanayak 40). Vanayak critiques Arun Shourie's metaphor (Shourie is a minister in the BJP majority government) of the religious essence being the "gene" of the country, thereby "escaping all control of historiography and history" (43). The making of an identity for Hindu women on the right is forged by traditional family discourse. But political sensitivity to the modern—equality and democracy—prompts the right to explain the obnoxious gendered prescriptions of ancient texts as necessitated by the presence of foreign influences, especially Buddhism and Islam.

It is perhaps to counter this increasingly powerful politicocultural rhetoric that scholars on the left tend to represent the text as univocal and misogynist. The left assert, for example, that the *Manav Dharmasastra* denies evidentiary value to women's testimony in court. "In the ultimate analysis, we are told that the evidence proffered by even a number of women should not be accepted owing to the instability of their intellect (*Manusmriti* vii.77)" (Roy 25). The text, however, contains contrary injunctions. Certainly, women's fickle nature is adduced to denigrate their testimony, but in the absence of other witnesses, women's testimony may be accepted.

Traces of family discourse, particularly constructions of female nature, still have power to subjectify women. Among the "truths" that constitute family discourse are: women are by nature sexually promiscuous and need to be guarded at the three stages of life by their fathers, husbands, and sons; women are pure, sexually fulfilled in the marital relationship and without desire for any male outside it; and women are weak of character and therefore no responsibility attaches to them for their sexual excesses. In cases of sexual congress or molestation outside marriage, it is a husband's honor that is at stake. He is responsible for avenging the wrong done to his wife. Men are considered to be, by nature, sexually aggressive and not to be held culpable for sexual excess. It is always the woman who is responsible for what is done to her. Disputes within the family must be settled within the family. True women shun the public. Those who do go public with grievances and seek redress from public law courts are, therefore, unwomanly. The right also believes that women's intellect is unstable, only women can do justice to women, women's preferred place is in their homes, women's preferred speech is silence, and women are talkative.

Alternative Judiciaries/Multiple Epistemologies

The number of alternative judiciaries that function in India today make it clear that the state and its modern law do not, so far, enjoy hegemonic epistemological status. The relation between the state and private dispute-settling bodies has sometimes been viewed as harmonious, with those bodies functioning "within the interstices of modern law" and "subject to its jurisdiction" (Gallanter 15). The source of that theory is liberal ideology, and the theory has been critiqued for not exploring the role and function of the law in maintaining patterns of power in the economy (Dhavan xliii–xlviii).

When the state cedes juridical powers to the religious establishment, it suspends an epistemology. The state, for example, upholds monogamous marriage as the family norm. Under existing rules, government servants who contract for second marriages are liable to be dismissed from service. The constitution, however, gives minority rights to tribes and their marital practices. A tribal officer of the government in Hyderabad had contracted a second marriage and was legally proceeded against by his first wife. The Supreme Court ruled that the laws of the tribe should take precedence over state law, and the state had to drop legal proceedings. Similarly, when the state reclaims a ceded power, it claims the right to know better. The final decree granting divorce in the Christian community rested with the church under Christian personal law, but it is being reclaimed.

Feminist campaigns were influential in the perception of religious establishments as having a history of gender discrimination. That militates against modern belief in equality upheld in modern law. Yet the state recognizes and seeks to protect the family and its adjudicatory procedures that favor conciliation in the case of marital discord. To that end, it has set up family courts and given them the powers of civil courts and the right to determine their own procedures. The adversarial procedures of modern law, confined to the question of guilt and innocence, are thought to be not consonant with Indian culture.

It might be supposed that conflicting value systems and multiple epistemologies result in existential angst. Would-be litigants, however, confront the proliferation of dispute-settling bodies pragmatically, strategically selecting those they believe will serve their interest. A *dalit* (outcast) who believes his village *panchayat* (elected council) contains too many Brahmins to make for a just verdict can bypass it and choose another tribunal. Terrorists in Andhra Pradesh are reported to hold periodic sittings and are approached for justice by litigants dissatisfied with the verdict of civil courts—in rape cases, for example. The ideology of one such group, the Peoples War Group (PWG), is being challenged by feminist critique from within and without. "A paradox of sorts has emerged," Vindya observes. "On the one hand . . . the term patriarchy is rather freely used in party documents and other writings to describe the totality of women's oppression. On the other hand the PWG has reacted negatively to the current feminist literature in Telugu, with the very term feminism being termed as diversionary, imported or as concerning a tiny majority [*sic*] unrelated to the reality and struggles of the working class and toiling women" (170).

One of the first women's groups that came up under PWG auspices took up individual cases of violence against women and the family. Similarly, a political party in Maharashtra has also been approached to adjudicate matters of family when a speedy settlement, not available in the state court of law, is desired. Women's courts are functioning in Gujarat on the premise that women cannot find justice from males.

The Manjunatha temple at Dharmastala in Karnataka is a unique legislating body where guilt is established by confession of the accused under the pressure of faith, even in disputes of a public nature such as the recovery of loans. The aggrieved party—of any religion—presents his *hoilu* (petition) to the *dharmadhikari* (religious head of the temple). The dharmadhikari sends a summons to the accused party—and leaves it at that. Most accused hasten to answer the summons, so potent is the fear and awe of Lord Manjunatha. If they falsely deny the accusation they are taken to the inner sanctuary and asked to repeat their denial—in the presence of the lord. It works. There are stories of accused answering the summons decades later, a run of misfortune over the years having been astrologically attributed to some *dosha* (sin committed in the past).[4]

These alternative judiciaries may be considered as the material structures where discursive truths are given body and circulate. The engendering of the legal subject by discursive truth has been excoriated by many within the modern legal system. Verdicts, perceived to be shaped by discursive reasoning, are described as biased, the bias considered sometimes as buried or deeply rooted. The case of *Neera Mathur v. Life Insurance Corporation,* for example, produced a verdict that a legal luminary castigated for being gender-biased. Mathur was found to be pregnant and dismissed on grounds of inefficiency. The Supreme Court ordered her reinstatement without commenting on the pregnancy. As Sathe observes:

> The Supreme Court ultimately revealed its hidden bias rather crudely . . . the court could have clearly stated that such a policy could not be adopted by any public corporation which was "State" for the purpose of Article 12 of the Constitution because such sex discrimination was totally forbidden by the constitution. Should the court wait for such a declaration until the issue is raised before it in an adversary proceeding . . . [which] is totally unsuited to Indian conditions? What was the justification for such judicial restraint in this case? Was it not merely sexism under the guise of legalism?

Other critics, too, have figured accounts for bias in judgments by using a metaphor of deep and surface structure. An essay by Flavia Agnes, for example, "goes below the surface of legal discourse to reveal assumptions and embedded in this discourse and to ask how law operates in women's lives" (Kapur and Cossman 37).

Distinct from these psychic and structural explanations is an epistemological one. It is being increasingly recognized that bias, prejudice, is constructed by what is called "ordinary social knowledge": "decision making is not a simple result of [justificatory] legal reasoning. . . . It necessarily takes account of the subconscious as well as conscious reasoning of the judge and this subconscious reasoning is necessarily informed by ordinary social knowledge constructed and maintained by narrative frameworks" (Jackson 25). These two types of reasoning are described as "those factors in decision making which conventionally remain private and those which might be used publicly in the process of justification" (26).

The State as Parens Patriae

When transgressive sexual practices move out of the private, women who suffer from the exclusionary practices of family discourse are newly subjectified. Resistance is constructed by imperatives of the modern welfare state: freedom, equality, and the possibilities they offer for a new life. Yet for all the prestige of modern law, and with state power behind it and the institutionalization and professionalization that attend it, discursive truths contest the claim of modern law to rationality and the claim of the state to be protector of the violated. The state in criminal law is ipso facto protector. Nevertheless, discursive truths lodge in the epistemological private of modern law and exert power to engender legal subjects: judge, counsel, prosecution and defense, accuser and accused.

Marked by traces of family discourse, women are immediately alerted and responsive to the silent functioning of the true woman in judicial functionaries. This ontological being, inferred from a context of ancient texts and cultural practices, produces behavior that is enigmatic and not accessible to the categories and classification of modern law. Epistemological confusion created by the confrontation of discursive truths and modern knowledge unsettles accepted categories. What is the nature of the offense? Who is the victim, and who the offender? How is guilt constructed? What is the nature of proof? What counts as evidence? Of what evidentiary value is a woman's testimony? Is a hostile witness inevitably guilty of perjury?

Marriage is widely perceived as the cornerstone of the family, notwithstanding the different forms of family that obtain in India (Kapur and Cossman 87–99). Conservatively sanctioned heterosexual relations operate normatively in the political rhetoric across political parties. This is obviously prompted by the desire to communicate immediately and effectively to a nationwide electorate, which family discourse ensures. The stories that follow make a study of the extent to which "the feeling of identification which individuals once had with the private domain and local community is transferred to the State" (Rex 212).

The Cases

The three stories that follow articulate cognitive dissonance and its management. The three women at the center of the three lawsuits were all implicated in violence, directly or at a remove. As educated, economically independent, professionally successful, middle-class women—a stage artist, an administrative officer in the government, and a badminton star—they are popularly designated as "modern." The term has accumulated derogatory meanings: empowered and therefore unwomanly, or Westernized and therefore deracinated and decultured, not Indian. The three women replace this opposition with a plurality of behaviors that differentiate them from the commonplace. At the same time, they all bear traces of family discourse that produces them as Indian women. By choosing to speak in different voices—interrogating, accommodating, and refusing—in their struggle for modern freedoms, they dissolve the ontological assumptions that define the true woman and destabilize the attempt to give modern Indian women fixed identities.

Interrogating Difference: Misra and Karanth

In 1986 the Madhya Pradesh government instituted a criminal case against B. V. Karanth, director of Bharat Bhavan, a state-run institute for the performing arts at Bhopal. Karanth was accused of attempting to burn Vibha Misra, a stage actress and his colleague. On May 24 of that year, Misra's landlady—the actress lived in a rented flat—and some of the landlady's relations heard screams issuing from the flat. The landlady's nephew rushed to it and knocked repeatedly before the door was opened by a "scared-looking" Karanth, his beard visibly singed. Misra also had burn marks.

The police were called, and on interrogation Misra accused Karanth of attempting to burn her. Later, upon medical examination, Karanth admitted (an admission he subsequently denied) to having acted out of sudden anger because Misra refused to take part in a play he was planning to stage. When the case came up for hearing at the Sessions Court in March 1987, ten months later, Misra retracted her statement. Karanth was, she declared, innocent. Moreover, the burns were the result of an accident at the stove, an incident arising from her own negligence.

The prosecution counsel wanted Misra to be declared hostile and urged that the evidence of the landlady and her relations be recorded, but the trial court rejected the prosecution's case. The state government then filed a revision petition against the trial court's order under section 284 of the Criminal Procedure Code, claiming that the evidence was critical to the case because the landlady and her relations were the first on the scene after the incident.

The case then came before the High Court, where again Misra insisted on Karanth's innocence. The prosecution counsel had sought to establish an amorous relationship between the couple as a motive for the violence and had Misra's letters to Karanth read out in court. Eventually, Karanth sought compromise. On the day his arguments were to be heard, the Madhya Pradesh government prayed for the withdrawal of the case in the public interest.

Why did Misra retract? More important, how was her retraction framed? Misra's behavior clearly represented a problem in understanding. Literary discourse has pioneered shifts in the understanding of enigmatic behaviors. They are historically and culturally conceptualized and epistemologically related. Sklar has investigated how hypocrisy moves from a moral category to a social one. Castigated as falsity and dissimulation, hypocrisy in novels and plays signifies "a covert form of pride" and operates as a "form of coercion." Eventually, it is perceived as socially produced and signifying "a whole culture of fear" (Shklar 23). If Misra's behavior can be considered hypocritical, how was it socially produced?

The linear legal narrative of indecision, accusation, and withdrawal of charge has become classic among women in India and other disadvantaged groups. After the initial hesitation, the decision to prosecute does not quite amount to faith in justice under the law. On the contrary, it is accompanied by skepticism, even fear, about the law's intentions. Legally, Misra was in strong position. Her charge against Karanth—that he attempted to set her on fire—was corroborated by eyewitnesses. Moreover, Karanth had confessed to the police that he had done so out of anger.

Legally, then, Misra was a victim of violence. Discursive constructions of guilt, however, intervened to construct her as the offender, In India, the behavior of libidinous females is believed to provoke and justify male anger. The history of case law in sexual violations attests to the lenience with which offending males are let off, with sometimes only an injunction for good behavior. Compounding Misra's guilt was the fact that she was the other in Karanth's marriage. The premium placed on marriage, on virginity and chastity, are reflected even in the amended laws (Kapur and Cossman 37). Mira was discursively categorized as the offender, and her retraction was produced by a gendered subjectivity.

But with a difference.

In criminal law in India, power to withdraw rests with the state, which is the complainant because its monopoly on legitimate violence has been encroached. In a welfare state, the state enters as *parens patriae.* When an accuser, as chief prosecution witness, withdraws a charge, the state cannot proceed because grounds for the complaint have been removed. Thus the state of Madhya Pradesh attempted to have Misra declared hostile. Such hostility, however, if inserted into the category of the confession, discursively constructs her as virtuous. In a court of law, denial of statements made in prior investigations may be actionable as perjury within modern law. Misra appears to have banked on the discursive effect of her retraction. Confession signifies the admission of a wrong done to another. It bonds with the accused against the state, reproducing the heterosexual normative relation of husband and wife.

Her retraction produced Misra as a real woman in the tradition of female nature as being forgiving and self-sacrificing. She occupied the space of a wife, in willing submission to her lord, her honor bound up with his. She pleaded with the court not to refer to Karanth as "the accused" and maintained that her burns were caused by an accident with a stove. She attributed Karanth's burns, his singed beard, to an attempt to rescue her. She described their relationship as the socially sanctioned pedagogical one of father and daughter, of guru and *chela* (disciple). Karanth, she told the court, had even intervened to save her intimacy with one of her peers. Misra's retraction, construed as a remorseful admission of unnatural behavior, returned the crime to the space of the private. In doing so, it exposed the falsity of the state's pretensions and verdicts to accord justice.

Two epistemologies were in conflict. Modern law classified Misra as a victim of violence, whereas the state moved to protect her interests as a citizen. The state's effort was repulsed. The discourse of family had constructed her as an offender; she was the other in a marriage. By appropriating the space of a wife and speaking from it, she was mimicking that discourse and undermining it. The tactic seems to have been conceived as a strategy to command a hearing. Her claim that the burns were caused by an accident with a stove could have been doubly produced. It is so common an alibi provided to culpable husbands by injured wives that it discursively produced her as a true woman. At the same time, her wifely performance unsettled the ontological assumptions in which the true woman is premised.

Gender is performativity. As Deborah Cameron says, paraphrasing Judith Butler, "The repeated stylization of the body, a set of repeated acts within a rigid regulatory frame which congeal over time to produce a natural kind of being" (Cameron 444). Speech-act theory tries to grapple with the problem of sincerity, without which the speech-act is infelicitous. The natural and the sincere are united in the concept of habitus: "Structural structures pre-disposed to function as structuring structures . . . which generate practices and representations that can be objectively adapted to their outcomes without supposing a consciousness. . . . It is of course never ruled out that the responses of the habitus may be accompanied by a strategic calculation tending to perform in a conscious mode the operation that the habitus performs quite differently" (Bourdieu, *The Logic* 53).

When the objective conditions that produce the habitus—marriage, chastity, decorum, and silence—do not obtain, the sincerity condition is violated. Patterns of listening built into the utterance are disrupted. Speech floats free of its culturally determined act and can be heard only in another speech genre. Here, in all likelihood, is the mocking or the jocular. Misra brought considerable theatrical talent to the cross-examination. Confronted with a colorful metaphor she had used of Karanth, "you have trampled on so many buds," she admitted being absorbed at the time in a play she was rehearsing under his direction and identifying with her character. The words she had used in court were in the script. At one point during the cross-examination the judge had to enjoin her from using the court as a stage. The courtroom was packed with spectators, and acting came naturally to her in such a milieu. A media report the morning after her testimony expressed the general response to it: "quite a performance." Misra's "performativity" may well have decontextualized a gendered speech-act to represent "nature" as art.

Difference Pathologized: Kulkarni-Modi-Singh

On July 28, 1988, Syed Modi, a Muslim badminton star, was leaving K. D. Babu Stadium in Lucknow, Uttar Pradesh, on his scooter when he was shot dead at point-blank range. Modi was married to Amita Kulkarni, a Hindu badminton player, in Mumbai in 1984, and the couple had a daughter a few years later. A close friendship developed between Kulkarni and Modi's friend Sanjay Singh, a politician and son of the raja of Amethi in Uttar Pradesh. Modi's murder presented an opportunity for Singh's political rivals, the Congress Party then in power at the center and fearful of his clout in Amethi (Rajiv Gandhi's constituency) to cripple him for the coming elections by implicating him in the murder. The Central Bureau of Investigation (CBI) took over the case from the Uttar Pradesh Police, to the dismay of the latter.

The major pieces of evidence at the trial were the murder weapon used by the killers, Kulkarni's private diary, and some personal letters. As the investigation proceeded it was found that contradictions in eyewitness reports and a lack of important details made the prosecution's case a weak one. The CBI was driven to pursue a new strategy—to use Kulkarni's diary against Singh as providing evidence for instigation and a motive for conspiracy to murder. The CBI raided Kulkarni's house in Lucknow and her flat in Mumbai and seized her diary; a personal letter from her mother, advising her and Singh to exercise restraint; and another from her husband, threatening suicide.

On the basis of those documents Singh and Kulkarni were charged with conspiracy to commit murder, and arrest warrants were issued. Kulkarni was picked up immediately, but Singh's political clout delayed his arrest. They were later released on bail. In September 1988 the Sessions Court at Lucknow exonerated them, and they were discharged. In 1990 the CBI filed a revision petition in the High Court of Allahabad, but that court upheld the decision of Sessions Court. In 1994 the CBI moved to the Supreme Court, which upheld the discharge but pointed out that a discharge did not amount to acquittal. Even if a motive were proved, conspiracy to murder could not be assumed. Some two years later Modi's assets were awarded to Kulkarni, his widow, by the additional civil judge of Lucknow. Toward the end of the long judicial battle Kulkarni and Singh were married; Singh had divorced his wife of fifteen years but not without another legal drama.

This is a telling example of how private passion can leave the family domain and move to the center of a public enquiry as a result of electoral ambition. In the process, difference was constructed and pathologized. The political necessity to prove adultery on the part of Kulkarni and Singh so as to establish a motive for the murder of Modi and justify the charge against Singh led to a focus on the private writings—chiefly Kulkarni's diary. The document became caught up in conflicting discourses that interrogated its evidential value—the legal and the literary. Sexuality is articulated with other discourses. The epistemological contest centered on the authority accorded in the two discourses to the first-person singular, the "I." The regimes of the law take it as expressing a unified, rational subject of free will, present to itself. In literary discourse on fantasy it is termed the "split subject."

It was important for the CBI to be able to use the diary as evidence, because it documented a fulfilled sexual relationship with Singh. In the absence of eyewitness evidence the confession carried legal weight. The dying declaration of a woman who is the victim of dowry violence, for instance, is given the status of truth if it is made to a magistrate or police officer or given freely. The diary could be taken as confession. It was widely suspected that the appearance of Kulkarni's diary in the media was a leak inspired by the CBI in the interests of its brief. It was viewed as an attempt to initiate a trial by media that would, the CBI hoped, convict Kulkarni and Singh of adultery and provide a motive for conspiracy.

According to the elaborate plot that the CBI fabricated, Kulkarni had sent Singh out of Lucknow so he could not be implicated in the murder. She had remained at home that morning, feigning illness so as not to accompany Modi to the stadium as she often did and thus giving the hired killers a clear field. For the CBI, Kulkarni's complicity had been circumstantially established. Multiple semiotic codes constructed her as "modern." She had made an unconventional marriage, marrying by choice out of her religious community. She wore jeans, jogged, attended evening parties, and even kept a diary without inhibition. Her account of herself in the diary as "independent" and "liberated" finished the job for the CBI: Agency was established, and adultery could be proved.

But literary discourse undermines the certitudes of legal discourse and repudiates traditional verities of character and narration. The narrator is distinguished from the author. All narration is narrativization. The "omniscient narrator" is a fiction; third-person narration does not amount to an objectivizing distancing. Literary forms are cut off from the moorings that sustained their identity: the realistic novel as fact, the fantastic as fiction. In a generic shakeup, claims of the novel to realism have been qualified. It does not reflect unmediated reality, despite using identifiable events and recognizable characterization. Autobiographical writing is no nearer the truth than third-person recounting. Fantasy poses a discursive dilemma. If it is true, it can not be fiction; if it is fiction, it cannot be fact, the legacy of the science-ideology opposition.

Kulkarni asserted in vain that her diary was fantasy and should be understood as "not all reality, not all imagination, a mixture of both, . . . a kind of rambling." As Copjec notes,"The subject position inscribed by a discourse is not the same as the subject who is engaged by that discourse, no more than the 'I' of the statement is the 'I' that makes it. The ex-centric or equivocal relation of the subject to discourse is never made audible and the nature of the conflict in the social is seriously misconstrued" (12). But the play of anxiety and desire can hardly be accommodated in the legal system's certitudes.

In the sexual economy of the Hindu scriptural texts, desire had been accommodated by its distribution over two categories of women: wife and nonwife. The wife "naturally" felt desire only in the marital relation; indeed, she was enjoined to pleasure her husband. The nonwife was publicly available, and the supply of her services, and demand for them, was sometimes regulated by the state. What this binary structure repressed was the autonomy of desire from the rigidity of regulatory systems. Referring to the romanticism that informs contemporary feminist narratives of public women in precolonial cultures—as, for instance, the *devadasis* (temple dancer or female servant of the diety)—and contrasting these with the unromantic accounts of the devadasis themselves, Mary John and Janaki Nair conclude, "It is clear that feminist narratives fail to acknowledge the ways in which wife and non-wife are constituted by the same patriarchal authorities so that they are structurally yoked in fundamental ways, making the securities and pleasures of one domain unavailable to the other" (11–12).

That issue seems to be the premise of Kulkarni's dilemma. She wanted both men in her life and believed in her powers to make that possible. Desire could be sublimated in a friendship that would neutralize its threat to chastity. As she noted in the diary, "We are both married to other individuals and our first duty is to them." The diary in which the desire is avowed and presented as experienced was a necessary means to order the self—a means through which this culturally induced compromise, encompassing both desire and duty, could be effected.

Kulkarni appeared confident of constructing a narrative of self-identity different from those discursively available. "In a post-traditional order," Giddens maintains, "an indefinite range of possibilities present themselves not just in respect of options for behavior but in respect also of the 'openness of the world' to the individual. The world intrudes into presence via an array of varying channels and sources" (417). One such is electoral politics. Giddens thinks that diversification of context is as likely to lead to a promotion of the integrity of the self as to its fragmentation. That self, however, must be cognizable as difference. All the world could go on was the proliferating information about Kulkarni that never seemed to come to rest in an epistemologically accessible self-hood. She would not disavow desire. Moreover, she refused to destroy her diary, knowing that it could incriminate her, when she had the opportunity to do so before it fell into the hands of the police. She voluntarily accepted chastity as a wifely duty and was ready to undergo a paternity test to prove that her daughter was Modi's.

These contradictions could not be reconciled in court, and the prosecution and defense produced different orders of understanding on the basis of heteroglossia. The prosecution interpreted the word *liberated* as a belief in free sex, which framed Kulkarni as a nonwife in opposition to the wife/nonwife of traditional discourse. The defense interpreted the word as women's right to have platonic relationships with men, placing Kulkarni in the discourse of modernity. That fragmented fractured self could only be perceived as deviant and aberrational.

"All self development depends on the mastering of appropriate responses to others," Giddens notes, "an individual who has to be different from others has no chance of reflexively developing a coherent self-identity. Excessive individuation has connections to conceptions of grandiosity. The individual is unable to discover a self-identity 'sober' enough to conform to the expectations of the others in his social milieu" (427). In his exposition of another dilemma of modernity, powerlessness versus appropriation, Giddens puts the sense of omnipotence at one end of the spectrum and engulfment at the other. Both are seen as pathological. Kulkarni, in her search for wholeness, could be said to have journeyed from one end of the spectrum to the other. The media reported that she sat through the court sessions with a stony face. Toward the end of the trial she was reduced to wearing white and removing the *bindi* on her forehead, thus denoting widowhood—public acceptance of the dictates of tradition. Difference had been pathologized because it could not make sense.

Domesticating Difference: Deol-Bajaj-Gill

In early July 1988, the financial commissioner (home) of the government of Punjab gave a dinner party for friends and colleagues. Rupam Deol Bajaj (Deol), the senior Indian administrative officer in the government, and K. P. S. Gill, director general of the Punjab police, were present as invitees. Deol was accompanied by her husband, Bajaj, and Gill came without his wife. Drinks flowed. Soon Gill asked Deol to sit with him, but she responded with a polite negative. He attempted to pull her chair closer, and she pushed it away. When he tried again, she rose to sit with other women. When Gill followed and asked her to return, she again rose to leave him. He stood above her to block her way, and when she pushed back her chair and turned to leave he slapped her on her bottom.

On July 20, Deol lodged a protest with the inspector general of police and the administration at Chandigarh, alleging that Gill's actions had outraged her sense of modesty. The advisor to the governor of Punjab noted on the file that he had occasion in the past, as inspector general of police, to reprimand Gill for his behavior, when under the influence of alcohol, with women. In November the investigating body concluded that the evidence on record did not substantiate Deol's allegations, and the governor let off Gill with a reprimand. Deol then lodged a First Information Report with the police on July 29. Bajaj, himself a senior administrative officer with the Indian government, filed a criminal complaint in the court of the chief judicial magistrate, Chandigarh.

Gill pleaded that the note of the inspector general of police and the governor's order were privileged documents, which the magistrate did not accept. In December, Gill petitioned the Punjab and Haryana High Court to quash the First Information Report because no offense had been disclosed against him. He claimed that Deol's complaint was false and frivolous—unnatural, absurd, and made with the intention to harm him. He also advised that the law should not concern itself with allegations of a trivial nature. The Punjab and Haryana court set aside the magistrate's order supporting the offense as trivial and upheld the claim of privilege. Gill made a contempt petition against Bajaj for quoting from the official note, an act the court held was now unnecessary.

Bajaj then appealed to the Supreme Court, which in October 1995 took cognizance of his petition and directed the chief judicial magistrate, Chandigarh, to take up the case. Under section 354 of the Indian Penal Code the CJM found Gill guilty in August 1996 of outraging the modesty of a woman and, under section 509, of indecent behavior. He was awarded two prison terms of three and two months, respectively, to run concurrently, and fined. In January 1997 the Chandigarh district and sessions judge upheld the decision of the chief judicial magistrate and ordered that Gill be placed on probation for three years. The judge also directed him to pay Rs. 200,000 as compensation to the victim and to deposit a sum of Rs. 50,000 to cover legal expenses.

In October, a division bench of the Supreme Court ordered Gill's prosecution. It described the slapping of Deol's bottom as the finale of earlier overtures and therefore proof of culpable intention. It further held that "even if we had presumed he had no such intentions he must be attributed with such knowledge, as the alleged act was committed by him in the presence of a gathering comprising the elite of the society." It described the act as an affront to the dignity of a woman. The court also dismissed the claim of privilege, holding that the encounter was a matter between two individuals and in no way affected the national interest.

The Hegelian doctrine of the rational state and the citizen-subject has hierarchized the public and private domains, implicitly placing the private as irrational and inferior and women outside the citizen-subject. Its "stipulated meaning of non-regulation by law" (Edwards 14) renders invisible the multitude of alternative judiciaries that proliferate in India, along with their material support of discourses.

The sovereignty of the state, its epistemological hegemony, is always threatened and often displaced by the different orders of rationality that prevail in private. The Deol-Bajaj-Gill case documents the contest of discourses on the grounds of the state: the civil services—the bureaucracy and police in this instance and management of contradictions. Violence is the differential that governs the division of law into private and public in matters of sexual transgression. "Sexual harassment in the workplace" conflates the two and gives new meaning to violence.

Naming is a political practice the effect of which depends on the power of cultural patterns of meaning that often lag behind modernist perceptions. "Sexual harassment," particularly when its designation connotes violence, challenges the prevalent construal of the same situation as "teasing" ("eye-teasing" generally targets women in public places). After the Supreme Court's guidelines in *Visakha Kumark and Others v. the Government of Rajasthan,* the increase in litigation by Indian women molested in the workplace has been considerable. It is shadowed, however, by discursive truths about the proper place for woman being the home, and those "truths" engender the subject of law.

Deol was a senior officer in the Indian Administrative Service and Gill in the police. Of the three arms of the civil service, the administrative, the foreign, and the police, the first is the most prestigious. Its prestige is officially recognized in the framing of rules, following court cases, which govern vertical and horizontal mobility in allied services with a view to ensuring opportunity for upward mobility for the police. Gill's rage at Deol's resistance to his importunate behavior may have been produced by her gender and by professional rivalry.

In traditional Indian discourse, the culpability of the woman is established by virtue of her female nature; she is believed to have in some way incited the man to misbehave. A class differential appears to operate in case law now that, ironically, colludes with tradition. Educated, economically independent, middle-class working women are perceived to be different, less subject than other women to restraints on movements outside their homes, in their social relations with men, and in their speech. Such deviations are considered to mislead men and surprise them into committing an offense. Deol's voluntary attendance at a mixed party—where drinks are commonly served—was sought to be construed in Gill's defense as misleading him. When the attempt did not succeed, another was made to locate the offense as having taken place at a private dinner party because in private space, this behavior could not be regulated by the law. That attempt, too, did not succeed.

Deol's initial response to the harassment was produced by the discourse of family, according to which sexual aggression is considered as male nature and not actionable. "Gill will be Gill" was how Deol was reported to have dismissed the event at the hearing of some invitees to the party. Even when her perception of it changed and she decided to seek justice, she preferred the comparative privacy of a departmental inquiry. If women are considered to be responsible for what happens to them, then to make experience public is to court shame. It was only when Deol's attempts within the service were frustrated by officials covering up for Gill that she was induced to go public. Predictably, the path was strewn with obstacles. The police had recommended that the First Information Report she lodged with them be quashed because there was no evidence to substantiate her allegation, witnesses having turned hostile or being unavailable. Vital information was sought to be suppressed as privileged. The governor was alleged to have suggested withdrawing a case registered against her husband some time previously if she withdrew hers as well. Given the skepticism of women about the state's claim to be their protector, and also perhaps to minimize the possibly adverse effects of the case on her career, she chose to remain in the discourse of family that casts violation of a woman as a matter between the two men concerned. The case was instituted by her husband, who declared in traditional style that he was fighting for his honor.

In spite of this orchestration, Deol could not escape the charge of narrow self-interest, even shameful publicity-mongering, that so often inhibits women from preferring charges in court. Among the most virulent attacks on her was one by Tavleen Singh, a well-reputed woman journalist for the *Indian Express* who had been called to account by her editor when a piece she had written on the Supreme Court verdict aroused considerable ire among readers. "We now have it from the highest court in the land," Singh reported on July 13, 1995, "that when a man slaps a woman's bottom it constitutes a crime known as 'outraging the modesty of a woman.' This is a matter so serious that the Supreme Court believes K. P. S. Gill, top cop, super hero, national icon should be prosecuted for the outrage." Gill, Singh conceded, had been guilty of "bad behavior." Her advice that such matters are better settled by "throw[ing] your drink in his face or kicking him where it hurts" (ibid.) indicates how powerful is the ideology and widespread the practice of keeping sexual harassment confined to the private and to its ways of redressal.

Singh also mocked the feminist campaigns that asserted women's right over their bodies. "Let's begin with the wrath of the sisterhood which, when I wrote my politically very incorrect speech, I had expected to descend on me by the bucketful," she wrote on December 3, 1995. (Women's organizations had rallied in protest against the government's reported intention of decorating Gill for his services to the nation.)

For Singh, the bottom line was that "justice for a slapped bottom is not a giant step for mankind." Her elision of gender in a statement clearly intended to be reductively funny was even more deplorable in the context of the debate in the media, which, sensitive to the issues involved, asked pertinent questions. If he had slapped her on some other part of her anatomy, would it amount to sexual harassment? Moreover, would he have slapped the home secretary on the bottom had the latter tried to avoid him at a party?

Sexuality is articulated with other discourses. The most intimidating of those brought to bear on Deol was the discourse of the nation. Gill had become a national icon for his role in suppressing militants in the Punjab who were agitating for a Sikh state, Khalistan. In its earlier avatar, the Punjabi Suba, the demand was culturally framed based on a common language and culture. The later demand for Khalistan was for a sovereign religious Sikh state. That set off waves of gruesome violence on Hindus in the Punjab and outside, and the government of India, under pressure of public opinion, dispatched Gill to the Punjab as inspector general of police. The movement was crushed. It was inevitable that Deol's struggle for justice would be dismissed as narrowly self-interested and trivial.

On the plea of the "national interest" information vital to Deol's interests, which described and recorded Gill's history of being under the influence of alcohol and misbehaving with women, was sought to be withheld as privileged. It came to nothing. The Supreme Court ruled that it concerned the matter as being between two individuals and could not be considered as pertaining to public interest.

The question of what constitutes political dissent was also raised. Balagopal, a political activist speaking about the terrorist movement in Andhra Pradesh, deplored the tendency of Gill and others like him to see separatist movements as anything other than a problem in law and order, ignoring the political dissent aspect. Gill and the government of Punjab could speak from the discourse of nation and national interest only because nationalists made icons of women during the struggle for Indian independence. In the process, Deol's action as voicing dissent was nearly obliterated.

"Modesty" is a key term in family discourse that defines a true woman in India. Modesty is the dharma, understood as both nature and duty, of women. The case demonstrates the ways in which discourse grows around a word and unsettles any systematic attempt to fix a signified to it. "Modesty" was once construed by external markers such as confinement to the home, restricted movements and wearing the veil outside it, silence in the presence of men, and so on. These came to rest in a hegemonic conception of female nature that internalized these rules and rendered them "natural." In urban areas, many women employed in offices and at other public organizations have either pragmatically disregarded some of these constructs or retained them for equally pragmatic reasons. External markers of wifehood, for instance, which announce a protector—the *mangalsutra* (necklace of black beads set in gold), the *kumkum* in the hair part, and red bangles, all of which denote the married state according to religious or regional affiliations—are retained because they discourage unwelcome male attention. And strategic representation of modern freedoms enables these freedoms to be retained. Rubbing shoulders with men in the workplace is offset by voluntary segregation during the lunch hour, a space for womanliness through exchanged recipes and shared lunch-packets, confided intimacies and offered advice, and appeals for help and receiving it. Such practices go along with statements endlessly repeated that women's interest in employment is purely in terms of economic betterment for their families and that they are not interested in careers or competition with male colleagues. In other words, the more things change the more they remain the same. It also remains reassuringly true that rules of seniority prevent gender discrimination in service and so ensure women's promotion over eligible male colleagues in the same category.

"Modesty" continues to be a worried term in the law. Case law—as in rape—has sometimes defined it as biological and inherent. A girl child, that is, is considered to be modest from the day she is born. At other times a class differential constructs evidence of immodesty. In some cases, the mere fact of disordered clothing can constitute evidence of adultery; in others, however, a man caught holding a woman's breasts is not thought to be guilty of outraging her modesty (Kapur and Cossman 104–5).

To inhabit family discourse, to speak modestly, is to command a hearing. "Retributory logic operates with the structures of patriarchy which pose the State as guardian of a certain kind of women," Baxi observes. "Further, it enhances the patriarchal common sense that women who do not enact patriarchal standards of morality . . . do not deserve retributory justice. The objective of retributory justice here is a certain kind of law and order, which on the one hand posits the State as the guardian of the chastity of a certain kind of women and on the other increases its disciplinary power over all women" (1199).

Deol's behavior remained within the discourse of modesty. The case was instituted by her husband, and it closed when he declined compensation awarded by the court, declaring that he had been fighting only for his honor. Retributory justice was due to Deol, and she got it. In the course of the judgment, modesty was given a new meaning—dignity. Deol's lawyer had feared that it would be understood as prudery. The court-given meaning of dignity goes beyond physical manifestations of violence to include violence against a woman's sense of self-esteem and sense of herself.

Agency: Deferring the Modern Indian Woman

The three preceding examples describe how modern freedoms can be staked within family discourse in India. Refusal of subjectification, the autonomy of desire, and freedom from sexual harassment at the workplace are all contemporary concerns that can be described as modern. The strategies involved in the achievement of these freedoms may be dissimilar, the voices may appear as contradictory. But they are neither opposed nor cacophonous. They are absorbed in a structure of difference where resistance is produced not in the space between ontological being and transgressive women but in the relations between them. These differential relations are both produced and agential. The relation of trace to resistance is to acknowledge one's history, refuse to be subjectified by it, and move beyond it. It is to defer the meaning of the modern Indian woman.

It is critical that the Hindu right seeks to fix meaning for its political ends by using the discourse of the nation, which itself is homogenized. Nationalists believed that national interests could be served by removing women altogether from the civil sphere and installing them outside bourgeois time as Grihalaxmi (the goddess of the household), a compound word that can "imagine a connection between the mythico-religious-social, often equated in conscious nationalist writing with a 'community' or 'Nation'" (Chakrabarty 80–81).

Such constructions have been critiqued for exiling Indian women from history. Radhakrishnan notes:

> The locus of the true self is exiled from processes of history while the locus of historical knowledge fails to speak for the true identity of the nationalist subject. The result is a fundamental rupture, a form of cognitive dissidence, a radical collapse of representation. Unable to produce its own history in response to its inner sense of identity, nationalism sets up women as victim and goddess simultaneously. Women becomes the allegorical name for a specific historical failure . . . the failure to co-ordinate the political or the ontological with the epistemological within an undivided agency. (85)

A passionate critique comes from a Marxist-feminist perspective. Congratulating Kamala Visveswaran for acutely perceiving the inability of subaltern historians to break away from the discourse they analyze and therefore their inability to theorize a general subaltern subject, Himani Bannerji comments: "The new woman of the nationalist imaginary is meant to disrupt and subvert the main enemy, modernity. . . . As reform seeking—thereby dubbed 'westernized,' 'inauthentic' and 'anti-national'—women, voicing demands for their own economic and social independence and aspiring to a citizen-individual status, they emerge as the enemy of the Nation" (914).

The productions of subjectivities carry their own form of agency. If women speak from within family discourse, it is the better to command a hearing. To push against borders that define the private is to radically threaten juridical and political constraints those boundaries guarantee. Conciliatory procedure is believed to be responsive to the needs of the Indian psyche, but to take up adversarial positions is not. Agency answerable to trace, resistance, history, and politics may work more effectively to expose (at the micro-level) the gendered assumptions of family discourse and thus interrogate the ontological being of the True Woman. Such agency must be construed as feminist.

Conclusion

To tell stories of women's experiences as they move from the private domain into the court of public law is feminist political practice. "At bottom, feminism is a mode of analysis, a method of approaching life and politics, rather than a set of political conclusions about the oppression of women. . . . Examining and understanding experience and connecting personal experience to the structures that define our lives, is the clearest example of the method basic to feminism" (Hartsock 36). Developments in theory have legitimized telling stories about the individual and her experience as a political practice. The hegemony of what is called "realpolitik" in appropriating the term *political* is assailed. "How have we come to associate politics with a limited range of activity within a specific location?" Mandaville asks. "The political should be viewed as comprising spaces of interaction situated across and between territories" (673). "Experience" has been retrieved from its idiosyncratic mooring. It is "a process by which, for all social beings, subjectivity is constructed" in interaction (de Lauretis 159). "Experience is a subject's history," adds Scott (34). "By virtue of the languages spoken," Bourdieu states, "the speakers who use them and the groups defined by possession of the corresponding competence the whole social structure is present in each interaction and thereby in the discourse uttered" ("Language" 503).

The title of this essay, "De-casing Women," is intended to resonate with the meanings of the word *case.* A case is a container, a kind of box. To "de-case" women, therefore, is to open Pandora's box and release the furies of multiple subjectivities from the confines of definitions of female nature. A case is a single instance, an example of something. To de-case, then, is to destroy the singularities of these women and return their experience to history. A case is a specific condition or state of affairs. De-casing opens it to genealogy.

NOTES

Words fail to carry the weight of my gratitude to Joan Scott for the invaluable recognition she has accorded to my work in meaningful ways. She is not accountable if this essay fails to live up to her assistance. Thanks to the community of the Society for Informal Education and Development Studies (SIEDS), Bangalore, for the hospitality of their library and kitchen. Special thanks to B. L. Kumar for so generously sharing his time, his books, and his readings. Sanjay and the Alternative Legal Forum (ALF), Bangalore, helped with legal details and provided stimulating discussion, and the library staff of the National Law School of India (NLSI) helpfully provided information. Thanks also to Rekha for her patience in typing several revisions of this essay and to Uma who completed the job. Shankar Pathak, as always, brought me through.

1. I use "local knowledge" and "alternative knowledge" interchangeably and as producing discursive truths in an untidy relation to the systematized knowledge of modern law.
2. The *Sankhya* is a theory of evolution, and according to it the universe consists of two eternal realities, one conscious (the *purusha*) and the other unconscious (*prakriti,* or matter). Prakriti is sometimes translated as universal matter or energy and sometimes as essential nature. Prakriti has three *gunas* (qualities or modes): *sattwa,* which is understood as harmony and equilibrium; *rajas,* which is activity and passion; and *tamas,* which translates as intertia or incapacity. Their interaction produces the evolution of human qualities. The dualism of purusha-prakriti, consciousness or self in relation to nature, is traditionally figured as the relation of male to female.
3. "The Dharmasastra sought to create an enduring set of attitudes and beliefs rather than to supplant customary practices with the imperatives ordained by the *rishis* . . . a unified even if seemingly amorphous set of beliefs" (Dhavan xv).
4. For more information on this, see *The Week,* July 30, 2000, 18–21.

Works Cited

Bannerji, Himani. "Projects of Hegemony: Subaltern Studies Resolution of the Women Question." *Economic and Political Weekly,* March 11–17, 2000, 914.

Baxi, Pratiksha. "Rape, Retribution, State: On Whose Bodies?" *Economic and Political Weekly,* April 1, 2000, 1199–23.

Bourdieu, Pierre. "Language and Symbolic Power." In *The Discourse Reader.* Ed. Adam Jaworski and Nikolas Coupland, 502–13. London: Routledge, 1999.
———. *The Logic of Practice.* Trans. Richard Nice. Palo Alto: Stanford University Press, 1980.
Cameron, Deborah. "Performing Gender Identity." In *The Discourse Reader.* Ed. Adam Jaworski and Nikolas Coupland, 442–58. London: Routledge, 1999.
Chakrabarty, Dipesh. "The Difference/Deferral of a Colonial Modernity: Public Debates on Domesticity in British Bengal." In *Essays in Honor of Ranajit Guha.* Ed. David Arnold and David Hardiman. New York: Oxford University Press, 1997.
Chatterjee, Partha. "The National Resolution of the Woman Question." In *Recasting Women: Essays in Colonial History.* Ed. Kumkum Sangari and Sudesh Vaid, 223–53. New Delhi: Kali for Women in Association with *The Book Review* Literary Trust, 1989.
Copjec, Joan. "m/f or Not Reconciled." *The Woman in Question.* Ed. Parveen Adams and Elizabeth Cowie, 10–18. London: Verso Press, 1990.
de Lauretis, Teresa. *Alice Doesn't: Feminism, Semiotics, Cinema.* London: Macmillan, 1984.
Dhavan, Rajeev. "Introduction." In *Law and Society in Modern India.*
Doniger, Wendy, and Brian Smith. *The Law of Manu.* Delhi: Penguin Books, 1991.
Edwards, Susan S. M., ed. *Policing "Domestic" Violence: Women, the Law, and the State,* 14. Newbury Park, Calif.: Sage, 1989.
Gallanter, Marc, ed. *Law and Society in Modern India.* New York: Oxford University Press, 1999.
Giddens, Anthony. "Modernity and Self-Identity: Tribulations of the Self." *In The Discourse Reader.* Ed. Adam Jaworski and Nikolas Coupland, 415–27. London: Routledge, 1999.
Hartsock, Nancy. "Fundamental Feminism." In *Building Feminist Theory: Essay from Quest.* Ed. Charlotte Bunch et al. New York: Quest, a Feminist Quarterly, 1981.
Jackson, Bernard. "Narrative Theories and Legal Discourse." In *Narrative in Culture: The Uses of Story Telling in the Sciences, Philosophy, and Literature.* Ed. Christoper Nash, 23–50. New York: Routledge, 1990.
Jaworski, Adam, and Nikolas Coupland, eds. *The Discourse Reader.* London: Routledge, 1999.
John Mary E., and Janaki Nair, eds. *A Question of Silence: The Sexual Economics of Modern India.* London: Zed Books. 2000.
Kapur, Ratna, and Brenda Cossman. *Subversive Sites: Feminist Engagements with Law in India.* Delhi: Sage, 1996.
Mandaville, Peter. "Territory and Translocality: Discrepant Idioms of Political Identity." *Millenium* 28, no. 3 (1999): 653–73.
Natarajan, Kanchan. "Gendering of Early Indian Philosophy: A study of Samkhyakarita." *Economic and Political Weekly,* April 28, 2001, 1398–404.
Omvedt, Gail. "Towards a Theory of 'Brahmamic Patriarchy.'" *Economic and Political Weekly,* Jan. 22, 2000, 187–90.
Radhakrishnan, R. "Nationalism, Gender and the Narrative of Identity." In *Nationalisms and Sexualities.* Ed. Andrew Parker et al., 77–95. New York: Routledge, 1992.

Rao, C. N. A. "Letters to the Editor." *Deccan Herald,* Bangalore, India, June 9, 2001.
Rex, John. "The Concept of a Multicultural Society." In *The Ethnicity Reader: Nationalism, Multiculturalism, and Migration.* Ed. Montserrat Guibernau and John Rex, 205–19. London: Quality Press, 1997.
Roy, Kumkum. "'Where Women Are Worshipped, There the Gods Rejoice': The Mirage of the Ancestress of the Hindu Woman." In *Women and the Hindu Right: A Collection of Essays.* Ed. Tanika Sarkar and Urvashi Butalia, 10–28. New Delhi: Kali for Women, 1995.
Sathe, S. P. "Sexism in Law and Justice." *Indian Journal of Social Work* 53, no. 3 (1992): n.p.
Scott, Joan W. "Experience." In *Feminists Theorize the Political.* Ed. Judith Butler and Joan W. Scott, 22–40. New York: Routledge, 1992.
Shklar, Judith. "Let Us Not Be Hypocritical." *Daedelus* 108, no. 3 (1979): 1–25.
Singha, Radhika. *A Despotism of the Law: Crime and Justice in Early Colonial India.* New York: Oxford University Press, 1998.
Singh, Tavleen. Column in *The Indian Express* (Delhi), July 13, 1995, n.p.
———. Column in *The Indian Express* (Delhi), Dec. 3, 1995, n.p.
Vanayak, Achin. "Deconstructing *Hindutva.*" *Lokayan Bulletin* 11, no. 4 (1995): n.p.
Vindya, U. "Comrades in Arms: Sexuality and Identity in the Contemporary Revolutionary Movement in Andhra Pradesh and the Legacy of Chalam." In *A Question of Silence: The Sexual Economies of Modern India.* Ed. Mary E. John and Janaki Nair, 167–91. New Delhi: Kali for Women, 1998.

7 Enabling Disability: Rewriting Kinship, Reimagining Citizenship

RAYNA RAPP AND FAYE GINSBURG

> In trying to portray my son in the literary model known as a novel, I have passed through . . . stages. In the case of a person like him with a mental disability, it isn't the individual himself but rather his family that has to pass from the "shock phase" to the "acceptance phase." In a sense, my work on this theme has mirrored that process. I have had to learn through concrete experience to answer such questions as how a handicapped person and his family can survive the shock, denial, and confusion phases and learn to live with each of those particular kinds of pain. I then had to find out how we could move beyond this to a more positive adjustment, before finally reaching our own "acceptance phase"—*in effect coming to accept ourselves as handicapped, as the family of a handicapped person.* And it was only then that I felt the development of my work itself was at last complete.
>
> —Oe, emphasis added

IN 1963, WHEN THE JAPANESE NOVELIST Oe Kenzaburo's son Hikari was born with a dangerous brain tumor, Oe and his wife chose to have it removed, a process that, along with a range of other kinds of supports, enabled the infant Hikari to survive, but with a profound disability. Since then, the family has had to recreate itself and its narrative. In his book, *A Healing Family,* Oe describes his family's capacity to embrace Hikari.

Healing is used here in two senses that draw our interest as researchers. The word's immediate referent would seem to be the capacity of parents and siblings to help heal the wound of difference for the affected boy. But Oe also emphasizes the work the family has undertaken to heal the wound of difference incurred to its own kinship narrative and practice. Oe, who won the Nobel Prize in literature in 1994, has written several other books chronicling the transformations in their familial universe inaugurated by the birth of Hikari. His works have helped his family and, at a remove, his readers to imagine an unanticipated cultural future that could give meaning and possibility to the reshaped habitus of daily life with a disabled family member.[1] Oe's compassionate and frank story of how his family came to embrace "being handicapped" is representative of a kind of shift in consciousness—disability consciousness—suggestive of a more expansive sense of kinship across embodied difference that, we argue, is essential to the growing public presence of disability in contemporary postindustrial democracies.

The proliferation of publicly circulating representations of disability as a form of diversity we all eventually share—through our own bodies or attachments to others—offers potential sites of identification and even kinship that extend beyond the biological family. In the United States in particular, such public representations of the connections (and disconnections) of disabled people and their families across embodied difference have helped to introduce a sense of public intimacy that, we argue, is crucial to redeeming the ADA promissory note of a polity "beyond ramps" (Russell). The simultaneous emergence of the U.S. disability rights movement along with the escalation of reproductive and neonatal technologies has intensified cultural awareness of a range of broader issues. These increasingly both shape and destabilize contemporary kinship practices as well as debates among disability rights activists, feminists, bioethicists, and health service providers.

Such concerns engage questions about medical ethics and the complexities of reproductive choice; concrete dilemmas about how to organize the practical logistics of care for disabled children; political and distributive queries about what citizens are owed; and conceptual questions about how disability is figured discursively. While such issues are often made the subject of public policy debate, they come already anchored in the daily and intimate practices of embracing or rejecting kinship with disabled fetuses, newborns, and young children. We suggest, then, that disability criticism should encompass not only the public arenas of law, medicine, and education, or the phenomenology of embodiment. It also needs to engage the intimate arena of kinship as a site where contemporary social dramas around changing understandings and practices of reproduction and disability are often first played out. Although the term *kinship* is conventionally associated with the private or domestic sphere, we stress the cultural work performed by the circulation of kinship narratives through various public media as an essential element in the refiguring of the body politic as envisioned by advocates of both disability and reproductive rights.

The efforts of families to "rewrite" kinship are crucial to creating a new cultural terrain in which disability is not just begrudgingly accommodated under the mandates of expanded post–1970s' civil rights legislation, but is positively incorporated into the social body. Likewise, rejection of the disabled from the familial and social body continues to occur, occasionally played out in the public media as scandals of exclusion[2] and in more intimate arenas as the conventional limits of kinship are sustained rather than transcended.

When we began to explore the world of disability—both as parents of disabled children and as anthropologists interested in reproduction, kinship, and social activism—we were struck by narratives like Oe's and their proliferation in a world in which constructions of the body and identity are increasingly mediated by biomedical technologies.[3] We were particularly interested in contradictions between, on the one hand, burgeoning genetic knowledge and the neoeugenic practices it has fostered and, on the other, the expansion of more inclusive democratic discourses—in particular, that of disability rights. To explore this tension, in this essay we foreground the domains of kinship and reproduction as key social sites at which many disabilities are initially assigned cultural meaning in the United States. We focus in particular on contemporary dilemmas surrounding pregnancy and the care of newborns and children with disabilities, which in turn underscore questions concerning the social location of caretaking and its political economy.

We locate our work at this nexus not only because reproductive choices—and the role played in them by the possibility of disability—are increasingly implicated in the new genetic knowledge but also because the parent-child relationship is a nexus at which dramatic alternatives are articulated: dependency versus autonomy; intimacy versus authority; the acceptance of caretaking versus its rejection; normative cultural scripts versus alternative, more inclusive "rewritings." Clearly, the "passions and interests" (cf. Hirschman) at work here can divide the points of view of children and parents. These potential divisions can be particularly acute in the case of children with disabilities, whose bodily and sensory (and, eventually, social and political) experiences may be profoundly different from those of their parents. Recent debates about cochlear implants for deaf children or facial surgery for children with Down syndrome highlight divisions over the value of mainstreaming technologies. Such issues divide families who differ over what constitutes "the best interests of their children." While conflicts between the perspectives of parents and children are typically associated with the separation and self-definition that intensify at adolescence, we focus here on dilemmas that emerge much earlier—indeed, from the embryonic stage or before.

Rewriting Kinship

The birth of a child who is, in one sense, profoundly different from other family members can pose an immediate crisis to the nuclear and extended family. In addition to providing medical support for the affected child, families face the task of incorporating unexpected differences into a comprehensible narrative of kinship (Landsman, "Does God Give," "'Real Motherhood'"; Layne). The birth of anomalous children is an occasion for meaning-making, whether through the acceptance of "God's special angels" or the infanticide of offspring deemed unacceptable. And in millennial America, new technologies have made the domain of kinship and reproduction—the locus classicus of anthropology—particularly charged with cultural contradictions surrounding questions of bodily difference.

A wide variety of contemporary cultural production testifies to this intensification. It is our argument that such public storytelling—whether in family narratives, memoirs, television talk shows and sitcoms, movies, or, most recently, through Websites and Internet discussion groups—is crucial to expanding what we call the social fund of knowledge about disability. In opening up the experiential epistemology of disability, as shaped by and shaping the intimate world of nonnormative family life, such forms of public culture widen the space of possibility in which relationships can be imagined and resources claimed. We underscore the significance of this burgeoning public circulation of intimate disability stories, expanding the arguments of others regarding the place of intimacy in constituting subjectivities of all sorts. As Lauren Berlant writes in her introduction to the special "Intimacy" issue of *Critical Inquiry*, "Rethinking intimacy calls out not only for redescription but for transformative analyses of the rhetorical and material conditions that enable hegemonic fantasies to thrive in the minds and on the bodies of subjects while, at the same time, attachments are developing that might redirect the different routes taken by history and biography. To rethink intimacy is to appraise how we have been and how we live and how we might imagine lives that make more sense than the ones so many are living" (286).

In the expanded domain of "public intimacy" linked to disability, different forms of embodiment are represented within the context of domestic routines and subjectivity. If this is true of information-sharing magazines such as *Exceptional Parent* and the slick and upbeat activist publication and Website *WeMedia*, it is no less characteristic of academic writings by scholars who may themselves be disabled (Asch, "Reproductive Technology"; Asch,

Women with Disabilities; Charlton; Fries, ed.; Handler; Hockenberry; Kuusisto; Linton; Mairs) or caring for disabled family members (Beck; Bérubé; Featherstone; Finger; Jablow; Kittay; Seligman and Darling). We suggest that such representations—what we call disability narratives—are foundational to the integration of disability into everyday life in the United States, a process that is in turn essential to the more capacious notions of citizenship championed by the disability rights movement. As authored by disabled people and/or their family members, these narratives offer revised, phenomenologically based understandings which at times also anchor substantial analyses of the social, cultural, and political construction of disability. The dissemination of such intimate insights among a broader public has helped to mobilize an extraordinary and rapid transformation since the 1970s in the way such notions as rights, entitlement, and citizenship are conceived—a transformation that is shaping public policy in areas such as health care, education, transportation, and access to built, aural, and visual environments.

Of course, not all disability narratives are so inclusive. A very different discourse about disability has emerged around the proliferation of reproductive technologies, in particular prenatal testing for detectable fetal anomalies. Certain assumptions are foundational to these processes. While U.S. genetic counselors are trained to express neutrality about the choices a pregnant woman and her partner may make around amniocentesis testing, the very existence of such a technology and the offer of such tests under the terms of consumer choice are premised on the desire for normalcy and fear of unknown abnormalities (Parens and Asch, eds.). As anthropologists, our task is to understand how these neoeugenic technologies come to make cultural sense despite the emergence of more inclusive discourses of disability in other cultural domains. Prenatal screening, for example, is attractive to cost-accounting health care bureaucracies in which market forces increasingly stratify the "choices" made available to different constituencies as medical care becomes subject to the spreading hegemony of neoliberal practices and ideologies. The attractiveness of prenatal screening to cost-conscious health bureaucracies is a case in point: with the administration of medical care increasingly under the sway of hegemonic neoliberalism, market forces come to dictate what choices are available to different constituencies.

In the United States, and increasingly throughout the postindustrial world, the anxieties that accompany pregnancy are, we argue, exacerbated by the individualized and privatized nature of medical decision-making. When it comes to information about the forms of medical and community support that might be available to the family of a child with a stigmatized difference, the access of prospective parents is limited. They are often unaware of the social fund of knowledge that would help them make a more knowledgeable choice (Ginsburg and Rapp). This de facto segregation is apparent in narratives elicited by researchers from pregnant women and their supporters about their attitudes and aspirations regarding prenatal testing (Browner and Press; Kolker and Burke; Press and Browner; Rapp; Rothman). Unlike the stories discussed earlier, few encounters with prenatal testing are rendered as public narrations. While the social science literature suggests that awaiting the results of an amniocentesis is quite stressful, the stress turns out to be ephemeral for those who receive normal diagnoses of their fetuses. They retrospectively experience the test as a nonevent; amniocentesis is quickly subsumed within the schedule of now-routine health procedures whose presumed outcome is a "normal" baby. By contrast, most of those whose diagnosis turns up positive choose to end the pregnancy. Such events generally pass unmarked, as is the case with most abortions in the West (for the counterexample of Japan, see Hardacre). Writing about abortion, especially under circumstances such as these, when the pregnancy was initially desired, is fraught with personal and political risk. Those few pregnant women who have breached the veil of privacy surrounding prenatal testing and abortion tend to circulate their stories only in specialized medical contexts (Brewster but cf. Rapp; Green). In describing their decision-making processes, they tend to emphasize the limits of caretaking within an available family structure and concern for a child's potential suffering.

> Some people say that abortion is hate. I say my abortion was an act of love. I've got three kids. I was forty-three when we accidentally got pregnant again. We decided that there was enough love in our family to handle it, even though finances would be tight. But we also decided to have the test. A kid with a serious problem was more than we could handle. And when we got the bad news, I knew immediately what I had to do. At forty-three, you think about your own death. It would have been tough now, but think what would have happened to my other kids, especially my daughter. Oh, the boys, Tommy and Alex, would have done okay. But Laura would have been the one who got stuck. It's always the girls. It would have been me, and then, after I'm gone, it would have been the big sister that took care of that child. Saving Laura from that burden was an act of love. (Rapp 247)

Such stories provide an illuminating, if stark, comparison to the more established and more acceptable genre of disability narratives. The themes shaping these different genres of narratives about disability reveal the crucial role that kinship plays in social exclusion, on the one hand, and as a site for the transformative cultural work that can help resituate disability in contemporary American social life, on the other. Clearly, disability stories are complex and variable. The parenting literature, for example, is fraught with the tensions between efforts to normalize the experience of disability and the need for advocacy and special resources to accommodate those who cannot enter mainstream American society through the same pathways or trajectories as most others.

These tensions are themselves a reflection of the way that consumer capitalism is shaping the experience of reproduction in the United States. Perhaps the starkest examples are provided by the contemporary trend of increasingly aggressive medical intervention, with the new reproductive technology of prenatal testing conjuring up a familiar specter from dystopian science fiction: that of designer babies for the market (McGee). At the same time, large numbers of compromised babies are able to survive thanks to advances in medicine and in therapeutic regimes such as occupational therapy and infant stimulation programs (Landsman, "Does God Give," "'Real Motherhood'"). These diverging sociomedical practices, which are increasingly part of normal obstetric and neonatal medicine, embody a doubled telos of modernity and technology. The practices of genetic testing, and other genetic research, seem to promise perfectibility for those who choose and can afford cutting-edge interventions (although what "perfectibility" might mean in practice is highly contested, as we discuss below). Concomitantly, other new technologies, medical and otherwise, offer another promise of expansive democratic inclusion and improved quality of life for those marked by difference from a hegemonic norm of embodiment (Blair).

Suppressed in these narratives of modernity, which stress individual choice and achievement, is the crucial place of kinship and gender in structuring these possibilities. Specifically, this doubled telos places pregnant women under the very American pressure of "choice." Many women, and especially women with first pregnancies, imagine themselves entering the workplace of contemporary mothering in one of two ways. Most plan to control the balance between participation in wage labor and the domestic economy. They use prenatal testing hoping never to face a pregnancy whose outcome would demand more caretaking than they feel they could provide; selective abortion haunts this dilemma. This model of rationality fits easily with the one that has emerged with genetic counseling, which assumes the power of individuals, no matter how constrained, to make rational choices that will "improve the quality" of their lives. A minority of women approach these tests differently, without intent to abort. They view the test as a technology for appropriate preparation should they need to provide specialized support for the birth of a child with a serious disability. In both cases, the assumption endures that infant and childcare is primarily the responsibility of the individual mother, with support from other kin and recourse to the marketplace, if finances permit.

The caretaking of a disabled infant requires different and expanded resources than can be provided by most kin groups without additional forms of support. The complexities of mobilizing the necessary medical, therapeutic, and social support reveal the limits of kinship within a gendered nuclear family structure. It is through this revelation, we suggest, that some begin to reimagine the boundaries and capacities of kinship and to recognize the necessity of broader support for caretaking. On occasion, they are motivated to rewrite kinship in ways that circulate within larger discursive fields of representation and activism.

The Limits of Kinship

Despite a quarter century of activism, policy innovation, and the substantial provision of public services in the United States, the securing of care for disabled members rests with the family. A vast gap remains between the rhetoric of public inclusion that mandates everything from universal design to inclusive classrooms and the battles that still have to be fought on a daily basis to ensure their availability—battles which not everyone can or will fight. As a mother and aunt of a child with significant disabilities point out in an article on "Uncommon Children":

> Laws attempt to provide parity in society for disabled individuals, but do they go far enough? Underfunded and understaffed public schools may be hard-pressed to meet sophisticated or extensive needs. Parents of "special ed" children become angry at the lack of responsiveness while parents of typical children grow resentful of monies seemingly diverted from regular ed. The very people who need to work together to meet these complex challenges are often pitted against each other.
>
> We expect parents of children with disabilities to "rise to the occasion," but some don't or can't. As a nation we were recently horrified by the Kelsos, who left their profoundly disabled ten-year-old at a Delaware hospital with a note saying they could no longer care for him. Certainly, they did the wrong thing. But their desperate act should not be dismissed lightly as simply aberrant. (O'Connell and Foster 18)

When we step back from this impassioned description of a grim social landscape, we recognize this narrative as grounded in a potentially productive tension between a capacious view of liberal democracy, in which law and social services are expanding to accommodate the needs of people with disabilities, and the reality of the daily tasks of caretaking, which remain in the household and dependent on family—and overwhelmingly female—labor. At the same time, biomedical technology holds out utopian promises that elide the dilemmas of caretaking while raising others about perfectibility, exemplified in a variety of sometimes controversial supports to people with disabilities, from cochlear implants for the hearing-impaired to computer resources for "fast-forwarding" learning-disabled students. Technology has also delivered a rapidly expanding panoply of reproductive choices. Reliable and inexpensive birth control, infertility treatments, and safe and legal abortion have greatly enhanced women's ability to control the circumstances of mothering. The prenatal diagnosis of disabling conditions in fetuses is surely part of this technological modernity. The common choice to abort based on such diagnoses suggests the limits of the expansion described above and the implicit recognition that much of the labor of caretaking, especially in infancy and childhood, still falls on mothers.[4] In a sense, technologies such as amniocentesis are allowing pregnant women and their partners to construct the limits of kinship on their own terms, however constrained. Realistically, many fear that the social support that they would need for a disabled child might be difficult to obtain. This was true in many of the narratives of working-class women who chose amniocentesis, who had vivid images of what a chronically ill child might do to their lives. One woman explained her decision to have prenatal testing this way: "With my other two, Lionel worked nights, I'm on days, we managed with a little help from my mother. When Eliza was three, my mother passed on, then my sister, she helped me out as much as she could. With this one, we're planning to ask for help from a neighbor who takes in a few kids. I couldn't keep a baby with health problems. Who would baby sit?" (Rapp 145).

Such stories poignantly illustrate how close to the edge many parents feel when they imagine the juggling of work and family obligations should disability enter an already tight domestic economy. Such stories can also mask deep-seated prejudices against the imagined "courtesy stigma" incurred by those close to people with "spoiled identities" (Goffman). Yet it is important to highlight the material pressures under which many families with two working parents find themselves and which serve as the matrix in which the decision to use prenatal testing is made.

As we noted above, some have argued that, in an upper-middle-class environment where children are increasingly regarded as commodities, genetic testing raises expectations among parents that they can "choose" to have a "perfect" baby (Browner and Press; Corea; Press and Browner). A more complex scenario emerges when women of diverse class, racial, religious, and national backgrounds who were offered prenatal testing were interviewed (Rapp). Whatever their cultural background, most pregnant women and their supporters are concerned not so much with perfection but seek basic health and "normalcy," recognizing the limits of the material circumstances within which they undertake mothering. Indeed, some were willing to live with a range of disabling conditions if they could manage it practically and if the child could enjoy life. Nonetheless, most were frightened by the stigmatizing conditions that the test might predict, about which they knew almost nothing and whose consequences they could only imagine (Rapp). Such conflicted responses are not surprising, given that the survival of disabled infants has escalated dramatically thanks to improvements in infant surgery, antibiotics, and life support technologies. At the same time, the knowledge of what is entailed in caring for such children remains absent from mainstream discourse, underscoring a sense of social segregation and stigma. On the genetic frontier, where the use of prenatal diagnostic technologies is rapidly becoming routine, a gap exists between the medical diagnosis of a fetal anomaly and social knowledge about life with a child who bears that condition. In this gap, the use of amniocentesis and selective abortion becomes perfectly rational. This tendency to marginalize and segregate disability issues will continue, legal progress and expanded public consciousness notwithstanding, until the conditions of care are less privatized and the social fund of knowledge is increased. It is this disjunction, then, between neighboring fields of social knowledge that animates the narrative urgency of those compelled to tell what might be termed their *un-natural histories,* as they struggle to represent the difference that disability makes in the domain of kinship.

Changing Cultural Scripts

The cultural dialectic between perfectibility and inclusion has often animated the work of the activist individuals, families, and groups who are the crucial link between the intimate domain of kinship and the broader public sphere. The utopian promise of perfectible children has had a longstanding hold on the American cultural imagination and is particularly powerful under current technoscientific regimes. At the same time, the ideal of equality has been the touchstone of a range of social movements that demand inclusion for those excluded on the basis of differences coded as biological deficiencies. Over the last twenty-five years, they have helped to catalyze policy initiatives that offer a potentially radical challenge to the boundaries of citizenship and the relations of obligation between (temporarily) able-bodied and dependent people across the life cycle. The IDEA, or Individuals with Disabilities Education Act (1975), followed by the ADA, or Americans with Disabilities Act (1990), are the two key pieces of postwar federal legislation that have established the framework for the civil rights for Americans with disabilities. These accomplishments have dramatically transformed both the institutional and intimate frameworks within which American families operate.

The responses of what Oe calls "disabled families" have shaped and been shaped by these historically shifting conditions. In the 1950s and 1960s, for example, many middle-class parents were commonly advised to institutionalize "non-normal" children whose survival rate was rising due to aggressive medical innovations, erasing their presence from the household and muffling their voices in family stories. Since the 1970s, however, deinstitutionalization and early-intervention programs have increasingly supported families in keeping disabled children at home. Responding to these changed circumstances, some families have begun to articulate new and public versions of domestic life with disabled children in an effort to reconfigure the discursive space defining these social fields. At the same time, a combination of forces—the *Roe v. Wade* decision legalizing abortion in 1973; the international development of prenatal genetic testing; and the rise of second wave feminism, with its advocacy of broad-based options for women's public and private lives—increasingly medicalized and individualized the cultural salience of reproductive choice. Twenty years on, the dilemmas of such "choices" have become a staple of public debate, as powerful medical, genetic, and prosthetic technologies extend and enable fragile lives even as prenatal screening technologies give prospective parents the option to terminate an anomalous pregnancy. Citizens of this "republic of choice" (after Friedman) face contradictory options that exceed the extant frameworks for ethical deliberation. In the contemporary scenario, it is women in particular who have thus been cast as moral pioneers. These anxiety-provoking circumstances generate and are reflected in contemporary public testimony about disability, whether in the work of accomplished writers such as the Nobel Prize–winning Oe or less prominent forms of cultural production. Such narrative engagements with unanticipated difference within the intimate culture of the family can be understood as interventions into the public sphere that—whether intended as such by their authors or not—work to subvert the hegemonic discourse of perfectibility disseminated by such sites as obstetric medicine, middle-class parenting literature, and, more generally, contemporary U.S. models of personhood that valorize celebrity and individual will.

The cultural activity of rewriting life stories and kinship narratives around the fact of disability, whether in memoir, film, or everyday storytelling, enables families to comprehend (in both senses) this anomalous experience, not only because of the capacity of stories to make meaning but also because of their dialogical relationship with larger social arenas. Indeed, the transformation of both emotional and technical knowledge developed in kin groups with disabled family members can foster networks of support from which activism may emerge. In other words, the way that family members articulate changing experiences and awareness of disability in the domain of kinship not only provides a model for the body politic as a whole but also helps to constitute a broader understanding of citizenship in which disability rights are understood as civil rights (Asch, "Reproductive Technology"; Asch, *Women with Disabilities;* Bérubé and Lyon; Kittay; Linton).

Mediating Disability

The creation of kinship ties between nondisabled and disabled people requires the imagining, for many families, of an unanticipated social landscape. This sense of reorientation to a place of possibility, as opposed to disappointment, is evident in the text of a flyer posted prominently in many American pediatric wards. It offers families of chronically ill and disabled children a parable of an unexpected journey to an unknown world, a counternarrative of hope in the face of the sense of crisis experienced by many families with hospitalized offspring:

> *WELCOME TO HOLLAND*
>
> Imagine you have planned a vacation to Italy, to see the rose gardens of Florence. You are totally excited, you have read all the guide books, your suitcases are packed, and off you go. As the plane lands, the pilot announces, "Sorry, ladies and gentlemen, but this flight has been rerouted to the Netherlands." At first you are very upset: the vacation you dreamed about has been canceled. But you get off the plane, determined to make the best of it. And you gradually discover that the blue tulips of Holland are every bit as pretty as the red roses you had hoped to see in Florence. They may not be as famous, but they are every bit as wonderful. You didn't get a red rose. But you got a blue tulip, and that's quite special, too. (Emily Kingsley)[5]

The almost invisible yet widespread circulation of this endlessly xeroxed document joins a range of popular imagery in which people with disabling conditions are becoming ever more visible in the public sphere. There is indeed often a direct relationship between the initial efforts of families to reimagine their narratives and the more public actions they undertake to help rescript narratives of inclusion at a broader cultural level. But the call to rethink kinship enacted in the posting of the Blue Tulips flyer is relatively recent and very much the product of the activism of families who have struggled against the categories imposed by medical and bureaucratic regimes.

The example of Down syndrome can illustrate the negotiation of such a category. Until the 1970s, many U.S. doctors would not treat the esophageal and heart problems for which newborns with DS are at increased risk, although the procedures for repair were increasingly well known. Parents of such children were encouraged to "let go" and often had no source of knowledge with which to dispute medical experts. The result was passive infanticide, or what medical historian Martin Pernick has called the "Black Stork." For children who survived, institutionalization was common; removal from their families was considered the responsible action to take for their care. Children with DS were regarded as incapable of emotional attachment or education. It is only since the 1970s that the conjunction of the deinstitutionalization movement, the creation of early-intervention programs for developmentally delayed infants and toddlers, and the passage of federal and state laws protecting the civil rights of the disabled have provided a social environment in which most families of DS children are now able to take them home at birth. This remarkable shift in biomedical, legal, and familial discourse and practice can be attributed in part to the direct activism of parents' groups such as the Association for Retarded Children (now the ARC) as well as to the indirect impact of writings by the kin of DS people—and eventually by affected individuals themselves—particularly in the form of memoir. Such rescriptings present an alternative world of kinship based on a shared difference, a phenomenon common to many disability support networks (Rapp, Heath, and Taussig). The following quote from two authors who recently became disability activists on behalf of their child clearly acknowledges an indebtedness to those authors whose narratives have created a sense of kinship that spans generations and crosses biological family lines:

> Like all parents of children with Down syndrome, we owe a great deal to the authors of books like *Count Us In*—themselves young men with Down syndrome—and their families for having transformed the social meaning of Down syndrome by helping to develop what's now called "early intervention

> for infants with disabilities." But we also find ourselves *the unwitting heirs of people and movements we never knew we were related to.* We saunter with our Jamie publicly largely thanks to Dale Evans who, in 1953, wrote *Angel Unaware,* a best selling memoir of her daughter Robin who was born with Down syndrome and died at age two. (Bérubé and Lyon 274)

Despite the progress that has been made since the publication of *Angel Unaware,* bringing a child with DS home is still an act of personal assertion in the United States; in New York state and many other places, the mother of a newborn diagnosed in hospital is always offered fosterage or adoption placement. While this practice is shockingly offensive to many new mothers, we should point out that it developed with "the best interests of the child" in mind. Hospital personnel know that disabled babies are at high risk of being abandoned; as they grow older and more difficult to care for, they also grow harder to place in a good home. As newborns are the easiest babies to place, social workers offer information on adoption right away. But the practice has an unintended consequence. The task of composing a normalizing narrative that can create a space of inclusion for the DS child within the family circle is immediately thrust upon the mother, who has to justify to medical personnel the otherwise unproblematic action of taking her newborn home with her.

Constructing such a normalizing narrative is an ongoing process. Down syndrome affects the full spectrum of class and ethnic differences in the United States, and parents of DS children pursue a correspondingly wide variety of strategies for expanding the reach and support of their children's lives. The established script of Down syndrome is being rewritten across a range of sites in a way that opens up a supportive universe for disabled people and their kin. The Special Olympics, infant stimulation programs, consciousness-raising and other sorts of events organized by the disability-rights community, and Internet chat groups are all examples of sites that can help reconfigure community for dubious family members.

These forms of positive public mediation of disabled people play an important role in refiguring the cultural landscape for new generations of families engaging with the social fact of disability. The activism of one parent, Emily Kingsley, a scriptwriter for the children's television program *Sesame Street,* is exemplary of this process. Kingsley was told that her son "would never have a single meaningful thought" when Jason was born and diagnosed with Down syndrome. She was counseled to institutionalize Jason immediately and to "try again" (Kingsley and Levitz 3). Instead, she wrote him into the script of *Sesame Street,* where he appeared throughout his childhood. Contrary to the dire predictions for his intelligence, at age six he was "counting in Spanish for the cameras" (4). The Kingsleys' cultural activism opened the door for people with other disabilities—people using wheelchairs, braces, and seeing-eye dogs—to appear as part of the quotidian world of mass media that is now an integral part of the public sphere of most postindustrial countries. Jason himself went on to coauthor the aforementioned book, *Count Us In,* with his friend Mitchell Levitz, who also has DS. Later, his mother scripted a prime-time docudrama based on her family's experiences, entitled *Kids Like These* (CBS, 1991). Of course, this ability to work in (and have access to) such media venues is not simply a matter of individual achievement but also of the cultural capital of activist families. As Bérubé and Lyon (282) point out: "Their fame . . . depends on their good fortune: not only were they born into extremely supportive families that contested the medical wisdom of their day, but they were born into families well-positioned for activism." Another mother, Gail Williamson, whose son Blair has DS and has also appeared on television, was moved to establish Hollywood's first talent agency for disabled actors in the entertainment industry (Gray).

Many Americans met their first person with Down syndrome in the late 1980s through the virtual presence in their living rooms of Chris Burke, who became a teen star in NBC's *Life Goes On.* Introduced by the Beatles' popular song, "Life Goes On," the show provided a realistic depiction of disability as part of everyday family life, while indexing, as the theme song's lyrics do, an optimistic message of possibility. But Chris's story is not only about his heroic triumph over adversity as an individual (Burke and McDaniel). It is imbricated in the complex nexus of changing contexts sketched above that have radically altered the biomedical, familial, practical, and legal narratives structuring disability in America over the last three decades.

Inevitably, the advertising industry was quick to follow the lead of *Life Goes On,* recognizing the potential for growth not only in direct sales to market niches ranging from psychotropic pharmaceuticals to adaptive technologies but also in a more indirect appeal to the loyalty of families with disabled members, through the inclusion of DS kids and teens in commercials for McDonald's, Benetton, and even in popular advertising circulars. Such efforts have been subject to criticism from some activists for reducing issues of citizenship to consumption. Yet the presence of people with visible disabilities in the landscape of popular and commercial culture has been embraced enthusiastically by many families as a sign of the growing public incorporation of this historically stigmatized difference. It speaks as well to the erasure of disabled characters that continues to prevail in the popular media since the appearance of such figures, even in advertising, is still regarded as exceptional.

"What Are You Staring At?"

Whatever progress has been made, there are still relatively few televisual spaces for children that regularly feature kids with disabilities talking about their own lives (as opposed to what some disabled children refer to as "models in wheelchairs"). The shows discussed above are salient exceptions, as is the Nickelodeon children's cable network's magazine program *Nick News.* "What Are You Staring At?" was an innovative special produced by *Nick News* and aired repeatedly during 1999. The half-hour program featured a group of kids and teens with a range of disabilities—DS, hearing and visual impairments, cerebral palsy, polio, burn injuries—talking about their lives with celebrity crips, journalist John Hockenberry and actor Christopher Reeve. The anecdote that follows, an account of one youngster's experience of this show, may be read as an illustration of the way that such public interventions can help to create an alternative horizon of kinship extending beyond the nuclear family.

In the summer of 1999 in New York City, ten-year-old Samantha Myers surfed onto "What Are You Staring At?" and was riveted. When the final credits ended, she announced to her mother that she wanted to talk about her disability on television. Samantha's disorder, Familial Dysautonomia (FD),[6] is an extremely rare condition of the involuntary nervous system that affects all forms of body regulation, including temperature, blood pressure, swallowing, and respiration. With some adult assistance she found the Website for the Make-A-Wish Foundation, a group that grants "wishes" to children with life-threatening diseases. She e-mailed them, explaining that her wish was to go on *Nick News* and talk about her life with FD. Within two weeks, she was working with a friend and a Make-A-Wish volunteer, making a pitch book with Polaroid photos and handwritten text about her life and disability. Sam's inventory of her life included police-style pictures she took of all her medical equipment, as well as photos of her dog, friends, and relatives.

By her eleventh birthday, she was working with a producer from *Nick News* to make a five-minute segment that she narrated, replete with footage of her school, doctor, friends, and some whimsical computer animation to make it kid-friendly. In late April of 2000, the show was broadcast; as a result, over the next few months Sam was invited to show her tape and to talk to a number of groups. Of greatest significance to Sam was that so many FD kids were able to see another child like themselves on television. She was deluged with e-mail from families with FD children around the country who were thrilled to see an image and story that for once included their experience. Many, like Sam, went on to use copies of the tape to help teachers and classmates at school understand the particular issues that kids with FD face on a daily basis.

Mediated Kinship

The media world into which Sam surfed at the end of the twentieth century is evidence of a transforming public culture in which disability is becoming a more visible presence in daily life. This anecdotal evidence—Sam's immediate sense of kinship with the disabled kids she saw and heard on television and her desire to join that process—suggests how significant such imagery can be to those who do not see themselves regularly in dominant forms of representation. Indeed, much of the early writing in disability studies focused not only on the need for changes in civil rights legislation but also on the absence of disabled people from literature and popular media—or, where present, the negativity of their portrayal, citing the legacy of freak shows, circuses, and asylums (Bogdan; Thomson). Others were working actively to alter the media landscape itself. Along with parent-activists who worked in the mainstream media such as Emily Kingsley, there were people like Mary Johnson and Cass Irvin, who founded in 1980 the alternative journal *The Disability Rag* (Shaw). Nowadays, the work of activists in visual media is increasingly evident in the plethora of photography shows and film and video festivals devoted, in part or entirely, to the topic of disability. And, of course, the Websites, e-lists, and chat groups of the Internet have dramatically expanded the range of sites at which images of disability are being negotiated.

The circulatory reach of electronic media is the key factor in the creation of what we call *mediated kinship*. Emerging as a neighboring—and sometimes overlapping—field to the formal, institutionalized discourse of disability rights, mediated kinship offers a critique of normative American family life that is embedded within everyday cultural practice. Across many genres, a common theme is an implicit rejection of the pressure to produce "perfect families" through the incorporation of difference under the sign of love and intimacy in the domain of kinship relations. We suggest that these mediated spaces of public intimacy—talk shows, on-line disability support groups, Websites, and so on—are crucial to building a social fund of knowledge more inclusive of the fact of disability. These media practices provide a counterdiscourse to the naturalized stratification of family membership that for so long has marginalized, in particular those disabled from birth. It is not only the acceptance of difference within families but also the embrace of relatedness that such models of inclusion present to the body politic that makes these spaces potentially radical in their implications. As sites of information and free play of imagination, these cultural forms help to create a new social landscape.

The struggle to form inclusive familial units takes place within an increasingly complex discursive world, a terrain in which the so-called genetic revolution—and the part played within it by prenatal testing—cannot be ignored. One suggestive source of images by which that revolution is imagined is via a classic trope of science fiction: the neoeugenic dystopia, as portrayed in such books as *The Handmaid's Tale* (Atwood) and films as *Gattaca* (Andrew Niccol, 1997); these are stories of monstrous kinship. But a more common discursive field is the science or business page of the newspaper, where advances in scientific knowledge, especially genetic technologies, are regularly reported yet the social dilemmas they index go largely undiscussed.

These dilemmas beg questions about who is entitled to make interventions into reproduction, the capacity of kinship to encompass difference, and the social location of care. While these are experienced as private, family matters, they cannot be contained within domestic domains. Caretaking is perhaps the most naturalized of these, conventionally attached to the unpaid labor of women in the home. Yet, in the United States, it is rapidly becoming a politicized arena in a privatizing economy in which families are expected to be "always on call," as Carol Levine argues in her book of that title, to care for disabled kin (Levine, ed.; see also Nussbaum). If paid, the labor of family caregivers would cost about $200 billion a year (Langone). Nevertheless, while health insurance increasingly covers the routinization of new reproductive technologies (NRTs) and the costs of neonatal intensive care units (NICUs), most home-based personal assistance—a need estimated at twenty-one billion hours yearly—goes unpaid by public funds despite the demonstrable bodily, emotional, and economic benefits of deinstitutionalizing support (Johnson 14; Linton; Russell). This is a skeletal sketch of the political economy of health care and assisted living "choices" that affects all Americans. Yet it is a barely visible landscape to most people unless and until their own or a family member's disability reveals its limitations on a practical, daily level.[7]

These revelations of the limits of kinship-based caretaking and the need for broader social recognition and resources for people with disabilities fuel the narrative urgency we have described throughout, beginning with Oe's compelling story of a "healing family," offering stories of familial inclusion that can serve as models of social inclusion as well. Additionally, progress in legal arenas has problematized the presumption of American citizenship as the exclusive entitlement of a normative able-bodied, non-dependent, wage-earning individual. At best, this model of personhood describes only a portion of the normal human life cycle. At worst, it systematically erases the rights of the disabled and their caretakers to have their fundamental needs addressed in the public arena.

While we have focused here on the nexus of disability rights and reproductive decision-making as highlighted in the parent-child relationship, kinship and disability—as instantiated by congenital difference, accident, illness, infancy, or old age—remain entwined throughout the life cycle. Thus, the disjunction between the aspiration for democratic inclusion and the fantasy of bodily perfectibility through technological intervention has energized much popular cultural expression, creating a growing sense of public intimacy with experiences of disability. In this gap, disability narratives offer what we have called unnatural histories, visions of lives lived against the grain of normalcy. It is here, we have argued, that the relations of kinship have the capacity to enable disability, giving narrative shape and cultural imagination to efforts to form a more perfect union.

NOTES

We have many people to thank, first and foremost our children, who have opened our eyes to worlds more exotic than we ever imagined we would encounter as anthropologists. We thank Carol A. Breckenridge, Candace Vogler, and the Board of Public Culture for helpful comments and Barbara Abrash and Simi Linton for their constructive engagement with the final draft.

1. Oe's writings point to the impossibility of individual solutions—even at the level of narrative—to what are cultural and social dilemmas. In a kind of parallel process, Oe has also written movingly on the aftermath of Hiroshima, an assignment he began the same year Hikari was born. This project enabled him to cope with the incomprehensibility of his son's condition by placing it in an even more inexplicable context of social suffering.

2. For example, national attention was riveted on the upper-middle-class Kelso family of suburban Philadelphia in December 1999, when they abandoned their ten-year-old son, Steven, with his diapers, medications, toys, and medical records, at the Dupont Hospital for Children in Wilmington, Delaware. Their nursing schedule had fallen apart over the holidays, and the parents claimed they could no longer cope with the intensity of their child's needs. While stories of abandonment are not uncommon, this one made public headlines in part because the mother had been a prominent volunteer on the Pennsylvania Developmental Disabilities Council.

3. The recent explosion of U.S. writing on disability, building on the groundbreaking work of scholars/activists who have been writing since the 1970s, is reflected in such developments as the dramatic growth of the Society for Disability Studies, the launching of new book series such as Corporalities: Discourses of Disability (edited by David T. Mitchell and Sharon Snyder for the University of Michigan Press), and the creation of university-based disabilities studies programs such as the one at the University of Illinois at Chicago. All are founded on a commitment to the centrality of disabled people, both as researchers and subjects (e.g., Charlton, *Nothing about Us without Us*). In anthropology, the efforts of pioneers such as Robert Edgerton (first published in 1967) and Henri-Jacques Stiker (first published in 1982) have been joined by an emerging scholarship focusing on issues ranging from stigma (Ingstad and Whyte, eds.), to cultural communities of difference (Groce), to the phenomenology of differently abled bodies (Frank; Murphy).

4. Of course, fathers have frequently been deeply involved and committed to this kind of labor, and have played exemplary public roles as well (e.g., Bérubé; Oe). However, the high divorce rates in families with disabled children is one indication that such fathers might be more the exception than the rule. We also note the gendered nature of caretaking and the professions associated with it, such as nursing, home health care, special education, and occupational and physical therapy.

5. Rayna Rapp first heard this parable at a Down syndrome parent's support group in 1985. It was plastered on the walls of the pediatric ward Faye Ginsburg occupied with her daughter for most of 1989. More elaborate versions have since appeared in print, at sites as diverse as the Brooklyn waiting room of a school board committee on special education and the back of a newsletter for parents of disabled children.

6. Information on FD is readily accessible at two Websites: <http://www.familialdysautonomia.org> and <http://www.FDVillage.org>.

7. In the United States and throughout much of the world, the tasks of caretaking continue to be naturalized in the domain of unpaid domestic labor. Increasingly, however, challenges to this situation are emerging as a result of the expanding needs of caretaking over the life cycle. The increased rate of survival among such formerly high-risk groups as low-birth-weight babies, the chronically ill, and the elderly make claims on public resources, usually mediated through their kin. Advocacy groups such as the growing movement for Independent Living seek public support for personal assistance, a policy which, they argue, "would relieve an enormous amount of stress on families and, over time . . . would begin to alter the public perception toward significantly disabled people and the people who relate to them" (Marca Bistro, head of the National Council on Disability, quoted in Johnson 14).

Works Cited

Asch, Adrienne. "Reproductive Technology and Disability." In *Reproductive Laws for the 1990s.* Ed. Sherrill Cohen and Nadine Taub, 59–101. Clifton, N.J.: Humana Press, 1989.

———. *Women with Disabilities: Essays in Psychology, Culture, and Politics.* Philadelphia: Temple University Press, 1988.

Atwood, Margaret. *The Handmaid's Tale.* Boston: Houghton-Mifflin, 1986.

Beck, Martha N. *Expecting Adam: A True Story of Birth, Rebirth, and Everyday Magic.* New York: Times Books, 1999.

Berlant, Lauren. "Intimacy: A Special Issue." *Critical Inquiry* 24, no. 2 (1998): 281–88.

Bérubé, Michael. *Life as We Know It: A Father, a Family, and an Exceptional Child.* New York: Pantheon, 1996.

———, and Janet Lyon. "Living on Disability: Language and Social Policy in the Wake of the ADA." In *The Visible Woman: Imaging Technologies, Gender, and Science.* Ed. Paula. A. Treichler, Lisa Cartwright, and Constance Penley, 273–84. New York: New York University Press, 1998.

Blair, John. "Online Deliveries Lighten Burden for the Disabled." *New York Times,* Sept. 5, 2000, B1, B5.

Bogdan, Robert. *Freak Show: Presenting Human Oddities for Amusement and Profit.* Chicago: University of Chicago Press, 1988.

Brewster, Arlene. "After Hours: A Patient's Reaction to Amniocentesis." *Obstetrics and Gynecology* 64, no. 3 (1984): 443–44.

Browner, Carol H., and Nancy Ann Press. "The Production of Authoritative Knowledge in American Prenatal Care." *Medical Anthropology Quarterly* 10, no. 2 (1996): 141–56.

Burke, Chris, and Jo Beth McDaniel. *A Special Kind of Hero: Chris Burke's Own Story.* New York: Doubleday, 1991.

Charlton, James. *Nothing about Us without Us: Disability, Oppression and Empowerment.* Berkeley: University of California Press, 1998.

Corea, Gena. *The Mother Machine: Reproductive Technologies from Artificial Insemination to Artificial Wombs.* New York: Harper and Row, 1985.

Edgerton, Robert B. *The Cloak of Competence: Stigma in the Lives of the Mentally Retarded.* 1967. Reprint. Berkeley: University of California Press, 1993.

Evans, Dale. *Angel Unaware.* Westwood: Revell, 1953.

Featherstone, Helen. *A Difference in the Family: Life with a Disabled Child.* New York: Basic Books, 1980.

Finger, Anne. *Past Due: A Story of Disability, Pregnancy, and Birth.* Seattle: Seal Press, 1990.

Frank, Gelya. *Venus on Wheels: Two Decades of Dialogue on Disability, Biography, and Being Female in America.* Berkeley: University of California Press, 2000.

Friedman, Lawrence. *Republic of Choice: Law, Authority and Culture.* Cambridge: Harvard University Press, 1990.

Fries, Kenny, ed. *Staring Back: The Disability Experience from the Inside Out.* New York: Plume, 1997.

Ginsburg, Faye, and Rayna Rapp. "Fetal Reflections: Confessions of Two Feminist Anthropologists as Mutual Informants." In *Fetal Subject, Feminist Postions.* Ed. Lynn M. Morgan and Meredith W. Michaels, 279–97. Philadelphia: University of Pennsylvania Press, 1999.

Goffman, Erving. *Stigma: Notes on the Management of Spoiled Identity.* Englewood Cliffs: Prentice-Hall, 1963.

Gray, Barbara. "They're Her All-Star Kids." *Family Circle,* July 13, 1999, 15–18.

Green, Rose. "Letter to a Genetic Counselor." *Journal of Genetic Counseling* 1, no. 1 (1992): 55–70.

Groce, Nora. *Everyone Here Spoke Sign Language: Hereditary Deafness on Martha's Vineyard.* Cambridge: Harvard University Press, 1985.
Handler, Lowell. *Twitch and Shout: A Tourreter's Tale.* New York: Dutton: 1998.
Hardacre, Helen. *Marketing the Menacing Fetus in Japan.* Berkeley: University of California Press, 1997.
Hirschman, Albert O. *The Passions and the Interests: Political Arguments for Capitalism before Its Triumph.* Princeton: Princeton University Press, 1977.
Hockenberry, John. *Moving Violations: War Zones, Wheelchairs, and Declarations of Independence.* New York: Hyperion, 1995.
Ingstad, Benedicte, and Susanne Reynolds Whyte, eds. *Disability and Culture.* Berkeley: University of California Press, 1995.
Jablow, Martha Moraghan. *Cara: Growing with a Retarded Child.* Philadelphia: Temple University Press, 1982.
Johnson, Mary. "The 'Care' Juggernaut." *Ragged Edge* 21 (Nov.–Dec. 2000): 10–12, 14.
Kingsley, Emily. "Welcome to Holland" at <http://www.nas.com/downsyn/holland.html>.
Kingsley, Jason, and Mitchell Levitz. *Count Us In: Growing Up with Down Syndrome.* New York: Harcourt Brace, 1994.
Kittay, Eva Feder. *Love's Labor: Essays on Women, Equality, and Dependency.* New York: Routledge, 1999.
Kolker, Aliza, and Meredith Burke. "Grieving the Wanted Child." *Health Care for Women International* 14, no. 6 (1993): 513–26.
Kuusisto, Stephen. *Planet of the Blind: A Memoir.* New York: Delta, 1998.
Landsman, Gail. "Does God Give Special Kids to Special Parents? Personhood and the Child with Disabilities as Gift and as Giver." In *Transformative Motherhood: On Giving and Getting in a Consumer Culture.* Ed. Linda L. Layne, 133–66. New York: New York University Press, 1999.
———. "'Real Motherhood': Class and Children with Disabilities." In *Technologies and Ideologies of Motherhood: Race, Class, Sexuality, Nationalism.* Ed. France Winddance Twine and Heléna Ragoné, 169–90. New Brunswick: Rutgers University Press, 1999.
Langone, John. "When Friends and Family Fill Most of a Patient's Medical Needs." *New York Times,* Oct. 12, 2000, F6.
Layne, Linda. "'How's the Baby Doing?': Struggling with Narratives of Progress in a Neonatal Intensive Care Unit." *Medical Anthropological Quarterly* 10, no. 4 (1996): 624–56.
Levine, Carol, ed. *Always on Call: When Illness Turns Families into Caregivers.* New York: United Hospital Fund of New York, 2000.
Linton, Simi. *Claiming Disability: Knowledge and Identity.* New York: New York University Press, 1998.
Mairs, Nancy. *Waist-High in the World: A Life among the Non-Disabled.* Boston: Beacon, 1996.
McGee, Glenn. *The Perfect Baby: A Pragmatic Approach to Genetics.* New York: Rowman and Littlefield, 1997.
Murphy, Robert. *The Body Silent.* New York: Henry Holt, 1987.

Nussbaum, Martha. "Disabled Lives: Who Cares?" *New York Review of Books,* Jan. 11, 2001, 34–37.

O'Connell, Linda G., and Lisa G. Foster. "Uncommon Children." *Mt. Holyoke Alumnae Quarterly* (Spring 2000): 13–18.

Oe, Kenzaburo. *A Healing Family.* Ed. S. Shaw. Trans. Stephen Snyder. Tokyo: Kodansha International, 1995.

Parens, Erik, and Adrienne Asch, eds. *Prenatal Testing and Disability Rights.* Washington: Georgetown University Press, 2000.

Pernick, Martin S. *The Black Stork: Eugenics and the Death of "Defective" Babies in American Medicine and Motion Pictures since 1915.* New York: Oxford University Press, 1996.

Press, Nancy Ann, and Carol H. Browner. "The Normalization of Prenatal Diagnostic Screening." In *Conceiving the New World Order: The Global Politics of Reproduction.* Ed. Faye D. Ginsburg and Rayna Rapp, 307–22. Berkeley: University of California Press, 1995.

Rapp, Rayna. *Testing Women, Testing the Fetus: The Social Impact of Amniocentesis in America.* New York: Routledge, 1999.

———, Deborah Heath, and Karen Sue Taussig. "Genealogical Dis-ease: Where Hereditary Abnormality, Biomedical Explanation, and Family Responsibility Meet." In *Relative Values: Reconfiguring Kinship.* Ed. Sarah Franklin and Susan MacKinnon, 384–409. Durham: Duke University Press, 2002.

Russell, Marta. *Beyond Ramps: Disability at the End of the Social Contract: A Warning from an Uppity Crip.* Monroe, Maine: Common Courage, 1998.

Seligman, Milton, and Rosalyn Benjamin Darling. *Ordinary Families, Special Children: A Systems Approach to Childhood Disability.* New York: Guilford, 1989.

Shaw, Barrett. *The Ragged Edge: The Disability Experience from the Pages of the First Fifteen Years of* The Disability Rag. Louisville: Advocado Press, 1994.

Stiker, Henri-Jacques. *A History of Disability.* Trans. William Sayers. 1982. Reprint. Ann Arbor: University of Michigan Press, 1999.

Thomson, Rosemarie Garland. *Extraordinary Bodies: Figuring Physical Disability in American Culture and Literature.* New York: Columbia University Press, 1997.

8 Virtuous Cuts: Female Genital Circumcision in an African Ontology

ROGAIA MUSTAFA ABUSHARAF

The only basis of power is "virtue."
—Bourdieu

MUCH HAS BEEN WRITTEN on gender violence in Africa. In this burgeoning literature, African women are repeatedly painted as downtrodden, forlorn, helpless casualties of male dominance. Their confinement in antiquated customs and cultural practices is viewed as puissant testimony to their eternal vassalage to patriarchy and, consequently, of their subjugation within both the so-called "public" and "private" spheres. This view is exemplified in the following passage from the *Hosken Report:*

> Genital and Sexual Mutilation of Females: [Africa] is a region where absolute patriarchy is the rule, where women are deprived of property and land rights, where polygamy and wife abuse are the rule and where male domination is absolute both in the village as well as in national governments. It is, therefore, clear that men are responsible for the worsening conditions in Africa: women and children are the abused and voiceless victims. The time to blame colonial powers is long since over—but the time for African men to take a look at themselves as persons and human beings in our modern world is long overdue. (Hosken 69)

When the report discusses female circumcision, it treats it as the violent sexual mutilation of females and contends that the operation has been perpetuated by the male-dominated tribal societies of Africa to suppress women's sexuality. To readers of Fran Hosken's *Report,* Esther Hicks's *Infibulation: Female Mutilation in Islamic Northeastern Africa,* or Alice Walker and Pratibha Parmar's *Warrior Marks: Female Genital Mutilation and the Sexual Blinding of Women,* the tyranny of patriarchy and the oppressive nature of gender relations in African cultures are evidenced most dramatically in the cultural practice of female circumcision. These representations stress a notion of patriarchy in which the African woman is seen as wholly subservient, passive, "voiceless": someone whose sexual and reproductive potential is controlled by men and whose genitals are mutilated in silence and without protest. However, as the narratives below make clear, African women, not men, insist on circumcising their daughters. Through ritual performance, these women ensure the transmission of cultural ethos within their lifetimes. As philosopher Diana Meyers argues, "Many Euro-Americans might doubt that there is any basis for the women of Douroshab ascribing autonomy to women whose cultures mandate [female genital mutilation]. Yet, the feminist literature on the [practice] provides ample evidence that many exercise effective agency with respect to this practice. One striking finding is that autonomy is to be found among accommodators as well as resisters" (1). In this essay, I want to shift the emphasis from agency and autonomy to a discussion of the ideology that shapes women's participation in the ritual.

Is circumcision a vicious act of mutilation and injury or a virtuous act of purity and rectitude? I have collected the personal narratives of a group of African women in order to untangle the ideology that lies beneath the persistence of this ritual. The ethnographic material presented here was gathered in the Arabic-speaking Muslim township of Douroshab, Sudan, during two periods of fieldwork in 1996 and 1998. I have focused on this township because of the ubiquity of infibulation, the most drastic type of genital surgery performed on girls. Before I proceed, a brief overview of the ritual in Africa, in general, and Sudan, in particular, will help put this material in context.

Female Circumcision and the Controversy It Has Engendered

For many years now, female circumcision has had "only paradoxes to offer"—to borrow from Joan Scott's provocative title. While viewed by the international community and many feminists as a disquieting, misogynous ritual, circumcision is defended by its practitioners as an act of virtue. This controversy is not recent. Historical documents from various parts of colonial Africa suggest that angry reactions toward the practice were frequent, especially in the case of European missionaries, who played an integral role in the work of the "civilizing" colonial apparatus. In large part because of the European animosity toward circumcision, the practice became a focus of African resistance to foreign encroachment and interference. For the Africans in question, female circumcision was largely seen as a revered rite rather than a senseless act devoid of meaning or significance. It was (and still is) viewed as belonging to the domain of African indigenous personality known as "Africanity" (Conteh 223). The term *Africanity* denotes "the variety of indigenous customs that has provided Africans with answers to the basic questions of their existence, from how they came into being to how they cope with the problems of daily life" (Skinner 60). From the perspective of Africanity, female circumcision expresses the significant tension that erupted between new, imported colonialist structures and old, resilient African cultures (Mazrui).

The angry emotional responses to female circumcision did not end with missionary efforts or colonial occupation. These feelings continue to be expressed at various feminist gatherings, such as the World Conference of the United Nations Decade for Women held at Copenhagen in July 1980, in which discussions of genital cutting, which became known as female genital mutilation, not only sent shock waves through angry delegates but also provided the forum for the first international conflict between African and Western women (Thaim). As Sudanese scholar and activist Nahid Toubia argues: "[These feminists] have acted as though they have suddenly discovered a dangerous epidemic, which they then sensationalized in international women's forums creating a backlash of oversensitivity in the concerned communities. They have portrayed it as irrefutable evidence of the barbarism and vulgarity of underdeveloped countries. It became a conclusive validation of the view of the primitiveness of Arabs, Muslims and Africans, all in one blow" (101).

This feminist discourse, which is closely associated with liberal/individualist ethics and as such exemplified in the democracies of the Western world, has undeniable implications for molding and texturing modern debates about female circumcision in the West (Abul Fadl, "Revisiting"; Abul Fadl, "Sexuality in Islam").

In many countries of the developing world, where specific forms of cultural expression such as female circumcision are often perceived by the international community as violence against women, liberal rights discourse is now seen as an ethnocentric condemnation of cultural difference. In these debates, not only is a unified, undifferentiated image of the "African woman" cultivated in the popular imagination. The increasingly informed efforts of African women and men to extirpate circumcision, which testify to new forms of *internal* cultural critique, are also rendered trivial and inconsequential.[1]

Whether genital cutting is called "circumcision" or "mutilation" is in and of itself telling of the inimical ideological debates and contrasting systems of knowledge at stake in the controversy. As David Fraser correctly argues,

> What is at stake in each deployment, each signifying debate, is clearly a battle over the characterization of a complex and nuanced set of social and cultural practices which will best capture the "reality" of what is "happening." In other words, the terminological debate is occurring in the rhetorical sphere of political and ideological phenomenology. At the same time, the linguistic strategy is also to obtain and maintain a canonical textual interpretive status, to define and to confine, to establish the boundaries and borders which in turn define strategies of exclusion and alterity. (338–39)

It can be argued that the differences in terminology not only reflect two divergent systems of knowledge, but also indicate some of the shortcomings of the feminist emphasis on the global uniformity of women's oppression irrespective of culture, class, or ethnic differences. Although the Arabic term for circumcision, *tahara,* also means purification, many feminists see it *only* as mutilation: a brutal act of dominance, violence, and transgression. One of the most significant aspects of this controversy has raged in anthropology, whose tradition of cultural relativism stresses the importance of understanding the human condition in all its manifestations and variations. Thus anthropologists argue that to understand female circumcision properly, we must grasp it in its context. Interest in the practice originates from an anthropological preoccupation with both rituals and bodies, the latter of which has been raised "to the status of a primary category of social and cultural theory . . . over the past two decades" (T. Turner 143). As a form of bodily modification in many societies, the circumcision ritual of male and female has captivated the ethnographic imagination. From Arnold van Gennep's *Rites of Passage,* Victor Turner's *The Forest of Symbols,* and Hamid Ammar's *Growing Up in an Egyptian Village* to Maurice Bloch's *From Blessing to Violence,* anthropologists have focused on circumcision as a cultural expression involving the body, its modifications, and the ensuing cultural and sociopolitical implications.

These scholars, then, have attempted to offer theoretical frameworks within which the body's symbolic, cognitive, political, and aesthetic processes can be explored. For example, in a recent essay, "Body and Mind in Mind, Body and Mind in Body," Michael Lambek demonstrates the ways in which "the body substantiates socially significant distinctions and relationships" (108). Descriptions of the body "as representation," as "a medium of social value," and as "community" are prevalent in detailed ethnographic accounts of local ritual surrounding the body, including circumcision rituals (T. Turner passim).

Feminists and other human rights activists, however, are often indifferent to these considerations; they consider circumcision a form of violence against women, indistinguishable from murder, rape, trafficking, forced prostitution, physical and emotional abuse, stalking, and sexual harassment. The recent criminalization of the practice in the United States, Canada, and Western Europe is an outcome of this position. These activists argue that female circumcision transgresses three primary, *universally accepted* articles of human rights protection: the right to health, the rights of children, and the right of bodily integrity.[2] The reason this controversy has been so significant, then, is that many of the issues it raises do not address genital cutting as ritualized surgery. Rather, this controversy encompasses a concatenation of issues relating to culture, gender, feminism, context, anthropology, human rights, women's agency, self and other, civilization and barbarism.

Circumcision in Sudan: An Overview

The practice of female circumcision is not universally practiced in Sudanese society. As in other African communities, the origin of these practices cannot be ascertained or pinpointed with any certainty. In part, this obscurity can be attributed to the marked sociocultural and religious diversity of Sudanese society. Most ethnographic studies of Sudan have judiciously distinguished Sudanese peoples according to discrete primordial cosmologies and social categories based on ethnic, religious, and regional distinctions. Sudanese ethnic structure is, however, even more complex than these studies acknowledge; it includes Nubians, Arabs, Nuba, Niolitics, Beja, and Azande, among other groups too numerous to enumerate.

Among the groups that observe genital surgeries, both boys and girls undergo circumcision rites. While most observers point out the negative attitudes toward uncircumcised women, Sudanese linguist Abdallah Eltayeb points to similar reactions to uncircumcised males: "Male circumcision was believed by the pre-Islamic Arabs to have something to do with the moon. They believed that the moon would partly circumcise an uncircumcised causing the foreskin to contract, hence the abusive remark 'he is uncircumcised but for the portion taken by the moon.'"

For women, the practice comprises a variety of ritualized surgeries, including clitoridectomy, excision, and infibulation, all of which have been performed for thousands of years. These operations are performed on girls ranging in age from a few days old to puberty. Trained or untrained midwives, traditional healers, barbers, and occasionally doctors may perform the surgeries. The ritual itself is a source of joyous celebration and elaborate festivities for males. However, with some exceptions, for females it is concealed and shrouded in secrecy. The reasons for female circumcision and the age at which it is performed differ across Sudan by regional, ethnic, and class differences. There is also variation in its prevalence, in the exact type of surgery practiced, and in the rituals associated with it. And, as we will see from the narratives gathered from Douroshab, even women of similar regions and backgrounds may understand the practice and its effects in vastly different ways. Despite the prevalence of the ritual, historically there has also been strong opposition that can be traced to the precolonial era, when indigenous efforts attempted to extirpate it. The first resolute and strong anti-circumcision movement in precolonial Sudan was religiously galvanized in the name of Islam. Before the annexation of the Sudan by Mohamed Ali, in the Turco-Egyptian Empire in 1821, El Sheikh Hassan wad Hassona, then a powerful religious cleric, initiated a campaign to exonerate Islam and redefine its position, especially in the eyes of people who attributed circumcision to Islamic religious ideology. To this day, older women avow the miracles of this cleric, who convinced many that people can be circumcised without genital cutting, when they utter the following words: "Ya Barakat elsheikh Hassan" (The infinite funds of blessings of Sheikh Hassan) / "Wad Hassona," (the son of Hassona) / "Tabab el majnnona" (the curer of the deranged) / "El sabbah el bit mahssona" (whose female client woke up one morning beautified by *sunna* circumcision even without cutting).[3]

Other equally influential religious clerics, such as Sheik Hamad wad Umm Marioam and Farah wad Takttook, also voiced their vehement opposition to female circumcision. These holy men influenced local discourses on culture, tradition, religion, and sexuality as early as 1861. But colonial intervention helped to engender opposing forces. In 1945, during the British colonial rule that began in 1898, a law was passed prohibiting infibulation, the most extreme type of genital operation. Subsequently, a midwife in the town of Ruffaa, on the eastern bank of the Nile, was sentenced to six months in prison for circumcising a girl. Mahmoud Mohamed Taha, the leader of the Republican Brothers political group, led a protest against the British action—a protest that soon developed into a popular uprising (El-Beshir). It is important to note, however, that Taha's protests had little to do with male supremacist tendencies; rather, they followed inevitably from his view of British intervention in the cultural life of Sudanese people as a vile, disparaging attack on Sudanese sovereignty and identity. His action should therefore be situated within the context of the nationalist anti-colonial struggles being fought at the time.

Despite Sudanese disdain for, and resistance to, colonial intervention, the British steadfastly pursued their anti-circumcision campaign (Beasley). On December 30, 1945, an ordinance making pharaonic circumcision illegal was adopted. The British were still seeking the support of prestigious political and religious figures with sizable followings to support the law in 1946, however, and Imam Abdel Rahman Almahdi of the Ansar sect and Ali El Merghani of the Khatmiya, two men wielding considerable power in Sudanese society because of their social positions, wealth, and piety, were asked to approach their followers and others who invoked religious arguments in support of circumcision. These two men contested the authenticity of the most famous sayings of Prophet Mohamed that appeared to pardon and condone female circumcision. In the end, the British laws were far from effective. Colonial rule had brought to Sudanese society the notion that things could be different, that nothing was given and that whatever existed was subject to challenge and transformation, so it should come as no surprise that many people harbored a deep suspicion of British proscriptions, which they were reluctant to heed. Despite the ban and the threat of incarceration, the majority of Sudanese women continued to practice infibulation (*elkhifad elpharoni*). Fifteen people were reported to have been prosecuted for infibulating their daughters in 1948, which testifies to the fact that the law did not end the practice. The ritual was simply practiced clandestinely. From the time of Sudan's independence in 1956 until the end of the 1970s, new plans were formulated to stop female circumcision. Attention now focused on those social and cultural aspects of the practice that accounted for its endurance in Sudanese society. More recently, several organizations, including the Sudan National Committee for Traditional Practices Affecting the Health of Women and Children, the Red Crescent, and the Mutawinat Group have identified research strategies and adopted a variety of approaches to female circumcisions, the most notable of which include community outreach through the use of mass media, audiovisual aids, and publications. Another approach aims to incorporate efforts to end female circumcision into existing programs concerned with public health, family planning, maternal and child care, midwifery training, and nutrition. Despite the strong anti-circumcision campaign in the Sudan, however, female circumcision has persisted.

The Ethnographic Context: The Place Called Douroshab

From Khartoum, the capital city of the Sudan, one travels about fifty miles northward, crossing the Blue Nile Bridge, to reach historic Halfi at Elmoolouk and then Douroshab Township. Home to some three thousand residents, it is considered to be a semi-urban community comprised of ethnically diverse residents. Yet reciprocity, mutual interdependence, and equanimity mark social life, where kinlike links and a deep sense of collective identity are constructed and fostered. Ethnic differences notwithstanding, Douroshab represents an exemplary gemeinschaft, one in which human relationships are warm, enduring, and based on a clear understanding of where each person stands in the community. The majority of these residents live in extended families in households where few women work outside the home. Most of the predominantly working-class men, however, fill the lower echelons of the Sudanese labor force in the capital city, although others have migrated to oil-rich Arab countries, such as Saudi Arabia, United Arab Emirates, and Yemen, leaving women and children behind. The township has a local marketplace, a small health clinic, and a municipality, which serves the government in collecting taxes and regulating land registration, use, and tenure.

Although I have focused in the material below on the experiences of individuals, their experiences can hardly be detached from the socioeconomic milieu of Douroshab as a semi-urban township at the outskirts of a "third world" city. In Douroshab, one is immediately aware of the existential realities of women's lives, lives that are bordered by poverty, morbidity, and social inequality. By focusing on individual women, I hoped to understand how these women emerge as the primary brokers of cultural reproduction and gender ideology in the various narratives they offered in the course of this ethnography. I follow anthropologist Susan Sered's definition of gender ideologies as "ideologies of difference that elaborate and legitimate the attribution of a range of traits, roles, and statuses either to men or to women. Gender ideologies are how societies establish and justify the links between bodies, laws, emotions, customs, and behaviors; between sex and gender" (8). Therefore, to comprehend the ideas of Douroshab women, we need to examine the constituents of this gender ideology, specifically the manner in which these women view themselves, their society, their universe, and their place in it. I have selected the narratives that I think effectively illuminate this ideology for discussion because they best clarify the place of circumcision in their lives.

Women's Narratives: Why Circumcision Is a Virtuous Act

My use of personal narratives is prompted by several considerations. First, by quoting direct speech at length, I aim to highlight the ideological complexity within which decisions to engage in this practice are undertaken. After two periods of fieldwork, it became clear to me that the status of women in the Douroshab community is not low, as a text like *The Hosken Report* might lead us to expect. As far as this ritual is concerned, women have the upper hand in determining when, how, and where a girl will be excised.

The considerable influence of women in their community is evident from the wide range of their responsibilities and from the roles they play in family and community life. In the context of female circumcision, women wield a particular power, for they alone perform the operations. Of course, the ritual becomes an important affirmation of one generation of women's authority over another; however, as the narratives below will show, this authority should not be dismissed as an expression of false consciousness in which women perpetuate their own subjugation. Nor can the motives behind genital surgeries be traced to a single patriarchal value, for as these narratives will show, there is no singular, oppressive patriarchal discursive practice that leads women to perpetuate their own injury. Within the complex symbolic and social context of circumcision practices, women see their participation as voluntary. It reflects, after all, the "law of the Mother," as we shall see below. A second reason for using personal narratives prominently in my work replies to the tendency in much literature on female circumcision to speak for the excised women. Third-person reporting, as a rhetorical strategy, reflects not only the shortcomings of certain feminist discourses but also demonstrates their inability to comprehend the complexity of life experiences in modern African societies. Finally, the meanings of female circumcision to its adherents are best illustrated through narratives. If British anthropologist Marilyn Strathern is correct in her belief that "in people's lives, of course, ideas cannot possibly have a life of their own," then perhaps these ideas will come to life in the context of the elaborate and nuanced narratives that describe them (310). I employ these narratives to provide an understanding of the ritual as presented in women's own words, which reflect their own truths.

The Predicament of Femininity

One of the most prevalent cultural justifications for circumcision is the belief that female genitalia are ugly and misbegotten and the clitoris "revolting." If left unexcised, these women say, it can continue to grow and will ultimately "dangle" between a woman's legs. Here the ritual enters the realm of the cosmetic: it is a repudiation of the otherwise loathsome appearance of female genitalia.[4] This perception, as Sudanese women confirm, is not to be belittled. I was told by an older woman that the midwife who performs the surgery is often reminded by the kinswomen of the soon-to-be circumcised to *sawihoo amalas wa samih zai dahar elhamama,* meaning "make it smooth and beautiful like the back of a pigeon." It could be argued that the ritual is not only a fastidious tactic in pursuit of an aesthetic but also that it is related to the very process of the cultural construction of the body. From this point of view, circumcision is the machinery that liberates the female body from its masculine properties. This idea is related to the belief found in ancient Egyptian mythology that stresses the bisexuality of the gods.[5] One of the women I interviewed, Saadia, aged sixty-two, told me that "circumcision is what makes one a woman." Her narrative reflects her ideas on circumcision as a vehicle to achieve femininity.

> Saadia: Our mothers and grandmothers taught us that circumcision is very important for women and girls. I was given pharaonic circumcision when I was eight years old living in Shendi. I still remember the operation being painful, but to this day I believe it is necessary, and it is more effective than the sunna that people want to follow these days. In the Sudan, our ancestors *zman* (of a long time ago) knew better than people these days, who do not want to keep their customs. Female circumcision is a good custom because the removal of the external genitalia is necessary for girls. These parts, especially the clitoris, can get very big. I heard from some people that women who are not circumcised have clitorises that are as big as a little boy's penis. I haven't seen it myself, but people who told me swore that this is the case. Now do you think a woman should allow that to happen to her daughters? I believe it because just as the rest of a girl's body parts grow when she grows up, her clitoris also grows. But these days people don't want to pay attention to that. People try to do the sunna, but the real circumcision is pharaonic because a lot of doctors and some women are trying to teach people that their ways are wrong. Circumcision is what makes one a woman because by removing the clitoris, there is no way that her genitals will look like a man's. The woman with a big clitoris is just like a man. How can a woman carry such a long organ between her legs and pretend that things are normal? That is why we say that pharaonic is good because after it is done the girl's genital area becomes very beautiful and smooth, *malsa.* For this reason, all my daughters were given pharaonic. None of them had any complications. Of course during the first days after the operation, they were not very comfortable. But when their wound healed, they were fine. I continue to believe in it and I hope that people don't abandon it. It is an old Sudanese custom that should not be changed because without it, women's bodies are not as beautiful. A woman should do everything in her power to keep her body beautiful and she should do the same for her daughters, too. But uncircumcised women will not have nice bodies; they are just like men. I don't know how they can accept the appearance of genitals that look like those of their husbands.

In a society where a strong belief about the clitoris being homologous to the penis exists, it is not surprising to encounter strong feelings of fear, anxiety, and discomfort over the possibility of clitoral growth. Not only is excision an effective way of removing an excessive organ, but the surgery also comes to represent the ultimate seal of femininity. The flat patch of skin created through clitoral excision and infibulation becomes that "symbolic wound" which speaks volumes to the specificity of cultural constructions of gender and womanhood. The narrative above is a powerful reminder of how female bodies are re-created and socialized in different cultural contexts.

The Virtue of Purity

From the perspective of the Douroshab women, the virtue of purity is also best achieved through circumcision, which is seen as closely related to cleanliness and purification. These women refer to the genital operations as "circumcision," tahara, which in the etymological sense denotes cleanliness and purification. Anthropologists such as Soheir Morsy, Mary Douglas, and Anne Sutherland have painted elegant portraits of how notions of purity and impurity operate as elaborate moral codes and as cherished cultural ideals in the cultures they examined. To paraphrase Morsy, the importance of social personhood in Douroshab lives is manifested on a daily basis and informs their concept of the human body—its need for purification and cleanliness (79). Sudanese justifications of circumcision as a purificatory operation are no different. External genitalia are seen as potential sources of pollution and defilement, *najasa,* which is a much-deplored state to be avoided at all costs. The concept of najasa denotes the antithesis of tahara; thus circumcision is a tool for avoiding najasa. As a statement of both physical and moral impurity, the concept of najasa extends to diverse situations. For instance, women are implored by religion to perform ritual purification known as *ghusl,* or bathing, after menstruation, intercourse, parturition, and other activities deemed polluting or *najis.* For these women, becoming pure and clean not only helps them establish their social personhood but also differentiates them from other women who do not practice circumcision and are therefore impure. Below are two narratives that highlight the importance of circumcision for enhancing cleanliness and purification.

> Aziza: [I] was born in Kassala in 1974. I lived there until I was married at the age of nineteen and moved with my husband to El Douroshab six years ago. I do not work outside the home. My Jaleen family will not allow me

to do that. Now I have three daughters of my own. Their ages are five, four, and one years old. I live with my in-laws in Douroshab. My husband takes care of me, my children, and the other people in the household. When I was eight years old, in third grade, I was circumcised. At that age you don't know what circumcision is about, but you know it is coming when people start drumming the *nugara* the week before the operation takes place. Then you know that the day of somebody's circumcision is approaching. A midwife was summoned to our house. A short time later, I was held by family members, three women. My face was covered and my legs were held apart firmly. I was thin and could not kick or do anything. The midwife gave me an injection before she circumcised me, but it seemed like the anesthetic was not very strong. I still felt some pain and afterwards, the pain was very bad. I remember that I had to stay in bed all month, because this is the habit in Kassala. The circumcised girl can't run around and ruin her surgery. Especially if she is stitched, it is very likely that she would hurt herself. I got married and from the first day, I suffered. After giving birth, like the rest of women I demanded re-infibulation. I have to tell the truth: circumcision does not allow women to want sex. Now, I only have relations on Thursdays, because my husband's job in Khartoum is demanding. Being in transit and in crowds every day from the Douroshab to Khartoum is a big problem for him. When he comes home, he just wants to rest. I have no problem with this, because I believe that having sex all the time is bad. It reduces a woman. Once a week, once every two weeks is okay. I am convinced that circumcision is a good practice. Maybe not the pharaonic but just the sunna. I am planning to circumcise my daughter during Eid Ramadan, because the weather is cool then. Also to get it over with right away, the two older ones will be done together. My year-old daughter will wait for two more years. My family and my in-laws are in favor of pharaonic circumcision because it is considered a beautiful circumcision. I am not going to have pharaonic done to my daughters, so I will just lie to them and say that I did. I think pharaonic is very cruel. I don't say that to the people in the family because they could circumcise my daughters without my knowledge, or they might insist on it. Right now, I say yes pharaonic is good, so that I can prevent it from happening to my daughters. If I do sunna, I think that will be enough for the girls. The most important reason for me to circumcise my daughters is to keep them clean.

Zakia: Most of the people in Khartoum do not practice pharaonic circumcision because they believe that it is not necessary. A lot of people I know who live there practice sunna for cleanliness. There is a big difference as to why some people insist on sunna while others insist on pharaonic. The people who support the sunna (I am one of them) believe strongly that it keeps the genital area clean. By removing the clitoris, which is the source of bad smells and secretions, a woman's body becomes very good smelling and clean. Although I was circumcised pharaonic, I allowed my daughter to be circumcised sunna for that reason. That is why I think pharaonic is unnecessary and painful, and in many cases it causes infections, very bad ones. But I don't think there's anything wrong with keeping the vaginal area clean. Now the new generation here follows the sunna, and some have stopped altogether. I don't believe that the sunna should stop. The woman who is uncircumcised in comparison to one who is circumcised sunna is not clean no matter how hard she tries. This is my opinion. A lot of people here now are trying to stop female circumcision. They visit schools and go to the different neighborhoods to talk about the problems. In my opinion if they just talk about pharaonic circumcision, people will be more willing to listen, but to teach them to stop, this is a problem. I believe that if they tell people that the sunna is better, this will be reasonable. The people who believe in pharaonic are hardheaded; they will not change just because they hear something bad about it. My view on sunna is very favorable because I do not believe in the sewing and stitching. A woman should not be left uncircumcised but at the same time her body should not be injured badly like in pharaonic. She can have a good marriage, and does not have to suffer from pain. I think that if women believe in the benefits of sunna, men will not have any problem. The sunna is good. The pharaonic is harmful. More people should know that now.

Female circumcision as a practice is a mirror image of prevalent gender ideologies, politics, and values regarding femininity and sexuality. To Saadia, Aziza, and Zakia, circumcision is important because it gives voice to gender and collective ethnic identity, serving to distinguish the border between themselves as pure *taharat* and others as polluted *nijsat* women. The politics of conformity go beyond keeping clean; they have to do with one's character, sociality, and personal and collective identity.

To Suaad, female circumcision is not a symptom of women's oppression but a potential source of their power. This is why she supports the tradition.

Suaad: Many people in the Sudan are starting to change their views about the circumcision of girls. They tell us that it is painful and violent. My own view is that there's no difference between boys' circumcision and girls' circumcision. Both are painful, so how come they're not saying boys' circumcision is also violent? Ask any man about their experience and they will tell you that they still remember the day of the event. A lot of people don't go to doctors, but to the person in the neighborhood who is *Basir* (a traditional healer). When the Basir circumcises a boy he does not use anything to ease the pain. I don't support ending this custom because I don't believe in the new message. I am

> one hundred percent behind pharaonic circumcision. My reasons are simple: sex with an infibulated woman is more enjoyable than with uncircumcised or sunna circumcised woman. When the vaginal opening is narrow and tight, the woman enjoys the friction, and the man enjoys a long intercourse rather than *akhtif wa aajri* (hit and run). This is my experience from two marriages. In the beginning, when my daughter was six years old, I decided to give her sunna because I was almost brainwashed by some people. A year later, I changed my mind when it became clear to me that the sunna circumcision was very mild, and in appearance she looked as if she were uncircumcised. I brought her to the midwife to perform infibulation. My main motive was that the genital area did not look nice with the sunna. Infibulation is smoother and much nicer looking than having big labia. The other reason is that sex is better with pharaonic. Now my daughter is married and she did not suffer from anything. As a grandmother now, my infibulation did not eliminate my desire to have sex even at this age. People say that if you cut the clitoris you don't enjoy sex, but we can say to the same people: do you think if your tongue is removed you will stop feeling hungry? The same with sex. These people need to know that if a woman has a good husband, sex can be good even if she is circumcised, and can be very bad if she is uncircumcised and has a selfish husband. The issue is a good marriage. Now I have sex almost five times a week. It is very enjoyable and I know too about orgasm, *tharwa.* I have *tharwa jinsia,* that indescribable sense of pleasure that gives one the feeling of touching the sky. It makes one shiver.

What Suaad's narrative powerfully problematizes is the notion of sexual pleasure itself. Michel Foucault is correct to argue that there is no "pathology of pleasure," no "abnormal pleasure" (quoted in Halperin 93–94). The fact that circumcision reduces desire is not reflected in Suaad's story. A similar observation was reported by Heidi Skramstad's research among Gambian women who believed that genital cutting did not reduce their enjoyment of sexual intercourse.

To Najat, "circumcision is a source of empowerment and strength." One of Foucault's most significant ideas is his conceptualization of power as neither an institution nor a structure but a "complex strategical situation," a "multiplicity of force relations," as simultaneously "intentional yet 'nonsubjective'" (Foucault quoted in Smart 77). The question then becomes, How is power exercised? By what means? The following narrative suggests an answer to this question in the Sudanese context. Circumcision is believed to endow women with a remarkable ability to exert self-control and power, to take charge of their "natural" desires and to display restraint over their sexuality. Self-mastery, a disposition seen as a virtue and as one promoted through genital surgery, is Najat's reason for her undeviating support of pharaonic circumcision. Infibulated women, she maintains, are able to drive hard bargains and have a say in household politics and decision-making processes. Their controlled sexuality allows them to achieve these goals in the face of scarce resources, hardship, and constrained socioeconomic circumstances. This is how women exercise power not only over their sexuality, but also over their spouses.

> Najat: I am twenty-six years old. I was married in Dongula before moving to Douroshab with my husband. I was married at the age of twenty-one. My husband is an accountant in Saudi Arabia. I was not able to accompany him for financial reasons. We wanted him to have roommates to save money, so that we can build a house. He visits me once a year. Now I have one son who is almost two years old. In Dongula I was circumcised at age six, pharaonic. Before I got married I had a different idea about marriage. I thought it would be all *henna* and *dukhan* and about staying beautiful. No, marriage proved to me to be a big responsibility. About my experience, I remember the day when I was circumcised. I cried and cried till I lost my energy. My memory of it is that it was very painful, and that other neighborhood children who underwent it were also in a lot of pain. The people around you pay no attention; to them it is good to be circumcised, so as to find a husband. But for men the story is different. When I got married and went on my honeymoon to a hotel in Khartoum, my husband was very angry. He told me that among men there is teasing about one's sexuality and ability to have an encounter without being rejected by the wife. I did not allow my husband to come near me because of my fears. It took several months for me to have normal relations with my husband. But in spite of this, after I gave birth, I wanted to be reinfibulated. I did it for myself, for I wanted to restore my body. I managed to have the *adal* (re-infibulation). Because after the midwife delivers the baby, the genital area becomes ugly-looking. Pharaonic circumcision is good for women. It protects the dignity of women. The woman will have control over her body and she will not run around with men. I think that a woman who is not *mukhafada* (reduced) has endless problems. I want to say to everyone who does not prefer circumcision that it gives women a lot of power in the household. For example, if she has a fight or if she wants her husband to do something for her, her circumcision will allow her to take control and be able to refrain from sex for a long time until she brings him to see the problem exactly from her view. I don't think that uncircumcised women can do that; those women, when they fight with men, maybe two days later after a fight, if the man touches them, they become aroused and immediately forget the problems just to have sex. That is why in Sudanese families, women are very, very strong. I swear that in some houses the woman is so strong that her husband can't breathe without her consent. I think this is true because of her power over her sexual desire. Men are weak, weak, and weak. They will

> do everything to appease a woman for sex. And the circumcised woman understands how to take advantage of the problem and turn it around for her own ends. A woman can make her husband wait for a long time, till he is no longer able to stand it. I think that because of these things, pharaonic circumcision is something good for women, because it helps your relations with the husband. Although I suffered on my honeymoon, I remember, on the way to the airport when my husband's vacation ended and he was on his way to Saudia, we were sitting next to each other in a van. He whispered to me that he was happy to see that I was a strong person. And that he admired my strength. My view about the circumcision of women is that I don't have a problem with the pain experienced. I think the pain goes away, but the relationships between men and women become very equal and strong. Circumcision gives a woman that power.

Najat's narrative represents a statement about the exercise of power in specific sociocultural contexts. She not only sees circumcision as an effective tool for controlling her "natural" desires but also as a way for women to exercise power in their daily affairs. This narrative contradicts the feminist assertion about circumcision as the signifier of women's victimization by male dominance. In so doing, the narrative illuminates an alternative view regarding cultural differences, women's agency, and autonomy in the household and beyond.

Najat also contradicts the narrative of Suaad just prior to it. Although Suaad's and Najat's narratives make opposing claims about the effects of circumcision on women's capacity for sexual pleasure, one can identify the differences behind the performance of the ritual in the same community.

"Marriage is the destiny traditionally offered to women by society" (de Beauvoir 425). Marriageability is an integral aspect of gender ideology among women in Douroshab and others throughout circumcision-practicing societies. The maintenance of circumcision as a way of protecting propriety, morality, and marriageability in Sudanese cultural understanding should not be unheeded or glossed over. The following narrative concurs with the previous one in proposing that female sexuality can be manipulated to gain respect and to attain status within the community and in the family. Faiza, a fifty-five-year-old mother of five girls, indicated to me that "circumcision protects the girls from getting in trouble and protects them from engaging in sex. I think that it is very important for the virginity of women to be protected if they want to get husbands who respect them." It is no wonder that the most impassioned, ardent advocates of the ritual are women themselves, who hold that by perpetuating circumcision they are protecting their daughters' virginity and hence their reputations. Here, ritual becomes a mirror for larger conceptions of what constitutes morality, good behavior, and sexuality.

> Faiza: I agree that pharaonic circumcision is painful. But still I am for it. I am also for having big celebrations of circumcision, because it is a very important occasion in a girl's life, just like a wedding. These days midwives can do it with anesthetics; the operation itself is easy. I chose pharaonic circumcision for my two daughters. I thought of their future. The woman who is circumcised behaves in a way that forces people around her to respect her. But a woman who is not circumcised cannot enjoy the same status. Men respect women who have self-respect and who do not get involved in sexual relations. We know that when a woman gets married, this background is important. If a woman protects her virginity, she becomes highly valued and *mashkora* (praiseworthy) by the whole community. When my daughter got married, some of my friends and I advised her not to yield to her husband's sexual advances the first night. She should play hard to get, because the way that you act towards sexual matters can be important afterwards. If she gives in from the first touch, as a woman I think that can be seen as a sign of weakness. But the more the woman resists, the more powerful she is. This was my behavior in my own marriage. I have been married for thirty years and to this day my husband runs after me and respects me very much. For this reason, pharaonic circumcision cannot just disappear like that. It is a good practice that we inherited from our grandmothers, people who knew how to handle men. None of the Sudanese women who are pharaonically circumcised are weak or powerless. They know what they are doing and pharaonic circumcision has not stood in the way of accomplishing their goals in life. If you look around, you can see that Sudanese women work hard and many hold high positions in society. Look at women in places where women are uncircumcised. Some of them can't leave the house without their husbands. We don't have these problems in Sudanese society. Pharaonic circumcision ensures the woman's strong place in the family. She is very trustworthy because she does not allow men to take advantage of her. She is her own person, even for the man she is married to. This is a source of respect and I think it is more important than how painful it is. The wound heals, but the relationships remain strong. By preserving her reputation, a woman will become powerful and respected by members of the community. Look at other countries. Premarital sex is common in places where women are uncircumcised, which not only undermines the reputation of the woman but taints the entire lineage by her uncontrolled sexuality and lack of control.

In these conversations sexuality is represented as a double-edged sword. It can be a source of tremendous strength if controlled and safeguarded, but it can also be a source of weakness, deviance, and feebleness.

Circumcision: A Collegial Act

In analyzing individuality and community in Marx's theory of social reality, Gould points out that for Marx there is an "ontologically independent entity that one could characterize neither as an individual nor as society, but only as a system of relations." Gould continues: "[in that sense] we would have an ontology of pure relations, with 'entities' having no independent ontological status whatever except as modes of relations or moments of relationship" (31). Marx's theory of relationality is helpful in shifting our emphasis from the question of individual agency to one of overdetermined social formation. Moreover, this critical approach has the advantage of enabling the particular form of social organization of Douroshab women to emerge more fully. Contrary to the widely held views found in most Euro-American literature on the subject, the relational rather than the individual context is the most significant aspect of circumcision rituals. Asha, a fifty-year-old Douroshab resident articulates her own social reality when she declares: "Customs are unbreakable. That is why I believe in circumcision." This statement highlights the philosophy of the individual-in-relation. As with many of the women I interviewed, Asha placed significant emphasis on personhood, bonding, and the maintenance of conventions and boundaries. The following narrative by Asha puts the custom in perspective, as an act of collegiality and community:

> Asha: I am forty-eight years old. I was born in Wad Elhabashi in Shendi. I finished middle school and am now a typist at the Ministry of Education. I have three children: two girls and a boy. When I was six years old, a traditional midwife circumcised me and I suffered from pain and from *akias eltuhara* (fistulae). I remember that before my circumcision, no one told me about it or explained why it was important that it be done. This is something people do all the time, it is part of their old customs, which do not need to be explained. My memory of it is that it was a painful thing and that other neighborhood children who underwent it were in a lot of pain. Also my memory of it is that it involved gifts and feasts. No one can deny that circumcision is a painful experience: you can't urinate, you can't walk, and you can't have anything to ease the pain. The nights were very long when as children we were not able to sleep because of the throbbing pain. You have to understand why our mothers were keen to do it. They did it out of concern because they did not want to break with their tradition. I can say that in spite of my suffering during delivery, which was also a problem, I was determined to have the adal. Because when they cut you open, the genital area becomes ugly-looking. Again, in my view, this was necessary because the women I know do it to

look good. When I got married we moved to Dongula, where my daughter was born. In Dongula, pharaonic circumcision is the norm. To circumcise as sunna seems as if you left your daughter uncircumcised. Although I know it is painful, and I know it causes problems, I know that circumcision has many benefits, which are more important than its troubles. For that reason I did not object to my daughter's circumcision. I supported her circumcision because it is the custom, and I wanted to be like everybody else in my family and my neighborhood. My daughter is now experiencing trouble; when she gets her period she can't move. I think that the problems I would face with my family would be greater and harder to deal with had I decided to abandon this custom altogether. The pressure did not come from my husband. My husband did not have any say when our young daughter was circumcised. I did not consult him or let him know, because this is a sensitive issue and it was my decision. My husband does not usually interfere in my business. But my relatives, especially my mother and my aunts, were the ones who wanted pharaonic. Now they want pharaonic for my young one, too. They will be unhappy if I choose other types, because the opening is not as small as in the pharaonic. I am convinced that circumcision is painful, but our relatives do not want to do it to us to hurt us. They are just following their community and their families. I feel that in the name of custom my relatives did that to me, and in the name of custom I did it to my daughters. All of these things are in my mind. I understand them, but I have no way of changing them because other more educated women come to tell us how bad circumcision is. If I leave my daughters uncircumcised, my relatives will talk and gossip about me. I will not be able to bear it. In the future, if my daughters want to change I might give them advice, but I will not try to change their ways because the new generations have different ideas.

Intimately linked to the idea of community solidarity is the indigenous conceptualization of rights. Since the individual lives within a larger collectivity, these rights are not seen as individual rights that are indivisible and inalienable, as commonly held in Western thought. People take greater freedoms within this community to instruct and advise each other about every facet of their lives. A long-established tradition of mutual cooperation and interdependence stresses a fundamental point: that the concept of rights "as inalienable, interconnected, and indivisible" cannot be grasped in isolation from the dynamic social relations of the collectivity. A common remark that I heard over and over again was that the persistence of female circumcision is attributable to the fact that "customs are not easy to break," as Asha told me. The acceptance of "customs" prompts many like Asha to continue the practice in order to secure social belonging to the community, kinship identification, and loyalty.

Epilogue

Almost eighty years ago, Franz Boas, the founding father of American anthropology, observed that when a dominant way of thinking pervades all of cultural life it often persists over long periods, surviving changes to the ways people live. Certainly, genital excision practices in the township of Douroshab thrive in spite of sweeping transformations in Sudanese society, including the "modernization" and Islamization of the country. The case of Douroshab suggests that the tenacity of this ritual cannot be understood in isolation from emotional and cognitive processes, kin and social relationships, accountability, morality, ideas about femininity and masculinity, or from the relations of power that prevail in the community. For example, as we have seen from the preceding narratives, in Douroshab, women's rationale for the continuation of circumcision is articulated in terms of its symbolism as an act that commemorates virtue and hallows morality. Female circumcision is a ritual contributing to the cultural construction of gender, womanhood, and "appropriate" sexuality, a part of the process of achieving full personhood within this culture. Simply stated, female circumcision has no meaning apart from other dominant ideologies, and these ideologies in turn combine to shape common moralities and codes of ethics in the communities in which circumcision is practiced. As political theorist Mona Abul Fadl argues ("Revisiting"), it neither strains our credulity nor does it tax our imaginations to acknowledge that every aspect of life is connected to every other and that, somehow, reality is a seamless web out of which all life proceeds. These narratives, therefore, ought to be understood in this spirit. As a ritual device, circumcision exemplifies a distinctive body of teachings; it is an "ontological mutation in existential conditions" (Auge 61) that gives the circumcised common recognition of a set of changing relationships within her community. Understood as a ritual, the practice is not seen by the people in Douroshab Township as a violation of human rights. Although most of the female interviewees acknowledged the extreme nature of the practice, they made no connection between its "violence" and a human rights violation. For example, women admit that circumcision has caused them a tremendous number of ailments, but because it is a cultural practice, the practitioners are not accused of violating their children's rights. Though painful and drastic, it is by no means seen as contravention or violation. On the contrary, in Douroshab terms, circumcision has many benefits for girls and women.

Abdulahi An-Na'im argues persuasively that "unless international human rights have sufficient legitimacy within particular cultures and traditions, their implementation will be thwarted, particularly at the domestic level, but also at the regional and international levels" (172–73). Without such legitimacy, it is almost impossible to improve the status of women through the law or any other agent of social change. Indeed, the very use of law in many African societies requires a prior conviction that the right to be protected is inalienable. The question then becomes how human rights can be legitimized in contexts within which violations take place. If such legitimacy does not already exist, and the whole community believes in the virtue of a practice like female circumcision, who is left to implement the law? Within communities that adhere to circumcision, this tradition is perceived *as a cultural right* and not as a breach of rights. The narratives of Douroshab women not only convey the meanings of circumcision but are couched in powerful terms that reveal how women construct multiple identities in an ever-changing social world. Genital modification is not only important in producing "socially informed bodies," but as a vehicle for creating meanings "that bound and represent the socialized self by mediating its relations to the ambient social world" (T. Turner 149). Attention to social reproduction is essential for understanding the politics and aesthetics embodied in the modification of women's bodies. Further, as I have argued elsewhere (Abusharaf), elucidating women's perspectives within societies rather than criminalizing them is not only a pressing political issue, but also the only strategy for the formulation of a sound anti-circumcision policy in the new millennium.

NOTES

I would like to thank Ellen Rooney, Elizabeth Weed, Denise Davis, Lloyd Pratt, Rosalind Shaw, and Nancy Chance for helpful comments. Many thanks to Fatima Osman and the women of Douroshab whose hospitality and support allowed me to write about the most private aspects of their lives.

1. The BBSAWS (Babikir Bedri Scientific Association for Women Studies) organized a workshop called African Women Speak, in which women from twenty-eight African countries drafted letters of appeal to their heads of state and ministries of health. The most important letter is the one sent to the registrar of the Nursing and Midwives Council in All African States. It reads: "We, the participants of the African Women Speak workshop, held in Khartoum, organized by BBSAWS, to discuss strategies regarding the eradication of female circumcision, appeal to the Midwives Council to condemn, disqualify, or take appropriate action against midwives who practice female circumcision. And this in light of the fact that the medicalization and modernization of fc is giving undue support to this unnecessary and harmful practice. We count on the support of the Midwives Council in our efforts to eradicate this unwarranted human suffering." This document reflects the increased tendency toward medicaliza-

tion, in which midwives more often than not practice these surgeries. The efforts of BBSAWS continue to reflect the importance of incorporating local knowledge into anti-circumcision programs. I had the opportunity to see the collection of statistical data and extensive ethnographic research conducted by Sudanese anthropologists and sociologists such as Samia Elhadi Elnagar, Idris Salim, Haj Hamad Mohamed Kheir, and Amna Bedri, among others. One activist told me, "Our identification of strategies depends on the views of the communities themselves."

2. The call for criminalization of the practice received considerable validation in the 1995 Beijing Decade of Women's Conference Platform for Action, which states that "Women's Rights are Human Rights." This slogan is founded on a basic truth: that the full and equal enjoyment of rights and freedoms by women and female children should top the list of priorities for governments and United Nations agencies. In this respect, the international human rights movement is ethically and ontologically geared to the moral conviction that men and women have equal rights by virtue of their humanity. As Machan acknowledges, "the idea [of human rights implies that] certain unifying principles of social conduct based on our understanding of what it is to be human, deserves systematic protection by legal enforcement" (479). The notion of women's rights as human rights therefore not only expands the scope of international law, but also allows women the possibility of making international legal claims (Charlesworth). The identification of female circumcision as a human rights violation reemphasizes the philosophical view that since human rights are derived from a shared human nature, these rights are indispensably universal, indivisible, and interconnected. However, the debate over women's human rights raises complex issues surrounding the applicability and relevance of human rights law under specific cultural, political, and economic conditions, especially in the developing world. According to a Nigerian lawyer, as reported by Rebecca Cook, "The rights discourse in Africa is not meaningful." She goes on to explain that "the severity of socioeconomic problems faced by women in countries undergoing structural adjustment may require basic needs strategy rather than a rights strategy" (479).

3. Sunna circumcision, or clitoridectomy, is the removal of the prepuce of the clitoris. It is considered to be the mildest form of genital operation. Excision is the removal of the prepuce of the clitoris, the clitoris itself, and all or part of the labia minora. Pharonic circumcision, or infibulation, includes excision of the clitoris, the labia minora, and parts of the labia majora, followed by the stitching of the vaginal opening, leaving a small opening for the passing of urine and menses.

4. This notion is not unique to these women. Similar ideology is found among the Dogon and the Bambara of Mali, and the Saney people of Uganda, among others. Thomas Lowry has shown that the ancient Chinese "did not mutilate the clitoris, but did consider a large one unsightly; classical Chinese erotic art almost never shows the clitoris" (195).

5. According to folk wisdom, circumcision may have been introduced to establish the femininity of girls. This explanation can be attributed to the mythology of the bisexuality of the gods. Meinardus argues that in ancient times, numerous gods of the Heliopolithic Mephitic and Thebaic pantheon were considered to be hermaphrodites. Genital excision was introduced to eliminate this condition.

Works Cited

Abul Fadl, Mona. "Revisiting the Woman Question: An Islamic Perspective." *Chicago Theological Seminary Register* 83, no. 1 (1998): 28–64.

———. "Sexuality in Islam." Given at the annual meeting of the American Anthropological Association, Washington, D.C., 1998.

Abusharaf, Rogaia M. "Revisiting Feminist Discourses on Female Infibulation: Responses from Sudanese Feminists." In *Female "Circumcision" in Africa: Culture, Controversy, and Change.* Ed. Ylva Hernlund and Bettina Shell-Duncan, 151–67. Boulder: Lynn Reinner, 2000.

Ammar, Hamid. *Growing Up in an Egyptian Village.* New York: Octagon Books, 1961.

An-Na'im, Abdulahi. "State Responsibility under International Human Rights Law to Change Religious and Customary Law." In *Human Rights of Women: National and International Perspectives.* Ed. Rebecca Cook, 167–89. Philadelphia: University of Pennsylvania Press, 1994.

Auge, Maurice. *The Anthropological Circle: Symbol, Function, History.* New York: Cambridge University Press, 1979.

Beasley, Ina. *Before the Wind Changed: People, Places and Education in the Sudan.* New York: Oxford University Press, 1992.

Bloch, Maurice. *From Blessing to Violence.* New York: Cambridge University Press, 1986.

Boas, Franz. *Anthropology and Modern Life.* New York: W. W. Norton, 1928.

Bourdieu, Pierre. *Outline of a Theory of Practice.* New York: Cambridge University Press, 1977.

Charlesworth, Hillary. "What Are Women's International Human Rights?" In *Human Rights of Women: National and International Perspectives.* Ed. Rebecca Cook, 58–85. Philadelphia: University of Pennsylvania Press, 1994.

Conteh, Sorie. "'Circumcision and Secret Societies' from West Africa." In *The Africans: A Reader.* Ed. Ali Mazrui and Tobey Levine, 223–36. Westport: Praeger, 1986.

Cook, Rebecca, ed. *Human Rights of Women: National and International Perspectives.* Philadelphia: University of Pennsylvania Press, 1994.

de Beauvoir, Simone. *The Second Sex.* 1952. Trans. H. M. Parshley. Reprint. New York: Vintage, 1989.

Douglas, Mary. *Purity and Danger: An Analysis and Concepts of Pollution and Taboo.* New York: Praeger, 1966.

El-Beshir, Hamid. *Women and the Agony of Culture: SNCTP and the Eradication of Harmful Traditional Practices in the Sudan 1992–94.* Khartoum: Assessment Report, 1994.

Eltayeb, Abdallah. "The Changing Customs of Riverain Sudan." *Sudan Notes and Records* 35 (1955): 146–58.

Fraser, David. "The First Cut Is (Not) the Deepest." *Dallhousie Law Journal* 18, no. 7 (1995): 310–79.

Gennep, Arnold van. *The Rites of Passage.* London: Routledge, 1977.

Gould, Carol C. *Marx's Social Ontology.* Cambridge, Mass.: MIT Press, 1981.

Halperin, David M. *Saint Foulcault: Towards a Gay Hagiography.* New York: Oxford University Press, 1995.
Hicks, Esther K. *Infibulation: Female Mutilation in Islamic Northeastern Africa.* New Brunswick: Transaction Press, 1994.
Hosken, Fran. *The Hosken Report: Genital and Sexual Mutilation of Females.* Lexington: Win News, 1993.
Lambek, Michael. "'Body and Mind in Mind, Body and Mind in Body': Some Anthropological Interventions in a Long Conversation." In *Bodies and Persons: Comparative Perspectives from Africa and Melanesia.* Ed. Michael Lambek and Andrew Strathern, 103–23. New York: Cambridge University Press, 1998.
Lambek, Michael, and Andrew Strathern, eds. *Bodies and Persons: Comparative Perspectives from Africa and Melanesia.* London: Cambridge University Press, 1998.
Lowry, Thomas. *The Clitoris.* St. Louis: Warren Green, 1976.
Machan, Tibor. "Human Rights Reaffirmed." *Philosophy* 69 (1994): 479–90.
Mazrui, Ali. *The Africans.* Boston: Little, Brown, 1986.
Meinardus, Otto. "Mythological, Historical and Sociological Aspects of the Practice of Female Circumcision among the Egyptians." *Acta Ethnographica* 16 (1967): 387–98.
Meyers, Diana. "Feminism and Women's Autonomy: The Challenge of Female Genital Cutting." Typescript, 1999.
Morsy, Soheir. *Gender, Sickness, and Healing in Rural Egypt: Ethnography in Historical Context.* Boulder: Westview Press, 1993.
Scott, Joan W. *Only Paradoxes to Offer: French Feminists and the Rights of Man.* Cambridge: Harvard University Press, 1996.
Sered, Susan. *Women of the Sacred Groves: Priestesses of Okinawa.* New York: Oxford University Press, 1999.
Skinner, Elliot. "The Triple Heritage of Lifestyles." In *The Africans: A Reader.* Ed. Ali Mazrui and Toby Levine, 60–74. Westport: Praeger, 1986.
Skramstad, Heidi. "The Fluid Meanings of Female Circumcision in a Multiethnic Context in Gambia: Distribution of Knowledge and Linkages to Sexuality." Working paper. Bergen: Michelsen Institute, 1990.
Smart, Barry. *Michel Foucault.* London: Routledge, 1988.
Sutherland, Anne. *The Gypsies: The Hidden Americans.* Long Grove, Ill.: Waveland Press, 1976.
Strathern, Marilyn. *The Gender of the Gift: Problems with Women and Problems with Society in Melanesia.* Berkeley: University of California Press, 1988.
Thaim, Awa. "Women's Fight for the Abolition of Sexual Mutilation." *International Social Science Journal* 35, no. 4 (1983): 747–56.
Toubia, Nahid. *Women of the Arab World.* London: Zed Press, 1996.
Turner, Terrence. "Social Body and Embodied Subject: Bodiliness, Subjectivity, and Sociality among the Kayapo." *Cultural Anthropology* 10, no. 2 (1995): 143–70.
Turner, Victor. *The Forest of Symbols: Aspects of Ndembu Ritual.* Ithaca: Cornell University Press, 1967.
Walker, Alice, and Pratibha Parmar, eds. *Warrior Marks: Female Genital Mutilation and the Sexual Blinding of Women.* New York: Harcourt Brace, 1993.

9 Feminist Family Politics

JOAN W. SCOTT

THE DEBATES ON THE PACS in France have occasioned an outpouring of opinion about the nature of families. Particularly vexing has been the question of the status of same-sex couples. For purposes of inheritance and other legal questions, same-sex partnerships may be recognized as "unions" governed by certain contractual arrangements, but the line has been drawn at calling these unions "families" because of the question of children. All manner of expert testimony has been brought to bear on the matter of "lineage" and "kinship," most of it seeking to prove that there is something either unnatural, culturally deviant, and/or psychologically damaging about children being born to or raised by two parents of the same sex. Some have written of the "right" of children to live in heterosexual families; others have objected to homosexual parenting as a distortion of the facts of nature. Sylviane Agacinski put it this way, "I don't believe that it will be good for children in the future to be placed within an asexual or homosexal lineage that effaces the fact that all human beings are born of a man and a woman."[1]

Agacinski's comment leaves aside the ways in which reproductive and cloning technologies have already altered the meaning of this "fact" (it may be more precise, for example, to say at the present time that all humans are produced by a sperm and an egg) and it rests on the questionable assumption that both members of a child's "real" parents are present in today's "families." Such families are actually now in the minority in France and elsewhere. Most interesting from the point of view of a historian of women and feminism, however, is the way in which Agacinski (who identifies as a feminist and is committed to equality between the sexes) links childbearing to childrearing, taking it for granted that the two tasks are necessarily (and ideally) performed by the same people. Not only does this distort the historical record (an issue to which I will return shortly), it also naturalizes the heterosexual nuclear family by making the social roles of parents and the sexual relations between them depend entirely on reproductive biology. Since it has long been a claim of feminists that families are precisely social and thus mutable institutions, it is surprising to find someone who calls herself a feminist lined up on the side of what amounts to biological determinism (although, of course, feminists have rarely been unanimous on any issue). Still, reform of the family by means of a separation between women's reproductive functions, on the one hand, and their sexual activity and social responsibility, on the other, has been at the heart of feminist critiques of modern patriarchy. Olympe de Gouges's eloquent refusal of nature as the ontological ground of the social organization of sexual difference is only one of many feminist arguments I could cite: "Look, search, and then distinguish if you can, the sexes in the administration of nature. Everywhere you will find them mixed up [*confondus*], everywhere they cooperate harmoniously in this immortal masterpiece" (101, my translation).

Agacinski would argue, I think, that although she seems to endorse the overwhelming importance of reproduction in the constitution of families, her concern is more for the symbolic representation of sexual difference than for strictly biological or genetic issues. This is also the position of the sociologist Irène Théry, whose report *Couple, filiation et parenté aujourd'hui: Le droit face aux mutations de la famille et de la vie privée* paved the way for the legislation that has now passed. Théry makes a strong case for the need for law to take into account the changes that have made legal, stable, and enduring marriage an institution of the past. Acknowledging that children now live in a variety of situations ("If you take a family today, an ordinary kinship group, you'll find married couples, divorced couples, remarried couples, single parent families, and never-married couples. That's what today's classic family is!") and that norms have changed dramatically, she nonetheless refuses the idea that a homosexual couple should be deemed parents by any social or legal standard: "No one is the child of two men or two women. I can well understand that some people are shocked to discover that homosexuals cannot together adopt a child. But to allow that would be to put back into question the mixed sex nature of our geneological system. If we allow adoption by homosexual couples, those children will have two mothers or two fathers. There would result a denial of sexual difference. But humanity is sexed; that's how it reproduces. How, and why, should we negate that?"[2]

One is tempted to ask naive questions about these assertions: Why assume that childrearers will claim to be childbearers and that children will be unable to tell the difference? Why assume that physical differences between the sexes will be "effaced" or "denied" by homosexual parents? How is a homosexual household different from one in which two women—sisters, or a mother and grandmother, say—are raising the children? Or from a household with a single mother raising children fathered by different men, none of whom has ever been present? Or from a family where children are being raised by a widowed father? Or from a household presided over by a heterosexual couple, one of whom also has a homosexual lover? The answers (for Théry and Agacinski) seem to lie less in the issue of who cares for and rears the children than in their objection to homosexual desire itself, an objection they cannot make directly because they do not want to be perceived as homophobic. Instead, they make the "sexual difference" of parents the requirement for a "family," a sexual difference that means both the literal presence (at some point) of a man and woman and a sexual relation between them. Calling a homosexual relationship a "family" will, in their view, confuse the issue of how babies are born and also violate the rules of "notre système généalogique." But unless one believes that this "system" is immutable, the insistence that the rules must be preserved is blatantly ideological; it is simply the defense of normative regimes of heterosexuality against challenge and change.

Those who argue for the system's immutability often invoke "the symbolic" as an alternative to biology, seeming to introduce the authority of psychoanalysis into the controversy about homosexual parenting. The suggestion is that in any culture children deprived of their natural heterosexual parents (the embodiments of sexual difference) will become, if not psychotic, then badly confused about their own sexual identities, for (in these distortions of psychoanalysis) the sociological and the psychological, the literal and the symbolic, are made to depend upon one another. The term *the symbolic* seems to refer to the theories of Jacques Lacan, but in fact Lacan's work does not substantiate the use being made of his ideas. According to Lacan, sexual difference is grounded not by anatomy but by symbolic articulation. Neither the biological nor the sociological family has much to do with the symbolic positions of "mother" or "father." To take one example, in Lacan's discussion of the symbolic order the father plays a key role; but this father—this agency that establishes the law that regulates desire—is a *position or function,* and it can be occupied by a subject who is not necessarily a father nor necessarily male. The symbolic father, writes Jacqueline Rose, represents "an insistence that the father stands for a place and a function which is not reducible to the presence or absence of the real father as such" (Mitchell and Rose, eds. 39). While it is true that Lacan maintains that the absence of a symbolic father is a factor in psychosis, he never says that this symbolic father must be the progenitor of the child. Moreover, when Lacan does refer to real fathers, he notes first that the reality of their position is established not by biology but by language. He adds further that their presence in a household is no guarantee that they will fulfill their Oedipal role (as agent of castration); indeed, the child may experience this castration in the physical absence of the real father. The apprehension of sexual difference by children does not require role models in the family, and it is not achieved by one-to-one correspondence (girls identifying with their mothers, boys with their fathers). Rather, the process of formulating a sexual identity is a complex one, an ongoing (and variable) negotiation among social norms of gender, unconscious desires and modes of identification, and individual life histories. Put more simply, neither the sex, gender, nor sexuality of the parents are predictors of the relation to sexual difference or the sexual choices of their children.

Charles Shepherdson reminds us that for Lacan and for Freud, there is "an explicit separation between biological origin and symbolic identity." The definition of the modern family as a biological unit, he adds, "sustains an illusion of 'nature' that conceals the true function of the family as a cultural institution" (see chapter 4). As a cultural institution, moreover, the family is a changing institution. Even if one grants that "the symbolic" is a factor in all human psychic processes, it does not follow that it operates outside of historical and cultural contexts. The symbolic does not translate into a single set of social institutions or individual psychologies. Which is why the evocation of "the symbolic" does not relieve us of a need for history.

The notion that "our genealogical system" is fixed or natural denies the historicity of family and kinship arrangements, a historicity that Théry acknowledges when she talks about the need to bring law into conformity with new demographic and social realities. These new realities, one might argue from a feminist perspective, involve the decline of patriarchal considerations, at least as they aimed at consolidating social alliances and transmitting property and power from one generation to the next. Once feminists railed against the "name of the father" as an appropriation by men of women's reproductive labor (Jeanne Deroin, writing in the 1830s called it "the branding iron that imprints the initials of the master on the forehead of the slave"), today women avoid this subjugation by not marrying.[3] (The children of married couples still must carry their father's name.) To a large extent, the old preoccupation with establishing the legitimacy of children (and thus of their claims to paternal inheritance) has also declined; in its place we have an obsession with genetic legacies and sexual identities.

Why the weakening of patriarchal forms and practices has been accompanied by anxiety about retaining the marks of sexual difference seems to me an important question to ponder—but not one I will take up until the end of this essay. First I want to explore some of the history of the relationship between childrearing and childbearing and suggest that this relationship depends not on the "natural" laws of sexual difference—whether biological or psychological—but on changing views about parental responsibility for children and changing regimes of patriarchal law.

"A man of the sixteenth or the seventeenth century would be astonished at the exigencies with regard to civil status to which we submit quite naturally. As soon as our children start to talk, we teach them their name, their age and their parents' name." So begins Philippe Ariès's monumental study, *L'enfant et la vie familiale sous l'ancien régime* (15). Ariès examines all manner of evidence to establish that the family form we have idealized (nuclear, child-centered, private) dates only to the seventeenth century. At that time "the family ceased to be simply an institution for the transmission of a name and an estate—it assumed a moral and spiritual function, it moulded bodies and souls" (412). The modern family was, moreover, "originally a middle-class phenomenon"; there was, Ariès tells us, "a connection between the concept of the family and the concept of class" (414). The nobility and the lower classes held different ideas and implemented different forms of family life, some aspects of which persisted despite the increasing standardization effected by the Civil Code after 1804. One of the marks of the new middle-class vision of family was an increasing emphasis on the role of women as childrearers. Tasks that had been hitherto dispersed—to wetnurses, nannies, servants, schoolmasters, fathers, clerics, neighbors, relatives and others—were gathered up under the rubric of maternal responsibility. Concomitantly, reproduction, one of many activities associated with women—and not exclusively with them—became the defining aspect of their characters and their lives. The economic value of women (variously measured for the nobility by dowries, family connections, and the production of legitimate heirs and for the lower classes by dowries and many forms of value-producing and wage-earning labor) was now calculated by reference to the "quality" of their children. The presence of the mother in the home with her children became a sign of the physical, economic, and emotional health of the family.

Although some historians (feminists among them) have argued that combining the jobs of childbearer and childrearer gave women a new and higher social status (because it was one that pertained solely to the female sex), it is also true that the equation of reproduction and childrearing narrowed the roles that had, in the past, been ascribed to women, and interpreted these roles purely as a function of biology (see Degler; Offen). In addition, it introduced a far more rigid sexual division of labor in definitions of reproduction. Once, a father's part in and responsibility for the conception of his child had been taken for granted by religious and state authorities who endorsed "la recherche de la paternité" as a way to compel paternal contributions to the support and education of children, whether or not they were legitimate. In contrast, by the early nineteenth century, under the provisions of the Civil Code, recognition of the father's role and attribution to him of responsibility for his progeny depended not on the fact of his biological contribution but on the legal status of the woman he "got with child." If married to the woman, the child was his, whether or not he was the biological father; if not married, the child belonged entirely to her. Unlike the maternal function that was taken to be an unquestioned result of biology, paternal function was entirely a matter of law. And the family established by this law (as I have argued elsewhere) was taken to be a form of men's property, important not only because it permitted transmission of material goods from one generation to the next but also because it was the tangible emblem of masculine personhood (Scott 62–64).

It is worth looking at the history of "la recherche de la paternité" even though it deals with exceptional aspects of the relations between heterosexual couples and their children. Often it is in dealing with what are taken to be exceptions that the basis for the rules governing normative arrangements becomes clear. I want to argue that these normative arrangements not only had a history, they also constructed biology to suit a particular vision of "the family."

By a law of 1556, a pregnant unmarried or widowed woman had to appear before a magistrate and answer three questions regarding her condition. The first was about when she had become pregnant; the second about the identity of the child's father; and the third about the place and circumstances of the intercourse. To verify the information, the magistrate was to be summoned by the midwife when the woman was in labor, where he would then repeat the questions. Under conditions of pain and suffering, it was thought, the woman was more likely to speak the truth. The purpose of this law (which has provided rich documentation for histories of early modern sexuality) was to prevent secret confinements and the infanticides they might conceal as well as to relieve local religious and/or political authorities from financial responsibility for the child by forcing the father either to marry the mother (if he was not already married) or to pay some child support. Another law, in 1670, allowed the mother of a child born out of wedlock to sue the putative father for financial damages (on such grounds as breach of promise, abduction, rape, seduction, and deception) and to gain some legal standing for the child. Depending on her testimony, on the witnesses she could summon, on her own reputation, on the reputation and social status of the man sued, and on the sympathy of the magistrate, a woman could prevail. And although it was rare for a father in these circumstances to be awarded custody of the child, his role in its conception, and thus his legal and financial relationship to it, was acknowledged (Hufton; Traer).

During the eighteenth century, the period that, according to Ariès, saw the emergence of middle-class notions of the family, there was great pressure for legal reform. Rousseau worried about the unreliability of women's testimony about the paternity of their children (there was no way, finally, to prove they were wrong, thus all the more reason for them to lie), and some magistrates tended to be more skeptical of women's claims (see especially Book 5). Legislation at the time of the French Revolution was driven by two conflicting principles: one that sought to equalize the status of all children by eliminating the distinction between legitimate and illegitimate children (at one point, illegitimate children were, for example, granted the right to inherit from both parents provided they had evidence of paternity, the search for which was briefly permitted), the other that sought to strengthen the affective and legal bonds of legitimate families. Napoleon's Civil Code resolved the tension between these two claims in favor of legitimate families. Article 340 prohibited mothers from seeking paternal support for children born out of wedlock and absolved the father of legal, fiscal, moral, and social responsibility for these children. Mothers, on the other hand, could neither disavow maternity nor responsibility. While "la recherche de la maternité" was mandatory, "la recherche de la paternité" was forbidden. Mothers of illegitimate children were held to a standard of nature (the fact that such children were legally referred to as "enfants naturels" makes this explicit); fathers were protected against "nature" by law. (That a legal and not a sexual relation was at the heart of the marital bond is demonstrated by the sections of the code on adultery: while a wife's adultery justified her husband's killing her, a husband's adultery was sanctioned—unless he introduced his mistress into the household where his wife and family lived [see Fuchs; Picq]).

The point of this example, so far, is to demonstrate that family norms are put in place legislatively and then justified by reference to biology and that families are organized in reference to legal, not sexual, relations; they are not (as Agacinski and Théry imply) incarnations of the truth of nature. This means, in general, that families are infinitely malleable institutions (as demonstrated by laws on adoption, which have long permitted single adults as well as couples to establish legal kinship with people biologically unrelated to them).[4] It means specifically that the link between childbearing and childrearing is a product of history—the result of highly contested social policy decisions—not a requirement of nature or of its alter ego in the current debate, "the symbolic." This insight is not new for either historians of the family or for feminists; but another look at "la recherche de la paternité"—this time at the discussions about how to reform section 340 of the Civil Code—might illuminate it more completely.

In the course of the nineteenth century, feminists, social reformers, and legislators came up with ideas for changing the Code's provisions on paternity. Courts were already modifying these provisions by invoking other articles of the Code and awarding indemnities to women and children who were "hors mariage"; the indemnities were paid (sometimes only to the child, sometimes also to the mother) by the man proven to be the father of the child. (Paying the indemnity followed not from avowing paternity, but from having been responsible for unspecified "damages.") Reformers sought to bring the Code in line with juridical decisions; laws were proposed, but not passed, beginning in 1878. Some reformers were moved by moral considerations, wanting either to reign in men's promiscuity or to hold them accountable for (what feminist Jeanne Deroin referred to in 1883 as) their "égoïsme bestial." (Deroin, in fact, maintained that while fathers ought to be held accountable for the support of their children, mothers should not. If mothers abandoned their children or turned them over to others to raise, this was a decision that should be respected and considered in the best interests of the child ["La recherche"].) Others objected to the heavier burden a woman had to bear caring for the offspring of a sexual encounter (be it rape or seduction) or a longer-term relationship that had involved two people. Still others depicted women as the victims of male power, unwittingly or unwillingly seduced and then abandoned not only by the fathers of their children but by the law. When legislation finally passed in 1912, it held strictly to the juridical precedents, requiring not recognition of paternity but financial contributions to the support of children from single men only (to require such contributions from married men would be to destabilize their legitimate families). The illusion that children were the legitimate product only of marital sex was thereby maintained.

Feminists were divided in their opinion about how to change the law. Some wanted to punish men's depravity, others to vindicate women, but the more serious discussion had to do with the institution of marriage and the well-being of children. Would "la recherche de la paternité" end up endorsing the marital hierarchy feminists sought to change, or would it introduce greater equality into the parental relationship? Was there something other than a financial advantage to be won for the child? Did his well-being entail knowledge of his father, or would the removal of the epithet "bastard" be enough to guarantee social acceptance and emotional stability?

At the second Congrès International des Oeuvres et Institutions Féminines, held in Paris in 1900, these and other matters were discussed at length.[5] Jeanne Chauvin, the first woman to complete legal studies in France, urged that "la recherche de la paternité" be limited to the assessment of "damages" and that these be awarded to women as well as to children. This would involve neither legal recognition by the father of his child nor force the introduction of the "natural" child into the father's legitimate family. The goal was at once financial support for the mother, provision of the child's subsistence and education, and protection of "the family." As M. Bonzon put it: "To require child support from the father rather than paternity . . . also protects the legitimate family. That must be our aim: there are legitimate wives and children whose honor is every bit as important as that of the unmarried mother. We must think to this stranger whom you would have enter into the family, and of the odious union of bastards and legitimate children which would result" (*Congrès* 1:271). For reasons such as these—which distinguished between moral obligation and legal paternity—Chauvin's resolution was endorsed by a majority of the assembled delegates.

At the other end of the spectrum was the proposal of Maria Pognon. It gained few votes but elicited heated and sustained discussion. Pognon represented the Ligue pour le Droit des Femmes, which scoffed at the utility of "la recherche de la paternité." Not only was it a waste of time to track down delinquent fathers, Pognon pointed out, it also would not yield much money if the father was a worker and poor. Moreover, asking women to identify their sexual partners and to explain the circumstances under which they became pregnant was insulting and demeaning, and women were not always the victims of male predators; pregnancy could also be the unanticipated by-product of love. "The child that requires your attention is born of love, not of your social concepts" (*Congrès* 1:277). The consummation of loving relationships did not require marriage, Pognon implied. And concern for children—the future of any society—ought not to be determined by the legal status of their parents. "Whether a child be acknowledged by any particular father is not important; what is important is that child's subsistence and education" (*Congrès* 1:277). The word *bastard,* Pognon told M. Bonzon, does not belong in our vocabulary. "The child is to be respected no matter the condition in which he is born. He is a small being whose future remains unknown and who might, some day, be of great service to all men and women" (1:277). To care for all children, Pognon proposed bypassing families entirely, relying instead on a "Caisse de la maternité" open to all mothers "sans exception" and supported by the state. Pognon's proposal substituted the state for the father as financial guardian of the child, but it did not entirely endorse the paternalist rhetoric so evident among republican legislators at the turn of the century. And while it took for granted the fact that mothers would apply for the funds, it did not assume that they were entirely responsible for childrearing. That, too, should be supplied by agencies of the state.

Like feminists before and after her, Pognon defined reproduction as a social function and sought social compensation for women who performed this labor, a labor in the interests not of individuals or families, but of society as a whole. In 1853, Jeanne Deroin (informed by the teachings of Saint-Simon and Fourier) had proposed something like a "Caisse de la maternité" in these terms: "Each infant born is one more worker who will augment the social wealth in proportion to that which society is willing to advance her to assure the complete development and free exercise of all her capacities. When a woman becomes pregnant, bears a child, and nourishes it, she has done a job that profits everyone. It is therefore up to society to provide for the needs of mother and child" ("A l'auteur" 75).

From this it followed that marriage and inheritance laws ought to be replaced by "l'adoption des enfants par la famille sociale"; only then would women be emancipated and children equally treated. In the name of securing support for illegitimate children and their mothers, these feminist proposals called into question the entire rationale for the structure of the middle-class family and they envisaged the state (a state in which they would be represented as citizens) as the answer to patriarchy. While they seemed to appeal to the prevailing idea that mothers were solely responsible for the upbringing of their children, they, in fact, held out what seemed to be a more subversive plan. It was based on a social vision that separated childrearing from childbearing and refused legal regulation of sexual relationships while asking for state-supported childcare and education. Who raised the children was less important than that they all have equal access to the resources that would make them productive citizens and that no legal stigma attach to the circumstances of their birth or "family" life. This feminist politics assumed that families existed by law and that law could be changed to implement new social visions.

These feminist proposals, which sought to enlarge the conceptual terrain of "the family," were offered in response to the constrictions brought by the generalization of middle-class ideas and practices. Ariès ends his book with a description of what was involved in this transformation. Under the old regime, he says,

> People lived in a state of contrast; high birth or great wealth rubbed shoulders with poverty, vice with virtue, scandal with devotion. Despite its shrill contrasts, this medley of colours caused no surprise. . . . The old society concentrated the maximum numbers of ways of life into the minimum of space and accepted, if it did not impose, the bizarre juxtaposition of the most widely different classes. The new [middle-class] society, on the contrary, provided each way of life with a confined space in which it was understood that the dominant features should be respected, and that each person had to resemble a conventional model, an ideal type, and never depart from it under pain of excommunication. The concept of the family, the concept of class, and perhaps elsewhere the concept of race, appear as manifestations of the same intolerance towards variety, the same insistence on uniformity. (415)

I would add that the concept of normative heterosexuality, with its insistence that the genital difference of partners is the only proper basis for a "family," is also the product of this middle-class ideal type, another manifestation of "the same intolerance towards variety, the same insistence on uniformity" that made its appearance some two centuries ago.

In the nineteenth- and early-twentieth-century debates on the family, the good of the child, especially her psychic health, was largely absent from consideration. It is, in contrast, one of the central issues in today's discussions. One reason, of course, has to do with our late-twentieth-century preoccupation with psychology and with the incorporation of some psychoanalytic thinking into "common sense." Yet another, it seems to me, has to do with the anxiety that accompanies the loss of structures once taken for granted as defining features of social life. The passionate defense of heterosexual parenting comes at a moment of exhaustion for the family form that required it. That nuclear family is neither a realistic model nor a lived reality anymore. What will succeed it? This is one of the issues in the current debates. But there is another issue that extends beyond the question of who can appropriately adopt, bear, and raise children, and that has to do with sexual difference. The middle-class family was understood as the crucible of sexual difference, the place where reproduction happened—reproduction both of the species and of the social forms that guaranteed it. To the extent that this family was taken to be the only natural form for the expression of "natural" difference, its disappearance suggests the disappearance of sexual difference as well. The extreme anxiety that responds to this suggestion reveals what it seeks to conceal: that sexual difference is socially, culturally, linguistically produced. Drawing the line at homosexual parenting is not at all about the good of children, as Agacinski and Théry want to maintain. It is rather a way of protecting us from the knowledge—a knowledge feminism has been at great pains to produce—that the social organization of sex and sexual desire can take (and has historically taken) many different forms.

NOTES

I would like to thank Charles Shepherdson for his critical suggestions on the first draft of this essay, and Didier Eribon, Eric Fassin, Francoise Gaspard, and Claude Servan-Schreiber for helping me understand the nuances of the PaCS and the current debates about "the family" in France.

1. Agacinski spoke in *L'Express,* March 5, 1998, 38.
2. This appeared in *Le Nouvel Observateur,* June 11, 1998, 18.
3. Jeanne Deroin, "Profession de foi," 40. I used a copy of this handwritten document from the Fonds Enfantin, 7608, no. 39, at the Bibliothèque de l'Arsenal, which was made by Claire Goldberg Moses, to whom I am grateful for sharing it with me. Another version of the text is available as "Profession de foi de Mlle Jenny De Roin" in *De la liberté des femmes: Lettres de dames au Globe (1831–32),* ed. Michèle Riot-Sarcey (Paris: Côté-femmes, 1992), 116–39.
4. It is only in recent years that sexual identity—that is, heterosexuality—has become a prerequisite for those wishing to adopt. In the past homosexuals (without avowing their homosexuality) constituted families and secured the right to inherit property by one partner's adoption of the other. This is still possible if homosexuality is unacknowledged or concealed from the authorities.
5. The proceedings have been published as *Congrès international des oeuvres et institutions féminines,* 4 vols. (Paris: Blot, 1900).

Works Cited

Ariès, Philippe. *L'enfant et la vie familiale sous l'ancien régime* (Centuries of childhood: A social history of family life). Trans. Robert Baldick. New York: Vintage, 1962.

Congrès international des oeuvres et institutions féminines, 4 vols. Paris: Blot, 1900.

Degler, Carl. *At Odds: Women and the Family in America from the Revolution to the Present.* New York: Oxford University Press, 1980.

Deroin, Jeanne. "A l'auteur du *Douaire Universel.*" *Almanach des Femmes.* London: J. Watson, 1853.

———. "La recherche de la paternité." *Le Droit des Femmes,* Aug. 5, 1883.

———. "Profession de foi de Mlle Jenny De Roin." In *De la liberté des femmes: Lettres de dames au Globe (1831–32).* Ed. Michèle Riot-Sarcey, 116–40. Paris: Côté-femmes, 1992.

Fuchs, Rachel. *Poor and Pregnant in Paris: Strategies for Survival in the Nineteenth Century.* New Brunswick: Rutgers University Press, 1992.

Gouges, Olympe de. *Déclaration des droits de la femme.* 1791. Reprint. *Oeuvres.* Ed. Benoîte Groult. Paris: Mercure de France, 1986.

Hufton, Olwen. *The Poor of Eighteenth-Century France, 1750–1789.* New York: Oxford University Press, 1974.

Mitchell, Juliet, and Jacqueline Rose, eds. *Feminine Sexuality: Jacques Lacan and the École Freudienne* New York: Norton, 1983.
Offen, Karen. "Depopulation, Nationalism, and Feminism in Fin-de-siècle France." *American Historical Review* 89 (June 1984): 648–70.
Picq, Françoise. "Par delà la loi du père: Le débat sur la recherche de la paternité au congres féministe de 1900." *Les Temps Modernes* 34 (Feb. 1979): 1199–212.
Rousseau, Jean-Jacques. *Émile; or, On Education.* Trans. Allan Bloom. New York: Basic Books, 1979.
Scott, Joan W. *Only Paradoxes to Offer: French Feminists and the Rights of Man.* Cambridge: Harvard University Press, 1996.
Shepherdson, Charles. *Vital Signs: Nature, Culture, Psychoanalysis.* New York: Routledge, 2000.
Théry, Irène. *Couple, filiation et parenté aujourd'hui: Le droit face aux mutations de la famille et de la vie privée.* Paris: Odile Jacob, 1998.
Traer, James F. *Marriage and the Family in Eighteenth-Century France.* Ithaca: Cornell University Press, 1980.

PART 3

Changing Paradigms, Reconfiguring Boundaries: Social Practice and Social Science

10 Usages of Science and Science of Usages: On Homoparental Families

ERIC FASSIN

Translated by James Swenson

ONE OF THE MERITS OF the public debate in France over the Pacte Civil de Solidarité (PaCS) is that it has made the self-evidence of our definitions of marriage and the family open to question. Given that the law was intended to have no effect on marriage and even less effect on the family, this merit is something of a paradox. Still, whether we approve of or deplore this development, the definition of marriage and the family in terms of the "difference between the sexes" (to use the phrase employed in the controversy), or—if we are ready to abandon euphemisms—by the heterosexuality of the parental couple, can no longer go unsaid; we have shifted from the realm of the implicit to that of the explicit. Thus, no longer invisible, the definition can become the object of a public discussion, which means, properly speaking, that it has become debatable. The new social and political visibility of homosexual couples, and more particularly of families calling themselves "homoparental" (a neologism that has been spread by this debate), forces us to rethink our presuppositions.

The only common character of these homoparental families is the parents' homosexuality as is shown by the heterogeneity of the ways they are composed: the children can come from a past heterosexual life, from adoptions by single persons, artificial insemination for women, or projects for coparenting between gays and lesbians. In other words, at issue is less the inscription of the difference between the sexes in kinship than the admission of different sexualities within the family. The current social and political state of affairs thus raises important questions. Is the family heterosexual by definition, or rather is the "heteroparental family" not the model but one model among others (including a homoparental variant), however dominant it may be?

Does the definition of the family make the reality of homoparental families unthinkable? Or does the reality of homoparental families lead us to rethink our definition of the family? In this case, is the issue simply broadening the definition, making space for newcomers, or do we need, in a more radical way, to question the function of definition itself? Clearly, when society calls something into question like this, it is not without effects on the sciences of society. The sociological or anthropological definition has been shaken every bit as much as the social definition.

There is nothing surprising about this. The history of the social sciences does not take place outside the world. To the contrary, knowledge about society is enriched by the questions society poses to it. This does not mean that the scholar merely responds to a social demand; the scientific enterprise is characterized by its reformulation of questions. A defense of the autonomy of science does not require that we bracket the society we are talking about—or the society we are talking in. There is no need to imagine science on the model of a fortress erected against the tumult of the age, safeguarding its eternal truths from the century's turbulence. Science cannot be a fortified camp; its provisional constructions allow it to move on and, hopefully, advance. Far from being immutable, the social sciences move—they can move and therefore they must move. Anthropology and sociology, no less than history, have a calling for movement rather than immobility. How could we believe that social evolutions could fail to affect them?

The Abuse of Social Science: A Political Critique

In today's French society it seems quite natural, in preparation for a democratic debate on marriage and the family, to ask social scientists for a definition. What seems particularly obvious is the order: first the scientific definition, then the political deliberation. Nonetheless, this obviousness can be challenged and the question posed to us by current affairs displaced. We might indeed ask not how to define but rather, What does it mean to define marriage and the family? Need they be defined? Who ought to do the defining? In other words, the operation of scientific definition itself is perfectly capable of entering into our field of vision and becoming an object of reflection.

The issue here is not to propose, in the name of science, an alternative definition of marriage and the family that would open a door for homosexuals instead of refusing them access. Opening marriage and filiation to couples of the same sex is a matter of political choice and not some scientific necessity. This is a responsibility that falls upon the citizen rather than the scholar.[1] As Claude Lévi-Strauss recalled when asked about the PaCS, "Social choices do not belong to the scholar as such, but to the citizen (and the scholar is a citizen too)" (*Au-delà du PaCS*).[2] This does not mean that the social sciences must be condemned to an academic ivory tower. It is out of the question to reject, on this essential point, the heritage of Durkheim, who wrote a century ago, "We would esteem our research not worth the labor of a single hour if its interest were merely speculative" (xxvi). We do not mean to install an absurd division between the scholar who is deaf to politics and the politician who is blind to knowledge. It is thus entirely legitimate for sociologists and anthropologists to intervene as experts in order to inform public decision making—but not to claim to determine it scientifically.

The problem, in fact, stems from a confusion of roles.[3] In her 1998 report to the government on the family, the sociologist Irène Théry—taking up word for word the definition she had proposed of the family in 1996 and of marriage in 1997—tries to define kinship in the following terms: "In the most universal sense of the word, beyond all differences between cultures, kinship is the institution that articulates the difference between the sexes with the difference between generations" (*Couple* 21).[4] *Couple, Descent, and Kinship Today*—the title of her report—thereby appear as anchored, sheltered from the winds of history, in the so-called anthropological (a frequently repeated term) harbor of a universal and immutable—that is, ahistorical—definition.

Such a definition must, of course, be understood as a reaction to the emergence of the homoparental question, in opposition to demands for innovation in the domain of the family. Its value lies less in what it allows us to think than in what it makes unthinkable. Its normative character appears clearly in the stigmatizing effects it has not only on homoparental families but also on monoparental ones, neither of which is founded on "the difference between the sexes," that is, on both maternal and paternal filiation. Moreover, legal as well as social norms are at stake. Thus, adoption by an unmarried person, which is currently legal in France, would have no place in this model, as the National Union of Family Associations, among other groups, noticed during the recent debates.

Whereas the counsel a scholar may give to a politician gives us no grounds for speaking of usurpation, we must be vigilant against the abuse of scholarly authority when it claims to provide a scientific determination of political decision making. Expertise is legitimate only when it recognizes itself for what it is. When, on the contrary, it passes definitions off as truths engraved in the eternal marble of nature or culture and thus replaces democratic deliberation with an "anthropological" determination, the expert is usurping the prerogatives of representative democracy. Indeed, under the guise of a preliminary definition, the very order of things is ordained; the parameters and perimeter of political debate are imposed as if they were axiomatic and not subject to reflection (as a working hypothesis might be). Such an abuse of scholarly authority occludes the political choices behind the definition. Pierre Bourdieu had already drawn this "lesson" in 1982:

> When the sociologist claims the right—which is sometimes actually granted to him—to state the limits between classes, regions, or nations, to decide upon the authority of science whether or not social classes exist, and how many, or whether such and such a social class—proletariat, peasantry, or petty bourgeoisie—, such and such a geographical unity—Brittany, Corsica or Occitania—, is a reality or a fiction, he assumes or usurps the functions of the archaic *rex,* who, according to Benveniste, is invested with the power of *regere fines* and *regere sacra,* that is, the power to establish borders and limits, to establish the sacred. (*Leçon* 12)

In the same way, stating the limits of the family does not mean describing what is but prescribing what ought to be—and thus what is and what is not a family. The delimitation of an inside and an outside, of a zone of inclusion and a zone of exclusion, is, as we have said, a properly political task not a scientific one.

Irène Théry herself has given us one of the most severe warnings against the dangers of expert opinion, particularly in the domain of the sociology of the family. In her work on divorce she demonstrated the harm that can result from an abuse of scientific authority:

> Such so-called expertise (*ces prétendus savoirs*) are the defeat of scientific knowledge (*connaissance*), just as psychobabble is the defeat of clinical psychology, psychiatry and psychoanalysis, just as sociologism is the defeat of sociology. Transformed into social expert opinion, always saying something more and different than what they are competent to say, it only provides support and nourishment for moralism, that degraded form of morality. It gives people the impression that they need to know when in reality they need to choose, that is, make a determination of values. Expertise thinks for other people. (*Le démariage* 422)

What is true of invocations of "the best interests of the child" is no less true when it comes to drawing the limits of the family; what is true of psychologistic expertise is no less true of the "anthropological" illusion.

The warning, moreover, is valid for everyone. Scholars as such have no more of a vocation to legitimate the demands of homoparental families than to oppose them. What I am proposing here should not be seen as a "contrary expert opinion," given in the service of an association, for example, against the expert opinion submitted to the government. The critique of abuse of expertise is equally valid whatever the policy or political agent for whose legitimacy it claims to provide a scientific foundation. This critique is necessary to preserve democratic deliberation from being overtaken by science. It is no less indispensable to preserve the autonomy of scientific debate from the intrusion of politics and thus protects the specificity of both scientific work and political choice. When it goes too far, expertise abuses both scholarly and political legitimacy.

The Sciences of Social Usages: An Epistemological Critique

To avoid this abuse, would the social sciences have to renounce the practice of definition? Or would they perhaps have to revise their definition of definition? In fact, the political critique is indissociable from an epistemological critique. On the one hand, it is not up to scholarship to define the rules of the social world—this is the political critique. On the other hand, even if there is no attempt to impose them in political debates, the scholar's vocation is not necessarily to propose scientific definitions of the social world—this is the epistemological critique, which we now need to set out in detail.

Definition in the Social Sciences

What if the task of the social sciences was not to produce definitions of the social world, to trace the limits of the thinkable and the unthinkable, those of the licit and the illicit? Doubtless, proper method seems to call for a preliminary definition of the object—in this case the family but also any social group—whether intensively by means of a theoretical proposition or extensively by means of a statistical category. After all, is not knowing ahead of time what we are talking about the minimal requirement of rigor? Still, we might suggest that this is not how the social sciences, insofar as they are historical, actually proceed. The most fruitful works in the tradition, even when they bear on a social category, do not give a priori definitions but rather seek to define the group historically so that the labor of definition itself becomes the object of research.

Two exemplary works give a good illustration of this procedure, one in the field of history and the other in sociology. The first one analyzes the elaboration of the working class in England: E. P. Thompson's *The Making of the English Working Class.* The second traces the constitution of a new social category in France: Luc Boltanski's *The Making of a Class: Cadres in French Society.* In both cases the definition is not posed at the outset but rather emerges in the course of research, since the authors see the labor of representation as political in nature, which means that the labor of definition is historical in nature. Before the social sciences, it is society that is engaged in a permanent labor of definition and redefinition; social history and historical sociology attempt to account for this "work in progress."

For the scholar it is not only bad politics but also bad methodology to supplant social agents by using science to impose a representation of the social world. Definition is not an objective and neutral scientific instrument but the stakes of political struggle. The social sciences, in order to avoid being instrumentalized, need to take the political history of definitions as their object. The scholar ought not to define the family. He or she cannot speak the "truth" of the family; his or her first task is to study the battles that take place around such representations. We again encounter here the warning of Pierre Bourdieu, echoing the thought of Michel Foucault: The relations between knowledge and power are played out in the very idea of truth. This is why the sociologist (and the same can be said of the anthropologist) "is he who attempts to speak the truth of the struggles concerning, among other things, the truth" (*Leçon* 16). However much of an expert he may be, he must refuse the temptation, inherited from the philosopher-king, to define the truth of society in the place of social agents. Here the epistemological critique leads to the same conclusion as the political critique.

But how can we talk about something in the absence of a preliminary definition? If we must renounce giving a preliminary definition, how should the scholar proceed, particularly when talking about "the family"? We would propose the following response: Anthropology and sociology are based on description rather than on definition. Or rather, far from replacing description, definition is indistinguishable from it. The social sciences are, in fact, sciences of social usages. They give an account of these usages—not in the sense of the usual and customary but in the sense of utilizations. In this sense, a definition is not the principle of a practice but the converse. For example, it is familial practices that define, not "the family" but the "family" of families (we shall return to this point). How do social agents play upon "the family" to "make families"?

Anthropological Universality

However, this is neither the way in which the question is posed to the social sciences today, nor the way they themselves pose it when confronted with the new reality of "homoparental" families. It is true that sociological expertise finds itself in a disadvantaged position. It is used to working with statistically significant realities, based on demographic data, which presuppose quantitatively substantial transformations. The transformations accompanying divorce and the recomposition of families, cohabitation, and births outside of marriage are clearly visible in this way. With homoparental families as well as with new techniques for medically assisted procreation, sociology finds itself faced with the difficulty of phenomena that are statistically invisible. The question then is not whether law needs to catch up to mores but of making a juridical choice that anticipates social evolution. In other words, the expertise demanded is no longer a posteriori but a priori.

This is why the demand for expertise, as was also the case in debates in bioethics, is primarily oriented toward anthropology.[5] It is well known that the arguments about the "symbolic order," articulated in opposition to homoparentality, whether coming from politicians, intellectuals, bishops of the Catholic Church, or psychoanalysts, have constantly made reference to the "anthropological foundations" of culture (Fassin, "L'illusion anthropologique"). Here the adjective *anthropological* refers to a universality transcending cultural specifities that allows for the definition of the norm in an intangible way. This is how Irène Théry justifies the political function of her definition: "It is unclear, *a priori,* why an abstract definition based on *all the known forms of family and kinship in the world* would be 'an abusive use of the social sciences.' It would seem more reasonable to think that this is the best of scientific (and even political) uses of anthropology, since the goal of the universality of the category is to set aside ethnocentric temptations, insofar as a more restrictive category risks assigning the Other to foreignness [*l'étrangeté*]" ("PaCS, sexualité" 166, emphasis in the original). Anthropological universality is then assigned a normative value. The common denominator of the definition indicates the minimal characteristics that are and must always and everywhere be present.

There is good reason to be surprised when we see "anthropological" logic identify the universality of the norm in order to pose and impose "the difference between the sexes" as the principle of marriage, the family, and kinship. We might recall that for Claude Lévi-Strauss, far from being identical with it, the norm is, in fact, opposed to universality as culture is to nature: "Let us suppose then that everything universal in man relates to the natural order, and that everything subject to a norm is cultural and is both relative and particular." The argument of *The Elementary Structures of Kinship* rests precisely on this opposition, which is transcended in only one case: "The prohibition of incest . . . presents, without the slightest ambiguity, and inseparably combines, the two characteristics in which we recognize the conflicting features of two mutually exclusive orders. It constitutes a rule, but a rule which, alone among all the social rules, possesses at the same time a universal character" (8–9). For Lévi-Strauss, the prohibition of incest is the only example of a universal rule. It is, moreover, necessary to understand clearly the nature of this universality, which is by no means an invariant; it presupposes no hard kernel, not fixed content or common denominator transcending cultural particularities. "The *fact of being a rule*, completely independent of its modalities, is indeed the very essence of the incest prohibition" (32, emphasis in the original). In other words, even though the rules are different everywhere, the rule is absent nowhere. If the rule must always be present, it may never be the same.[6]

An approach that attempts to found the familial norm on the universality of the rule thus could not be based on Lévi-Strauss's work. The invocation of the universality of the difference between the sexes in debates on the PaCS refers instead to Françoise Héritier's analyses of the "differential valency of the sexes."[7] In her work on kinship, Héritier does indeed recall Durkheim's axiom that "all kinship is social," which, she comments, is what justifies the fact that "it can be said that kinship systems only exist in the consciousness of men and are arbitrary systems of representations." And, she acquiesces, "all this is certainly true." But her agreement leads immediately to a qualification: "Still, we claim that it is on the basis of a biological given, which can only have been the same from all eternity, that human thought has refined and symbolized by exploring all of the logical possibilities for paradigmatic combinations that this substrate offers" (*L'exercice de la parenté* 15–16).[8] This implies that Lévi-Strauss's analysis is incomplete. "We will thus introduce here a *second fundamental law* of kinship, which is in fact the very condition of the first and which is every bit as deeply disguised and ignored, for the same reasons, namely the apparently natural force of its self-evidence: the *differential valency of the sexes* or, if you prefer, the *different place of the two sexes within a table of values*, more generally the domination of the masculine principle over the feminine principle" (ibid. 50, emphasis in the original).

Héritier's addition represents a substantial movement away from the principles of Lévi-Strauss's analysis. It is true that in the *Elementary Structures* it is always men who exchange women: "The total relation of exchange which constitutes marriage is not established between a man and a woman, where each owes and receives something, but between two groups of men, and the woman figures only as one of the objects in the exchange, not as one of the partners between whom the exchange takes place" (115). Elsewhere, Lévi-Strauss explains, "Women readers, who may be shocked to see themselves reduced to being objects of exchange between male partners, can be reassured that the rules of the game would remain unchanged were the opposite convention adopted, with men being exchanged between women's groups. As a matter of fact, a few societies of a highly developed matrilineal type have, to a limited extent, expressed things that way" ("The Family" 60). But it is not a matter of a simple permutation, for the reasoning can be pushed even further: "And both sexes can accommodate themselves to a slightly more complicated description of the game, which says that groups consisting of both men and women exchange among themselves kinship relations" (ibid.). Conversely, for Héritier, "the facts are stubborn. . . . If logic implies the total reversibility (or reciprocity) of the formula without doing any harm to the system as a whole, reality stubbornly continues to show that the overwhelming majority of human societies has illustrated only one of the two logically possible sides of a single realization" ("La citadelle imprenable" 78).[9] The "differential valency of the sexes" is indeed the "second fundamental law of kinship."

Héritier does not see the biological universality of the difference between the sexes as directly determining kinship; otherwise, its variations would be incomprehensible. Still, the "basic givens" of this substrate constrain thought. Certain figures, "logically possible and thinkable in conceptual terms," thus remain "unthinkable in natural terms, viscerally unallowable and technically impossible to realize" (*L'exercice de la parenté* 51). In other terms, "The observation of the difference between the sexes is the foundation of all thought, scientific as well as traditional. . . . sexual difference and the different roles of the sexes in reproduction" forms the "final stumbling block of thought" (*Masculin/féminin* 19). The normative possibilities of this cognitive constraint have appeared quite clearly in the recent debate. Thus Héritier, in an interview with the Catholic newspaper *La Croix,* recalls her conception of the difference between the sexes as "inescapable stumbling blocks of thought" to explain (the expression is used as the title of the article) that "no society allows homosexual kinship." She goes on to comment upon this refusal: "Thinking means, first of all, classifying, and classifying means discriminating, and the fundamental discrimination is based on the difference between the sexes. This is an irreducible fact. We cannot decree that such differences do not exist; they are inescapable stumbling blocks of thought, like the opposition of day and night." And, the anthropologist adds,

"Our modes of thought and our social organization are founded primarily on the observation of the difference between the sexes. It is impossible to maintain reasonably that this difference can be displaced upon the homosexual couple" ("Aucune société" 16). "Homosexual kinship" would thus be impossible because it is unthinkable.

We should note in passing that if the universality of the difference between the sexes, defined as a fundamental law of kinship, can, as is the case here, result in a normative anthropology, this consequence is not inevitable. Indeed, a program for a critical anthropology can be found in Héritier's work. In *Masculin/féminin* she calls for a logic of "unveiling": "The permanence of ideas and thoughts about difference that we have described should not lead to the conclusion that every effort to make established disparities disappear is doomed to inexorable failure, but should rather lead to the certainty that struggle requires a knowledge of the nature of the enemy that will allow us to adapt our combat appropriately" (10). In this case the object is less the difference between the sexes itself than the "thinking of difference" (as Héritier's subtitle puts it), that is, "representations" and "interpretations." The author thus appeals to Voltaire in order to fight "prejudice." In this case, anthropology can contribute to "changing things" rather than insisting on their immutability.

Redefining Definition

Clearly, it is no more necessary to identify empirical universality and social norm than to suppose that behind a definition, however universal it may be, lies an invariable common denominator. To escape this double identification we can begin by looking for cracks in the wall, that is, exceptions to the universality of the rule. Take the phenomenon, well known among anthropologists since the 1930s, of "woman-marriages." The most famous example was reported by E. E. Evans-Pritchard: "What seems to us, but not at all to the Nuer, a somewhat strange union is that in which a woman marries another woman and counts as the pater of the children born of the wife" (108).[10] In Héritier's eyes this is not truly an exception because, as Evans-Pritchard had clearly stated, one of the two women who is barren "for this reasons counts in some respects as a man."

To return to the current situation, this logic would seem to make it necessary (but also, no doubt, sufficient) for one partner in a lesbian couple to "be" the man, and, in a gay couple, for one to "be" the woman" for homosexual kinship to become thinkable. Indeed, according to Héritier, the problem (contrary to the situation among the Nuer) is that "there is in our societies no social rule stating which partner in a homosexual couple is the father and which the mother" ("Aucune société" 16). But it would be overly hasty to conclude that this filiation is only possible in inegalitarian societies that assign the two sexes clearly distinct roles and that as a consequence "no society admits homosexual kinship." Perhaps the reverse is true, and it is in our societies featuring undifferentiated filiation that the difference between the sexes (establishing who is the father and who is the mother) is less indispensable than in societies featuring unilinear descent. In any case, today, even in the United States, "homosexual" kinship exists not only in practice but also in the eyes of the law.[11] This fact is no less stubborn, and anthropology must take it, too, into account, even in France.[12]

The ultimate interest of such exceptions is not that they require a reformulation of the definition but rather that they put into question the universality of any definition, none of which can speak the universal (and thus definitive) truth of marriage and descent. This tendency can be seen in the critical reflections proposed by some British anthropologists who are particularly close readers of Lévi-Strauss's work. As early as the 1950s Edmund Leach suggested that marriage is nothing more than a "bundle of rights" and drew the conclusion that "all universal definitions of marriage are vain." He thus dismissed the definition given by a then-current English anthropology textbook, the substance of which is widely accepted in France today: "Marriage is a union between a man and a woman such that children born to the woman are recognized legitimate offspring of both partners" ("Polyandry" 105).[13] The empirical critique thus leads to a rejection of the universalist definition (or perhaps of a particular conception of universality). The same thing is true of marriage that is true of the incest taboo: The *fact* is universal but not its character, which is infinitely variable.

This theoretical attitude was subsequently taken up by Rodney Needham, leading him to rethink the definition. Beyond technical debates on particular points, the anthropologist proposes a "skeptical" approach to kinship. For Needham, "The phenomena classed as 'kinship,' for instance, do not in all cases possess any specific features such as could justify the formulation of general propositions about them." More generally, "there need not be . . . anything that the phenomena of 'kinship' have in common, or that the phenomena of 'marriage,' 'descent,' 'relationship terminology,' or 'incest' respectively have in common." The problem stems from our way of thinking about classification: "We are inclined by our conceptual habits to assume that there must be something in common to all the phenomena that we class together as 'kinship' and the rest, and it is this unanalyzed premiss that leads us into theoretical difficulty" (*Remarks* 30). In matters of kinship we must give up the search for common denominators.[14]

In short, "there is no such thing as kinship, and it follows that there can be no such thing as kinship theory." This does not, however, require us to give up talking about "marriage," "the family," or "kinship." As Needham puts it, "If an ethnographer sets out to tell us about marriage, we have at least a preliminary indication that he is not going to focus directly on dam building." To put it another way, words like "marriage" are useful provided that we take them for what they are and do not attribute to them a theoretical function unifying the diversity of their usages. They are, in fact, "'odd job' words." Needham borrows the expression, and beyond it the whole theory of "family likenesses," from Wittgenstein ("Remarks" 5). The critique bears on an illusion found in both science and ordinary language that makes us seek a common denominator in all of our "collective representations, whether they [be] the quasi-technical generalizations of social anthropologists or the ordinary resources of everyday language," where, in fact, there are only "family likenesses" ("Polythetic Classifications" 65).

Wittgenstein's contribution can be a decisive one for the social sciences, as Jacques Bouveresse and Pierre Bourdieu have understood in France (Bouveresse, "L'animal," *Le mythe;* Bourdieu, *Craft of Sociology, Logic of Practice;* Bourdieu, Chamboredon, and Passeron). Wittgenstein proposes a critique of the illusions inherent in philosophical language and in particular of our "craving for generality": "the tendency to look for something in common to all the entities which we commonly subsume under a general term.—We are inclined to say that there must be something in common to all games, say, and that this common property is the justification for applying the general term 'game' to the various games; whereas games form a *family* the members of which have family likenesses. Some of them have the same nose, others the same eyebrows and others the same way of walking; and these likenesses overlap" (*Preliminary Studies* 17). In this sense, but in this sense only, "'games' form a family" (*Philosophical Investigations* §67, 32). The abstraction of definition is always a misinterpretation claiming to give a word a unique, universal, and definitive meaning. In reality, it would be better to make an inventory of usages, united by only partial resemblances.

As Bouveresse writes, "The error committed here is the belief that the task of philosophy is to disengage unitary concepts or essences from the extreme diversity of usages and examples." Not that we need to renounce using these words: "one can perfectly well use them, and even give them a central place in philosophical research, without feeling obliged to define them in advance" (*Le mythe de l'intériorité* 211). The problem is not words but the illusion of definition. "We are unable clearly to circumscribe the concepts we use; not because we don't know their real definition, but because there is no real 'definition' to them" (Wittgenstein, *Preliminary Studies* 25). The common denominator of definition does not exist; between usages there is only an *"air de famille."* Still, and this is the last point we must now address, the critique of universal definitions does not reduce the anthropological project to nothingness by condemning it to cultural relativism. Indeed, taking inspiration from Wittgenstein, anthropology could take as its object of study, rather than invariants, the grammar of social usages.

Un air de famille: How to Say Things with Acts

The goal of the twofold critique that we have sketched out here is to trace the limits not of the family but of the power and knowledge wielded by the social sciences. The political critique bears upon the use of scholarly authority. Scientific reason should not be called upon to decide democratic debates. Expertise is abusive when it substitutes a self-proclaimed scientific necessity for a political choice. The epistemological critique could be summarized as "the most perfect science in the world cannot give what it does not have." We should not ask the sociologist or the anthropologist to give us universal and immutable definitions of the social world. That is not their job. It is important to recall both what science ought not to do and what it cannot do. Still, the positive vocation of this twofold critique is to open up a reflection upon what the social sciences *can* say and do—on the condition of taking into account the place of social actors and the role of social practices in the definition not of "the family," as we have seen, but of the "family of families."

For Wittgenstein, apprehending the meaning of a word does not imply a definition that would be the principle of its different usages. The philosopher insists upon this point: "Let's not forget that a word hasn't got a meaning given to it, as it were, by a power independent of us, so that there could be a kind of scientific investigation into what the word *really* means" (*Preliminary Studies* 28, emphasis in the original). The political critique can always invert the epistemological critique. At the moment that sociologists and anthropologists think that they have disengaged an absolute definition of marriage, the family, or kinship they are, in fact, only rediscovering not their universal signification but the definition imposed by "a power independent of us"—namely, the state. As a matter of fact, the administration that requests an expert report finds it all the more authoritative insofar as it gives an explicit, scientific formulation to the implicit definition and categories that already organize the state's thinking.

This is the argument of Pierre Bourdieu's text "The Family Spirit." Faced with the definition of the family, scepticism is more reasonable that realism, at least during a first moment. Indeed, "If it is true that the family is only a word, it is also true that it is an active 'watchword'" (66). This category has on its side the weight of institutions; this fiction is quite real. The agents of the state—statisticians, social workers and judges, but also sociologists—"help to reproduce the institutional thinking that is part of the conditions of functioning of the family." To sum up, "The family is indeed a fiction, a social artifact, an illusion in the most ordinary sense of the word, but a 'well-founded illusion,' because, being produced and reproduced with the guarantee of the state, it receives from the state at every moment the means to exist and persist" (72–73).

Still, a somewhat different lesson, not entirely in agreement with Bourdieu's analysis, can be drawn from Wittgenstein's thought. The epistemological critique, together with the political critique, opens the possibility of conceptualizing not only the reproduction that would condemn the family never to change but also a transformation. After all, "the family" never stops changing. It is in history, traversed by history. New usages do manage to impose themselves—that is, new actors manage to impose them. Social actors can shake up the circular definition that is passed back and forth between the state and institutional forms of knowledge; sometimes they disturb this reproduction of the same. In other words, we ought to replace the analysis of definitions with the study of usages. The truth of the family is no more inscribed in the eternity of the categories of the state than in the Platonic heaven of abstract ideas. Families are incarnated in practices and thus liable to change.

And we can see today, in fact, a new social evolution and political transformation. The social evolution refers to changes in homosexual lifestyles consisting of a reappropriation of coupledom and, via children, the family. The political transformation comprises the work of representation before the media and in the political sphere, properly speaking, that makes such changes visible. The Association of Gay and Lesbian Parents is one vector of this movement, along with other associations and a few politicians and intellectuals. As we have seen, this novelty is expressed by a neologism: the homoparental family. The acceptance of this new usage represents a substantial victory. Yesterday, the idea of a homoparental family seemed to be an oxymoron; today, it is the affirmation that homoparental families are not families that is beginning to seem like a contradiction in terms. Social and political practices have transformed language and definition through usage. The way in which the truth of the family is generally imposed by legitimate instances has been interrupted, their performative magic disturbed by the play of the actors. The classic proposition about speech acts can be reversed. Here, doing is saying.

To illustrate this appropriation of language by practices and the renewal of representations resulting from it, we can take the example of a contrast between two important French daily newspapers. In the wake of the debate on the PaCS, *Le Monde* recently devoted its lead article to "Homosexual Couples Who Want Children" (Krémer). The articles on the topic, of course, recall the existence of debates ("sociologists, psychiatrists, and psychoanalysts are divided") but also present an image of ordinary families—families like any other. This banalization forms part of a decision to adopt a descriptive approach. Even if it is "statistically invisible," it is nonetheless a "reality." *Le Monde*'s readers can recognize themselves in these portraits and feel that, in the end, the difference is not that great. The surest sign of the "normalization" of the homoparental question is that laughter without homophobic sarcasm has become possible, as can be seen in the cartoons by Plantu and Pessin.

A few months later, *Libération* decided to include the homoparental family in a series devoted to "the century's families" (Daumas). For *Libération,* the example of Carla and Marie-Laure does not illustrate the new banality of homoparentality but rather emphasizes the difference of "the life of this family unlike others." "Children of May 68, Carla and Marie-Laure lived in a threesome (with Carla's boyfriend), then as a couple, and now have a family of five, since they have had three children together by means of artificial insemination." *Libération*'s readers, in contrast to *Le Monde*'s, may recognize themselves more easily in this freedom of desire, presented as a legacy of the 1970s. The questioning of the norm rather than the normality of the homoparental family is highlighted. These two articles represent opposite but complementary ways of inscribing the homoparental family in the general landscape of "the family." The difference between these examples clearly shows the acceptance of the usage. Everyone can have his or her own image of the homoparental family.

We can now return to our starting point. What is a family? We all know that the singular is deceptive since there are so many different families. But we must push the analysis of the plural even further. Behind the diversity of families no minimal definition is to be found. Homoparental families thus hold a great interest for the social sciences. They help rethink the definition, not only with a view toward broadening it, as was already the case with recomposed families, but in order to call into question our definition of definition. Indeed, the difference between the sexes is perhaps the last common denominator that is in the process of disappearing from the principle of the family. It is true that we could have learned it long ago from ethnology, but we were not ready to listen. The well-anchored self-evidences of our own societies prevented us from hearing what Leach had to say in the 1950s and Needham in the 1970s. Our culture had to change in the 1990s before we could understand what other cultures clearly called into question—namely, the idea of a unitary definition overarching the diversity of families.

Of course, no model of the family incarnates the family by uniting all of its traits. This ideal model is not an ideal-type—a legitimate norm, perhaps, but not a definition. Homoparental families have in common with other families only (but this is certainly enough) *"un air de famille"*: the mouth of one, the eyes of another, this one's chin and that one's nose.[15] Like heteroparental families, they can be recomposed. Like monoparental families, they can be constructed with a single parent, and in any case without dual descent from a father and a mother. Like families that have recourse to *adoption simple,* they can be based on plural descent and coparenting. Like heteroparental families resulting from medically assisted fertility, or using the route *adoption plénière,* they sometimes bracket biological origins—and sometimes not.[16] In short, homoparental families find their place in a "family of families," with no presupposition of a common denominator going beyond partial resemblances being either necessary or possible. We must thus renounce the idea of substituting some other hard kernel for the difference between the sexes in order to account for this new reality. The description of the usages of the family is enough of a definition.

Moreover, this is why, even though it is statistically marginal, the example of homoparental families leads us to reconsider the totality of familial configurations. They point out clearly what remains to be thought in the family, what just yesterday we believed was unthinkable. As always, the social sciences have much to learn from social reality. And while they can study the transformations of the definition of the family, they must not be allowed to prevent such transformations from occurring in the name of the definitions they give. Whether we are anthropologists or sociologists, we should not mistake our vocation; our definitions are never definitive because they are always descriptive. History imposes regular revisions on us by making us account for a constantly shifting reality. We need to renounce the idea that definitions are the defining principle of reality. The job of the sociologist or anthropologist is to study the grammar of social usages. If the social sciences can thus modify their definition of definition, we are allowed to think that they could more easily escape the normative temptation to define "proper usage."

NOTES

1. On this distinction, I would refer in particular to my testimony ("Pour l'égalité des sexualités") before the Commission des Lois of the Senate during public hearings on the PaCS (Jan. 27, 1999): "I am a sociologist, but if I am appearing before you today it is in the name of a political principle and not a scientific one: equality" (Senate [France] 176).

2. The sentence is drawn from a letter dated July 19, 1999 (*Au-delà du PaCS* 109–10), which Lévi-Strauss sent in response to my questions.

3. I will only recall briefly here the political critique of the abuse of expertise that I have developed elsewhere as a prelude to another critique, this one of an epistemological nature. Recalling it is necessary, because we will eventually need to articulate the two critiques. For my analysis of the work of Irène Théry, see Fassin, "Le savant"; in "L'intellectuel spécifique,'" I propose a way of going beyond the choice between "pure scholarship" and expertise.

4. Théry first proposed these definitions in two articles that were also published as "Notes of the Fondation Saint-Simon." "The family can be considered as the institution that articulates the difference between the sexes with the difference between generations" (Théry, "Différence des sexes" 68). Moreover, "Marriage is not the institution of the couple, but the institution that links the difference between the sexes with the difference between generations" (Théry, "Le contrat d'union sociale" 181).

5. I have tried to analyze this contrast between anthropological and sociological forms of expertise in Fassin, "La voie de l'expertise."

6. Similarly, in order to conceptualize the universality of the symbolic function, Lévi-Strauss refuses to accord it any content. In contrast to the subconscious, full of images accumulated during an individual life, "the unconscious . . . is always empty—or, more accurately, it is as alien to mental images as is the stomach to the foods which pass through it" ("The Effectiveness of Symbols" 203).

7. We will not discuss here the other half of the definition ("the difference between generations"), whose political role is far less prominent. Still, we can again refer to Lévi-Strauss: "On the very occasion of marriage, numerous societies practice the confusion of generations, the mingling of ages, the reversal of roles, and the identification of what we regard as incompatible relationships" (*The Elementary Structures of Kinship* 487). Lévi-Strauss is here critiquing Malinowski, who had imprudently affirmed that "no society could exist under such conditions" (486).

8. The citation from Durkheim is taken from his review article, "Prof. J. Kohler."

9. Héritier is discussing the analysis of François Héran.

10. We could also look at the radical example of the Na of China: Cai Hua suggests that it is, in fact, a "society without fathers or husbands," in other words, a radically matrilineal society in which the difference between the sexes does not define descent and marriage does not exist (*A Society without Fathers or Husbands*). Regardless of

the theoretical or empirical criticisms that can be made, the example is at the very least thought-provoking.

11. Moreover, this is not only the case by means of successive adoptions by the two parents, but also, in New Jersey since 1997, by means of joint adoption. The unthinkable is already thought.

12. The first works by American anthropologists are already several years old (Lewin; Weston). In France, Anne Cadoret is conducting research on homoparental families. Since this article was first published, the Netherlands, the U.K., and Sweden have authorized adoption for same-sex couples—all three countries belong to the European Union just as France does.

13. Leach returns to the controversy his article generated, and continues that argument, in "Marriage, Legitimacy, Alliance."

14. This book is dedicated to Leach, and the references to him are important; see also Needham, *Remarks and Inventions: Skeptical Essays on Kinship.* Despite the fact that *Rethinking Kinship and Marriage* has been translated into French as *La parenté en question* (Paris: Seuil, 1977), Needham's arguments appear to be ignored to an astonishing degree in current French debates. Thus Francis Zimmerman, in his synthesis *Enquête sur la parenté,* does not list this book in his bibliography nor discuss this line of argument. He only mentions Needham's more technical contributions and describes him in a biographical note as a "vigorous defender of structuralism and the theory of *alliance* in the Anglo-Saxon world" (228).

15. Should the metaphor of the *air de famille*—especially as applied to a family of families—suggest a naturalization of kinship (biological ties causing such "physical" resemblances), it is worth bearing in mind that the perception of likeness is indeed a social construction, related to kinship systems rather than biological laws (Vernier).

16. The distinction in French family law between *adoption simple* and *adoption plénière* corresponds roughly to that between "open" and "closed" adoption in the United States, but the distinction is legal rather than pragmatic and social. Thus in an *adoption simple* both birth and adoptive parents are considered to be legal parents of the child, whereas in an *adoption plénière* the birth parents cease to have any legal relation to the child whatsoever.

Works Cited

Boltanski, Luc. *The Making of a Class: Cadres in French Society.* Trans. Arthur Goldhammer. New York: Cambridge University Press, and Paris: Éditions de la Maison des Sciences de l'Homme, 1987.

Bourdieu, Pierre, Jean-Claude Chamboredon, and Jean-Claude Passeron. "Appendix: The Family Spirit." In *Practical Reason: On the Theory of Action,* 64–74. Stanford: Stanford University Press, 1998.

———. *The Craft of Sociology: Epistemological Preliminaries.* Trans. Richard Nice. New York: Walter de Gruyter, 1991.

Bourdieu, Pierre. *Leçon sur la leçon.* Paris: Minuit, 1982.

———. *The Logic of Practice.* Trans. Richard Nice. Stanford: Stanford University Press, 1990.

Bouveresse, Jacques. "L'animal cérémoniel: Wittgenstein et l'anthropologie." Post-script to Ludwig Wittgenstein, *Remarques sur le rameau d'or de Frazer* (Paris: L'Âge d'Homme, 1982), 39–124.
———. *Le mythe de l'intériorité: Expérience, signification et langage privée chez Wittgenstein.* Paris: Minuit, 1976.
Cai Hua. *A Society without Fathers or Husbands: The Na of China.* Trans. Asti Hustvedt. New York: Zone Books, 2001.
Daumas, Cécile. "Mémoires intimes d'un siècle bouleversé: Mes deux mamans, et moi, et moi, et moi." *Libération,* Aug. 24, 1999, ii–iv.
Durkheim, Émile. *The Division of Labor in Society.* Trans. W. D. Halls. New York: Free Press, 1984.
———. "Prof. J. Kohler, Zur Urgeschichte der Ehe." *Année Sociologique* 1 (1898): 316–18.
Evans-Pritchard, E. E. *Kinship and Marriage among the Nuer.* 1951. Reprint. New York: Oxford University Press, 1990.
Fassin, Éric. "La voie de l'expertise et les silences de la science dans le débat démocratique." In *Au-delà de PaCS,* 89–110.
———. "Le savant, l'expert et le politique: La famille des sociologies." *Genèses* 32 (Sept. 1998): 156–69.
———. "L'illusion anthropologique: homosexualité et filiation." *Témoin* 12 (May 1998): 43–56.
———. "'L'intellectuel spécifique' et le PaCS: politique des saviors." *Mouvements* 7 (Jan.–Feb. 2000): 68–76.
Héran, Françoise. "De granet à Lévi-Strauss: 1. L'échange à sens unique." *Social Anthropology* 6, no. 1 (1998): 1–61.
Héritier, Françoise. "Aucune société n'admet de parenté homosexuelle." Interview with Marianne Gomez. *La Croix,* Nov. 9, 1998, 16.
———. "La citadelle imprenable." *Critique* 620–21 (Jan.–Feb. 1999): 61–88.
———. *L'exercice de la parenté.* Paris: Hautes Études, Gallimard/Le Seuil, 1981.
———. *Masculin/féminin: La pensée de la différence.* Paris: Odile Jacob, 1996.
Krémer, Pascale. "Ces couples homosexuels qui veulent des enfants." *Le Monde,* March 14–15, 1999, 1, 8–9.
Leach, Edmund R. "Marriage, Legitimacy, Alliance." In Edmund Leach, *Social Anthropology,* 176–211. New York: Oxford University Press, 1982.
———. "Polyandry, Inheritance and the Definition of Marriage: With Particular Reference to Sinhalese Customary Law." *Rethinking Anthropology.* London: University of London Press, 1961.
Lévi-Strauss, Claude. "The Effectiveness of Symbols." In *Structural Anthropology.* Trans. Claire Jacobson and Brooke Grundfest Schoepf, 186–205. New York: Basic Books, 1963.
———. *The Elementary Structures of Kinship.* Rev. ed. Trans. James Harle Bell and John Richard von Sturmer. Ed. Rodney Needham. Boston: Beacon Press, 1969.
———. "The Family." *The View from Afar.* Trans. Joachim Neugroschel and Phoebe Hoss. New York: Basic Books, 1987.
———. "Introduction." *Au-delà du PaCS: L'expertise familiale à l'épreuve de l'homosexualité.* 2d ed. Ed. Daniel Borello, Éric Fassin, and Marcela Iacoub. Paris: Presses Universitaires de France, 2001.

Lewin, Ellen. *Lesbian Mothers: Accounts of Gender in American Culture.* Ithaca: Cornell University Press, 1993.
Needham, Rodney. "Polythetic Classifications." In Rodney Needham, *Against the Tranquility of Axioms,* 36–65. Berkeley: University of California Press, 1983.
———. "Remarks on the Analysis of Kinship and Marriage." In *Rethinking Kinship and Marriage.* Ed. Rodney Needham, 1–19. London: Tavistock, 1971.
———. *Remarks and Inventions: Skeptical Essays on Kinship.* London: Tavistock, 1974.
Senate (France). Report 258. "Annexe au procès-verbal de la séance du 10 mars 1999." General session 1998–99. Available online at <http://www.senat.fr/rap/198–258/198–2580.html>.
Théry, Irène. *Couple, filiation et parenté aujourd'hui: Le droit face aux mutations de la vie privée.* Report to the Minister of Employment and Solidarity and to the Garde des Sceaux, Minster of Justice. Paris: Odile Jacob and La Documentation Française, 1998.
———. "Différence des sexes et différence des générations: L'institution familiale en déshérence." *Esprit* 227 (Dec. 1996): 65–90.
———. "Le contrat d'union sociale en question." *Esprit* 236 (Oct. 1997): 159–87. Followed by documentation prepared by Marianne Schulz (188–211).
———. *Le démariage.* 1993. Reprint. Paris: Odile Jacob, 1996.
———. "PaCS, sexualité et différence des sexes." *Esprit* 257 (Oct. 1999): 166.
Thompson, E. P. *The Making of the English Working Class.* London: V. Gollancz, 1963.
Vernier, Bernard. *Le visage et le nom: Contribution à l'étude des systèmes de parenté.* Paris: Presses Universitaires de France, 1999.
Weston, Kath. *Families We Choose: Lesbians, Gays, Kinship.* New York: Columbia University Press, 1991.
Wittgenstein, Ludwig. *Philosophical Investigations.* Trans. G. E. M. Anscombe. New York: Basil Blackwell, 1958.
———. *Preliminary Studies for the "Philosophical Investigations," Generally Known as the Blue and Brown Books.* New York: Basil Blackwell, 1958.
Zimmerman, Francis. *Enquête sur la parenté.* Paris: Presses Universitaires de France, 1993.

11 A Semiotics of the Public/Private Distinction

SUSAN GAL

THE DISTINCTION BETWEEN public and private is a ubiquitous feature of everyday life, where the terms are used in multiple and seemingly contradictory ways. "Private property" is a defining feature of a capitalist economy, but in capitalist systems participants also consider "private" those intimate relationships that are ideally protected from economic calculation. This combination is neither careless confusion nor a regrettable inconsistency. On the contrary, I argue that when the public/private distinction is analyzed as a communicative phenomenon—a product of semiotic processes—it shows a complex and systematic logic that explains this usage. The logic undergirds a great deal of social reasoning in everyday life as well as in political and social theory. To explicate the semiotics of the public/private distinction, one must first be clear about what it is not.[1]

Since the emergence of the doctrine of "separate spheres" in the nineteenth century, social analysts in Europe and the United States have repeatedly assumed that the social world is organized around contrasting and incompatible moral principles that are conventionally linked to either public or private: community vs. individual, rationality vs. sentiment, money vs. love, solidarity vs. self-interest. The belief that these values are antagonistic continues to generate heated political argument. It motivates the widespread fear that practices such as money payments for intimate care will contaminate the trust and love of private life. There is also the parallel fear that expressions of emotion and the mobilization of intimate ties will weaken the fairness and rationality of politics. Narratives about the dangers of mutual contamination by public and private spheres are evident in both republican and liberal political thought. These traditions differ in the value and location they assign to the public good as opposed to private interest. Yet they agree on the centrality of the opposition. By contrast, feminist scholarship has made these dichotomies the center of its project of critique. First, feminist research has challenged the supposed incompatibility of the moral values associated with public and private. Despite the assumption of "separate spheres," most social practices, relations, and transactions are not limited to the principles associated with one or another sphere. Empirical research shows that monetary transactions of various kinds are common in social relations that are otherwise understood as intimate interactions within families: love and money are often intertwined. Similarly, the "personal is political" in part because private institutions such as families often operate, like the polity, through conflict, power hierarchies, and violence. By the same token, political acts conventionally categorized as public are frequently shaped by sentiment and emotion. Far from being incompatible, the principles associated with public and private coexist in complex combinations in the ordinary routines of everyday life. Second, feminist research has successfully shown the error of assuming stable boundaries between public and private. Legal changes are perhaps the best indicators, but the stigmatization of practices once accepted and taken for granted also provides important evidence. Activities such as wife-beating, which were considered a private concern a few decades ago, are now the subject of public legislation around the globe; conversely, consensual sexual activity among adults that was once more widely subject to legal prohibition has become a private matter in many locales.

However, historical changes in the "content" of what is legally or conventionally considered public and private have not undermined the distinction in normative discourse and social theory any more than has evidence about the inseparability of principles. This should not be surprising. As feminist theory has argued, the public/private distinction is an ideological one, hence not easily susceptible to empirical counterevidence. Yet the implications of this insight have not been sufficiently explored. Rather than mounting an analysis of the distinction as ideology, most feminist critiques have simply borrowed or extended the cartographic metaphors of everyday life. In a recent collection of key feminist texts, the excellent introductory essay by Joan Landes asserts as a cornerstone of current thinking that the "line between public and private is constantly being renegotiated"; it stresses the "stability and instability in the boundaries that separate these regions of social life" (3).[2]

These metaphors, however, hardly do justice to the regularity and conceptual subtlety of what we as theorists and social actors actually do with this ideological distinction. Public and private do not simply describe the social world in any direct way; they are rather tools for arguments about and in that world. Hence, to understand the persistence of the dichotomy and our sense of its constancy despite dramatic changes, we need an account of how it operates as ideological communication. Drawing on a Peircean semiotics as developed within linguistic anthropology, I suggest we look for the indexical properties of the public/private distinction. This will reveal that its referential content always relies on contexts of use and that the distinction is relative to those contexts. By using the public/private dichotomy, participants can subdivide, recalibrate, and thus make fractal recursions in their categorizations of cultural objects and personae. A Peircean approach also suggests that we can understand "ideologies" as metadiscourses that comment on and regiment other communicative practices. Only when a practice is labeled and named is it regimented referentially, thereby becoming relatively easy to discuss as a social reality. By contrast, fractal subdivisions enacted by participants through indexical signs are often hard to notice, even for the social actors who use and impose them.[3]

In what follows I clarify this discussion of semiotic processes, providing examples of how they work and relying on the two major approaches to "public/private" in current scholarship: the sociohistorical and the typological. As I have mentioned, the first of these has emphasized the ideological nature of the distinction, showing that supposedly incompatible principles are closely intermingled in daily life. It has traced how definitions of public and private have changed. Writings about this dichotomy, along with everyday practices and institutional/legal arrangements in different national traditions, are constitutive of capitalism and instrumental in the making of liberal and republican politics (Davidoff and Hall; Frader and Rose; Habermas; Landes). The typological approach is more normative, juxtaposing the writings of philosophers and social theorists from different periods. It points out the inconsistencies in definitions of public and private and draws implications for reform of social theory and of the social world (Benhabib; Fraser). The semiotic analysis I propose aims to unpack the way this dichotomy operates in categorizing and differentiating cultural "objects." It is meant to supplement and complement the other perspectives.

My examples in this essay will be drawn in part from East Central Europe because for those of us working in that region over the last two decades the changes consequent to 1989 provided a challenge: How is it that public and private are so different in state-socialist societies and in capitalist parliamentary democracies yet also eerily familiar? By including American examples as well, however, I suggest that the processes discussed here are not limited to one part of the world. They help us to make more rigorous comparisons across regions and political systems.

Fractal Distinctions

The establishment of a cultural distinction between public and private has been a prolonged and often conflictual sociohistorical process. Over the last twenty years historical scholarship has outlined the development of this conceptual pair in Europe and the United States. Descriptions of the struggles over gendered divisions of labor, the reorganization of the economy, and the emergence of civil societies and public spheres have all been part of these traditions of research. Recently, Gail Kligman and I have outlined the continuities between these Western European understandings of public and private and those that emerged in East Central Europe since the nineteenth century and during the communist era. My interest here, however, is not this important process of construction but rather the way that the categories operate communicatively once they are a taken-for-granted part of a cultural scene.

A semiotic approach to public and private suggests that, contrary to customary scholarly parlance and commonsense usage, "public" and "private" are not particular places, domains, spheres of activity, or even types of interaction. Even less are they distinctive institutions or practices. Public and private are co-constitutive cultural categories, as many have pointed out. But they are also, and equally important, indexical signs that are always relative, dependent for part of their referential meaning on the interactional context in which they are used.[4] First, then, the public/private dichotomy is best understood as a discursive phenomenon that, once established, can be used to characterize, categorize, organize, and contrast virtually any kind of social fact: spaces, institutions, bodies, groups, activities, interactions, relations.

Second, the historical creation of a distinction between "public" and "private" is not dependent on the use of these or even parallel lexical items, though for historical reasons cognates of the English terms are frequent all over Europe and in postcolonial regions as well. Rather, the historically locatable process of developing these categories into politically and economically significant distinctions appropriates or is parasitic on the much more widespread pragmatic possibility of using, in interaction, a variety of indexical signals for more proximate versus more distanced relationships or events. Linguistic resources for doing this are the deictics such as "here" and "there" as well as changes in gesture, posture, and what Bakhtin called "voicing." The ideological distinction is a metacommentary that regiments practices, sometimes implicitly, sometimes explicitly, mapping on them a grid of interpretation. Deictics and other indexicals most often use the speaker's body as an orienting center so that far from being "merely discourse," these processes of "pointing" away from self and toward self through speech have a strong materiality. Even when recruited—through metadiscursive commentary—for grand political projects, they remain available for creating embodied subjectivities.

Third, and most important for my purposes here, the public/ private dichotomy is what some of us, in theorizing processes of social, cultural, and linguistic differentiation, have called a "fractal distinction."[5] This means it is a particular kind of indexical. Whatever the local, historically specific content of the dichotomy, the distinction between public and private can be reproduced repeatedly by projecting it onto narrower contexts or broader ones. Or it can be projected onto different social "objects"—activities, identities, institutions, spaces, and interactions—that can be further categorized into private and public parts. Then, through recursivity (and recalibration), each of these parts can be recategorized again by the same public/private distinction. It is crucial that such calibrations are always relative positions and not properties laminated onto the persons, objects, or spaces concerned. They are like Bakhtinian voicings or perspectives rather than fixed categories. The term *fractal* is used in geometry to describe how a single pattern recurs inside itself—is self-similar—often with multiple nestings. But some venerable works in social science, such as the analysis of segmentary lineages in anthropology, have also explicated this logic without the handy "fractal" label.

A familiar, everyday example of how this works is the common conceptualization of American bourgeois domestic space. At a first look, the privacy of the house itself contrasts with the public character of the street around it. If we focus, however, on the inside of the house, then the living room becomes the public, that is, the public part of a domestic private space. Thus the public/private distinction is reapplied and now divides into public and private what was, from another perspective, entirely "private" space. But even the relatively public living room can be recalibrated—using this same distinction—by momentary gestures or utterances, voicings that are iconic of privacy and thus create less institutionalized and more spontaneous spatial divisions during interaction (Goffman). The whispered aside, the confidential turn of bodies toward each other at a company party, come to mind as familiar examples of privacy fleetingly created. Conceptualizations of the street, in turn, share this same fractal property. The distinction between a storefront swept and cleaned by a proprietor, as opposed to the sidewalk and road that are ideally the city's or public's responsibility, also relies on a public/private difference, this time projected onto spaces that, when calibrated to a more encompassing context, are all "public." Thus spaces that are undoubtedly public (in one context) can be turned into private ones by indexical gestures (the sweeping and caretaking) which are recalibrations that bring them into new contrast sets.

No matter how labile or "shifty" we imagine boundaries to be, the idea of boundaries does not do justice to this semiotic and communicative process. On the contrary, discussions of public and private spaces with unstable boundaries assume a single dichotomy, thereby collapsing the nested distinctions into each other, making the nesting processes and indexical recursions hard to notice.

An example shows the ways in which fractal thinking allows some distinctions to conveniently disappear. In an ethnographic study, Biggart (cited in Zelizer) describes the internal organization of direct-sales corporations in the U.S. such as Amway, Tupperware, and Mary Kay Cosmetics. Blue-collar women respond to their family's need for money by taking this kind of paid work. But they retain the ideals of a public/private divide in which women are supposed to be in the private, unpaid (home) sphere while waged work is public (away from home) and done by men. The women think of their jobs as sidelines, not "real" work. In choosing jobs, they recalibrate the public/private divide, applying it now in the context of the world of paid work. This allows and encourages them to distinguish among the jobs themselves according to the home/work principle. They declare that their satisfaction with direct sales comes in part from the fact that they are not away "eight to five," so their children are unaware they are working for money. As Zelizer remarks, it is ironic that while overstepping the bounds of the home these working women recreate a public/private dichotomy in which they can remain "stay-at-home mothers." Note also that it is not a single distinction they impose. Rather, their ideological move involves at least one recursion of the home/work distinction in order to create the desired impression and then requires a partial "forgetting" of that move.

In other cases the public/private distinction is less fluid and more firmly institutionalized. In these cases the institutions themselves show a fractal organization. Social science funding in the U.S. is a convenient example. There are public sources of social science funding and private ones: the U.S. federal government, say, versus the Ford Foundation. But within the U.S. government, there is once again a public/private distinction made, as the federal government distributes some of the money it spends on social scientific research through public organs such as the National Science Foundation but subcontracts other parts of that research money to private organizations such as the American Council for Learned Societies. In yet another fractal split, the ACLS also subcontracts some of its decision making to scholars who work for federal agencies (e.g., the Wilson Center in Washington) so that there is clearly a "public sector" as well as a private one inside the supposedly private ACLS. Nevertheless, the differences between the ACLS and the NSF—despite the same original source of some of their money—are consequential, carrying different rules for eligibility, for evaluating proposals, and for disbursement.

Thus, public funds get turned into private money at numerous sites but usually through nested subdivisions. It would seem that one can always deny the "publicness" or "privateness" of the funds by focusing on a higher or lower level of organization. Much intraorganizational strategizing focuses on such matters. Importantly, there are subtle changes at each embedding; it is not entirely the "same" public and private at each subdivision. Rather, the definitions of public and private are partially transformed with each nested dichotomy—each indexical recalibration—while (deceptively) retaining the same label and the same co-constituting contrast.

In all these examples of spaces, types of work, and institutions there is no simple continuum of public to private. No funding agencies, for instance, are "more" public or "more" private. Each is one or the other, by law. Nor are some forms of paid work "more" paid than others, though some are surely more lucrative. Here, as with the earlier example of bourgeois spaces, the issue is not one of unstable or fuzzy boundaries. Rather, the intertwining public and private is created by practices that participants understand as re-creations of the dichotomy. Yet, in part because these separations are indexical, participants can often collapse them into a single dichotomy, simplifying what is, in practice, complexly recursive.

The Public/Private of Social Science

Social science theorizing is as permeated by fractal thinking as the everyday practices and institutional arrangements I have already described. Indeed, theories about public and private have usually done little more than point to these nested distinctions, presenting them as analysis without explicating their logic. Carole Pateman's critique and reinterpretation of the classic Enlightenment theorists works by revealing the nested structure of their arguments. She shows that for Rousseau and others, the distinction between private property and public state rested on a previous (and unacknowledged) dichotomy between a more general private (the domestic) and a more general public (the social).

Fractal stories as analysis are evident elsewhere, too. Albert O. Hirschman, in a classic discussion of public and private action in European history, writes:

> The ancient contrast, much debated from Aristotle down to the Renaissance, was between *vita activa,* then understood precisely as active involvement in public, civic affairs, and *vita contemplativa* which referred to withdrawal from active life and studied abstention from participation in its futile struggles and excitement . . . in a more modern vein I distinguish here between *two varieties of the active life:* one is the traditional *vita activa* which is wholly concerned with public affairs; and the other is the pursuit of a better life for oneself and one's family. (7, emphasis in the original).

Similarly, Habermas's influential argument about the structure of the early bourgeois public sphere depends on a first distinction he draws between what he (and the social actors he is analyzing) thought of as the private realm and the sphere of public authority, made up of the state and the court. He writes: "Within the realm that was the preserve of private people we . . . distinguish again between private and public spheres. The private sphere comprised civil society in the narrower sense, that is to say, the realm of commodity exchange and of social labor; embedded in it was the family and its interior domain" (30).

Focusing on the public/private distinction as a semiotic or sign phenomenon in communication allows one to see the similarities among face-to-face deployments of these fractal distinctions, institutional examples, and the parallel moves of social theory. In having several "levels" of public and private in their theories, Rousseau, Hirschman, and Habermas are not being imprecise or confused, as some have argued. On the contrary, they show the same conceptual regularity evident in everyday usage. They, like all of us, sometimes take careful note of the embedded distinctions, but more often forget the various levels that are indexically signaled and collapse them into a single "public/private" distinction that is then referentially named and easily becomes the focus of discussion. This elision of fractal embeddings relies on the fact that indexical signals are difficult to discuss explicitly. Once named and thus semanticized, the fleeting distinctions of different roles, spaces, and categories indexically invoked in interaction turn into reified "objects" of the social world that seem solid and distinct. This quality of semantic distinctions, as opposed to indexical signals, is a quite systematic feature of communication and common in ideologies.[6]

In sum, public and private will have different specific definitions in different historical periods and social formations. But once a dichotomy is established, the semiotic logic forms a scaffolding for possibilities of embedding and thus for change, creativity, and argument. In these nested dichotomies, there is always some skewing or redefinition at every iteration. Furthermore, redefinitions that create a public inside a private or a private inside a public (be it in identity, space, money, relation) can be momentary and ephemeral, dependent on the perspectives of participants. Or they can be made lasting and coercive, fixing and forcing such distinctions, binding social actors through arrangements such as legal regulation and other forms of ritualization and institutionalization.

In the social world, many co-constitutive categories have the properties I have described and regularly intersect with public/private. Left/right in contemporary politics, modernity/tradition, and East/West (in the cold war cultural sense) are clear examples. We are not surprised to find that within any leftist group there are always those who think of themselves as the "real" left, in contrast to their insufficiently radical comembers. But if we were to isolate these "real" leftists in a room, the same distinction of lefter-than-thou is likely to reappear (given an actual dispute), once again dividing the group into left and right. Single individuals may be, on some occasions, "left" (depending on what group they happen to be with, what issue they are arguing) or "right"—these positions are indexical, that is, linked to occasion and situation, not fixed or permanently laminated to individuals. The same holds, of course, for the rightists.

Gender is another distinction that shows similar properties: it can be applied to virtually any "object" of social life (Scott). In a discussion of sex/gender dichotomies and their imitative, parodic, and undermining entailments, Judith Butler neatly shows how the male/female distinction is partially and complexly reiterated among "anatomical females" as butch and femme. But this is never the end of it since "there will be passive and butchy femmes, femmy and aggressive butches" (309), and the fractal play continues on the "anatomically male" side of the opposition, too. One can argue about the extent to which reiterations are fully imitations. I would argue that recursions (i.e., reiterations) are never entirely mimetic. They always introduce some change in meaning. One should also examine the political messages and implications of such reiterations and their effects on subjectivities and on how identity is established. My point is that we must theorize the fractal backbone.

East Central Europe

So far, I have sketched examples from social science and from American culture and institutions. The contrast with East Central European cases is instructive. The public/private distinction was one of the ones directly targeted by communist theorists in the nineteenth century—and by Soviet and, later, East Central European communist parties—as essential points for transforming bourgeois, capitalist society through social engineering. As is well known, the aim was elimination of the "private" through the extension of state control into activities, spaces, and relations deemed "private." The socialization of production and commerce—as much as of civil society, voluntary organizations, and housework—was understood as a means of ending or reducing social inequality, especially the oppression of women. Changing the conceptual or discursive linkage of women's work to private and men's to public was one of the goals of communist planners and ideologues.

Vast changes were attempted in political and economic arrangements, some successful, others notable failures. There were important differences in these social engineering projects between countries in East Central Europe and across historical periods. My goal here is modest: to provide a number of examples, mostly from Hungary, the case I know best, to illustrate my claim that despite enormous structural changes that created state-socialist societies, some features of the public/private distinction bear significant similarities to the capitalist examples mentioned above, with important consequences for further change. By the 1980s in Hungary, women were at least half the labor force, and over 80 percent of women worked for wages. All industry and virtually all commercial activity had been socialized for decades, and the interstitial, non-state forms of political activity such as unions, parent/teacher organizations, political parties, and professional organizations had been taken over by the state. Yet, as a result of the 1956 Revolution, a certain leeway in activity was allowed to Hungarians in what was deemed the private sphere, and the state to some extent turned its attention away from what was done by people after their official jobs, during their vacations, and in their households. The question here is how these changes were understood and how they were structured.

As in the West, the public/private distinction in East Central Europe was aligned with what were seen as opposed and antagonistic principles. However, in the communist period, these principles differed substantially from those common in the bourgeois world to the west. In the East, the public/private distinction was aligned with a discursive opposition between the victimized "us" and a newly powerful "them" who ruled the state. Private activities, spaces, and times were understood by people throughout the region as "ours" and not the state's. Different moral principles and modes of motivation and reward were considered appropriate to work, spaces, and social relationships considered "ours" as opposed to those considered the purview of the state. People loafed in official jobs but on their private plots practiced extremes of overwork ("self-exploitation"). The imperative to be honest and ethically responsible among those who counted as "us" contrasted with the distrust and duplicity in dealings with "them" and with the official world generally.[7]

An ethnographic example will show the implications of these dichotomies for the activities of everyday life. Janine Wedel reports an incident in Poland in the 1980s when "an employee took a desk from a state-owned factory, intending to resell it. He left the desk in a truck near his apartment building until it could be delivered to the intended purchasers. But to his dismay, it disappeared" (15). By the moral rules of public and private life, removing the desk from the factory did not count as theft at all since it was merely "taking" from the state. The disappearance from the street, however, was seen by the man himself as a violation of the moral injunction not to steal from "our own." As Wedel notes, "He complained bitterly to his neighbors that 'people are dishonest and immoral'" (15). This incident is by no means an illustration of hypocrisy or divergent moral frames. On the contrary, according to Wedel's account and my own parallel ethnographic experience in Hungary, the man who took the desk from the truck would have agreed in principle with the owner of the truck. For both there would be "theft" as opposed to justified "takings," the first relevant to private, the other to public situations. They differed, however, in their assessment of how to calibrate the nestings of public and private for that occasion. This is what explains the rage of the man who originally "took" the desk from the factory. What was private and "among neighbors" for him was subdivided by another person to create a "public" in which the desk was again available for righteous taking. Similar indexical calibrations help explain denunciations of kin, family, and friends under socialism as well as the apparently hypocritical participation in oppositional activities of families and individuals highly placed in the Communist Party (Gal and Kligman 51).

The fractal nature of public and private under socialism was important not only in interpersonal ethical decisions but also in implications for institutional change. By the 1980s, activities deemed "public"—understood to be properly the responsibility of and under the control of the state—were increasingly embedded in private life. Thus the private was understood as divisible into a private that revolved around reproduction and family life and a public-inside-the-private that used those same resources for production and politics. For example, one development (actually surreptitiously encouraged by the state) was the growth of various forms of production with what was understood as domestic (private) space/time/activity/personnel. Such household production, using household members, domestic spaces, and after-hours time, provided as much as 30 percent of Hungarian production by the 1980s (though exact figures were hard to come by, given the partially clandestine nature of the production) and included agricultural, small industry, and service industries.

A parallel development (in this case tolerated though certainly not encouraged by the state) was the growth of small dissident political organizations, voluntary groups of various kinds including *samizdat* publication ventures. Again, these were understood by actors as "politics" and hence public. Once again, the private was imagined as subdivided, having a public embedded within it. Like production within the household, which was labeled and discussed under the rubric of the "second economy," this kind of politics was heavily theorized by those engaging in it. They considered this public-inside-the-private as a significant dissident gesture and famously called it "antipolitics." For my purposes here the significant fact about antipolitics was that it created what everyone called public spaces within the private household. Incidentally, this form of politics was supported by the labor of women who did the scrubby work of antipolitics. In the process, they often became invisible as political actors exactly because they were understood to be in the private part of the private household, not its public part.[8]

These examples suggest that the description of the public/private distinction as fractal, and its organizational forms as embedded and self-similar, holds as much for the East Central European examples as for the earlier American ones despite the important substantive differences. Fractal distinctions describe well the structures of interpersonal morality and social change in late socialism, and they are just as adequate for describing those in capitalist systems. In some cases, the fractal outcome may have been historical accident or simply the result of a dearth of other possibilities (Stark). But in other cases, the cultural opposition itself inspired the form of social change. Embedding "public" activities in private spaces, thereby splitting the private space into both a public and a private, might well have occurred to people as a logic of their cultural categories and might have stimulated the forms of their dissent. There is ample evidence of just this process in discussions by Hungarian planners during the 1980s who were trying to save the socialist economy. Just as the private world of Hungarian life was being transformed in the 1980s by embeddings of public activities, so the "public" economy—in this case the great state-owned corporations—were also changing drastically. State planners and economists were arguing that to make the socialist economy more efficient they would have to add new structures to socialist enterprises. The compromise measures invented by planners were "work groups" within factories and other productive units. These work-cooperatives were small groups of workers operating within their own factory, often on subcontract from the factory itself. They used the machinery and time of the factory, and their own labor, but produced not for the benefit of the factory but for their own profit. Such social structures existed on an informal illegal basis for years before they were legalized and institutionalized in Hungary (Burawoy and Lukács).

It is hard to see this as anything other than the embedding of private enterprise (in a limited form, to be sure) within a (public) state economy. The discussions of the economists make it clear that they considered the possibility of subdividing and embedding to be a clever move, a compromise that would allow the semblance of retaining the communist system's public/private arrangement while importing into it much-needed motivation and efficiency considered characteristic of private economic activities (Seleny). I would argue that the fractal possibilities of the public/private distinction provided a resource and template for conceptualizing and then creating social change. Importantly, and as the economists emphasized in their discussion, the embedding itself allowed them to deny that anything really drastic had been done.

Implications and Comparisons

In both capitalist arrangements and state-socialist ones—which are, of course, vastly different in many ways—a fractal private/public distinction can be shown to operate, first of all as a discursive resource but one that can be turned into institutional structures and into routinized organizations. I suggest that this observation enables larger generalizations and also finer comparisons. For instance, in a discussion of the East Central European cases, Gail Kligman and I showed that while the standard bourgeois discursive pattern in Europe before World War II associated women with the private and men with the public, socialism reversed that association in many ways so that women came to be seen as allied with the state (public). It is often said that this discursive linkage of women with the state helps explain the difficulties of feminist organizing in the region after 1989. Thus, feminism has been seen as a communist project and therefore discredited along with communism. But because both gender and public/private are fractal distinctions, the situation was, in fact, much more complicated. During the final years of socialism, women were associated not with the state in general but with its redistributive, social support aspects; men were associated not with the private in general but with the antipolitics that was occurring within private spaces.

In addition to such comparative possibilities, I believe there are broader implications to such an analysis. Let me highlight just three I have already mentioned briefly. First, it appears that social theorists and ordinary people use the same fractal processes "to think." This means it is not enough to find the fractals. Even though social theorists have often noted that publics and privates are mutually embedded, they then usually revert to cartographic metaphors of shifting and unstable boundaries. Yet the imagery of shifting boundaries is a result and not an explanation of the ideological processes we observe and use.

Second, the fractal nature of distinctions such as the public/private one allows people to experience them as stable and continuous in spite of changes in the contents of the distinction. So we can see the nineteenth-century arrangements in Western Europe as the "same" as today's despite evident and enormous differences because the co-constitutive oppositions are still in place, and we collapse the embedded distinctions. In East Central Europe this continuity "effect" is currently quite important. For instance, it allows people to sense the family as stable in the midst of frightening political-economic change.

Third, and most generally, the indexical and fractal nature of the dichotomy allows for the denial or erasure of some levels or contexts of distinction as people focus on other contexts. It is generally the case, as I have suggested, that nested recursions are collapsed into each other and their differences elided, especially in explicit discussions. Participants often erase their own experience of embedded practices; in discussions that favor referentially stable categories they can easily ignore the indexical character of the dichotomy. This regularly results in the conflation of several nested public/private distinctions into a single distinction, hence the common illusion that there is only one division or distinction—and one shifting boundary to worry about—as the numerous levels of embedding disappear from view.

This latter erasure can have diverse political consequences. In the case of socialist planners in Hungary, it allowed them to deny that they were making radical changes in Hungarian economic arrangements when, in fact, they were introducing various forms of market economy. In the case of Rousseau's multilayered theory of the state, Pateman has shown that it allowed denial of the way in which the public/private of state/economy depended on a previously denied distinction between domesticity and society, with implications for the understanding of women's position in that ideological formation. It is from this Enlightenment tradition that we inherit the use of the category "private" in the apparently contradictory manner with which I started this essay. The example can stand for the larger point. My aim has been to argue that such supposed ambiguity and incompatibility—as between "private" property and private (noneconomic) relations—is, in fact, a predictable and unambiguous result of ideological communication in which social organizations are imagined in nested ways. Furthermore, such fractal imaginings—whether in bourgeois or in state-socialist societies—provide a productive point of comparison between regions. A further and important question is the redefinition of the contrast under multiple recursions (iterations) and when paired or laminated to other distinctions. As I have suggested, public and private can make contrasting bundles of oppositions in different political systems. Within single political systems, as well as across them, fractal processes provide fertile nodes for conflict and debate, as well as ways of creating differentiation and cultural innovation.

NOTES

1. An earlier version of my argument, further developed here, appeared in chapter 3 of Gal and Kligman. My thanks to Andrew Abbott, Judith Irvine, and Gail Kligman for discussion of these issues.

2. Although the phrases in quotation marks come from Landes's introduction, similar metaphors occur throughout her fine collection. A fuller survey would include the early feminist anthropological arguments about universals of public and private as well as the definitive retorts in Jane Collier and Sylvia Yanagisako's *Gender and Kinship.* My own argument is not a structuralist recapitulation of the earlier debate but rather what one might call metastructural, an attempt to sketch the semiotic conditions for making a structuralist argument of that kind.

3. Works that introduce and exemplify this kind of analysis of ideology are collected in *Regimes of Language,* edited by Paul Kroskrity, and in Bambi Schieffelin, Kathryn Woolard, and Paul Kroskrity's *Language Ideologies;* see also the earlier work of Michael Silverstein, "Language Structure."

4. In addition to indexicality as discussed by Peirce, I am drawing here on the further development of the notion of indexicality and shifter by Jakobson and then Silverstein.

5. The idea of fractal distinctions as a feature of language ideology and thus of linguistic and social differentiation is developed in Gal and Irvine's "The Boundaries of Languages" and Irvine and Gal's "Language Ideology and Linguistic Differentiation" (see also Gal, "Bartók's Funeral," for a political example). For a full-dress analysis of scholarly discourses in fractal terms and suggestive observations about

such analysis more generally, see Abbott. Numerous social theorists have written about what seem in retrospect like fractal processes. The most prominent of these are E. Evans-Pritchard and Gregory Bateson. Descriptions of such processes are not hard to find in ethnographic and sociological literatures.

6. The process outlined here bears some resemblance to what Bourdieu and others have called a "theory effect," though its communicative properties have not been described in this way (133).

7. This general issue has a large literature, and the phenomena have been noted by virtually every researcher of state socialism. Gail Kligman provides a close look at the duplicities of public and private in Romania, and János Kenedi describes the nestings of public and private provisioning in Hungary.

8. There is a large literature on the "second economy" and "antipolitics" in the former Soviet bloc. For instance, Katherine Verdery provides a general discussion of the communist and postcommunist periods. See also Gal and Kligman for an overview.

Works Cited

Abbott, Andrew. *Chaos of Disciplines.* Chicago: University of Chicago Press, 2001.

Bakhtin, M. M. *The Dialogic Imagination: Four Essays.* Ed. Michael Holquist. Austin: University of Texas Press, 1981.

Bateson, Gregory. *Naven.* Stanford: Stanford University Press, 1935.

Benhabib, Seyla. "Models of Public Space: Hannah Arendt, the Liberal Tradition and Jürgen Habermas." In *Feminism: The Public and the Private.* Ed. J. Landes, 65–99. New York: Oxford University Press, 1998.

Bourdieu, Pierre. *Language and Symbolic Power.* Cambridge: Harvard University Press, 1991.

Burawoy, Michael, and János Lukács. *The Radiant Past: Ideology and Reality in Hungary's Road to Capitalism.* Chicago: University of Chicago Press, 1992.

Butler, Judith. "Imitation and Gender Insubordination." In *The Second Wave: A Reader in Feminist Theory.* Ed. Linda Nicholson, 301–15. New York: Routledge, 1997.

Collier, Jane, and Sylvia Yanagisako. *Gender and Kinship: Essays Toward a Unified Analysis.* Stanford: Stanford University Press, 1987.

Davidoff, Leonore, and Catherine Hall. *Family Fortunes: Men and Women of the English Middle Class, 1780–1850.* Chicago: University of Chicago Press, 1987.

Evans-Pritchard, E. E. *The Nuer.* New York: Oxford University Press, 1940.

Frader, Laura, and Sonya Rose. "Introduction." In *Gender and Class in Modern Europe.* Ed. Laura Frader and Sonya Rose, 1–33. Ithaca: Cornell University Press, 1996.

Fraser, Nancy. "What's Critical about Critical Theory." In *Unruly Practices,* 113–43. Minneapolis: University of Minnesota Press, 1989.

Gal, Susan. "Bartók's Funeral: Representations of Europe in Hungarian Political Rhetoric." *American Ethnologist* 18, no. 3 (1991): 440–58.

———, and Gail Kligman. *The Politics of Gender after Socialism: A Comparative-Historical Essay.* Princeton: Princeton University Press, 2000.

———, and Judith T. Irvine. "The Boundaries of Languages and Disciplines: How Ideologies Construct Difference." *Social Research* 62, no. 4 (1995): 967–1001.

Goffman, Erving. *The Presentation of Self in Everyday Life.* New York: Beacon, 1959.
Habermas, Jürgen. *Structural Transformation of the Public Sphere.* Cambridge: MIT Press, 1989.
Hirschman, Albert O. *Shifting Involvements: Private Interest and Public Action.* Princeton: Princeton University Press, 1982.
Irvine, Judith T., and Susan Gal. "Language Ideology and Linguistic Differentiation." In *Regimes of Language.* Ed. Paul Kroskrity, 35–84. Santa Fe: School of American Research, 2000.
Jakobson, Roman. "Shifters and Verbal Categories." In *On Language: Roman Jakobson.* Ed. Linda R. Waugh and Monique Monville-Burston, 386–92. Cambridge: Harvard University Press, 1957.
Kenedi, János. *Do It Yourself: Hungary's Hidden Economy.* London: Pluto, 1981.
Kligman, Gail. *The Politics of Duplicity: Controlling Reproduction in Ceausescu's Romania.* Berkeley: University of California Press, 1998.
Kroskrity, Paul, ed. *Regimes of Language.* Santa Fe: School of American Research, 2000.
Landes, Joan. "Introduction." In *Feminism: The Public and the Private.* Ed. Joan Landes, 1–20. London: Oxford University Press, 1998.
Pateman, Carole. *The Sexual Contract.* Stanford: Stanford University Press, 1988.
Schieffelin, Bambi, Kathryn Woolard, and Paul Kroskrity, eds. *Language Ideologies: Practice and Theory.* New York: Oxford University Press, 1998.
Scott, Joan. *Gender and the Politics of History.* New York: Columbia University Press, 1988.
Seleny, Anna. "Constructing the Discourse of Transformation: Hungary 1979–82." *East European Politics and Societies* 8, no. 3 (1994): 439–66.
Silverstein, Michael. "Language Structure and Linguistic Ideology." In *A Parasession on Linguistic Units and Levels.* Ed. P. Clyne, W. Hanks, and C. Hofbauer, 193–247. Chicago: Chicago Linguistics Society, 1979.
———. "Shifters, Linguistic Categories and Cultural Description." In *Meaning in Anthropology.* Ed. Keith H. Basso and Henry A. Selby, 11–55. Albuquerque: University of New Mexico Press, 1976.
Stark, David. "Recombinant Property in East European Capitalism." *American Journal of Sociology* 101, no. 4 (1996): 993–1027.
Verdery, Katherine. *What Was Socialism and What Comes Next?* Princeton: Princeton University Press, 1996.
Wedel, Janine. *The Private Poland.* New York: Facts on File, 1986.
Zelizer, Viviana. "Intimate Transactions." In *The New Economic Sociology: Developments in an Emerging Field.* Ed. Randall Collins, Mauro Guillen, Paula England, and Marshall Meyer. New York: Russell Sage, 2002.

12 Rethinking Transition: Globalism, Gender, and Class

PEGGY WATSON

IN THIS ESSAY I DISCUSS some of the questions the ending of the cold war raises for the understanding of gender and politics. Because feminism cannot be understood except in its historical context, and because after communism that context itself stands in need of explicit theorization, exploring the possibilities of meaning for feminism goes hand in hand with a conceptualization of transition in the former Soviet Bloc.[1] The transition to democracy in Eastern Europe has not at all conformed to expectations, East or West. For one thing, whatever the gains, democratization has not been experienced as an unequivocal improvement on what went before. In a number of ways, the changes have brought disappointment—even hopelessness—to many women and men living in the new democracies. The sharp increase in premature mortality in the first half of the 1990s, particularly among men in the former Soviet Union, is perhaps the most telling indication of this.[2] Unemployment, civil strife, rising crime rates, and the transformation of prostitution into survival and big business sex—these have been some of the more obvious aspects of the downside of transition. Western observers have attempted to decipher the historical significance of the welter of contradictory and unpredicted events of postcommunism but have been notably unsuccessful in this. As the political scientist Stephen Holmes has written: "Not even a coherent disagreement about what cluster of factors triggered the earthquakes of 1989 and 1991 has taken shape, and informed observers readily acknowledge that the shattered and ceaselessly evolving ex-East bloc still lies beyond our powers of classification. . . . Our wholly unforeseeable *fin d'époque* still awaits its convincing observer. In the meantime, frequent references to 'chaos' accurately express a general lack of confidence about emerging patterns and long-term trends" (22–23).

A new field of scholarship, that of "transitology," has come into being—in some measure constituted by these confounded expectations. At the same time, one response to the persistent mismatch between expectation and event in postcommunism, has been to question the language of transition itself. Political scientists, sociologists, and anthropologists have argued that the term should be discarded on the grounds that the word implies an unproblematic trajectory and a destination that is known. Words such as "transformation" have been seen as more noncommittal and have been recommended instead. It is time to leave the notion of transition behind, it is said, since it focuses attention on the past and the future at the expense of the present. The latter, it is implied, can "speak for itself," if only we restrict ourselves to the role of neutral observer. The events themselves will then tell us what is really going on.

Here I engage critically with the wait-and-observe approach. For scholarly critiques of "transition" seem to presuppose a default line of objectivity in the study of postcommunism which is there to fall back on once the misleading term is removed. The American anthropologist Katherine Verdery has written that "[if Western leftists had] not been convinced of socialism's evolutionary teleology, they might have been less betrayed by the system's shortcomings. Observers who likewise expect from the present transition progress toward a specific end expose themselves to comparable risk. Attending to what is happening rather than looking for what ought to happen might be fairer, humbler, and more prudent" (228). One question being posed in this essay is, Just what is it that is assumed "ought" to happen after communism? What underpins this expectation, and how does it influence the way we read the events of transition?

In what follows it is my intention to show how the identity of the democratic West—the framing of "postsocialist" politics in the West and the New World Order—is itself at issue in the interpretation of postcommunist change. An oppositional construction of West-East difference (the difference between democracy and communism) in terms of the presence-absence of freedom underpins transition discourse. The corollary is that identities across this particular linear difference are constructed as essentially the same. I show how this discourse is characterized by "whiteness" and discuss the way this underlies tensions in West-East feminist exchange. The critique which is put forward in this essay interrogates the idea of absolute space on which the theory of liberal freedom rests as it has been articulated in civil society discourse. The essay discusses some of the political uses to which such civil society discourse is put. An alternative theoretical framework is put forward which draws instead on the notion of political "curved space." A transition from a communist to a democratic regime involves the re-curving of political "curved space; that is to say, transition can be understood in terms of the transformation of relations of power that comes with the redefinition of the state. In place of West-East identity sameness, I argue for pluralization (Connolly *Ethos*)—that is, the recognition of another—in this case West-East—dimension of identity difference through which gender has been experienced. This dimension of difference does not displace, but is fused with and makes more complex, already-recognized diversity. It is this expanded recognition, I suggest, that is needed in order to account for the surprises that democracy after communism brings. Instead of expectations based on the idea that democracy, in principle, represents the opportunity for people to be their "true selves," democratization can then be seen to itself involve a process of redefinition where a contest over identity transformation is central to the realization of change.

The re-curving of political "curved space" (that is, the redefinition of relations of power) which transition entails involves the rewriting of the terms of citizenship and the transformation of the state, a process which takes place within a global matrix of power. Integral to this process is the legitimation within postcommunist societies, of political hierarchy. In postsocialist transformation, gender is encoded within a broader state and supra-state project of political differentiation implemented through transformation of economies and states. Political hierarchies among women are in the process of being formed. The current global constellation presses for a focus on differences among women—after communism, the creation of such political differences is paramount and depends on the institutionalization of class.

The Epistemology of Transition

Epistemological issues are conspicuous by their absence in the study of postcommunism. Yet if one steps outside this particular field of academic discourse, there is a substantial body of work where claims to neutrality in knowledge have been successfully challenged and where the question as to whose knowledge will count as legitimate and approaching impartiality, has been linked to political location and relations of power (Foucault, *Archeology;* Said). This kind of framework has been fruitfully applied, for example, by feminist theorists who advocate an approach to analysis that focuses on differences among women, for example those expressed through race and class. Of central importance here is the way black feminists have emphasized how "whiteness" in academic discourse assumes the existence of a group of objective intellectuals who can identify and speak for the interests of others in a way that is not at the same time distorted by their own experiences and by who they are (Morrison). They have shown how whiteness involves implicit claims for the existence of an objective position outside relations of power—which is not involved in the production of, or itself defined by, the other. Because this is so, whiteness claims access to a more universal and objective moral and political standpoint (Flax).

The perception of events in Eastern Europe cannot be separated from their interpretation—and whether or not it invokes the language of "transition," the study of postcommunism, of system transformation, inevitably involves the active production of meaning. In this it reengages a theory of what essentially distinguishes Western democracies from a communist regime, thus reviving in a new mode the polarity that divided the globe and shaped politics within West and East during the cold war decades. Historically, the meaning of "Western" has undergone change (Williams). Since the 1950s it has first and foremost been formed through cold war opposition with a communist "non-West."[3] With the end of communism, "America," the "Free World," and the "West" stand in need more than ever of symbolic definition through contrast. In the New World Order the "West" has not disappeared, although the system against which its postwar identity was primarily defined, the "captive Soviet Bloc" and communism, no longer exists. In narratives of transition what is at stake is a process whereby the East should in theory become more like the West. However, *pace* Claus Offe, the discursive opposition between West and East did not disappear in 1990. Rather, the nervously premature announcement of the "end of history" recast this polarity by reasserting an unquestioned and often unspoken idea of the West as the democratic standard through which the East, and change in the East, could be evaluated and understood. As such, it was an assertion not of victory but of Western dominance in the New World Order.[4]

Although transnational feminism transcends the borders of any individual state, it is far being situated in a "power-free zone." Rather, it is produced by, and produces, transnational power relations, that is, a transnational "curved space." The curvature of this space is a function of asymmetrical global relations of power. That being the case, an idea of the West—even if implicit and unspoken—is inevitably part of the cognitive frame within which the feminist discourse of transition is constructed, just as this discourse itself produces "the West." Insofar then as this "West" is an unspoken point of reference for the representation of Eastern Europe, a Western-centeredness, analogous to whiteness, structures feminist interpretations of change. Recognizing this is a good place for a discussion of feminism in postcommunism to begin.

Second, however, the idea of the West that has been put beyond question in the study of postcommunism has not primarily been one where people are inherently different or culturally superior as in the orientalism discussed by Said (cf. Kideckel). Within the particular definitional context of transition, the West is first and foremost a "place" where people are *free.* In a reversal of Marx's view of communism as a state of freedom following capitalist alienation, the current rhetoric of change in Eastern Europe is replete with the captivity-into-freedom trope. For example, the Czech politician Jaroslava Moserova said at a recent conference on women's leadership in the new democracies that "some people find it hard to bear the responsibility of freedom . . . I call it the 'zoo effect.' When the doors to the zoo are opened and the animals are set free, it is the predators that make best use of their newfound liberty. The timid ones find it safer to go back behind bars."[5] In this vein the escalating levels of premature mortality among men in the former Soviet Union have been constructed as the result of a kind of natural selection. "There is no mystery," an Estonian woman sociologist asserted vigorously at an international meeting focusing on transition. "These men simply can't face the risks of freedom."[6]

What this means for feminist debate is that Western-centeredness, as well as structuring the understanding of feminism in Eastern Europe, at the same time produces an implicit theory of feminism in the West. Insofar as feminist discourse of transition is structured by a binary view that tacitly counterposes communism and democracy in terms of the absence versus presence of "freedom," it erases the political oppressions, including those enacted as race and class, that structure power relations among women within the democracies of the West. In other words, an important question to ask is how far Western-centeredness in postcommunist discourse—which equates freedom with "the West"—constructs a patriarchy that is universal and thus reproduces, in a transnational arena, the very whiteness—and middle-classness—made visible by feminists in other contexts (Frankenberg; Morrison).

This having been said, the consistent surprises brought by democratization take on renewed significance. They invite us to question the validity of the assumptions that determine how the stories of transition can, or cannot, be told. In other words, the significance of the theoretical impasse, both feminist and nonfeminist, which has been created in postcommunism lies in the fact that it bids us call into question the "truths" regarding Western freedom which shape our expectations of change. It is important to make explicit the way in which an understanding of "transition," which is couched in the specific oppositional terms of freedom versus its lack, rests on a "slippage" in the way the word *liberty* is used. The primary meaning of liberty in postcommunism is quite specific in time in that it refers to the ending of an unwanted political regime.[7] What are the implications when this historically distinct meaning is unjustifiably appropriated for the normative description of a postcommunist realm? One implication of encapsulating the difference between communism and democracy in these one-dimensional terms is that it constructs identities "West" and "East" as fundamentally the same. To put it the other way round, the congruence of identities across West-East difference—their universalization—is necessary in order to lend coherence to the notion of freedom which operates in postcommunist discourse.

(Anti)Feminism in Postcommunism: Suppressing the Paradox

The "surprise syndrome" has been as much a feature of the transnational discourse on women and postcommunism—which has not usually engaged explicitly with the language of "transition"—as it has been of nongender-centered transitology (Lepenies; Sztompka). "Americans," the U.S. ambassador to Austria pronounced in 1997, "have been stunned to learn that the fall of communism, a goal worked toward for so long, has in some cases meant greater difficulties for women."[8] Why, for example, had the prevention of abortion been the immediate policy concern of almost each of the newly democratized countries (Kiss)? What of the masculinization of parliaments? Where has the rollback of social services left women, and what can be done about rising levels of sexual harassment and violence against women? And—a question I raise in the present analysis—what are the implications of the conversion of state property to the private property of (mostly) men? But it is not just the fact that democracy has brought with it more difficulties for some women that has taken Westerners and others aback. Why, it has been asked, if feminism has been understood as a democratizing force in the West—an emblem of Western-type "civil society"—has there been relatively little spontaneous sign of it in the democratizing East? This palpable sense of a "lack" vis à vis Western experience, a kind of "phantom feminism" effect, has been graphically described by Agnieszka Graff, a young woman returning to Poland after studying abroad:

> I'm afraid that my feminism is very un-Polish. It was born in the States, and it was there and in England, during five years at college, that it grew up.

> Sturdy and strong—to end up in a fatherland, which poor thing, it had never seen in its life before. I must admit that my feminism felt strange and out of place in Poland. It got a bit thin and weedy before it found a few friends. People pointed at it, prodded it in the stomach. For the first time in its life it came up against opposition—no longer was it "politically correct." Some people actually thought it was funny—even worse, not sexy at all. It tried to adapt—but somehow that didn't work. These pathetic attempts made me wonder, and I now think I have formulated my own particular answer to the question: "Why is there no feminism in Poland?" . . . Because there just isn't. It is not in a mass movement, it is not in the bookshops; there is a trace of it in the universities—and sometimes it pops up in conversations and newspapers, but almost always in the form of a strange and alien being—something to be looked at, patted and nodded at with a greater or lesser degree of indulgence. (Graff, "Feminizm" 20)

A decade after the death of the communist body, the "authenticity" of feminism as a political movement in postcommunist democracies remains an audible subject of feminist debate.[9] For example, Slavenka Drakulic recently recalled an early West-East encounter at a conference in Belgrade in 1978 (44). She tells how the East Europeans at the meeting were told by an American woman delegate that what was really needed in Yugoslavia was a feminist revolution. The East Europeans present were amazed, but none of them dared to tell their foreign guests how they saw it for fear of appearing backward in Western eyes. In retrospect, Drakulic concludes, not without irony, that their "silence was a mistake. . . . Much later we realized that to stand up and speak in public was one of the toughest things women everywhere have to learn. [We also learned] how hard it is to convey what you think is inequality to someone who is from an entirely different part of the world" (44).

From the beginning, much of the transnational literature on women in postcommunism has reflected a need to account for the non-sequitur which (anti)feminism after communism appeared to represent. A good deal of the discussion in this literature, then, has looked for the reasons why the difficulties faced by many women both during and after communism did not lead to an embracing of feminist identity.[10] How were these events of postcommunism to be understood? The denial of any underlying political difference has been one response to this (anti)feminist paradox.[11] That is, the explanations that have been looked for are ones to account for postcommunist deviation from feminism as an unquestioned norm, while the expectations against which the "deviation" is defined have been taken as given.

There have been many, at times contradictory, suggestions as to what these blockages might be, most relying on the invocation of an ever-increasing "Soviet legacy."[12] The communist "suppression of civil society"; the widespread rejection of the communist regime and with it Soviet-type "state feminism"; too little time (the "double/treble burden"), or, on the contrary, too much (the generosity of communist welfare—especially in the GDR); and the prevalence of anti-individualism/collectivism or the unwillingness to form groups have all been put forward as possible causes. But whatever the cause, the underlying assumption has been a normative one. The feminism that *should have* appeared—given, for example, the obvious asymmetry of the sexual division of labor or the fact that the rulers were male—has in some way been prevented from its natural expression through the experience of communism. Long after the formal end of state socialism this mode of explanation still sometimes takes the form of identifying East European barriers to apprehending what "feminism" *in fact* means. What frequently comes across from this discourse—despite references to pluralism—is a feminism that is uncontested and white because all those accounts that look to a "lack of a language" (the communist contamination of the term or the failure of Western feminists to "properly explain" it) seem to posit—but not to define—an underlying truth for feminist identity which transcends political differences among women, those distinguishing women within the West as well as those which have distinguished West and East. A focus on differences among women is nevertheless crucial because it raises questions about relations of power that cannot be deemed to be constant across democratic and communist systemic contexts.

"Leaving Home": Disarticulating Feminism and Gender

The origins of the (anti)feminist paradox, according to many observers, lies with one-sided—that is, East European—problems in conceptualizing or naming. One early visitor to postcommunist Prague has eloquently described the difficulties she encountered. A self-identifying "political tourist,"[13] she writes:

> Roaming the beautiful, cobblestone streets of Prague . . . I came across an enterprising young man in a narrow alleyway who was pinning a banner to a clothesline that stretched across two lamp posts. The banner read: "The End of Totality." The makeshift exhibit . . . also displayed a poster of a woman in red, flowing skirts. She wore a red babushka wrapped round her crown like a bandana . . . and she stood, feet firmly planted, in the midst of an undulating

> line of women. Heavy chains bore down on the backs of these women. . . . With bare hands, this woman was ripping apart the chains that bound her sisters. She was liberating womankind.
>
> Standing in a crowded pathway that summer afternoon of 1990, where tourists bargained for posters symbolizing a quickly fading era, I worried. It seemed the association of women's rights with communism would jeopardize real women in Central and Eastern Europe, as their specific needs and rights became obscured in the rejection of a system that had coopted feminist values and claimed to have solved the "woman question." . . . Unfortunately, this seems to have been what has unfolded and shapes a primary challenge that feminists have been tackling since 1989: namely, having to deconstruct and disentangle feminisms from the communist experience. It's a Herculean task, is it not? . . . I can see that the challenge of the woman in red lives on, in the efforts of all who have been nurturing gender awareness and building women's movements in the societies that women, with men, helped to set free. . . . Standing among thousands of people in Wenceslaus Square on the first anniversary of the "Velvet Revolution," I joined the crowd in chanting "We shall overcome."[14]

I quote this passage because it expresses very well a widely felt wish to share the concerns and experiences of women in the new democracies. Yet at the same time, as an exemplary act of West-East political identification it raises some of the issues of perception and interpretation that are key to the discussion here. What the observer sees as real in this scene of the "End of Totality" are after-effects of communism which continue, in societies which have been "liberated," to obscure for women where their interests actually lie. In this way a dimension of postcommunist experience is defined: It is the confusion that has to be addressed for women in Eastern Europe to become aware of the reality of their gender oppression and the increased scope in "choices" which now offer the way to be "free." The strength of postcommunist resistance to this version of reality does not undermine this view but rather reinforces it—calling forth an intensification of the effort to make clear what is already known.

This is a knowledge that recognizes only *feminist* differences among women. The restriction of recognized differences among women to those expressible through feminism makes the apparent lack of enthusiasm for feminism in Eastern Europe (a fact often remarked upon by East European feminists themselves) inexplicable in its own terms, the result of "distortion" and not really "true." And the effect of this is to place limits on the possibilities of political debate.[15] The contradiction implicit in assuming that no feminist identity implies no gender awareness is that in constructing "women," in this sense, as a fixed and unitary political category, and otherwise excluding, it does precisely what the invocation of the notion of "gender" in Eastern Europe is intended to undo. But there is more than irony here. Accounting for the paradox in terms of East European women "not knowing what the term 'feminist' really implies" is another way of restating "reality," of prescribing a basic West-East political sameness for women and seeking to place it above contention in Eastern Europe. What this does in effect is to reestablish—in the face of paradox—the (teacher-pupil) terms of West-East structured feminist discourse. "Freedom" is what legitimates the Western-centered claim to greater access to "truth." As an early commentary on feminisms East and West put it, "Desires formed under the absence of conditions of free and open discourse, or in the absence of consideration of relevant issues, whether in the West or the East can hardly have the same status as those desires and beliefs women would be likely to have after fuller discussion" (Funk 325).

From a different analytical location, the (anti)feminist paradox is not something to be explained away. It is a voice to be taken at face value—that is, on an equal basis with other voices in transnational discourse. From this location the paradox raises questions as to how far feminist political identity can be accounted for purely in terms intrinsic to a given sexual division of labor given that there has been relatively little West-East difference in this material regard. Rather, it says something else: that an exclusionary construction of "women" is not universal and, further, that such a construction depends on the curvature of sociopolitical "curved space." (Anti)feminism after communism asks that we consider afresh the role of the workings of liberal democracy in defining the political differences that attach to bodily sex. It asks us to see what is much harder to discern without a perspective from democracy's "outside." That is, it indicates the role of the "system" to the extent that—putting communism aside—democracy's "freedoms" are a matter of relative advantage within a system that engages, and therefore also *produces,* relative political location—but where, normatively, political equality obtains.

Letting East European difference be heard is a real challenge and a risk because it means having to interrogate precisely what so far has been farthest from analytical view—the unspoken assumptions and interests that have kept ideas of the underlying sameness of West-East political identity after communism so firmly in place. Problematizing the transnational relations of power that structure postcommunist feminist discourse means opening a new set of issues for critical review. To what extent, for example, does thinking about transition in terms of linear West-East comparison have the effect of eclipsing class, race, and wealth—the differences of dignity and voice that in existing democracies adhere to these—from transnational debate? How far, then, is the political order *within* Western democracies also at stake in the discourse of transition, and how far does the erasure of such issues produce expectations of transition as an untroubled, nonconflictual process of change? Wouldn't an approach that is attentive to the indignities inherent in democratic regimes call for a conceptualization of "women" after communism that looks with an especially critical eye to the broader political/economic terms of transition rather than putting these beyond question or brushing them aside—as "postsocialist" politics in the West do—in terms of a "victory" or *fait accompli?*

And if feminism's raison d'être is specific to political exclusion in democratic regimes, as the (anti)feminist paradox suggests that it is, how far is feminist discourse of transition actively reproducing the preconditions of its own existence, in naturalizing competitive democracy through a categorical focus on gender and taking for granted the broader implications of the state-economy changes currently being put in place? Such considerations have been left outside the analysis of postcommunism, where intellectual inquiry has been overly restricted to the excavation of the kind of communist legacies which will explain failed predictions but leave presuppositions intact.

Rather than succumbing to a kind of "end of history" perspective whereby the end of the cold war is the end—bar abstract feminism—of the politics that matter, a challenge for feminism is to stand up to the renewed possibility after communism of conceptually—not just physically—"leaving home." The route proposed here travels via "political space."

Civil Society and the Concept of Space

In the last two decades there has been a revival of "civil society" as a way of signifying and implementing democracy. This has been accompanied by spatialization of the metaphor of political change (S. Hall). In place of the metaphor of "revolution," implying the inversion of a political order, social change has been figured in terms of the creation of civil society as a political "space." On the one hand, where civil society has been understood as an analytic concept or an ethical ideal there has been notoriously little agreement as to its substantive content. As Katherine Fierlbeck has written, "The mafia might, for example, be justifiably excluded from the groups making up civil society (on the grounds, perhaps, that this organization involves economic transactions); but the same cannot be said of the Ku Klux Klan or Hitler

Youth" (161). Entirely uncontroversial, however, has been the representation of civil society in terms of space. For example, the most thorough-going attempt to theorize civil society after the end of communism has been provided by Jean Cohen and Andrew Arato, who envisage it to take the form of "self-limiting, democratizing movements seeking to expand and protect spaces for both negative liberty and positive freedom and to recreate egalitarian forms of solidarity without impairing economic self-regulation" (12). Rather than seeking an analytical definition of "civil society," the question asked here is, What are the particular purposes of "civil society," defined as a "space for people's action" (Fowler 18) or as an "action space" (Edwards and Foley 125)?[16] What interests are served by this use of the concept, and how is it deployed?

In philosophical terms there are two possibilities for the conceptualization of space: relativistic "curved space" or "absolute space." Albert Einstein defined these two contrasting concepts of space as follows: (a) space as a positional quality and (b) space as a container of all material objects. He explained the first, "curved space," in terms of the "psychologically simpler" concept of place. Place, he said, is a small portion of the earth's surface, identified by a name, a thing whose place is specified is a material body or group of bodies. Does the workplace, he asks, have a meaning independent of this one? If not, then one has to conclude that space (or place) is a sort of material order of objects and nothing else. If the concept of space is formed and limited in this fashion, then to speak of empty space has no meaning. Concept (b) is quite different. If one imagines a box that contains so many grains of rice or cherries, the "space" of the box is a property that is as real as the box itself. Other boxes may have a "space" of the same size. Thus, the concept of space acquires a meaning that is independent of any material object. In this way, by a natural extension of box space one can arrive at the concept of an independent (absolute) space in which all material objects are contained. "It required a severe struggle to arrive at the concept of independent and absolute space," he wrote, "indispensable for the development of theory. It has required no less strenuous exertions subsequently to overcome this concept—a process that is by no means yet completed" (Einstein xvi).

In the field of physics the intuitive appeal of "absolute space" has been shown to have far-reaching implications for the understanding of time-space-matter relations, and its limitations have been convincingly transcended by the concept of "curved space." Still, the idea of absolute space as "emptiness" is compelling, and in social thinking it remains a prediscursive notion that informs ideas of political space, as in the case of an Arendtian or Habermasian public "sphere." In postcommunism, where the spatiality of discourse is exemplified by (but by no means confined to) civil society and third-sector narratives, it is the notion of "absolute space" that has come to the fore. As an idea that continues to influence the way the social world is apprehended, the notion of absolute space draws on a prerelativistic Newtonian concept, an abstraction which claims the existence of a void in which physical bodies are present, as it were, as "guests." In Newton's theory, which emerged from a theory of matter, heavenly bodies exist freely in "space," and their motion is read exclusively in terms of properties that are constructed as inherent in the bodies themselves (Jammer).

This way of talking about the universe gained currency in the field of physics in the seventeenth century for reasons that owed much to politics because of the model of society that it sustained: "The meaning of the Newtonian synthesis that was bequeathed to the Enlightenment, partly by Newton himself, was profoundly political. The Newtonian ideology was intended to promote liberal Protestant interests at home and abroad and to maintain and bolster the power and status of a pious and God-fearing elite" (Jacob 272; see also Jammer). This was because, for Newton, the idea of an eternal absolute space, the *sensorium,* was indispensable in allowing for the existence of God and hence the representation of society in the wake of the English Revolution in terms of a *natural order.*[17]

The importance of a theory of freedom after the revolution, which nevertheless would not lend itself to the concrete claims for equality being made at the time by the Levellers, has been discussed by Freudenthal. Newton's work was significant in this regard in that it put the idea of empty space, and God "within" it, beyond challenge through experimental "proof." This had important implications for the democratic theory of Newton's contemporary John Locke, as well as for the work of Adam Smith. The claim for the possibility of a "free" market economy which is able to exist outside relations of power as a self-contained "system" is one in which Adam Smith was also directly influenced by Isaac Newton's theory of the motion of celestial bodies in absolute space (Jacob).

"Absolute space," in liberal democracy, supports a cosmology where "sense is made" of the world in terms of the qualities of autonomous "selves" which are analogous to Newton's discrete bodies existing freely "in space." In framing action and identities in absolute terms, "absolute space" and the self-contained bodies within it make possible the idea of the existence an objective and "independent" scale in terms of which such selves may be ranked with respect to each other. Together, this creates the possibility of translating the perception of actually existing hierarchy into the reflection of an underlying natural order rather than as the enactment of politics. The existence of absolute (political) space is thus a crucial presupposition behind liberal democracy's hidden ideology.[18] What better means of concealment than as "emptiness"?

A subversion of the apprehension of the spatial as an idealized and absolute medium for identities and action and its corollary (identities that can be conceived of independently of specific relations of power) is, I think, what Foucault was advocating when he recommended the "desanctification" of space ("Other Spaces").[19] This desanctification can be achieved by drawing on the Einsteinian concept of curved space. In the physical world, the curvature of curved space may be experienced as gravitational effects. With political "curved space," political actors/identities, rather than acting "within" political space or being prevented from so doing by virtue of space's lack, instead *constitute* as they are constituted by a specific political "curved space." The characteristics of "curved space" are always specific in time because "curved space" depends on the particular players that constitute it and what they do. Like place, the relativized concept of "curved space" cannot be defined in the abstract—as something of which there can only be more or less—and with it political abstractions, such as the autonomous individual or the universal subject that whiteness presupposes, become impossible to conceive.

With the re-formed spatial metaphor, the "whiteness" that has been identified by feminists can be said to act like the gravitational pull that can be used to describe "curved space." This "pull" is an expression of unequal power. The one place this inequality in the terms of interaction is not felt is at the core of the identity that both exercises as it is constituted by this definitive force. This is what gives whiteness its invisibility to the "white." That is to say, whiteness depends for its invisibility on a depoliticizing ideology underwritten by the assumption of the existence of absolute space. Precisely because the latter is so apparently neutral it remains beyond question as a way of imagining "freedom," effectively masking liberal democratic discourses of power.

Transition, with its invocation of "freedom," has been constructed as an extrapolitical process, as what should be the unfolding of a natural order, one that should "emerge" with the "creation of space." However, what is at stake is not the removal but the reconfiguration of asymmetries of power, that is to say the re-curving of political "curved space." The source of the difficulties which arise in attempting to square Western expectations with the "realities" of the postcommunist condition do not lie with term *transition* itself but with a broader construction of change that denies that identities in liberal democracy are constituted by system-specific relations of power. Here, "civil society" has an ideological role to play. It is to this I now look, bearing in mind that in depending for its effectiveness on a West-East, freedom-unfreedom conceptual divide—in essence an assumption of the existence of "absolute space"—such discourse embodies an ideal that is not simply impossible in practice (cf. Hefner) but also theoretically suspect.

"Civil Society" as Ideological Discourse

The Identity of the West in a Globalizing Context

In March 1997 human rights for women was declared an official part of U.S. foreign policy, in effect constituting a kind of American "state feminism for abroad."[20] "Expanding the "circle of human dignity" requires far greater attention to the rights of women throughout the world, as Hillary Clinton emphasized in her speech to an audience of UN delegates and NGO representatives at the UN later in the year. "Let us say it loudly for the entire world to hear us," she went on to say. "[We] do not believe that violence against women is simply cultural; we believe that it is simply criminal."[21] Here then, as I see it, is a discourse where the construction of the New World Order—and the United States' role within it—is very much at stake. Here, it is a story of the struggle of "civil society" against "violence against women"—an issue that conveys powerful moral signals where the messages involved seem simple, unambiguous, absolute. Here, "civil society" stands for democracy and "freedom" because, as we can tell from the reference to a "circle of dignity," it continues to be defined in contrast to the no-longer-existing communist state—a definition that persists even though "civil society," now a *nonprofit* sector, has become in postcommunism what under communism it could never have been.[22] Here, then, is a definition of a New World Order continuing to push outward on the limits to freedom, a project over which the world's most powerful state presides.

Instead of falling, however, the reported incidence of violence against women during democratization has steadily increased. Still, when it comes to a description of what political change is "doing" in postcommunism, it is the term *making visible* that persistently recurs. West-East opposition in terms of the presence/absence of political "absolute space" is reflected in the fact that democracy after communism is seen as providing the transparency, the opportunity to "lift the curtain" and look straight through the present to the exposed reality of the communism of a decade before (Minnesota Advocates for Human Rights). The present becomes simply the medium. It affords the facility to view because democracy after communism is constructed as entailing "freedom of expression" where once there was none. This has impelled explanations of rising levels of violence against women in postcommunism in the direction of "more frequent reporting," excluding the possibility that democracy after communism can itself be associated with increases in violence against women—bound up with the new impulses and frustrations that democratization brings—that is, with the factors associated with the increases in other forms of crime.

According to a recent article in the *New York Times,* a 33 percent rise in domestic violence cases was reported in Poland in 1995, with steady increases since that time. What this showed—unequivocally to the author of the piece—was "that more women were reporting such incidents." As "the facade of the cohesive family is being rolled back," stated the report, what is being revealed is the fact that traditionally "women are expected to marry early in Poland, and submit to their husbands' will, even if that means harsh physical abuse" (Perlez A8). The point of analytical concern here does not devolve on the presence versus absence of physical abuse against women in East European countries prior to democratization. The point is rather to question the extent to which explanations of *change,* in this case rising levels of reported abuse after the end of communism, are constructed in terms of the presence/absence of "absolute space." Nevertheless, the *New York Times* article quoted above is a good example of the way in which the Western media, in producing a one-sided discourse of democracy as "revealing" rather than revealed, play an active role in "inventing" the "cultural legacy" they unmask—in this case, *a national tradition in eastern Europe.*[23]

In the current global context, civil society discourse produces and depends on a conception of "violence against women" that is very strictly defined. Excluded is violence against women that cannot be readily encapsulated in gender-categorical terms. An example of what is omitted is physical violence against women, where violence is perpetrated against both men and women for reasons of economy/state.[24] Second, "violence against women" is conceived of in terms that—again because of the way "gender" is used—are abstracted from broader aspects of experience. What is significant is the relative ease with which "violence against women" can be represented as a self-contained problem, an issue of "pure" gender untrammeled by considerations of broader political and economic context.

The "Platform for Action" which emanated from the 1995 Beijing Conference for Women defined violence against women as "a manifestation of the 'age-old inequality between men and women,' which has led to domination of and discrimination against women." The solution the document foresaw was to act to allow women to "control their own lives" to gain access to "economic and political power" (*Platform for Action*). As this formulation indicates, violence against women is an issue that fits neatly into, and reproduces, the kind of thinking that underpins the feminist ideas of West-East political sameness discussed above. That is to say, the problem of violence against women can very readily slip, and in transnational discourse has slipped, into an essentializing man-versus-woman frame.[25]

This is an irony of some proportions, given that a classic vignette of West-East feminist interchange has the "Eastern" response to feminism as an objection to pitting women against men and the "Western" counter-response as an often-frustrated attempt to explain that women-versus-men is *not* what feminism is about. Nevertheless, such is the "pull" of Western-centeredness in the discourse of transition that what it produces is an idea of gender that is ahistorical in every respect except for the cultural legacy of communism and the ameliorative impact that democracy is deemed to have on gender relations, in affording the opportunity to transcend that legacy through the benefits of publicity.

Here, then, is a concrete example of how an assumption of the existence of "absolute space" and its corollary, universal identity across communist-democratic frames, sustains a particular construction of democratic freedom, depoliticizing not only transition but also the West. It is this "whiteness" that offers the possibility, in the face of everything that has happened in the former Soviet Bloc over the last decade, of an unimpeached narrative of Westernization as progression being retained. In her capacity as roving U.S. representative promoting women's rights abroad, Hillary Clinton has given clear voice to the purifying value of such self-definition through global contrast: "When I think about the women who've been imprisoned, tortured, discouraged, barred from involvement in education or professional opportunity—what *any of us* go through in America is minor in comparison" (Eisenstein 150, emphasis added).

The Idea of the Independent Self

The abstractions of "civil society" and "freedom," the accompanying ideas of "empowerment" and "control," are surely at odds with the concrete situations of increasing stress and loss of control in which many women see themselves after communism. But more than this, they render such situations irrelevant, accidental, or avoidable if people do what they should. Underpinned by an assumption of the existence of "absolute space," these notions are used to suggest that now nothing, except people themselves, stands between the empowerment of some becoming the empowerment of all. At issue is the legitimization of transition by means of an ideology that puts in place an idea of nature so hierarchy is interpreted as nature's reflection and thus evaluated, notwithstanding democracy's norm of equality, as equitable or just. More often than not, what is at stake in transition is an individualistic ideology of self-blame. Outside civil society discourse, the message has been more overt. In the face of widespread popular dissatisfaction with the effects of democratization in Russia, the well-known liberal economist Alexei Uliakov, writing recently in *Izvestia,* has instructed those without the money for a flat not to accuse other people on this account, calling on the poor to blame only themselves for their misfortunes (Shlapentokh).

After communism, an ideological transition of this kind is not easy to achieve. It is not easy to rewrite the rules of perception whereby the socially problematic and its resolution are no longer seen in terms of the state but in terms of the underlying qualities of selves. The research I have conducted in Nowa Huta, Poland, has traced social change in the nation's "first socialist town" and offers many examples of resistance to such civil society discourse. For example, a woman in an administrative post in the local steelworks had left her husband when she was young ("violence?—there was that too"), and she described in some length the sense of independence that her job at the then–Lenin Steelworks had given when supporting her small children had been her prime concern.

The steelworks—much reviled by the local Krakow intelligentsia as the embodiment of communism—towers over the region and remains the linchpin of the local economy. As the enterprise continues to shed labor and many of its broader social functions with a view to privatization, she expressed concern for the increased difficulties of young single mothers and currently has two such women on her staff:

> And if you were to ask me, if I were in the same situation today as I was in 1970, would I have the courage to leave my husband—an engineer who earned a good salary—we had a beautiful flat, only he had a very bad character, he was a bad person. Now in 1998 or 1999, would I have the courage—then I can tell you in all certainty—*no.* I would try to struggle on. I simply would know that I couldn't afford a flat, that I wouldn't have one. I would know that on my own I would have no hope of providing for the children, giving them an education. . . . I would know that I couldn't condemn my children to hunger.[26]

Another young woman, a psychologist who had worked with the local woman's refuge and hotline for victims of violence, linked the problems of women she counseled with the "inequality that comes from the current economic situation in Poland." She looked back on her experiences of the last years:

> There's no low-cost house-building now. I mean now they're only building flats for people that are really rich. . . . There aren't any ordinary, low-cost flats—that's particularly visible in Nowa Huta isn't it, a lot of families living in the same flat—and that's a spatial problem too, because research shows that if you've got less than ten meters a head or whatever, it causes psychological problems. It's a terrible vicious circle and it really depresses me. After three or four years working in the refuge and with the hotline I have an enormous sense of ineffectiveness. . . . I have an enormous sense of ineffectiveness. Yes, maybe you do undertake work at the grass roots, so to speak—work like refuges for battered women or hotlines for victims of violence. But in a way we're doing the job of the Ministry of Health or the Ministry of Education. We're simply doing the job of the government institutions who should be dealing with these problems. They feel very comfortable because in their reports they can write—oh yes, here we have an organization doing such and such. . . . Without changes at the top you can have as many telephone hotlines as you like, or refuges for battered women, but without changes in the law, in political thinking, without rules, laws, and so on from the top, nothing will change—really. I simply don't count on it. That's just how it is. It depresses me.[27]

Rethinking "Transition": The Differentiation of Citizenship

Instead of concentrating so exclusively on ways of redefining the problematic in terms of what the removal of communism has "revealed" about what was really there before, a fundamental question for theorizing feminism in postcommunism is to reconceptualize the difference between communism and democracy so as to understand what qualifies as "(in)equality," "freedom/oppression," or "resistance" within either frame. In what way is political space under communism and democracy differently curved? What are the changing power relations of transition that "civil society" mystifies? In order to answer these questions, the broad differences between the communist and liberal state-economy should be defined.

The claim of state socialism was that the poverty and social inequality, including sexual equality, that were endemic to presocialist modes of production would be transcended by a communist regime. Key to this regime was a nonprofit, nonprivate-property economy and the relative absence of not agency but private rights. Under communism, the economy was recognized as overtly political. As an explicit aspect of the exercise of power it represented a core element of the party/state that defined its role as acting on behalf of society as a whole. Ultimately, social inequalities were reduced but not eliminated under socialism. Yet despite the existence of social differences including status groupings,[28] citizenship, which defined the relation of the citizen to the state and to other citizens under state socialism, was both universal and unitary because state power replaced the potential private rights of everyone and was unprecedented in scope.[29] Given the top-down, administrative, and collective nature of Party rule, the possibility and very point of differential citizenship and masculine "individuality" were effectively removed.

Parallels have been drawn with the French Revolution and the origins of modern feminism in discussing exclusions of women from a postcommunist "public sphere" as if the changes being experienced in Eastern Europe were analogous to those in the new French Republic but distanced from them in time (Watson, "Eastern Europe's Silent Revolution"). One limit, then, to the analogy lies in the fact that while the idea of universal citizenship was born during the course of the French Revolution (Fitzsimmons), citizenship that was formally *universal* preexisted democratization in the former Soviet Bloc.[30] Moreover, with democratization after communism, rights become conditional capacities dependent on the outcome of the interplay of social factors (cf. Barbalet). They describe horizons of possibility rather than self-standing entitlements under ostensible state guarantee. Insofar as the liberal democratic right to property, for example, is a right to gain property *if you can* (ibid.), after communism, social difference itself has been gaining the potential to *differentiate politically* (Watson, "(Anti)Feminism"; Watson, "Civil Society"). Thus, what women are being excluded from in postcommunist democracies cannot easily be framed—as it was after the French Revolution—as a broader process of political equalization. The novelty of masculinism after communism is that it is part of a broader process of sweeping political differentiation, the result of the unparalleled opportunity for *relative* political empowerment which democratization after communism brings. The process of relative political empowerment/disempowerment in Eastern Europe was enabled by the reintroduction of private rights, the privatization of the economy and liberalization of the law.

The significance of the patterning of extralegal action for differences between women, West and East, can be illustrated by comparing the varying exclusionary possibilities of a public/private conceptual divide. In democratic regimes, the public/private distinction has been one way of defining women out of politics and defining the political as masculine. That is to say, the identification of women with the private and personal has been part of a construction and a process—a mobilization of difference—whereby women's political identity, contrary to the universal tenets of the system, is diminished in favor of that of men. Because it has been constitutive of political difference in democratic systems, the public/private distinction structured representation and voice and has figured prominently in Western feminist critiques.

In communist countries, however, a public/private distinction could not be mobilized to subvert the universality of citizenship, as it could in the West. Political exclusion or inequality could not be defined in these terms under communism. Women could not easily be constructed as particular beings outside politics, or politics be defined as masculine, for the simple reason that in this system both men and women were outside politics insofar as representation and voice were the prerogative of the state. That is, the identification of women with the domestic—insofar as this was the case—could not incorporated within any exclusionary discourse that referred to women alone, for exclusion or inclusion was framed in terms of the "leading role of the Party," where the Party increasingly became what everyone resented the most. "Inequality" came to be defined in terms of the oppositional relationship between "society" and "state."

The state-society distinction was not congruent with a public-private divide. As the sociologist Jerzy Szacki has written, the politically constructed counter-society was itself both "social" and "private." Here, public or private were not necessarily contradictory or counterposed. In "society" possibilities for action and self-expression—whether at home or at work—were importantly inscribed in terms of personal trust and affective ties, as "the family" itself was redefined (Watson, "Explaining"). In this sense, whatever its superficial gender similarities with the West, the unintended consequence of communism was that the life of society was not—to borrow Marilyn Strathern's expression—the life of *men*. In other words, under communism, although the rulers were male it was not men who ruled.

Globalism, Gender, and Class

What, then, are the implications for conceptualizing feminism in "transition"? Ideas of sexual difference that serve inclusion/exclusion are not simply coded with the "atavisms" of Eastern Europe, newly revealed; they are coded with "Westernization" of state/economy, with private property and with "class." The political theorist Wendy Brown has drawn attention to the way in which the political effects of wealth and capitalism are among the issues most taken for granted in Western political theory.[31] In postcommunism, the generation of wealth/poverty constitutes the primary, if unanalyzed, site of current processes of political differentiation that democratization brings. The strategy for economic transformation in the former Soviet Bloc was an expression of the "Washington Consensus," the outcome of global relations of power.[32] In contrast to the facelessness of Party edicts, the strategy was constructed as having been "master-minded" by individual men.[33] In the case of Poland, it was alternatively Jeffrey Sach's or the "Balcerowicz Plan." The framing of this program of privatization of ownership and "market rationalization" in terms of "technical correction" meant removal from the arena of public discussion. Since the acceptance of such changes in Poland were by no means a forgone conclusion, the point of global strategy was to impose the rules of the game. Balcerowicz himself was to write that "it was easier for the supporters of the market-oriented reforms to defend them as *fait accompli* than it would have been to build reforms gradually in the face of strong populist opposition in the Parliament after the elections of October 1991" (307).

In the argument he puts forward, the inherent superiority of private ownership in this global strategy is conjoined with a hierarchy of sex to form a mutually buttressing set of fundamental "truths": "One widespread example of an erroneous generalization is to assert that form of ownership has no significance, by citing examples of certain state enterprises in the West which are just as good as private ones (the list is usually rather short). This procedure is just as absurd as pointing to a female shot-putter as proof that women are not physically weaker than men" (Balcerowicz 235).

Moreover, the economy is enunciated in terms of a "logical model," to be understood in counterposition to the distorting effects of "emotional appeal" that emanates from the word *social* (Balcerowicz 233). In this way the "social"—against which economic individuality is defined—is implicitly coded as feminine, disqualifying both the feminine and the social at the same time. In a formulation that—from the point of view of the framework of present essay—is aptly Newtonian, Balcerowicz expresses the view that "emotionally loaded terminology is not a mistake in itself, but a potential source of mistaken judgments. One of the advantages of mathematics is that its language is entirely emotionally neutral. In discussing social phenomena, such an advantage would probably be as great as that offered by the precision of mathematical relationships" (234).

A vision of the return of the individual informed the early deliberations of the new democratic Polish Senate, where only "the free market, based on private subjects, can guarantee the stability of the democratic transformation."[34] Here, the institutionalization of individual rights of property and the abolition of the right to abortion were the twinned legislative concerns of the new order, again coding the new subject as masculine. The full employment economy-state was to be superseded by an economic system oriented toward profit and risk. Western advisers involved in the process of economic transformation observed that they had to "work with companies who don't understand the profit motive . . . to keep expenses down, prices up, and make up the difference in the middle. In contrast to the old days, where the more people you employed, the better you were doing, . . . you have to take risks and hopefully you'll get rewards" (Robert Towbin, quoted in Wedel, *Collision* 176).

It has been the connection between a neoclassical notion of risk, on the one hand and, on the other, risk-taking as a sign of moral fiber and the masculine that has contributed to a discourse of the individual who is "up to" taking risks on behalf of society—the new, Western-type, entrepreneurial man. "What Poland still needs are stuntmen and daredevils, not somebody who will spend time putting on make-up or going to the hairdressers'," as Lech Wałęsa has remarked.[35] In Krakow, "Penetrator" is the name that has been given to a prominent brokerage firm, while the press features advertisements such as those for a new Polish fragrance called "Makler" (stockbroker), described as "being the scent of a man."

While private property and the "free market"—encompassing what in Poland has been called the "piratization" of the property that formerly belonged to the state (J. A. Hall)—is an important site of the current "rise of masculinism" (Watson, "Rise of Masculinism"), issues of gender redefinition are for women, not necessarily an area of primary concern. As a Slovakian woman explained to her Western interlocutors in 1996, "During Socialism, somehow, everything was settled, and especially the economy and the political situation—there was nothing to shout about. . . . But nowadays we have serious political problems and serious economic problems, privatization and things like this—so all the rest can go away" (quoted in Eliot et al. 23). Such views testify to the fact that as the changes take place, vividly contrasting fates are in view. Who will be in employment, and who will have unemployment "in their genes"?[36] Who will have a future, and who will have none? Will there be a middle class? If so, who will join its ranks and who will be left outside? In some cases, literally, who will survive? Insofar as "whiteness," metaphorically speaking, is what is being constructed, who will be "white"? Such issues—relating importantly to the formation of political differences among women—are still in the balance, and have an overriding salience.

Some women are carving out careers, paying others to work in their homes in their place. Others are networking with counterparts in the West.

Others again are being swept into a downward spiral of entrapment and despair. Unemployment has remained one of the most frequent subjects of the letters that women write to the editor of the popular Polish women's magazine *Kobieta i Zycie* (Gaińska). Many of these letter-writers try to recount their experiences and convey the shock of the new. According to the magazine, many women who had had problems trying to accommodate paid work and housework and dreamed of spending time at home feel terrible after a few days, even when money isn't a problem; they feel useless, unwanted, desperate. They suddenly realize what their husbands, sisters, or friends must have been going through. And when some find work again they find themselves in the oppressive position of having to agree to practically anything their employer wants—for fear of losing their jobs. At the beginning of the decade readers used to write to the magazine, asking it to intervene. Now few do.

How then should feminism frame this issue in an unprecedented context of change where for *all* women that are unemployed, unemployment is new? Is one to defer to the economists' notion of unemployment's "natural rate" or acquiesce in the view that natural differences in people's "entrepreneurial ability" are what now stand revealed? Is, then, the marker of "acceptability" and fairness in this situation the 50 percent figure, where unemployment levels of women are equal to those of men? Are differences that are to be regarded as not natural but political *only* those that exist between women and men? If so, then I would say that feminism becomes in some inevitable measure accomplice to the political processes behind the suffering endured by the women described above. If not, then a broader feminist critique of both the means and the ends of transition is overdue.

Both the empowerment and disempowerment of people are at stake in transition. In the interpretation put forward here, political differentiation after communism is linked to the redefinition of state and economy and the way the relation between these is undergoing change. The transition to democracy and the process of "deregulation" does not mean the removal of power from the economy but its denial through the reassertion of the notion of an economy that can be "free." One revealing irony of postcommunism being that the free economy has had to be introduced by supra-state fiat.

Given this setting, feminism's task is more daunting than the progressive exposure of a retrograde past. In the postcommunist democracies, where both masculinism and other modes of *relative* political inclusion are phenomena that are qualitatively new, masculinism, as it takes shape, is locked into the wider terms of inclusion. But equally, if some women complain bitterly about what is happening to them yet still feel relatively little "discrimination," then one reason is that the shock of their experience is part of a broader pattern of selective demobilization which also includes men. Paradoxically, to focus exclusively on a categorical idea of gender in postcommunism that compares "men" on one side and "women" on the other is to endorse the underlying terms of transition, terms which themselves are productive of masculinism. As I hope I have shown, it also means endorsing the wider political inequalities that inhere in the West.

NOTES

This essay is in part based on a talk given at the Center for Russian and East European Studies, University of Michigan, in March 1998, as part of the "Crossing Borders: Rethinking Area Studies" Program. The Nowa Huta study is based at the Faculty of Social and Political Sciences, University of Cambridge, and is funded by the U.K. Economic and Social Research Council, Grant Number R000222627, the British Academy, and the Isaac Newton Trust, Trinity College Cambridge.

1. See the Introduction in Scott (*Feminism*) for a discussion of how historicizing difference informs feminist history.

2. The average life expectancy of Russian men is now about twelve years less than that of women. A 1999 UNDP report calculates that there are now 5.7 million "missing men" in the Russian Federation alone as a result of premature deaths (*Human Development Report*).

3. This overlays older configurations of West-East difference. In the nineteenth century, the intellectual ideals of "Western Europe" were made possible by mobilizing the category of the (backward) East (Wolff). Compare David Kideckel's notion of "categorical orientalism" (Kideckel).

4. Earlier discussions of the importance of the West-East distinction for structuring the discourse of transition are presented in Watson ("(Anti)Feminism"; "Civil Society").

5. Jaroslava Moserova, vice president of the Czech Senate, speaking at the "Vital Voices Conference," Vienna, July 9–11, 1997.

6. Remarks made at the International Sociological Association's regional conference "Building Open Society and Perspectives of Sociology in East-Central Europe," Krakow, September 14–18, 1996. The idea of men not being "up to" the risks of freedom resonate with a number of commentators. For example, an analogy attributed to Nicholas Eberstadt has been drawn between increased mortality after the ending of communism and the increased mortality of blacks after the end of slavery in North America (Chen, Wittgenstein, and McKeon; see also Mueller).

7. Zygmunt Bauman conceptualizes this distinction in terms of his notion of a "two-step revolution," involving first, the toppling of the previous regime, and secondly, the emergence of the new one (Bauman).

8. Swanee Hunt, U.S. ambassador to Austria, remarks to a conference entitled "Vital Voices: Women in Democracy: Seeking to Strengthen the Role of Women," Vienna, July 9–11, 1997.

9. See, for example, the discussion of this subject in issues 4 and 5 of the Polish

feminist periodical *Penym Gosem* and the contributions to "Talking about Women and Men," a special issue of *Transitions* (5, no. 1 [1998]). One of the themes tabled for discussion at a conference entitled "Gender in Transition in Central and Eastern Europe," organized by the Centre for Interdisciplinary Women's Studies at the Humboldt University in Berlin in 1999, was the "viability of a serious East-Central European challenge to the international hegemony of Western feminist thought." In Poland, an exchange of views on the place of feminism was published in a series of articles in *Gazeta Wyborcza* during June and July 1999 (e.g., "Patriarchat").

10. The literature on women in postcommunism includes work by Corrin (ed.); Einhorn; Funk and Mueller (eds.); Rueschmeyer (ed.); and Scott, Kaplan, and Keates (eds.).

11. For a consideration of paradox in democratic politics see Connolly (*Identity*); for the centrality of paradox to feminism and democracy see Scott (*Only Paradoxes*).

12. I discuss a number of different explanations of the absence of feminism in postcommunism in "Eastern Europe's Silent Revolution."

13. The term *political tourist* was coined by Vaclav Havel.

14. E-mail message from S. Penn to Lenka, Nov. 17, 1997, "Network of East-West Women" <http://www.neww.org>.

15. It is, in William Connolly's terms, an "untruth," something, that is, "which cannot achieve sufficient standing within the terms of discourse of a time without stretching contemporary standards of plausibility and coherence to their limits of tolerance" (*Ethos* 523).

16. Compare Keith Tester's focus on the "why" rather than the "what" of civil society. He offers a somewhat different answer to the question that the one put forward here.

17. For a discussion of the importance of God and the individual freedom (but not "space") in the work of Locke, see Seligman.

18. I have in mind the notion of ideology espoused by Louis Althusser ("Ideology").

19. Pierre Bourdieu attempts to bring the idea of absolute space to the surface, but does so by means of a direct translation of the physical concepts of space, time and matter. He does not go far from the concept, however, as when he talks of positions "situated *between* the two poles of the field, in the *neutral* point of the space" (725, emphasis in the original).

20. "Advancing the status of women is not only a moral imperative, it is being actively integrated into the foreign policy of the United States," Madeleine Albright announced at an International Women's Day ceremony at the U.S. State Department on March 12, 1997. "It is our mission, it is the right thing to do and frankly it is the smart thing to do" (Lippman).

21. Hillary Clinton, speech to the United Nations, December 10, 1997.

22. This is a reference to Istvan Bibo's description of "civil society" under communism as "small circles of freedom," a key metaphor for the representation of NGOs in postcommunism (Les; Siegel and Yancey).

23. A similar point about the role of Western media has been made by Pasic and Weiss with reference to the construction of ethnic labels in the context of the former Yugoslavia.

24. The construct of "violence against women," as it figures in this U.S. foreign

policy discourse, leaves outside of view the U.S. claim to a monopoly over means of violence that remain legitimate, as in military interventions abroad.

25. For example, see some of the contributions to OŚKa (1998).

26. Author interviews with J.M., Nowa Huta, August 1996, December 1998.

27. Author interview with U.P., Krakow, November 1998.

28. Even where forms of private production existed, as in Hungary or rural Poland, this activity was framed and limited by the prescriptions of the broader economy-state.

29. This concrete and all-encompassing approach to citizenship was symbolized by Nowa Huta and the other state socialist new towns, where the city itself represented societal policy. Its architecture, facilities, and employment enterprises exemplified the new political order and the way the new socialist citizen would be produced.

30. For a discussion of the intelligentsia, workers, and peasantry status groups under state socialism in Poland see Staniszkis.

31. For her critique of the more general theoretical retreat from the problem of domination within capitalism, see especially Brown, chapter 1, "Introduction: Freedom and the Plastic Cage."

32. Transition strategies in Eastern Europe have been based on the "Washington Consensus"—opinion formed in Washington and involving the IMF, the World Bank, and the U.S. Treasury ("Economic Neoliberalism").

33. The title of Janine Wedel's "The Harvard Boys Do Russia" reflects the transnationally gendered nature of transition.

34. According to Poland's postcommunist legislators, "The idea of a democratic and pluralistic, law-based state, characterized by self-government . . [and] the social market economy, assisted by state intervention. . . . This model assumes the dominant role of private property, which enjoys full legal protection (1992 Legislative Council statement, quoted in Loś).

35. These remarks were made with reference to Hanna Gronkiewicz-Waltz, director of the Polish National Bank (quoted in Millard).

36. The Polish sociologist Maria Jarosz was asked in a 1998 interview whether unemployment in the country was hereditary. She replied that it was not, since it had not been experienced for long enough (interview with Maria Jarosz).

Works Cited

Althusser, Louis. "Ideology and Ideological State Apparatuses." In *Lenin and Philosophy and Other Essays.* Trans. B. Brewster, 127–86. London: New Left Books, 1971.

Balcerowicz, Leszek. *Socialism Capitalism Transformation.* Budapest: Central European University Press, 1995.

Barbalet, J. M. *Citizenship.* Milton Keynes: Open University Press, 1988.

Bauman, Zygmunt. "After the Patronage State: A Model in Search of Class Interests." In *The New Great Transformation?* ed. C. G. A. Bryant and Edmund Mokrzycki, 14–35. London: Routledge, 1994.

Bourdieu, Pierre. "The Social Space and the Genesis of Groups." *Theory and Society* 14 (1985): 723–44.

Brown, Wendy. *States of Injury: Power and Freedom in Late Modernity,* Princeton: Princeton University Press, 1995.

Chen, Lincoln, F. Wittgenstein, and Elizabeth McKeon. "The Upsurge of Mortality in Russia: Causes and Policy Implications." *Population and Development Review* 22, no. 3 (1996): 517–30.

Cohen, Jean L., and Andrew Arato. *Civil Society and Political Theory.* Cambridge: MIT Press, 1992.

Connolly, William. *The Ethos of Pluralization,* Minneapolis: University of Minnesota Press, 1995.

———. *Identity/Difference: Democratic Negotiations of Political Paradox,* Ithaca: Cornell University Press, 1991.

Corrin, Chris, ed. *"Superwoman" and the Double Burden: Women's Experience of Change in Central and Eastern Europe and the Former Soviet Union,* Toronto: Second Story Press, 1992.

Drakulic, Slavenka. "What We Learned from Western Feminists: Democracy and the Treason of Lipstick." *Transitions* 5, no. 1 (1998): 44.

"Economic Neoliberalism Became almost Irrelevant." Interview with Grzegorz W. Kołodko. *Transition* 9, no. 3 (1998): 1–5.

Edwards, B., and M. W. Foley. "Civil Society and Social Capital beyond Putnam." *American Behavioral Scientist* 42, no. 1 (1998): 124–39.

Einhorn, Barbara. *Cinderella Goes to Market: Citizenship, Gender and Women's Movements in East Central Europe,* London: Verso, 1993.

Einstein, Albert. Introduction. In Max Jammer, *Concepts of Space: The History of Theories of Space in Physics.* 1954. Reprint. 3d rev. ed. New York: Dover Publications, 1993.

Eisenstein, Zillah. "Women's Publics and the Search for New Democracies." In *Citizenship: Pushing the Boundaries.* Ed. Feminist Review Collective, 140–67. New York: Routledge, 1998.

Eliot, Jo, Tor Foster, Chris Hood, and Lynn R. Reed. "Gossip, Cake and Wine: Methodological Challenges for Feminist and Dialogic Research in Cross-Cultural Settings." In *Invitation to Dialogue: Beyond Gender (In)Equality,* ed. Ilze Koroleva. Riga: Institute of Philosophy and Sociology, Latvian Academy of Sciences, 1997.

Fierlbeck, Katherine. *Globalizing Democracy: Power, Legitimacy and the Interpretation of Democratic Ideas,* Manchester: Manchester University Press, 1998.

Fitzsimmons, Michael P. "The National Assembly and the Invention of Citizenship." In *The French Revolution and the Meaning of Citizenship,* ed. Renee Waldinger, Phillip Dawson, and Isser Woloch, 29–42. Westport: Greenwood Press, 1993.

Flax, Jane. "Race/Gender and the Ethics of Difference." *Political Theory* 23, no. 3 (1995): 500–510.

Foucault, Michel. *The Archeology of Knowledge.* Trans. A. M. Sheridan Smith. London: Tavistock, 1972.

———. "Of Other Spaces." *diacritics* 16 (Spring 1986): 22–27.

Fowler, Alan. "Strengthening Civil Society in Transition Economies—From Concept to Strategy: Mapping an Exit in a Maze of Mirrors." In *NGOs, Civil Society and the State: Building Democracy in Transitional Societies,* ed. Andrew Clayton. Oxford: INTRAC, 1996.

Frankenberg, Ruth. *White Woman, Race Matters: The Social Construction of Whiteness.* London: Routledge, 1993.
Freudenthal, Gideon. *Atom and Individual in the Age of Newton: On the Genesis of the Mechanistic World View.* Dordrecht: Reidel, 1986.
Funk, Nanette. 1993. "Feminism East and West." In *Gender Politics and Post-Communism,* ed. Nanette Funk and Magda Mueller, 318–30. New York: Routledge, 1993.
———, and Magda Mueller, eds. *Gender Politics and Post-Communism.* New York: Routledge, 1993.
Gaińska, Bozena. "Problemy Rynku Pracy w Listach Czytelniczek Tygodnika Kobieta i Zycie." *Rynek Pracy* 9, no. 81 (1998): 39–42.
Graff, Agnieszka. "Feminizm Ryzyka—i Dlaczego w Polsce Go Nie Ma." *Pełnym Głosem,* 4 (1996): 19–23.
———. "Patriarchat po Seksmisji." *Gazeta Wyborcza,* June 19–20, 1999, 20–23.
Hall, John A. "The Nature of Civil Society." *Transaction: Social Science and Modern Society* 35, no. 4 (1998): 32–41.
Hall, Stuart. "For Allon White: Metaphors of Transformation." In *Stuart Hall: Critical Dialogues in Cultural Studies,* ed. David Morley and K-H Chen, 287–308. London: Routledge, 1996.
Hefner, Robert. *Democratic Civility and the History and Cross-Cultural Possibility of a Political Ideal.* London: Transaction Publishers, 1998.
Holmes, Stephen. *The Anatomy of Antiliberalism.* Cambridge: Harvard University Press, 1996.
Human Development Report for Central and Eastern Europe and the CIS. New York: Published for the United Nations Development Programme, 1999.
Interview with Maria Jarosz, *Rynek Pracy,* 1998, 9.
Jacob, Margaret. *The Newtonians and the English Revolution 1689–1720.* Ithaca: Cornell University Press, 1976.
Jammer, Max. *Concepts of Space: The History of Theories of Space in Physics.* 1954. Reprint. 3d rev. ed. New York: Dover Publications, 1993.
Kideckel, David A. "What's in a Name? The Persistence of Eastern Europe as Conceptual Category." *Replika: Hungarian Social Science Quarterly.* Special ed. on "Colonization or Partnership? Eastern Europe and Western Social Sciences," 27–32. Budapest: Budapest University of Economic Sciences, 1996.
Kiss, Judit. "The Second "No": Women in Hungary." *Feminist Review* 39 (1993): 49–57.
Lepenies, Wolf. 1992. "Social Surprises. Germany in Europe—Three Years after the Revolution." Mimeo. Fritz Thyssen Stiftung, 1992.
Les, Ewa. *The Voluntary Sector in Post-Communist East Central Europe: From Small Circles of Freedom to Civil Society.* Washington: Civicus, 1995.
Lippman, Thomas W. "Albright Puts Women's Rights Top of the Agenda." *Washington Post,* March 20, 1997.
Loś, Maria. "Property Rights, Market and Historical Justice: Legislative Discourse in Poland." *International Journal of the Sociology of Law* 22, no. 1 (1994): 39–58.
Millard, Frances. "The Catholic Church and Women in Poland." Presented at the Centre for Russian and East European Studies, University of Birmingham, Nov. 15, 1995.

Minnesota Advocates for Human Rights. *Lifting the Last Curtain: A Report on Domestic Violence in Romania.* Minneapolis: University of Minnesota Press, 1995.
Morrison, Toni. *Playing in the Dark: Whiteness and the Literary Imagination.* Cambridge: Harvard University Press, 1992.
Mueller, John. "Democracy, Capitalism, and the End of Transition." In *Post-Communism: Four Perspectives,* ed. Michael Mandelbaum, 102–67. New York: Council on Foreign Relations, 1996.
Offe, Claus. *Varieties of Transition: The East European and East German Perspective.* Cambridge: Polity Press, 1996.
OŚKa. Special issue on Violence against Women 2, no. 1. Warsaw: OŚKa, 1998.
Pasic, A., and T. G. Weiss. "The Limits of Non-State Politics in the Former Yugoslavia." *Security Studies* 7, no. 1 (1997): 194–227.
Perlez, Jane. "Dark Underside of Polish Family Life." *New York Times,* May 8, 1998, A1–A8.
Platform for Action. Fourth World Conference on Women, Beijing, 1995. Text available at <http://www.un.org.womenwatch/daw/beijing/platform/plat.htm>.
Rueschmeyer, Marylin, ed. *Women in the Politics of Postcommunist Eastern Europe.* Armonk: M. E. Sharpe, 1994.
Sachs, Jeffrey. "My Plan for Poland." *The International Economy,* 3, no. 6 (1989): 24–29.
Said, Edward. *Orientalism.* New York: Vintage Books, 1979.
Scott, Joan W., ed. *Feminism and History.* New York: Oxford University Press, 1996.
———. *Only Paradoxes to Offer: French Feminism and the Rights of Man.* Cambridge: Harvard University Press, 1996.
———, Cora Kaplan, and Debra Keates, eds. *Transitions, Environments, Translation: The Meanings of Feminism in International Politics.* New York: Routledge, 1997.
Seligman, Adam B. *The Idea of Civil Society.* New York: Free Press, 1992.
Shlapentokh, Vladimir. "No One Needs Public Opinion Data in Post Communist Russia." *Communist and Post-Communist Studies* 32, no. 4 (1999): 453–60.
Siegel, Daniel, and Jenny Yancey. *The Rebirth of Civil Society: The Development of the Non-Profit Sector in East Central Europe and the Role of Western Assistance.* New York: Rockefeller Brothers Fund, 1992.
Staniszkis, Jadwiga. *The Ontology of Socialism.* Trans. P. Watson. New York: Oxford University Press, 1992.
Strathern, Marilyn. *The Gender of the Gift.* Berkeley: University of California Press, 1988.
Szacki, Jerzy. *Liberalizm po Komuniómie.* Krakow: Spoeczny Instytut Wydawniczy Znak, 1994.
Sztompka, Piotr. "Looking Back: The Year 1989 as a Cultural and Civilizational Break." *Communist and Post-Communist Studies* 29, no. 2 (1996): 115–29.
Tester, Keith. *Civil Society.* London: Routledge, 1992.
Verdery, Katherine. 1996. *What Was Communism and What Comes Next?* Princeton: Princeton University Press.
Watson, Peggy. "(Anti)Feminism after Communism." In *Who's Afraid of Feminism: Seeing through the Backlash.* Ed. Ann Oakley and Juliet Mitchell. London: Penguin, 1997.
———. "Civil Society and the Politics of Difference in Eastern Europe." In *Tran-*

sitions, Environments, Translation: The Meanings of Feminism in International Politics. Ed. Joan W. Scott, Cora Kaplan, and Debra Keates, 21–29. New York: Routledge, 1997.

———. "Eastern Europe's Silent Revolution: Gender." *Sociology* 27, no. 3 (1993): 471–87.

———. "Explaining Rising Mortality among Men in Eastern Europe." *Social Science and Medicine* 41, no. 7 (1995): 923–34.

———. "The Rise of Masculinism in Eastern Europe." *New Left Review* 198 (March–April 1993): 71–82.

Wedel, Janine. *Collision or Collusion: The Strange Case of Western Aid to Eastern Europe, 1989–1998.* London: Macmillan, 1998.

———. "The Harvard Boys Do Russia." *The Nation,* June 1, 1998, 11–16.

Williams, Raymond. *Keywords: A Vocabulary of Culture and Society.* London: Fontana Press, 1976.

Wolff, Larry. *Inventing Eastern Europe: The Map of Civilization on the Mind of the Enlightenment.* Stanford: Stanford University Press, 1994.

13 Making the Visible Invisible: The Fate of "the Private" in Revolutionary China

GAIL HERSHATTER

Neglect in Theory

For almost as long as the "public/private" discussion has preoccupied second wave feminist scholars it has vexed the subgroup of us whose research centers on China because of its awkward fit with what we think we know.[1] Comparing the separation of spheres in eighteenth- and nineteenth-century China to those in Europe and America, Susan Mann comments:

> [T]he distinction between *nei* and *wai*—between women's inner sphere and men's outer sphere—is quite unlike the Western dichotomy separating the "domestic" from the "public" sphere. Instead, in High Qing discourse the principle of *bie*—separate spheres—is invoked to stress that wives and mothers inside the home embody the moral autonomy and authority on which husbands and sons must rely to succeed outside. All are part of a family system that constitutes a seamless, unitary social order centered on the home and bounded by the outer reaches of the imperium. (15)

The issue here is not the absence of a gendered division of labor. Women in imperial China were certainly barred from access to the civil service examinations, formal office-holding, and untrammeled physical circulation outside domestic space (though this varied greatly with class). Yet at the heart of imperial political thought was the precept that activities and values inculcated in the family, usually by women, were the very foundation of social order and state function. The domestic, in this sense, was not at all private.[2] Women's role in household production was also linked to a wider public world. Late imperial statecraft writers ceaselessly promoted women's handicraft labor as crucial to the health of the agrarian economy and hence the stability of the state itself (Mann 143–65 passim).[3] Imperial state officials did not stop exhorting, rewarding, or regulating at the gate to a "private" or domestic realm. On the contrary, they regarded this realm both as the foundation of their power and as an appropriate subject for their encomia.

Activists in the early twentieth century, when they called for a new culture and for radical political change, reversed the positive valence that late imperial thinkers had assigned to the family as foundation of the state. Instead, they argued that the domestic realm was the source of China's weakness in the world. Men learned deferential, even slavish, behavior in the family and carried these bad habits into the public realm, making them into slavish citizens and China into a slavish nation (Schwarcz 107–17). Such thinkers made the liberation of women (and male youths) from an oppressive "Confucian" family system one of their key demands, linking it to the health of the nation.

The "traditional" women described by these reformers were not the moral exemplars and tireless household producers praised by late imperial writers. These women were footbound, confined to the inner quarters, denied the most rudimentary education, and economically unproductive. Empirically accurate in some respects (or about some women) and distorted in others, this representation shifted attention to the domestic as the source of public ills rather than the foundation of public order. Here *nei* and *wai* were linked as a source of national pathology rather than national health, and women were described as crushed by the weight of an oppressive "feudal" tradition centered on the family. The self-proclaimed task of reformers and revolutionaries was to remove this weight and liberate the potential of women as educated citizens, as laborers, and as human beings. The domestic realm was identified as a key node for the installation of modern practices, epitomized by the "small household" of a free-choice conjugal couple (Glosser).[4]

In 1927, early in his revolutionary career, Mao Zedong once again reconfigured the relationship between public and private, for the first time giving the latter a contingent and subordinate significance. He wrote: "A man in China is usually subjected to the domination of three systems of authority: (1) the state system (political authority) . . . (2) the clan system (clan authority) . . . and (3) the supernatural system (religious authority). . . . As for women, in addition to being dominated by these three systems of authority, they are also dominated by the men (the authority of the husband)" (44).

For Mao, political authority vested in the landlord class was the primary source of oppression for Chinese peasants, and its overthrow would weaken the other three forms of authority, liberating women as an almost incidental byproduct of a wider revolutionary process (Croll 189). The public realm of political and economic power attained a causative stature; it was there, not in the family, that the foundation of a stable state should be sought.[5] As the Communist Party shifted its main venue of revolutionary activity to the countryside after 1927, it experimented with marriage and family reform but came to focus its primary efforts on military strengthening, economic production, and local governance guided by the Party.

This emphasis on the public realm continued after the establishment of the People's Republic. In practice, Party policies in rural areas in the first decade after 1949 focused primarily on establishing Party and mass organizations, reconfiguring land tenure, establishing agricultural cooperatives, raising production, and incorporating women into collective structures. The reconfiguration of family relations was a far less prominent policy goal.[6] It received explicit attention, however, when the Marriage Law was promulgated in 1950 and publicized in 1953.[7] In this period was the vastly enhanced importance of the public realm. It was to be the locus of social change, the designated sphere of valued activity, the place where citizens would naturally invest their loyalty and love.

The socialist state did not recognize the domestic realm as the foundation of the state (as imperial thinkers had done) or as a key cause of social and political backwardness (as their revolutionary forebears had done). State policy pronouncements after 1949, while attending intermittently to questions of marriage reform and family harmony, deprived the domestic realm of causative status. The domestic was often described as the place where feudal remnants lurked, hindering the socialist project, but feudal remnants were a stumbling block rather than a deadly threat to state goals. As a realm that was supposed to lie back and be transformed, the domestic was not much theorized or even mapped. The labor conducted within its bounds was only intermittently attended to, mostly when it impinged on state notions of the public welfare (for instance, in periodic short-lived discussions of how to provide child care so that women could be mobilized for production). No longer a major location from which modernity was supposed to emerge, the domestic was regarded as a merely residual, reactive realm of human activity. Hidden from history, unvoiced, it became, arguably for the first time in Chinese history, private.[8]

And yet we have a paradox here. Even while deemphasizing the domestic realm, this same socialist state transformed it in ways more thoroughgoing and profound than any previous regime through its policies on production and its mobilization of women as state subjects (Barlow). In the 1950s, collectivization rendered the household a unit for redistribution rather than production. Women's spinning and weaving, once conducted in domestic space, was no longer a key indicator of prosperity and social order (and the ability to pay taxes); it became instead an outmoded form of small-scale production, to be displaced by the collective. At the same time, women's fieldwork (already common in poor peasant families) was destigmatized—in fact, lauded—and remunerated through the workpoint system.[9] Women were brought out of domestic space to work in collective groups, to attend political meetings (in the process being named political subjects *as* women and *as* peasants), and to attend literacy classes.

Now this can be summarized as a familiar story, one with a great deal of historical resonance: Marxist revolution sells out feminism.[10] But I want to shift attention from the analysis of state ideology and policy statements (where most accounts of China's early socialism are stuck) to the virtually unexplored realm of cultural history. What was the relationship between state pronouncements and what people inside and outside state organizations understood to be happening then, or what they remember now, when they recall the early years of socialism almost half a century later?[11] What transpired "on the ground" when the domestic realm was demoted from its status as foundation of social stability or engine of necessary social change? And what is the contemporary legacy of several decades of theoretical neglect?

In an effort to move away from the center of political power and its voluminous but unsatisfying written record, this inquiry focuses on rural China, specifically central and south Shaanxi province. It draws on archival research and interviews with women over sixty, conducted since 1996.[12] It thus places a doubly marginalized group—rural women—at the center of an inquiry about the cultural history of the 1950s. And in moving beyond official accounts—while never ceasing to ask about the effect those accounts produced in their own time—it confronts the dilemmas raised by live subjects, with living and changing memories, in the unmapped terrain of oral history. What do these life histories, read against each other and the written record, tell us about the categories of public and domestic?

Questions we should consider about the public include: How, when, and through what mechanisms do rural women see themselves as having been catapulted into the public realm? What is public for them? Of all the new languages provided by the state, which ones did they learn to speak? How did they receive or reconfigure the language and practices of that realm? How do they assess the reconfiguration of their lives?

About the domestic we need to ask: What happens to a realm that becomes unvoiced, that dips below the horizon of history even as it undergoes profound transformations?[13] If state discourse does not record those transformations except to applaud them as faits accomplis, then where else might we look for traces of them? How might we look at the undertheorized and unvoiced, at places where no official language was available to describe what women felt to be happening at the time or what they now remember as having happened? What areas of life seemed to them to remain untouched? Where did they want *more* state intervention?

Currently, "the private" has taken on new meanings in the reform era—from state endorsements of private enterprise to celebrations of intimate and affective life in a newly flourishing popular culture. We need to examine anew how "the private" is situated with respect to "the domestic." What are the consequences for rural women, particularly older women, of this late-breaking attention to a private realm (or, as some would have it, the return of two repressed "natural" desires, for capitalism on the one hand and a haven in a heartless world on the other)?

Public Space, Visible Labor, and the Language of Feudalism

When older rural women in Shaanxi remember the changes of the 1950s, many of their most vivid stories center on a newfound sociality of labor in the company of non-kin women their own age. Poor women in this region had often done farm work prior to 1949, and virtually all of them spun and wove at home both for family consumption and to earn income to pay taxes. Contrary to the image of footbound women cloistered inside the family compound, many of them had routinely ventured out into the fields and to the market to buy thread and sell thread or cloth. But women who moved through public space in prerevolutionary times knew that such travel was dangerous to their physical and social safety. Exposure to bandits, marauding soldiers, and predatory males of all sorts was always a possibility, and even if such an incident never occurred, a rumor to that effect could damage a woman's chances for marriage or her standing in her marital family. Prior to 1949, women who worked in the fields either did so in the company of male kin or remained unprotected because their households were deficient in male labor power. Women's presence in social space, then, was common but unlauded because of its associations with poverty, lack, and the potential for shame.

After 1949, in contrast, female labor was rapidly reorganized as groups of women formed spinning and weaving coops and agricultural mutual aid groups. The agents of this reorganization in central and south Shaanxi were many: male Party officials transferred down from the old liberated areas in the north, Women's Federation cadres recruited from cities and towns and deployed to villages, and local women activists developed by both these groups. All these people spent substantial time going from one household to the next, convincing anxious or recalcitrant parents and in-laws that it was both respectable and advantageous to allow their young women "out" (that is, away from the immediate supervision of kin) to work. What they offered in return was the assurance that young women would work under the watchful eyes of respectable neighbors, returning with income and virtue intact.

Cao Zhuxiang, who was later to become a regional labor model, was a thirty-two-year-old widow forced by family circumstance to do fieldwork before 1949. But her work organizing coops in the early 1950s had an altogether different feel to it, purposeful but no longer grim: "We were happy as we worked all day, and sang songs. As soon as it got dark we would go to school, and make up songs, and under these circumstances a day was very lively. We never stopped being busy, even at home. Time would pass without our noticing it—now you would need to go to the fields, now it would be time to go home.... We were always humming away as we went about our business."[14]

Singing, in fact, is featured almost as prominently as labor in women's contemporary memories of those days. Women sang not only at formal political meetings but also on sentry duty, in the fields, and at home: "Women in the old society were tortured. People made up the song 'The Feudal Society Has Many Evils.' We sang every day. We sang even when we were in bed at night. In the morning, my mother said, 'Fengcun, you still haven't gotten up? Are you still singing in bed?' I said, 'O.K., I am getting up'" (DFC 1999).

The point here is not that 1950s' China resembled the set of a giant socialist realist musical, full of happy singing peasants. Singing—which women remember as a gendered practice performed mainly *by* women (DFC)—was one of the means by which they were drawn into a public space. It linked the formal messages imparted in political meetings to the work of daily life. And as that work was reconfigured and women were drawn out in groups to work in the fields, the songs helped explain to them the significance of what they were doing.[15]

For young village women, both those who were waiting to marry out and those who had recently married in, the new activities are remembered now less as labor than as a form of social gathering in public space with other women of their own age. The fields, so recently regarded as a danger zone, were redefined as a safe space *because* they were public:[16]

> Working together, there were a lot of people and it was lively. Alone in the house, working by yourself, you felt nervous. I felt more comfortable working with a lot of people. (MJH 1996)

> It's good to work in the fields. When I stayed at home I felt unhappy. I felt comfortable when I was in the field. (BYL 1999)

Even as the fields became legitimate places for groups of unrelated women to work, sing, and chat, the significance of the domestic was shifting as well. In many women's stories, the home is talked about as a place controlled by fearful parents and anxious in-laws, worried that their young women would slip out of their control. For daughters, the main objection was that they would come to harm outside, especially at night:

> GXX: You weren't in school when you were young. After liberation there were literacy campaigns and night schools. Did you participate?
>
> ZQL: My mother didn't let me go. She said, "How can it be called school when men and women are mixed together?" She didn't let me go. So I didn't go to school. I can't even recognize my own name.
>
> GXX: You were an activist in the [Communist Youth] League. You didn't go to school?
>
> ZQL: My mother blamed me even when I went to meetings. . . . When people came to call me out, my mother said I was not in and I was out doing something. My mother was an old feudal. Later, Song Shifang was the director of the administrative district. She said, "You can ask Qilan do anything. But whenever her mother says anything, she will give up." She asked me to join the party. I was so scared. My mother said no. We had meetings till very late in the evening. There were so many meetings in those days. . . . She didn't let me go. Song Shifang, sometimes when there were league meetings, said to my mother, "Please let her go to the meeting tonight." My mother said, "She goes to meetings every day. She can't go at night. If someone comes to bring her to a meeting, you will have to accompany her when she comes back." (ZQL 1999)

For young married women the objection was somewhat different. Having recently paid considerable sums to acquire a daughter-in-law to carry on the family line, the elders were afraid of losing their investment:

> QZF: After liberation, they propagated equality between men and women and things like that and [my father-in-law] was afraid that I would leave. He was afraid of that. He meant to lock me in a cage and not let me go out. He didn't understand what was going on and was afraid of such things.
>
> GXX: He was afraid that you would divorce?
>
> QZF: Yes. Divorce, leave.
>
> GXX: What did your husband think? Did he simply listen to his father?
>
> QZF: Yes. He did what his father said.

GXX: Did he have any thoughts himself?
QZF: No. You have never seen husband and wife at that time. (QZF 1997)

Women speak frequently of coming home from nighttime meetings to find that no food had been left for them or that the door had been barred. Many of them quote their elders as uttering some variation of this "feudal" aphorism: "There are only men governors, but there are no women county heads. Women can only move around the kitchen stove." Whether this saying ever actually issued from the mouth of an older person or not (its ubiquity marks it as likely circulated by Party/state cadres), it encapsulates everything about the domestic as a space of confinement that these young women were learning to reject.

As their circulation in public engendered new domestic conflicts, young women learned a new language to name those conflicts: the language of feudalism and its remnants. Prior to the revolution, "feudalism" had been a standard piece of Chinese Communist Party (CCP) vocabulary, deployed by Mao Zedong in the phrase "semi-feudal, semi-colonial." In Mao's usage, "feudal" had referred to the entire set of power relations centered on landholding, patriarchal clans, and state authority. But in stories told by women about the 1950s, the specific content of "feudalism" is all about gendered experience centered on the domestic realm, both before and after the revolutionary divide known as Liberation.

Labor model Cao Zhuxiang uses the term, for instance, to refer to pre–1949 practices of confining girls to the home, buying child brides, mistreating daughters-in-law, and footbinding. After 1949, she uses "feudalism" to talk about a family that tries to prevent the daughter-in-law from attending literacy classes and also calls herself "feudal" for being embarrassed to attend a county meeting with very few women early in her cadre career (CZX 1996). A popular song remembered by former activists in south Shaanxi denounces the practice of arranged marriage in which young people did not see each other before their wedding day. It opens with the lyric, "Feudal marriage was really blind / who can see a cat if it's in a bag when you buy it?" In the 1950s, they recall, wedding sedan chairs were abolished because they were feudal conveyances that had to be carried by four people. The custom that a bride should cover her shoe soles with paper to avoid taking the dust (and symbolically the wealth) of her natal family onto the sedan chair and into her new home was called "feudal remnant thinking," and domestic ceremonies on the wedding day were labeled "feudal family rituals" (GYY 1997). A woman who didn't want her family mentioned on the radio because she thought it was shameful to have the family's name broadcast aloud "had feudal remnants in her head" (MJH 1996). Gender confined to a domestic context, then, was one of the crucial dimensions, perhaps *the* crucial dimension, in defining "feudalism" and marking feudal time off from the revolutionary present.[17]

Domestic Space, Invisible Labor, and the Language of Bitterness

As the main repository for feudal remnants, the household had no articulated place in time as marked out by the anticipated changes of the revolution. No one in 1950s' China predicted that the household would wither away, although the Great Leap Forward in 1958 grandly promised to socialize some of its functions with the unmellifluous slogan "eating will be dining-hall-ized, labor will be militarized, and wearing clothes will be sewing-machine-ized." But the dining halls were quickly disbanded after the debacle of the Great Leap, and commune sewing groups charged fees beyond the reach of many families (ZQE 1996). For most of the socialist period, then, farmers continued to prepare and consume food and to produce and wash clothing at home, as well as to raise large numbers of children. Homes were full of what one might call productive activity.[18] Yet theoretically speaking, the domestic was a residual space, and the many activities that continued under its aegis did not garner much attention in state discourse except in periodic campaigns to shorten the half-life of "feudal remnants." This meant that even while women's labor became more visible, and lauded, than had ever been the case before, the domestic as a site of labor virtually disappeared from state discourse if not from daily practice.

In tracing out the place of invisible domestic labor in memories of the 1950s, perhaps it is wise to begin with the remuneration women received for their visible public labor: workpoints. For much of the collective era, a day's labor was recorded in the form of workpoints. At the end of the year, when part of a collective's grain was sold to the state and income from sideline production was tallied up, each production team calculated the value of a workpoint in that place for that year and distributed cash and grain accordingly. Households short on workpoints had to come up with cash, or go into debt to the collective, to obtain enough to eat. How many workpoints a day's labor was worth was determined not by the length of the day nor by the task performed but by the person performing the labor. Periodic evaluations by the production team decided how many points a person's labor was worth, and the pattern across regions has been well documented. A man typically earned ten points per day, while a woman earned between six and eight.

In answering questions posed by suspicious Western feminists in the early 1980s, cadres and farmers (male and female) typically explained this disparity by reference to the need for physical strength in farm labor.[19] They proffered this explanation even in situations where the tasks in question required no brute force (e.g., tea-picking, where women's "natural dexterity" is said to give them an advantage), where men were paid ten points for technical tasks while women performed the physical labor (Wolf 83–84), or where women's production was bringing in more income to the collective than that of men. Margery Wolf, interviewing farm women about this situation almost twenty years ago, detected an undercurrent of resentment about it, but it was only an undercurrent. Our interviews were conducted more than a decade after the demise of the system, when presumably there was no political risk in denouncing it. Yet even then women were also matter-of-fact in recounting the disparity, with only an occasional hint of resignation:

WGH: If both men and women dug, a man could get ten points and a woman got eight?
ZXF: Yes.
WGH: Do you think it was good to do it this way?
ZXF: We could do nothing even if it was not good. It was the production team that made the decision. (ZXF 1997)

Women certainly did not keep silent because the workpoints were unimportant to them. Many of them told us that they wanted to do fieldwork because they liked earning workpoints, but a closer look at what they liked about it is instructive. In their stories, the cheerful, musical sociality of the first years after the revolution quickly gave way to a more practical imperative: Women's labor in the fields was absolutely necessary to keep their families from going into debt to the collective. The need for workpoints even overrode customary practices surrounding childbirth:

GXX: How long after you had your oldest did you start to go to the fields to work?
MJH: Forty days.
GXX: Isn't it the usual practice here to wait a hundred days? How is it that you started working after forty days?
MJH: At that time, who paid attention to such things?
GXX: Did you want to go because there was a lot of work in the fields, or . . . ?
MJH: I wanted to earn workpoints.
GXX: Who took care of the child for you?
MJH: I put him in the room and put him to sleep. (MJH 1996)

So women needed workpoints, depended on workpoints, fundamentally rearranged their lives around the need to earn workpoints, and yet do not appear to have fastened on the lower pay rate as a source of serious discontent.

Any attempt to map all the reasons for this silence across varied regions and thirty years of collective production would be hubristic. Nonetheless, it is clear that women and men alike understood women's participation in collective work to be "less than" that of men not because women were physically frail but because their time was divided between the public and the domestic. And women's ongoing domestic responsibilities, which utterly saturated their daily routines, *could not be voiced* much less addressed as a labor problem under the terms provided by the revolution. The chief form of household economic activity performed by women—spinning and weaving for the market—had been eliminated in the early years of the revolution. After that, in revolutionary parlance, there was no such thing as domestic labor. Domestic tasks were not spoken of as "labor" (*laodong*). That term was reserved for fieldwork and collective sideline production, just as the term "work" (*gongzuo*) referred only to salaried labor.

What place, then, does the domestic hold in women's memories of the collective period? Domestic tasks were, of course, unending, and no one in the rural environment—cadres, men, or the women themselves—questioned the division of labor that consigned virtually all of them to women. Childbearing, child rearing, preparing food, washing, and needlework bracketed the "working day" defined by workpoints and crept into all of its interstices as well. "I fed the pig first before I went to the field. On my way back, I collected some grass for the pig. I breastfed my kid first after I came back home. Then I cooked immediately," recalls one woman with a large extended family and several children (BYL 1996). Others talk about washing clothes at mealtime and performing other household tasks at night. Chief among these was the sewing of clothing for everyone in the family and shoes and shoe soles for four seasons for children who outgrew them every year. Needlework in these stories holds the place that singing does the fieldwork stories; it is featured in every account and encapsulates for the memories of an entire epoch:

WGH: Until what time did you sew at night?

ZXF: *Aiyao,* I never counted. When I felt sleepy, I lay down and slept. We had an oil lamp for sewing at night. When it was cold, I put my legs under the cover. I put a bench on the cover and placed the lamp on the bench. I was afraid the oil would splash on the covers when my kids turned. It is not true that it is difficult to do needlework nowadays. There are lights now. Lights are so bright.

WGH: When did you have electricity?

ZXF: I don't know when. I am afraid it was not many years ago. (ZXF 1997)

PQY: When [the children's] father was alive, I never slept at night. When there was no electricity, I lit a lamp. I did needlework. When my sons slept, I put them on the *kang*. When they woke up, I held them up to pee and then put them down. I worked after 12 o'clock at night. I made clothes for my sons. I worked in the collective during the day. I never slept. I was so pitiful. When I made winter clothes, if I had some time during the day I would spread it out and get it ready to sew. At night, I sewed it and sewed buttons on it. I was so pitiful. I had so many sons. I was so tired. (PQY 1999)

Needlework, along with child care, extruded into public meetings as well:

WGH: Were there many meetings?

ZXF: Many meetings. We had meetings every two days or so.

WGH: Could you do needlework at meetings?

ZXF: It was allowed originally. Later it was not allowed. I took needlework, such as the kids' shoe soles, to the meetings. I did some while we were waiting for others to come. I hid it as soon as the meeting started.

WGH: Did you bring your kids with you to meetings?

ZXF: I took the younger ones.

When women talk about the endless round of domestic tasks, they refer to them (or to the life dominated by them) as "bitter." They do not connect them to the state requirement of fieldwork or to the question of labor. Even in periods when the state permitted women to sell their needlework at rural markets, needlework was not construed as labor, and the state's silence on domestic tasks seems strange to no one.

Yet the state does not escape their ire. For these women, needlework was ineluctably associated with children, and it is in speaking of the state's role in birth control that their exasperation shows:

WFL: When we were working in the collective, the state was in charge of everything. They took charge of telling us to grow the grain properly, harvest more, and eat more. But they didn't take charge of births. They did not control childbirth. To have more children means to suffer more, to be worn out. I have eight children and you might think it's too funny, two sons and six daughters. I had lots of children, I starved, I endured extreme bitterness. After Liberation, I had so many children that I got angry. Why didn't they control it and tell people not to have more children? It was pitiful.

GXX: You had many children at that time. Did you ever think of having fewer children or planning births at that time?
Wang: What family planning? Finally when I had the tenth, family planning started. Who ever talked to us about family planning?
GXX: Were there any popular ways about how to have less children among the people?
Wang: People said to have a certain kind of medicine and to go to the doctors. But the doctor said why did you come to me—it was immoral and sinful. So, people were really pitiful.
GXX: So that means there were doctors among the people?
Wang: There were many barefoot doctors. Many. Everywhere. Later I heard that family planning came. I rushed to the hospital to get an IUD. Otherwise, I would have one or two more. It would have been unbelievable. Can you imagine there were some who had thirteen births?
GXX: When the family planning came, you rushed to get an IUD?
Wang: Yes. I rushed to get it.
GXX: When did the family planning came?
Wang: In the year my youngest child was born. In the year of the pig. In 1971 the family planning came. (WFL 1999)

In socialist China, women's labor was not discussed with respect to categories of equality versus difference much less a deconstruction of this binary. Rather, equality and difference were consigned to different domains. Equality was a feature of a public political domain, not an economic domain. The state proclaimed as an established fact that men and women were equal, meaning that they enjoyed equal political status (inflected, for both men and women, by class). The official Party-state analysis held that political equality had been achieved the moment the state stepped forward to guarantee it and that women's ability to enjoy this equal political status was limited only by feudal remnants located in the household, not by state-endorsed workpoint practices.[20] The women we interviewed also regarded themselves as the political equals of men and often praised the revolution for having created conditions in which women "dared to speak." Gender equality was assumed.

But gender difference in the public economic domain was assumed as well—physical difference, justified by reference to often irrelevant attributes—and was encoded in the workpoint system. And shaping women's participation in public economic activity, although seldom discussed, difference was also assumed at the level of a household division of labor. What is interesting and puzzling here is that no one articulated difference as a problem, either in state documents or in individual reminiscence. It was so much a part of the taken-for-granted arrangements of common sense that it merited virtually no comment, even as its consequences ramified throughout the stories told to us by rural women. This bedrock assumption that difference was immutable and had nothing to do with equality may help to explain why women did not object (or at least did not do so consistently and vociferously) to the workpoint gap which marked them as less valuable than men in the only recognized coin of the socialist realm: public labor.

Renegotiations of Public and Private: Contemporary Coda

It is well known that in the post-Mao period of economic reform the Chinese countryside has once again been transformed. Announcing that they had made a mistake in extending public ownership too far too fast in the countryside, state officials began in the late 1970s to preside over a return to family farming (based on long-term inheritable leases rather than private ownership) and to dismantle of most features of the collective. The results are mixed and complex; they include an improvement in rural living standards, large-scale migration of young rural people to the cities, and emerging inequalities between regions and between households.

The end of collective farming and the state enunciation of new visions of modernity accelerated a change in rural households that had begun during the collective period. When collectivization abrogated inheritance rights in the 1950s, it began to erode the previous practice in which married sons lived with their aging parents until the parents died. Although the constitution and various laws during and after the Mao years reiterated that adult children were responsible for the support of their parents, the economic underpinning of the multigeneration family began to erode. It became customary for young married couples to reside with the man's parents only until they had their first few children, after which they separated out. (There is considerable evidence in women's stories that with the proliferation of children, many grandparents were just as happy not to be living under the same roof with large broods of children needing care.)

With the economic reforms, the domestic unit has reemerged into public discussion as one sign of modernity, a modernity that socialism is now thought to have delayed. The repressed domestic realm has not only returned, it is everywhere celebrated. It appears in state writings, in an emergent social science, and in popular discourse as the location of consumption and the repository of affect. It is now also a sanctioned location for economic production and the creation of wealth, as evidenced in the state's periodic campaigns to publicize newly rich households. The household is one of the sites where the state locates fantasies of increasing prosperity for all. If the domestic is for the first time celebrated as a "private" realm, it is nevertheless one shot through with public dreams.[21]

In one of the revolution's bitter ironies, however, this domestic realm has reappeared in a form that excludes and penalizes the older women who kept it running in the years of its public invisibility. Our interviews included many women, many of them by now widowed, who complained of sons denying them support or refusing to speak to them, sons whose wives won't let them give their mothers grain, sons who curse and beat their parents in what would elsewhere be called elder abuse, and sons they occasionally take to court to sue for support.

Many lessons could be drawn from this conjuncture. Daughters, for instance, who customarily marry out and are not expected to provide old-age support, appear to be far more generous with their material resources and to have less fraught relationships with their mothers, confounding generations of preference for sons. But whatever else we may come to think about the changing configurations of public and private, it seems clear that the generation of women to whom the revolution promised equality were not well served by the disappearance of the domestic realm from revolutionary visions and are equally unlikely to be rescued by the return of that realm in the revolution's wake.

NOTES

The research on this project, carried out from 1996 to 2001, was largely funded by a grant from the Luce Foundation's U.S.-China Cooperative Research Program, with additional assistance from the Pacific Rim Research Program of the University of California. A sabbatical year of research and writing in 2000–2001 was supported by the U.C. President's Fellowship in the Humanities, the Chiang Ching-kuo Foundation, and the National Endowment for the Humanities. My most profound thanks go to my research collaborator Gao Xiaoxian (note 17) and to Wang Guohong and Zhao Chen for their assistance on two different fieldwork trips. I am grateful for the capable research assistance of Jin Jiang, Lyn Jeffery, Wenqing Kang, and Xiaoping Sun, funded in part by the Committee on Research of the Academic Senate at the University of California, Santa Cruz. I thank the participants at the international symposium on "Women, Nation and Society in Modern China (1600–1950)" held at the Institute of Modern History, Academia Sinica, August 23–25, 2001, for stimulating comments on an earlier version of this paper. The paper has also benefitted from the discerning comments of Emily Honig, Susan Mann, Lisa Rofel, and Wang Zheng.

1. In the title of this essay I use the term *revolutionary China* in a broad sense, to encompass the period from the late Qing to the present. During this entire period,

the questions of whether China is modern, how China can become modern, and whether China can become modern through a dynastic/communist/market socialist revolution have been key issues for intellectuals and other elites. I do not mean "revolutionary" to refer only to areas and time periods controlled by the Chinese Communist Party; I am using the term to point to a society's characterization of its own major problems and projects. A single essay cannot cover the entire twentieth century comprehensively. My intent in using this long historical lens is to raise the issue of whether the concepts "public" and "private" are useful to our understanding of Chinese women's history, and then to focus on rural women in the period of collective agriculture beginning in the 1950s, with a brief epilogue on changes in the reform era.

China scholars sometimes engage in an ornery Sino-exceptionalism, but I believe that this particular assertion of "not in our corner of the world" is not an instance of that. Rather, feminist scholars of China are simultaneously grateful for the issues raised in feminist scholarship on Europe and the U.S., and frustrated that the flow of issues and reconceptualizations has been largely unidirectional.

2. Patriarchs of elite families, many of whom held official posts, also emphasized the family/state linkage in written instructions to their families about appropriate domestic conduct (e.g., Furth).

3. Statecraft writings should not be taken as a straightforward account of practices in the political economy. Mann notes that even while statecraft writers were touting the beneficial effects of women's cotton and silk production—for household income and the prevention of female indolence alike—protoindustry and the growth of guilds were making women's work in China's most advanced areas less important. Nevertheless, she argues, the assiduous promotion of women's household labor by officials, combined with family practice that kept young married women at home serving their in-laws, may have "reduced the number of women available to work in China's factories on the eve of industrialization" (Mann 176).

4. Significantly, twentieth-century writings on the family also reversed the values assigned to urban and rural. In late imperial writings, agriculture had been regarded as more essential and more virtuous than trade, and farming families embodied society's core values, unlike urban dwellers who engaged in the suspect activity of commerce. By the twentieth century, however, many reformers saw the cities as the place where a Chinese modernity would be fashioned and believed that only after cities had become modern would rural families, mired in feudal thinking, be able to rise to the level of urban civilized practice.

5. Although Mao shifted attention away from the domestic realm as a source of political change, prior to the revolution he was as eloquent as any imperial statecraft writer in detailing just how much household economic activity was performed by women. Writing from southeastern Jiangxi in 1930, he noted:

> Women and men are equal partners in production in Xunwu. Strictly speaking, in terms of farming, women's duties are much heavier than those of men. . . . Women assist men in carrying the muck and grain, transplanting rice seedlings, weeding fields, uprooting the weeds in the paths between the fields and on the edges of the fields, turning over the soil, and cutting the grain. But although men help out, women are chiefly responsible for hulling grain, polishing grain, watering

gardens, transplanting vegetables, cutting wood, mowing grass, making tea, cooking meals, raising pigs and other domestic animals, washing and ironing clothes, mending clothes, making shoes, sweeping floors, and doing dishes. Besides these tasks, raising children is also a woman's duty; thus, the toil of women is harder than that of men. Women's tasks come one after another, and their work never ends. (1:212–13)

6. The 1954 Constitution of the PRC, in Chapter 3, "Fundamental Rights and Duties of Citizens," listed as Article 96: "Women in the People's Republic of China enjoy equal rights with men in all spheres of political, economic, cultural, social and domestic life. The State protects marriage, the family, and the mother and child." The 1975 and 1978 Constitutions reiterated this provision, although the article number changed. The 1975 version referred to "equal rights with men in all respects," rather than specifying realms, but the 1978 version restored the original language. The 1978 Constitution also added that "The state advocates and encourages family planning" (Qi Xin et al. 182, 198, 226). The 1950 Marriage Law devoted much attention to altering conditions of entry into marriage (child marriage, bigamy, concubinage, exaction of money and gifts) under the rubric of abolishing the "feudal marriage system." Chapter III of the law, "Rights and Duties of Husband and Wife," guaranteed equal status in the home; exhorted husband and wife to love each other, work together and care for children; specified that both had free choice of occupation; and guaranteed equal rights in the possession and inheritance of family property. Chapter IV, "Relations Between Parents and Children," prohibited maltreatment or desertion of children by parents and vice versa. All of these provisions, especially if they had been enforced (or even enforceable), would certainly have reconfigured family relations substantially. When read against the specificity and detail of other contemporaneous laws such as the Agrarian Reform Law (1950) or the Model Regulations for producers' cooperatives, however, the provisions about the family are striking for their lack of attention to domestic labor, both productive and reproductive. The 1950 Marriage Law comprises 12 English pages of text; the Agrarian Reform law 87 pages. For the text of the Marriage Law, see Wang, ed. 383–94. For the agrarian reform law and the coop regulations, see Wang, ed. 395–532.

7. Johnson argues that the party/state advanced its marriage reform agenda very tentatively, and only when it was considered not to conflict with the priorities of land reform and collectivization (93–153). More recent research by Diamant indicates that implementation of the Marriage Law was both more extended and more disruptive of social order than previously understood. My intention here, however, is not to accuse the PRC government of abandoning marriage reform, nor to defend it, but rather to assess the relative emphasis in state practice (discursive and mobilizational) on "public" and "domestic." Here Susan Glosser has a particularly helpful observation when she writes: "More than a vehicle for improving women's rights and weakening the power of patriarchal authority, the [marriage] law helped define the relationship between state and society. . . . The CCP extended these principles [that a reformed family would lead to a strong nation] to explicitly include nation-building as part of a couple's marital duties. By insisting on this tribute to the state, the CCP obliterated distinctions between private and public and absorbed the most interior aspects of the private world into the political realm. The private became more political than

anyone could every have anticipated" (169, 174). Glosser sees more continuity between Republican-era and communist family reform than I am claiming here, but an extended discussion of that point is outside the scope of this essay.

8. It is crucial to note that this is not a state silence about women. Women are everywhere visible—as state subjects, as producers moving happily through public space, as labor models, and as cadres. This is a silence about that sphere of productive and affective activity known as the domestic, which is, of course, an important sphere of gendered relations.

The issue of "the domestic" is further complicated by the fact that it is not a self-evident, easily delineated physical space but rather a cultural and ideological space whose boundaries must be mapped in a historically specific manner. Under certain circumstances (e.g., the feminization of agriculture in the late collective period of the 1970s and the early reform period of the 1980s), fieldwork itself became characterized as domestic labor. In an urban setting, as Wang Zheng shows (Lu Fang-Shang, ed.), the lanes of 1950s Shanghai were redefined as extended domestic space under the aegis of the residents' committees. Throughout the present essay, "the domestic" encompasses the household as a site of family relationships and labor but is not necessarily limited to its physical dwelling space.

9. In her study of Hangzhou silk workers, Lisa Rofel points out, as did Mann for the imperial era, that the inside/outside dichotomy did not map onto "an American middle-class cultural dichotomy of domestic versus public" and that "inside/outside was not based on a misrecognition of activities within the household as nonlabor" (72). Women in pre–1949 Hangzhou produced silk alongside male family members inside domestic workshops, and this did not challenge the accepted notions of gendered activity. It was only when women went "outside" to work among non-kin that they fell beyond the pale of respectability, and Rofel notes that older women worker's memories of pre–1949 times are still tinged with shame. Rofel argues that Liberation entailed for these women workers not a change of venue (they were already "outside") but a destigmatizing of "outside" activity (64–80). I make a similar argument about rural women and fieldwork in Hershatter (83).

10. The best exposition of this argument in English is Johnson; for important modifications of this thesis centering on the Party's gender politics in the 1920s, see Gilmartin.

11. Because this sort of project relies heavily on oral history, it is already not possible to ask similar kinds of questions for earlier periods. It is quite likely that huge disparities also existed between late imperial or republican theorizations of the domestic discussed above and the social practices inside Chinese households. We will never know if Qing farming wives felt themselves to be the pillars of the empire or if Republican rural women understood themselves as both instantiations and perpetrators of slavish thinking. My thanks to Emily Honig for her timely skepticism on this score.

12. Since 1996 I have been working on a joint research project with Gao Xiaoxian, Research Office director of the Shaanxi Provincial Women's Federation. This research, carried out in the summers of 1996, 1997, and 1999 and in the spring of 2001, was funded by a grant from the Luce Foundation's U.S.-China Cooperative Research Program. Its core comprises in-depth interviews with sixty-seven older women (most of them farmers, some former Women's Federation cadres) and several men (four

interviewed formally and at length, perhaps a dozen others in village briefings or informal conversations) in rural central and south Shaanxi, focusing on their memories of the 1950s. We have also collected regional and local policy directives; local records in city and county archives; Women's Federation work reports; and contemporaneous works of literature, art, and reportage about policies that affected women. We have spoken at length with men who held leadership positions at various periods in each village we visited. A fourth and final research trip was planned for the spring of 2001. Although our research has been shared and we are writing a coauthored essay about it, the ideas expressed in this particular essay are my sole responsibility and reflect my own questions about history, memory, nostalgia, and the state. Gao Xiaoxian plans to use the material from our joint research trips in preparing two projects of her own for publication in Chinese: a collection of oral histories and a history of rural women's labor in Shaanxi over the past half-century.

13. The reference here is to a foundational work in Chinese feminist literary criticism: Meng Yue and Dai Jinhua's *Floating onto the Horizon of History* (1989), sometimes translated as *Voices Emerging into the Foreground of History*.

14. Author interview with Cao Zhuxiang, 1996. Cao Zhuxiang is a public figure, and I use her name here. The other women we interviewed are referred to by initials only. The use of oral histories about the socialist period raises the usual questions about ventriloquization of state propaganda and restrospective romanticism. I discuss these questions elsewhere in the project. For purposes of this essay, the reader is just going to have to trust that I am neither a cold warrior nor a revolutionary sentimentalist.

15. Revolutionary singing should be seen as a practice that produces what Timothy Mitchell calls "the state effect." Mitchell suggests that we stop trying to draw a precise boundary between state and society, and that we stop thinking of the state as a "free-standing agent issuing orders" (93). Instead, he wants to begin with the "uncertain boundary" between the state and society and to ask, "How is the effect created that certain aspects of what occurs pertain to society, while others stand apart as the state?" (89). And he suggests that "the state should be addressed as an effect of detailed processes of spatial organization, temporal arrangements, functional specification, and supervision and surveillance, which create the appearance of a world fundamentally divided into state and society. The essence of modern politics is not policies formed on one side of this division being applied to or shaped by the other, but the producing and reproducing of this line of difference" (95). I pursue this theme at length in other sections of this project.

16. Before 1949, when women worked in the fields with their male family members, it is quite possible that this was not considered "public" space, but rather an extension of the domestic. It was, however, *exposed* domestic space and therefore not completely safe. Women who worked alone in the fields, even very close to their own dwellings, were considered to be beyond the margins of safety altogether.

17. This poses some unresolved questions. Was "feudalism" taken up in different ways by rural men and women, or did men, too, use it to refer to footbinding, female seclusion, and marriage practices? In other words, was it only women who were invited, even encouraged, to imagine modernity as a liberation from particular gender practices, or was this a crucial part of envisioning modernity for men as well?

18. With the regulation and restriction of markets, of course, sidelines run by wom-

en (spinning and weaving for the market, raising livestock, and handicrafts) assumed a much less important role in generating household income, leaving workpoints for collective labor (see below) as women's main means of contributing income to the household.

19. The most complete analysis and criticism of these practices in English is Wolf (79–111). As collective labor was replaced by the household contract system in the late 1970s and early 1980s, remuneration by workpoints disappeared.

20. The formulation "proclaimed by the state" glosses over a number of questions that require further exploration. First, what kind of speech act was state proclamation, and how did it work? By declaring women equal, did the state render inequality unspeakable? Was inequality thus masked and reproduced, even elaborated? (Thanks to Judith Butler for raising this troubling issue.) Second, how might we be more precise in talking about "the state," or the Party/state, in a rural context? Preliminary examination of published and archival documents at the national, provincial, and county level reveals a curious silence about the gendered division of labor in the household economy. Did policymakers or cadres at some levels, or in some government departments, worry about the questions of family reform more than others? If there were differences on "the family question" or the "household economy question" within the Party/state, where and how were they expressed, and what difference did they make? Did anyone see the closing down of markets as a blow to women's sidelines, or women's sidelines as an important contribution to the household economy, or the household economy as an important support to the collective economy rather than a hindrance? (Thanks to Susan Mann for helping to elucidate these questions.)

21. It is worth noting that while "the domestic" is now considered "private" in contemporary China, "the private" is not only located within the physical confines of household space. In urban venues, new forms of public intimacy, including but not limited to call-in hotlines and karaoke bars, are redefining the contours of "private" life, and my brief glimpses of rural dance halls and boomtown county seats suggest that similar redefinitions may become more pervasive in the countryside as well.

Works Cited

Barlow, Tani E. "Theorizing Woman: Funü, Guojia, Jiating." In *Body, Subject and Power in China.* Ed. Angela Zito and Tani E. Barlow, 253–89. Chicago: University of Chicago Press, 1994.

Croll, Elisabeth. *Feminism and Socialism in China.* 1978. Reprint. New York: Schocken Books, 1980.

Diamant, Neil J. *Revolutionizing the Family: Politics, Love, and Divorce in Urban and Rural China, 1949–1968.* Berkeley: University of California Press, 2000.

Furth, Charlotte. "The Patriarch's Legacy: Household Instructions and the Transmission of Orthoox Values." In *Orthodoxy in Late Imperial China.* Ed. Kwang-ching Liu, 187–211. Berkeley: University of California Press, 1990.

Gilmartin, Christina. *Engendering the Chinese Revolution: Radical Women, Communist Politics, and Mass Movements in the 1920s.* Berkeley: University of California Press, 1995.

Glosser, Susan L. *Saving the Nation: Chinese Visions of Family and State, 1916–1953.* Berkeley: University of California Press, 2002.

Hershatter, Gail. "Local Meanings of Gender and Work in Rural Shaanxi in the 1950s." In *Re-Drawing Boundaries: Work, Households, and Gender in China.* Ed. Barbara Entwisle and Gail E. Henderson, 79–96. Berkeley: University of California Press, 2000.

Johnson, Kay Ann. *Women, the Family and Peasant Revolution in China.* Chicago: University of Chicago Press, 1983.

Lu Fang-Shang, ed. *Wu sheng zhi sheng* (Voices amid silence). Vol. 1: *Jihdai Zhongguo de funü yu quojia (1600–1950)* (Women and the nation in modern China, 1600–1950). Taipei: Institute of Modern History, Academica Sinica, 2003.

Mann, Susan. *Precious Records: Women in China's Long Eighteenth Century.* Stanford: Stanford University Press, 1997.

Mao Zedong (Tse-tung). *Selected Works of Mao Tse-tung.* Vol. 1. 1927. Reprint. Beijing: Foreign Languages Press, 1975.

Meng, Yue, and Jinhua Dai. *Fuchu lishi dibiao: Xiandai funü wenxue yanjiu* (Floating onto the horizon of history: Research on modern women's literature). Henan Renmin Chubanshe, 1989.

Meng, Yue, and Jinhua Dai. *Fu chu li shi di biao: Zhongguo xian dai nü xing wen xue yan jiu* (Voices emerging into the foreground of history: Contemporary Chinese women's literature). Taibei Shi: Shi bao wen hua chu ban qu ye you xian gong si, 1993.

Mitchell, Timothy. "The Limits of the State: Beyond Statist Approaches and Their Critics." *American Political Science Review* 85, no. 1 (1991): 77–96.

Qi Xin et al. *China's New Democracy.* Hong Kong: Cosmos Books, 1979.

Rofel, Lisa. *Other Modernities: Gendered Yearnings in China After Socialism.* Berkeley: University of California Press, 1999.

Schwarcz, Vera. *The Chinese Enlightenment: Intellectuals and the Legacy of the May Fourth Movement of 1919.* Berkeley: University of California Press, 1986.

Wang, Joseph En-pao, ed. *Selected Legal Documents of the People's Republic of China.* Arlington: University Publications of America, 1976.

Wolf, Margery. *Revolution Postponed: Women in Contemporary China.* Stanford: Stanford University Press, 1985.

PART 4

Displacements of the Private/Public Opposition

14 A Semiprivate Room

ELLEN ROONEY

I am not inside anything.
I'm not outside it, either.
—Riley

JOAN SCOTT ENTITLED THE 2000 conference where the papers collected in this volume were initially presented together "Feminism and the Shifting Boundaries of Public and Private." The work of the participants repeatedly stressed the uneven, wavering, mutable quality of those boundaries, the phantasmatic nature of our obsessive reinvestments in their regularity and regeneration, and the uncanny power that the binary public/private has to make things of interest simply disappear, as Judith Butler observed. The semiprivate room is one such lost site. Although it insistently emerges in multiple forms, it repeatedly slips out of view as the powerful opposition of private to public is reinscribed. The semiprivate figures neither an inside nor an outside but the conscious practice of drawing boundaries in a field neither the private nor the public can anticipate or guarantee.[1]

The Semiprivate Room

The classroom is a semiprivate room. As such, it is a site of the peculiar intimacies and coercions, the self-revelations and decisive constraints, that characterize a space neither public nor private, both exclusionary (perhaps even exclusive) and impersonal. As a workspace, the classroom necessarily entails a relation to the unfamiliar, the as-yet unknown, the potentially difficult. Its very existence testifies that common sense is not enough and that ordinary language is what we speak at home. In other words, the semiprivate room is one site of the disciplines. As a form—and every discipline is first of all a form of discourse—it figures critical discourse in a mode that does not participate in the celebratory invocations of information, access, and speed (quantity) that so dominate our historical moment. While we congratulate ourselves for our mastery of "information technologies," the semiprivate room persists as another scene.

I propose that we adopt the semiprivate as a figure of critique that exposes the enabling presuppositions of our commonplace understanding of public discourse and defamiliarizes powerful myths concerning its limits and its modes. As a trope, the semiprivate room enables us to rethink our understanding of the work of rhetoric in our so-called public discourses and to reconfigure the relations among reading, rhetoric, interpretation, and argument in the field of political discussion "proper." Such a reconfiguration may of necessity involve a disciplinary clash, one that perhaps can be read as a contentious revision of the suspiciously smooth transition Habermas narrates in *The Structural Transformation of the Public Sphere* when he recounts the shift from a literary public sphere to a political one (43–56). But it is part of the burden of my argument that the conflict among disciplines is a powerful and productive effect of their semiprivate practices, one that we should not seek to rationalize away or to distribute definitively across the boundary that opposes public to private.

My essay will seek rather to displace the public/private opposition by elaborating the figure of the semiprivate as a unique location, one that is not graspable simply as a combination of or compromise among elements drawn from the familiar spheres of public and private. Ultimately, I want to suggest that the discursive practice proper to the semiprivate room can figure the collective discourse of the public sphere and serve as a critical resource for rethinking the practices of civil society. Insofar as the possibility of critical exchange is an essential component of any public sphere, however it is defined, the practice of a contemporary critical "publicity" may itself derive from the semiprivate: a field of acknowledged exclusions rather than porous flows, a site that we know not primarily as a set of protocols or rules or as a content or datum but as a form of rhetoric and a mode of address. Such a proposition obviously involves a certain impropriety in the face of commonplaces about what a public discourse ought to be. It entails, for example, reevaluation of the problematic of pluralism, its professed universalism and its ineluctable exclusions. But before beginning to unpack my sense of this possible discourse, its critical possibilities and modes of address, let me linger for a time in the semiprivate.

My *American Heritage Dictionary* tells me that the adjective *semiprivate* means "shared with usually one to three other hospital patients." The definition proper is followed by an example of use, so the entire entry reads: "shared with usually one to three other hospital patients: a semiprivate room." This use of illustration is not a feature that characterizes most of the definitions in the *American Heritage.* (In this respect, it differs, for example, from the *OED.*)[2] I notice, for instance, that semipermeable, semi-precious and *semper fidelis* (this last *sem-* is a different root) appear on the same page with the semiprivate; each is defined, but none is illustrated with a phrase or a sentence. I take this special emphasis on the exemplification of the semiprivate, its explicit restriction to the rooms of hospital patients, as a sign that this adjective is not widely used in American English to characterize other sorts of spaces or relations. My usage is thus, in some sense, a nonstandard one or a neologism, a kind of semiprivate joke. This circumstance precisely suits my purposes. The semiprivate room spawns neologisms.

Although it is common for people—traveling to conferences or for pleasure or both—to share rooms, they typically refer to their shared accommodations in hotels or inns as doubles or triples or even shares, *not* as semiprivate. This is due to what I have called the peculiar intimacy, quite different from the intimacy of friends or lovers or siblings who share a room, that marks the "semiprivate" as a distinctive locale. A semiprivate room in a hospital, for example, is exclusive, with obvious constraints on entry (and, for that matter, egress) and sometimes rigid protocols governing the timing and even the personal character of visitors. And yet it is also an open or "public" space, one in which strangers are proximate and inevitably interact and where only the very rash (or the very gravely ill) would assume any real privacy or confidentiality: after all, a text detailing one's bodily functions hangs in a folder on the door, which often stands ajar.

Yet the commonality of those who share such a room is at best partial, as the term semiprivate announces; *semi*—of course means half, partly, or partially. Indeed, the semiprivate room always has a wholly contingent or accidental aspect. To remain with the example of the hospital room for a moment, we note that patients are assigned empty hospital beds more or less as they arise, at random. Their common room has been configured by public interests in an indifferent public process, partly economic, partly epidemiological, partly cultural. Private interests are not part of this process—or at any rate the private interests of the *patient* are not a factor that is taken into account.[3]

Nonetheless, in some very broad sense, these accidental roommates do share an ontological condition: the semiprivate room shelters strangers who have in common the quite particular neediness that brings them there, in close proximity to each other and, crucially, available to a host of other people, most of them strangers as well. In the case of the hospital room, these other people include visitors (not excepting visitors to the other patients), nurses and doctors, aides and orderlies and, sometimes, students. The semiprivate is in this respect a structure that regulates and facilitates a certain mode of attention. It is a discipline, and, as such, it entails a mode of address.[4]

The particular quality of this disciplined or disciplinary address also marks the semiprivate of the classroom. Both sites are marked by an operation of power-knowledge that has become familiar to all of us: a certain discourse or "contract" of cooperation and compromise reigns although it is always and everywhere vulnerable to renegotiation even as coercion, legal and physical, remains a real possibility. The avenues for this coercion flow in many directions, which is not to say that the semiprivate room is an egalitarian space. There is always a ruling authority, so recognized, in the semiprivate room, but it is not lodged in a sovereign body, and the questioning of authority is also a regular, indeed, essential, feature of its disciplinary practice, a critical mode of the subjectivity that operates there. "Opinion" and the clash of opinions are critical elements here, too. (And so we seek second opinions.)[5] Some quantum of fear or anxiety accompanies this clashing of opinion, along with desire and hope, of course, and real dangers are by no means completely absent, whether from the intrinsic situation of those present—their prior conditions—or due to the specific procedures undertaken during their stays. "Testing" is only one we might name. Ultimately, the occupants of this space may even threaten one another. The semiprivate is not a utopian space; its partialities have costs.

The economy of the semiprivate room is also marked by a peculiar partiality. Commodity relations are hardly banished: by now no one in the U.S., at least, needs to be told that "health care" and education are growth industries. Yet public money is inevitably at stake in the construction of the semiprivate room, and a direct financial or economic relationship among its inhabitants is not generally the rule (though there are some who argue that this should change).[6] Teachers are, of course, paid; teaching is a job. Indeed, unions and strikes are more and more likely as forms of academic dissent.[7] However, the student rarely pays his teacher directly; and even in those important instances where an adult works and studies and pays her own tuition bills, those payments generally do not cover the full cost of maintaining the semiprivate room that houses study—and they most definitely do not create a relation of employee and employer between teacher and student despite energetic efforts on all sides to retool students as consumers. While the semiprivate room enables power and fear to flow in every direction even as it repeatedly breaks down and reestablishes figures of authority, direct economic exploitation is not the most salient form of power here. The injuries of class have a more significant if more elusive force.[8]

In the last few passages, I have tried to loosen the semantic restriction of the semiprivate to the space of the hospital and to enumerate qualities that also describe the semiprivacy of the classroom. A public space marked by essential exclusions; a familiar enclosure where the unknown or unfamiliar is a required, indeed welcome, presence; a site of fundamental individual (and individualizing) urgency and crisis where a certain impersonality and vulnerability to public scrutiny is the structuring principle of even the most deeply felt personal experience; a temporary enclave where everything that happens is overheard: this is a semiprivate room.

The urgency and individual crises of the semiprivate room are the consequences of the trial that is built into any experience of learning, the consciousness of unavoidable transformation and the risk of failure to which everyone in the semiprivate room is subject. The pleasures and the dangers of the encounter with the unfamiliar that the semiprivate room prescribes are simultaneously a matter of personal formation, of subjects coming into discourse as individuals, and a matter of a general—class—experience.[9] This formative experience is ineluctably etched with standardizations, regularities, and disciplines that are in no conceivable sense personal or unique, which is perhaps only to say that they are linguistic and that private language is an oxymoron. As Denise Riley observes, "Language goes with us into the house" (4)—and back out again. The pun of disciplinarity announces not only the coercion of the semiprivate room but also its intimacy, the discipleship that binds its cast of players, however random or arbitrary the process that initially draws them together. Paradoxically, seemingly coercive and indifferent discipline forges individual subjects and particular, sometimes beloved, objects. The relations among these individuals are never merely personal but always also exemplary; the objects they attend to are the product of their interactions rather than ready-made; and these interlocutors speak in neologisms, which form the bases for their critical discourse.

I am aware of the reductions involved in the pages above as a description of any classroom, even if we limit this description to the United States or to the university. I have bracketed a host of questions about the specificity of disparate classrooms, about public and private schools, rich and poor districts, elementary schools, graduate schools, trade schools. In this sketch, economics, the state, intellectual culture, teacher-training, ideological interpellation, and bodies inscribed with all their differences are subordinated to a general proposition: that is, in a space that straddles and deforms the public-private distinction in a particular, even peculiar way, a certain critical practice is possible. This semiprivate critical encounter or disciplinary practice, and the forms of address, appropriation, and exchange that emerge in its field, provide us with the means to a critique of the discourse of the "public sphere." While my account is stripped down and in that respect reductive, I do not think it is necessarily idealist or idealizing. The semiprivate room is no little Eden, free of conflict, resentment, or anger, and my intention is not to romanticize, etherealize, or even to *celebrate* it any more than one would celebrate the semiprivate hospital room. I am interested, though, in the way it works. Indeed, I am not ultimately concerned with the classroom per se, save as a universally familiar (in the U.S.) trope—one that enables us to nominate the semiprivate as a figure for critical discourse, a critical discourse that is by no means limited to the academy, to the university, or the school. The semiprivate room clarifies the sense in which the academy has never been an ivory tower and yet suggestively hints at the reason for the enduring power of the epithet.

Andrew Ross has observed that the academy "is a massive public sphere in itself, involving millions of people in this country alone, and so the idea that you break out of the academy into the public is rather nonsense" (quoted in Fish 118). This observation seems unassailable to me. The university is a workplace, as are all schools. These workplaces are per se no more isolated from the general field of the public (in its commonsense meaning) than any others: law firms, fast food restaurants, publishing houses, airlines, hog farms, car factories, and so forth. These workplaces and their "products" differ in myriad crucial ways, of course, but not in that some are de facto more "public" than others. Furthermore, the forms of discourse raised up in the university restlessly travel: "There are no private intellectuals" (Fish 117).

Yet, as the parodic notion of the ivory tower hints (and my elaboration of the figure of the semiprivate above tries to make explicit), the academy wields critical principles of exclusion, and this exclusivity, this insistence on limits (on the form of the discipline), structures its modes of address at both a practical and a theoretical level. Without this practice of limits, the enabling transformation that is essential to any classroom praxis (a college lecture, a grade school protocol, a seminar) would be unthinkable. Indeed, the configuration of the semiprivate room as I have briefly sketched it here effectively puts into question one of the mantras of the polemic against the academy and its specialized knowledges, a mantra often spoken by academics accusing other academics of being hopelessly constrained by disciplinarity, the mantra of "accessibility." Whereas the traditional polemic on behalf of the academic as public intellectual berates her for speaking in tongues, reveling in a jargon that is useless to civil society, that is, for her inaccessibility, I propose to read the inaccessible as both a lure and an indispensable border. In the dynamic moment when the lure of the not-yet-known draws its public across the threshold into the semiprivate room, the possibility of critical discourse takes flight.

In Lieu of a Frame: Are You Taking This Class?

As a semiprivate room, the classroom depends on public support, embodies public policy, and is shaped by public opinion. Yet it is by no means a freely entered space: not just anyone can walk into your classroom and take a seat. Those individuals who take a class (in every sense of the verb) both recognize and help to elaborate the practices of a kind of "public exclusion," an inaccessibility that gives the semiprivate room its form and format and makes it a familiar if peculiar space where an encounter with the unfamiliar is the norm. The impersonal intimacy that is established among a teacher and the students who take her class in this partially closed, but arbitrarily populated, semiprivate space creates an opening for the as-yet-unthought. This is the precondition, the disciplinary ground, for any "pedagogy" whatsoever and, I would submit, for critical discourse itself.[10] (I use the term *disciplinary* here in its most abstract, and inclusive, sense; chemistry, philosophy, and anthropology are all disciplines insofar as they produce theoretical objects, methodologies, and knowledge-claims and thus distinguish themselves from other disciplines. But so is sculpture.) The semiprivate room and the impersonal intimacy it engenders enable the *formal* specificity without which there can be no critique, indeed, without which discourse has no purchase, no reality effect, and becomes essentially uncritical—no matter how ironically worldly or luridly referential it is; no matter what its *content* may be. The semiprivate room supports, even seeks out—though in practice it can never guarantee—the new thought where new may sometimes indicate merely the previously unknown (the multiplication tables, the state capitals, how to read) and at other times the genuinely original, new objects of knowledge and theoretical paradigms, new arguments and modes of thought. This is a disciplinary space where access is radically redefined, where we find an impersonal intimacy in the form of something like an inside joke (Gallop, ed., *Pedagogy* 2–3), in the form of something we had never thought of before, a new reading. This *formal* experience, rather than any imaginable content, is the critical essence of the semiprivate room.[11]

The forms of discipline, address, and reading at work in this space figure an alternative to the models of public discourse that have animated previous polemics on behalf of the public intellectual at work in civil society and many historical accounts of the heyday of the bourgeois public sphere. If the semiprivate can defamiliarize our contemporary myths of public discourse, it is primarily thanks to those forms, which constitute its specificity and the particular contribution it could make to debates in the public sphere proper rather than to the content that might emerge from the work of its would-be public intellectuals—no matter how elegantly recuperated by an accessible idiom.

The proper understanding of the public sphere and its phantoms has, of course, been the topic of seemingly endless debate. In the United States as recently as five years ago, the status and nature of the public intellectual was of enormous concern, both inside and outside the academy.[12] Whether in the mode of cultural critic or scientific expert, university intellectuals were eagerly seeking wider venues for their work and polemicizing on the importance of their "public" roles, even as the demand for "content" in the entire range of media outlets exploded.[13] Rapidly shifting currents have displaced the most intense polemics on this issue, but this shift occurred before anyone satisfyingly answered the question of what defines the public intellectual. Academic intellectuals have opinions, of course, as well as particular expertise, for example, about alcoholism, or extinction rates, or dating Renaissance paintings. But insofar as there exists a public debate on issues of general importance, the public sphere suffers no shortage of opinion makers, and there are no grounds for the argument that the opinions of academic intellectuals are per se superior to others and therefore essential to public debate (Fish; Robbins; Sinfield). But if the university is itself a public sphere, and there are no private intellectuals, what does it mean to offer the figure of the semiprivate, abstracted from the practice of the classroom, as a critique of our current ideologies of the public sphere or civil society? What particular value in its disciplinary forms or modes of address can underwrite an effort to extend them, to encourage a public larger than our current enrollments to assert the idioms of the semiprivate in the realm of civil society? If the semiprivate is a space where accessibility is redefined, where a form of impersonal intimacy enables critical thought to seek out the unfamiliar, to displace the already known, and thus to *read,* it is still the case that the classroom has been a highly specific and even fixed locale. How can this figure reach beyond its familiar precincts to disrupt our hegemonic account of a porous and freewheeling market in unfettered information or to reorient our dreams of a "practical discourse" of the universal (McCarthy 51)? Does the fact that the public, so-called, is overwhelmingly composed of people with some first-hand experience (for good and for ill) of the classroom as a semiprivate room offer an avenue for this intervention? How is the power of the semiprivate to reanimate our public discourse bound to its standing as a field of readings, a hermeneutic intervention?

In December of the year 2000, it was possible to write of our epoch as one that announced itself in contradictory idioms. We lived in a moment of crises in public discourse, crises in education, crises in the realm of privacy. In the U.S., the list of ills was pure cliché: an apathetic electorate (seemingly resolute in its passivity even in the face of the Supreme Court's unprecedented intervention in the electoral process), a petty and gossip-driven media, a corrupt political elite, and a vulgar popular culture; general hysteria on the subject of academic standards, on preventing school violence, on admissions to elite nursery schools; anxiety about the security of our DNA records, our financial records, even the records of our purchases of records, CDs and books. The realm of civil society was depicted as suffering terminal decay in narratives that originated in all corners of the political spectrum.

But, in the U.S. context, this discourse of crisis coexisted with an equally clichéd counterdiscourse of prosperity and peace, innovation and stability: rising productivity, rising literacy rates, rising rates of homeownership, rising surpluses, rising numbers of Web pages, rising employment. Explicitly economic indicators were woven together with accounts of intellectual and intersubjective "networking" to suggest a democratic revolution in "public discourse" troped as information technology. Both the crises and the golden opportunities had particular, academically inflected forms for those who work in universities in the U.S.: distance-learning, Napster, the networking of basic research and academic publishing, course Web pages and chat rooms, the corporate university. But the distinctiveness of the university and of the situation of academics was not as remarkable as the way in which both were willy-nilly engaged with the popular terms in which the myths of access and the fantasies of utopian inclusion in the new civil society proliferate. The academy, too, dreams of a kind of universal pluralist flow in which everyone anonymously and instantaneously bathes, and all markets (especially the markets in ideas, in culture) are free. There is some expectation that this free-flowing knowledge will also make us rich, but friction—conflict understood as inhering in the production of knowledge as such—was dismissed as a twentieth-century problem, an old economy worry.

Late in the year 2001, the landscape has changed beyond recognition, not only because of the horrific September attacks on the United States, but because of recession, corporate fraud, deficit spending, and the nature of the American administration's response to the threat of terrorist attacks to come. Privacy, technology, ethnic profiling, globalization, freedom of movement, and the market itself all remain dominant topics and figures for our collective life; but with the rapid and dramatic change of so many fortunes, the articulations among these terms have twisted and in some instances even reversed. And yet, the utopian celebration of free markets and free movement and its concomitant vision of critical exchange as a matter of flow and data has not entirely been vanquished, which is testimony to its deep roots. Despite grotesque evidence of corporate fraud, many voices warn against the darker specter of re-regulation; the current scandal is a corporate one, not a political one, these commentators insist. No "political" response is warranted. Watching a television commercial enjoining Americans to travel that intercuts travel industry cheerleaders with shots of George Bush defying terrorism, one could be forgiven for having the impression that freedom to vacation was the single most dearly held value in the U.S.

The idiom of the semiprivate room pointedly interrupts these tropes of flow and simultaneity. As a figure, the semiprivate room defamiliarizes the standard metaphors that govern our narratives of public discourse across the fields of politics, media, culture, and intellectual debate. At the same time, it resonates with the ongoing struggle—in academic work and in our culture at large—to question accepted definitions of private and public, and with them the "crisis" view that civil society has withered in the shadow of the commodity.[14] The semiprivate is thus also a polemic, a critique of the myths of contemporary "publicity" as the flow of data, but also of our allegedly failed attempts to protect the virtues of the public sphere or to reinvent them in new and effective forms. The figure of the semiprivate intervenes in part by insisting that any typology of the social spaces of critical exchange must confront the question of form. The varied and sometimes utterly incompatible *forms* of public exchange that characterize civil society today are themselves a positive argument for its potential critical force. (That people discuss an infinite variety of *contents* in their web chat rooms is of no particular weight.) The figure of the semiprivate clarifies the way in which form constrains and enables by virtue of its power, never absolute, but never trivial, to include *and* to exclude. This power is of course not fixed. The work of form is only revealed in the act of reading, and just as no theory is ever fully adequate to a textual instance, no subject position ever fully realized in any individual, so no formal feature stands as the full expression of a text before reading has set it into motion. The articulation of form is itself the task of reading; form emerges as such from reading's work (Rooney, "Form and Contentment" 29–31). On this view, reading is a transitive verb, a practice of rhetoric and argument that takes up a text (any text) and represents it in an interested, or as Althusser puts it, a "guilty" manner; reading is thus of necessity intentional, that is, polemical, and textual form is its medium. And, despite grim accounts of the death of civil society and of rational-critical argument, reading is everywhere in profusion in our historical moment.

This is emphatically not to say that such reading is unfettered: the semiprivate room figures the situatedness of reading, its inescapable location in an untranscendable site. But it is this site that gives it its persuasive power and *ratio,* even as it sets limits to both. In this respect, the figure of the semiprivate room is as incompatible with the Habermasian narrative of universal reason seeking expression in the arguments of a rational-critical discourse addressed to a "formless humanity" (85) as it is hostile to the cyberplot of universal code amassing in the data pools of a technocratic discourse addressed to a disembodied globality. Disciplinarity is an economical term for the particular fetters or limits that structure readings, whether within the university or without. The discipline is easily the university's most perspicacious institutional form.[15] But disciplines are dynamic forms, constantly renegotiating their boundaries and investments, constantly revising their objects and methods, and constantly vulnerable to what Derrida has called "the paradox of the message transformed by the addressees" (85–86). Disciplinarity is in this respect a form that travels well beyond the disciplines. The disciplines open out to their publics, not in terms of their contents, but as powerful figures for contestatory and open-ended debate, for an embrace of the unfamiliar that is never formless, but that incessantly celebrates the logic of the supplement, of reading as a never-ending project. The academic discipline thus presents an exemplary instance of the logic of the semiprivate room, a space of production, exchange, and conflict. This explicitly bounded space, limited in a critical and untranscendable manner, requires us to acknowledge its impersonal terms of engagement as exclusive and thus as peculiarly intimate, that is, as semiprivate, and to attend to its unavoidable figuration of the subject of address.

Every form of (social) discourse entails a specific mode (or modes) of address. Address is thus an element of form. As a strategic gesture and a symptom, it reveals the investments and constraints of a particular discursive practice, even as it lends that practice coherence, persuasiveness, and the appearance of unity. There are of course many ways of conceiving the problem of address; for my purposes, address is fundamentally a rhetorical effect, a trope. Address must rhetorically constitute unanticipated subjectivities, proffering new positions to actual readers or empirical audiences. And address inevitably imposes exclusions in its projection of a reader/a reading. The addressee is never simply a mirror image of an already existing reader.

Given that it cannot simply reflect its audience, its literal readership, every address is necessarily a gamble, an open-ended gesture that always risks failure: readers may refuse to be addressed, may attack (or ignore) the addressor, and will without exception transform not only the "message," but its mode of address as well, all in the simple process of taking it up. Every address is thus also a reading, and as such, it is inevitably reread.

Ultimately, the practices of reading and address that characterize the figure of semiprivate intervene against what I have elsewhere described as an essentially "pluralist" mystification of public discourse that is particularly powerful in the United States (Rooney, *Seductive Reasoning* 1–63). This pluralist hegemony theoretically celebrates the universal reader and the author who "addresses" her. But in practice, pluralism enforces the exclusion of any position that foregrounds the possibility (or the necessity) of exclusion. This pluralist problematic of "general persuasion" thus imagines a universal community in which every individual is a potential convert, vulnerable to persuasion, and then requires that every critical utterance aim at the successful persuasion of this community in general, that is, in its entirety. No intervention that begins with the insight that exclusion is the theoretical and political ground for all forms of public discourse, hegemonic and counterhegemonic, can function within this pluralist problematic. Pluralism renders the "irreconcilable divergence of interests *within* the critical community an unthinkable form of discontinuity" (Rooney, *Seductive Reasoning* 5).[16] Within the pluralist problematic, the absent or excluded term is exclusion itself. Any discourse that challenges the theoretical possibility of general persuasion, that takes the process of exclusion—the form of the semiprivate—to be necessary to the production of meaning and publicity, is effectively barred.

Obviously, many of the current polemics on behalf of access, celebrating information as flow, confusing data with knowledge (or even with argument), and eagerly seeking to market knowledge and render "learning" as a process of information retrieval, share the fundamental assumptions of this pluralist model of universal persuasion. This is not, however, to say that the computer per se, as a technology, bears the burden of our current euphoria or that the semiprivate room is an anachronism, a retreat from the very terms of engagement with the present. It is to say that a certain kind of critical discourse—fundamental to civil society and visibly at work in the classroom—is impossible in a pluralist space that excludes exclusion, celebrates frictionless "access," and forgets the critical power (intellectual, political, and intimate) of the enclosure, the form of discourse and discipline. It is, of course, crucial that entry into the semiprivate room never be a matter of essential qualities—I am not covertly mounting a campaign for invidious exclusions or "separatism." But the semiprivate room is one that must be actively entered (or left empty). The semiprivate must manufacture the fiction of a provisional inside, imposing a form of engagement that is set into motion by a mode of address—not by means of a reflection, an echo or a miming, but by a projection, a call, an apostrophe, a seduction: the work of the semiprivate.

Not in Public: Feminism and the "Intimate Sphere"

The figure of the semiprivate room, as I have been elaborating thus far, must inevitably engage the animated debates on democracy and the decline of civil society, critical theory, and participation, where the meanings of privacy and of "publicity" in all of its senses have been so carefully examined. Perhaps most salient to my discussion is the argument about what exactly ought to count as the "public" in the phrase "public sphere." This question is unavoidable insofar as I hope to extend the figure of the semiprivate and to resist the suggestion that this trope is in essence merely another turn on the form of publicity. There is of course no consensus on the meanings of the couple public/private. From some perspectives, which we might gingerly call classic, the public sphere is the site of citizenship and free debate, as opposed to the state; in Habermas's words, the public sphere is "the sphere of private people come together to form a public." This view has been subject to intense scrutiny—celebrated, dismissed, extended, critiqued, recuperated. In *Feminists Read Habermas,* a range of feminist thinkers concede the limits of what even the late Habermas offers in the way of a discussion of gender, yet conclude, in the editor's words, that "his discourse theory is one of the most persuasive current reflections on politics and moral and social norms" (2; see also Fraser; Landes, ed.). Nonetheless, for many speaking in quite common feminist idioms, the public is precisely the world of labor and the state, while the private is the domestic or the family, only in living memory genuinely subject to the rule of law.

As Catherine MacKinnon puts it: "The private is everything women have been equated with and defined in terms of *men's* ability to have" (635). At the same time, in both the lingua franca and the technical idioms of capitalist democracy in the U.S., the private is nothing more or less than the market, and the public is merely the state and its interfering, tax-mad bureaucrats. (This is of course an idiom entirely familiar to the early capitalists Habermas describes.) The "classic" paradigm has also been challenged by work that emphasizes the existence of a plurality of public spheres, some of them in conflict with "the" bourgeois public sphere of Habermas's model and historical narrative; work that addresses "alternative public spheres" and frequently champions "counterpublics" (Negt and Kluge) has at the very least complicated and qualified Habermas's original analysis.

I am persuaded by Bruce Robbins's suggestion, in his survey of these contradictory views, that publicity "is a quantity appearing in the market as well as the state, and in numerous spots in between"; consequently, "no sites are inherently or eternally public" (xv). This view obviously offers encouragement to my suggestion that the figure of the semiprivate might reach beyond the classroom, outside the academy, and across the binary of private and public, into a nominally public sphere where public is taken only to mean beyond the confines of the university and the disciplines it shelters (in every sense of the term).

This commonsensical deployment of the term public does not exhaust my proposal's connection to this critical work, however. The semiprivate is not a compromise formation, a middle term blending the public and the private as they have been theorized historically; indeed, the terms in which I have tried to elaborate this figure have little in common with the critical vocabulary of democratic participation, private persons coming together, and the art of rational-critical public debate that marks debate, post-Habermas. There are, however, two terms vital to the operation of the figure of the semiprivate that seem to me also to be crucial to feminist work explicitly addressed to the Habermasian conceptualization of the public sphere: "exclusion" and "intimacy." This is hardly surprising, given that feminist discourse offers us so many privileged instances of the critical and essentially uncertain operations of reading and address that I have linked to the figure of the semiprivate. The figure of address has long been an element of the work of feminist theory.[17] Like many of its political and intellectual allies, feminism has made little progress in its anxious struggles with the question of *Who Can Speak?* as a recent title put it (Roof and Wiegman, eds.).[18] The resulting shift in focus away from the identity politics that underlie the "problem of speaking for" (Alcoff) has renewed interest in a politics of address that may take us further than our efforts to conjugate race, class, and gender have thus far. In this respect, certain traditions of feminist discourse stand for me as exemplary of the semiprivate. Their contending modes of address preclude it from evading the question of exclusions, and its practices of reading insist, at their best, on the impersonal intimacy and the formal situatedness that characterize the figure of the semiprivate. Indeed, feminist theories have repeatedly converged on the figure of the semiprivate: in both the affirmation and the critique of identity politics; the interrogation of the (phallocentric) universal; the complex articulations of "personal criticism"; and the intricate analyses of feminist pedagogy.[19] By virtue of its continuous engagement with and displacements of the opposition of public and private, feminist discourse has anticipated the figure of the semiprivate in myriad ways.

But to return to the more immediate question of the public sphere as such: the feminist critique of Habermas is not one. There are decidedly different degrees of dismissiveness and engagement with his model even in the work represented, for example, in a collection such as *Feminists Read Habermas.* Marie Fleming's "Women and the Public Use of Reason" stands out for the way in which it brings together the problem of exclusion—which every feminist commentator addresses—and the trope of intimacy, which has not been as extensively examined. Fleming teases out the contradictory claims that Habermas has made in the aftermath of criticisms that his original work "underestimated" (119) the significance of both plebian and gender exclusions from the fundamental structure of the bourgeois public sphere. In Fleming's view, Habermas's conclusion that he can nevertheless retain the basic outlines of his original analysis in *The Structural Transformation of the Public Sphere* is a mistake, the result of an ongoing misrecognition of the challenge of his feminist readers and of the nature of his own analysis. She then decisively links Habermas's misplaced confidence to his original claims concerning the category of the "intimate."

Fleming reminds us that Habermas interrupts his historical analysis of the development of the discourse of public and private when he arrives at the question of the specificity of the bourgeois public use of reason. At this point, he has recourse to a structural rather than a historical analysis and, simultaneously, to the figure of gender. As Fleming observes, in his argument, "the bourgeois public use of reason was not, in essence, a continuation of the salon-based, rational-critical public debate. According to Habermas, bourgeois subjectivity was structurally tied to a concept of 'humanity' that originated as a feeling of 'human closeness' in the innermost sphere of the conjugal family. That 'closeness' was apparently related to the 'permanent intimacy' characteristic of the new type of family life (in contrast to the 'playful' intimacy of the urban nobility)" (122).

This remarkable claim situates gender—and gendered "intimacy"—at the very crux of the bourgeois recuperation of publicity and is untroubled by the fact that the "permanent intimacy" of this "human closeness" conceals both the social subordination and economic dependence of women and children. Fleming stresses that "this explanation requires not only a detour to a structural argument, but also a temporary departure from the discourse of public and private. Habermas now distinguishes between the *public* (in its literary and political forms), the *private* (economic) and the *intimate* (conjugal family)" (122). While this complicating gesture admittedly takes place in plain sight in Habermas's text, Fleming argues that "the significance of Habermas's point that there is a transfer of experience from the intimate to the public sphere gets lost as he now effaces the intersection of the 'intimate' and 'public'" (123). Rather than conceding, in response to his critics, that the exclusion of women from the public use of reason was both structurally constitutive of the bourgeois public sphere (125)[20] and deeply destabilizing of his fundamental analysis and linking those facts to this peculiar eruption of a gendered category of the intimate, Habermas insists that it was precisely the bourgeois experience of intimacy that nurtured the *principle* of inclusiveness that is for him the hallmark and the absolute or transhistorical justification of the bourgeois model of the public sphere (despite its frankly admitted shortcomings in historical practice).

In Fleming's view, Habermas not only concedes but actually privileges "the informal (non-legal) regulation of *internal* family relationships" (131), genuinely "private" relationships. (Marx and Engels are cited as authoritative precursors in this regard.) As a consequence, "the view that the intimate sphere is basically resistant to the logic of public and private is implicit in the argument of *The Structural Transformation*" (131), and Fleming suggests that this view has also dominated the work of Habermas's critics. "The ideas of the private and intimate have generally been run together," while the "private sphere has been conceived to include everything that is a non-public matter" (133). The intimate sphere has been lost as a category, but its effects cannot be forgotten. Its structural association with a dependent femininity and with the definitively nonpublic underwrites the masculinism of the public sphere as such—this even in recent work that explicitly chastizes the actually existing public sphere for its great but merely "historical" error, the exclusion of women.

Turning back to the figure of the semiprivate, we can see that Fleming's reading illuminates its critique in two ways. Retrieving the intimate from the twin realms of the family and of permanence, the semiprivate simultaneously revises the very meaning of exclusion. The semiprivate room is emphatically not a room of one's own in the home of one's family. The cadre that gathers in the space of the semiprivate is contingent, impermanent, only partially identified with one another, in some respects, wholly antithetical to the permanently bound and legally protected intimates that make up the normative family. Rather than grieve over the exclusions that enable and constrain it, the semiprivate makes active use of its partialities, accidents, and historical limits in order to generate critical exchange—an impersonal intimacy. In the tripartite version of Habermas's narrative, the intimacy of the (conjugal) family, which is finally "excluded" from the working model that lives on in the Habermasian tradition, is supposedly a space of personal autonomy, of purely affective relations and of the end of history—intimacy flourishes there as the expression of "'human being' per se." While it may nurture the subject that eventually reasons in the bourgeois public sphere, intimacy has no properly public function, no direct recourse to publicity, despite what Fleming calls its transference to the public sphere (123), and the notion of exclusion within the field of the intimate or of exclusion as simultaneously the cause and effect of what we call intimacy is unthinkable.

By contrast, the figure of the semiprivate draws exclusion and intimacy into a close but uneven relationship with one another. While Fleming ties the constitutive exclusion of women to their status in the intimate, the semiprivate forces us to recognize the productive relation between exclusion and intimacy, as well as to see that today intimacy is abroad, roving beyond the confines of the "conjugal family" and functioning in an impermanent, even impersonal, and often "playful" *public* mode. Intimacy is not then simply undone by its movement outside the family or by contact with the juridical or with the formality marking the public sphere. In its new register, it figures the possibility of critique from a position that eschews the myths of universality and the purely human.

This is the position that Habermas is unwilling to think, even when his text points to its possibility. As Fleming's reading makes clear, he acknowledges not simply the role of the intimate sphere, but of women themselves, as part of the historically prior "literary" public sphere, in establishing the protocols of the public sphere proper. Women's essentially dependent and subordinate status did not apparently prevent them from serving as the support for the elaboration of the "public sphere in the world of letters" that is eventually translated into the political public sphere, or even as agents in that world. And yet, when Habermas comes to describe the social-structural transformation of the public sphere, that is, its degradation, he cites the loss of genuine autonomy and real authority that men (as bourgeois and as patriarchs) have suffered in the twentieth century as a major factor in their incapacity to sustain the discourse of the public sphere. Men become women, but they retain none of the powers that the women of the intimate sphere and the literary public wielded; not only the public sphere, but the intimate sphere that engendered it, is destroyed. The subject of publicity has lost his formative context.

Perhaps by rethinking all the forms of intimacy—and the historically marked exclusions that ground it and thus give it form as the purely private—outside the telos of universal reason, we can imagine another context and other forms. Impersonal intimacy makes possible the semiprivate's welcoming embrace of the unfamiliar and its appetite for the stranger: the unfamilial partner sets the scene of critical exchange and work, the forms of argument and conflict, the limits of reading. The semiprivate room does not represent the wholesale abandonment of what Michael Warner has called the structure of self-abstraction—but it does imply its radical reorientation and another rhetoric of subjectivities. Warner's "The Mass Public and the Mass Subject" characterizes the "self-abstraction" that is a condition for public address in just such terms of defamiliarization and de-identification: "We adopt the attitude of the public subject, marking to ourselves our nonidentity with ourselves" (234). According to Warner, this unrecognized "strategy of impersonal reference"—"the text addresses me" even as it also "addresses no one in particular—is a ground condition of intelligibility for public language" (235), where the "validity of what you say in public bears a negative relation to your person" (239). He is interested in the "vast range of everyday life [that has] the reference of publicity" and more specifically in the "mass cultural public sphere" and "mass public subjectivity" (242–43ff). In that respect, his attention is turned distinctly away from the figure of the semiprivate. But Warner's work does disclose the multiple forms of publicity and the de-rhetoricizing stratagems in which publicity encodes itself, tracing what he calls the specific rhetorics of personhood, which, in the context of the public sphere, are rhetorics of disincorporation (239). Finally, his analysis of the subject of mass publicity traces the contradictory movements of identification and alienation, movements that are revealed in part by what he calls "the intimacy of . . . collective witnessing." For Warner, this intimacy is a consequence of the way in which our "own" desires are "in most cases . . . public desires, even mass public desires, from the moment that they were our desires. . . . Our desires have become recognizable through their display in the media; and in the moment of wanting them, we imagine a collective consumer witnessing our wants and choices" (242). This collective witnessing has intimacy, in Warner's view, because subjectivity itself, including minoritarian subjectivity, is founded in this "field of choice," despite (or perhaps because of?) the fact that it is also a field of brand names. If critique can emerge (perhaps can only emerge) from the exclusive yet impersonal intimacy of the semiprivate, it must then be acknowledged that self-abstraction is at best a partial and positional achievement, a reading without guarantees. The semiprivate room makes such an acknowledgement "public," the explicit theme of its language of critique. What Warner calls the "unrecognized" strategy of address—"'The text addresses me' *and* 'It addresses no one in particular'"—is structurally unrecognizable in the classic formulation of the bourgeois public sphere, precisely because the rhetorical problem of address is by definition elided ("everyone had to *be able* to participate" [Habermas 37]). The semiprivate room speaks directly to this problem of address and confronts a field of heterogeneous addressees that may no longer be adequately named a "mass public." It thus situates argument in a shifting relation of address, where an impersonal (nonconjugal, impermanent, nonoriginary) intimacy can in principle be read—indeed, can only be read. It locates in that semiprivate reading the rhetorical ground for critical intervention.

Coda: In Seminar

A blunt spatial metaphor supports the figure of the semiprivate room: the semiprivate is a matter of location, of boundaries, of entries and exits, and negotiated forms of framing and exclusion. But the semiprivate is also always a problem of translation, and the term itself is by no means easily transplanted to other languages or contexts. Even in English speaking countries, the semiprivate's meaning and usage (where it is used at all) are far from uniform. This linguistic difficulty announces a parallel concern: that the figure delineated of the semiprivate room may "actually exist" only in very particular, even eccentric, locales. Drafted for delivery at another site, the original version of my essay bore a subtitle, so that it read: "A Semiprivate Room, or, who do you think you're talking to?" In American English, this latter expression is idiomatic, aggressive, more than slightly aggrieved. In the form of a question, it in fact asserts that you are talking but that you don't know to whom. In revising and retitling my paper, I again confronted its idiomatic quality and considered seriously whether its basic trope—the figure of the semiprivate room—would travel well or usefully address the broad theoretical topic of our conference: "feminism and the shifting boundaries of public and private."

I obviously retained the trope, but I considered my paper a kind of experiment in address, which is to say that I was prepared for it to fail rhetorically, not to translate. Miglena Nikolchina's stunning account of the work of the seminar in talking out the regime in Bulgaria puts this anxiety of translation (and its lingering hint of a hierarchy of transmission) firmly to one side: "while linguistic and translation problems were debated in the minutest possible details, the idea of language never disturbed our conviction that, in writing and speaking Bulgarian, we inhabited the same dimension as the texts that we read (in whatever language)" (115–16). In its place, Nikolchina puts the question of how, "through a curious move that reversed the actualization of theory into the terror of totalitarianism, the end of totalitarian terror took a theoretical turn" (97). She thus returns us to the place of the reader, neither inside nor outside. In rearticulating the seminar, Nikolchina reiterates its practical refusal of "hierarchies, borders, or compartmentalized zones" (115). She stresses the way in which, in this world of "thorough transmittability," "we could overhear anything and imagined ourselves overheard . . . from any given point in the continuum" (97). She recounts the multiplication of the seminar's centers and its other-than-official status: "what was going on could not fit into the temporal, spatial, and ideological limitations of institutions and expanded into private spaces" (100). The "promiscuous closeness" of the seminar meant that "the boundaries between the private and the public were blurred" (100). The seminar inhabited an impure border between private and public: "academic structures and, more importantly, the function that the regime ascribed to intellectuals were 'privatized,' and private life . . . was expropriated and all but erased" (113). The seminar pursued the work of the semiprivate.

But, if the seminar assailed boundaries and borders and talked through the incommensurable, it simultaneously occupied a particular political ground and faced a totalitarian regime with its own terroristic practice of discourse. The power of talking in seminar was appropriated directly from that regime, indeed, was cultivated in the very space the regime had imposed and in response to one of its forms of terror: "what made it possible to bring about the demise of a regime by theory (if we assume that this is, indeed, what happened) was the very structuring of the regime as total discursive control. Discursive control secures the prerogative of a particular discourse to emanate reality. The surest way for a discourse to be reality is through enforcing itself as the only discourse there is." (97)

Nikolchina demonstrates the way in which the seminar occupied the private/public borderland and enlarged its field as the regime reached its breaking point precisely by taking the implications of the terroristic imperative of discursive control literally: "the seminar was possible because of the premises it shared with the regime it was undermining: the belief in unassailable discursive power" (98). Turning the fundamentalist impulse to enforce itself as the only discourse, the *one* discourse, back on itself, the seminar "inhabited the discursive machine it was trying to outwit" (97–98). The seminar mimed the regime, as Nikolchina observed in Bellagio, expecting words to be things and things to be words. "When something's talked about for too long, / It usually turns into reality" (Stanev quoted in Nikolchina 96).

To turn the question with which I began back upon Nikolchina's account of the seminar: How does the figure of the seminar translate? How can it be read into a context where the regime seems to attribute no power to intellectuals or their discourse, where the celebration of the pluralistic multiplication of languages is the official line (however uneven its application may be)? I do not think that these questions are merely symptoms of a desire to collapse all our examples into a single, totalizing figure, or of my indifference to the historical and political specificity of the instance Nikolchina presents. On the contrary, the current political climate in the United States gives these questions a pointedness they lacked just one year ago. The official discourse remains one of pluralism and multiplicity, and the administration insists that it is only terrorists who promote a fundamentalist and monolithic discourse, who have only one way of seeing the world, and who would make the world one by attacking freedom itself, which is to say, by attacking plurality and difference. The terrorists will have one. But the administration has simultaneously assailed its critics as disloyal and reconfigured political debate as an attack on the unity essential for the defense of the "homeland," for domestic security. Nikolchina's intricate unraveling of the vulnerability of discourse-to-discourse illuminates this scene.

The discursive context that I have outlined as the ground of the semiprivate room is not one in which the strategy Nikolchina describes can powerfully intervene. But there is a vital point of contact between the seminar and the semiprivate room in the matter of thinking language. The semiprivate room insists that nothing can be taken literally: its formal practices (of exclusion) function precisely to establish the figures by which a particular reading moves forward. As the example of the disciplines makes clear, the semiprivate room *produces* its objects. But at just that conjuncture, Nikolchina's account of the seminar resonates, for the work of the semiprivate room also presumes belief in discursive power. In its very different context, this means recognizing the figurality of all of our words and of our reality as well. The semiprivate is the "area, almost unnamable, where metaphorical description bleeds into the nonmetaphorical" (Riley 3) and the possibility of shielding the real from its figures recedes.

To close with one last question: how is it that two radically different contexts, engendering (semantically) opposed strategies (literalism and figuration) should both come to the crux of the private and the public, seeking there another term that cuts across its oppositions, inner/outer, masculine/feminine? In lieu of an answer, a renewal of the questions: how is our every effort to think language-making (and language as making) bound to the opposition we call public and private and thus, perhaps, to sexual difference? how will the confounding of that opposition lead our reading of language onto a new terrain?

NOTES

1. I am grateful to Monique Roelofs for providing an earlier forum for this argument and for her critical commentary, and to Elizabeth Weed, who heard the semiprivate room and imagined a future for it.

2. The *OED* offers as its first example of "semiprivate" a reference to the play *Black Macap Violet,* which refers to a "semiprivate throughfare" (1876). "Semipublic" is an older term in the lexicon, appearing in the *Edinborough Review* in 1804. The *Oxford American Dictionary* ignores the U.S. referent of the hospital, defining the semiprivate simply as "having some privacy but not fully private." This is not a term that translates easily, even into the languages closest to English.

3. Private interests in the alternative sense of private *business* interests have, as is well known, intruded definitively into this space in the United States in recent years. This founding ambiguity in the concept of privacy will return to haunt us below.

4. The discipline that I intend to emphasize here is that of the semiprivate room, not of medicine as such, the latter having a field of play that includes but is hardly limited to the semiprivate hospital room. The disciplinary field that extends from the clinical spaces Foucault explores in *The Birth of the Clinic* (a text that is not one of his most frequently cited works, at least in the U.S. context) to the much wider sphere of professionalism itself, where an enormous body of feminist scholarship has addressed the effective marginalization of female practitioners in the course of the professionalization of medicine, is quite another topic.

5. Nothing about this process is simple, of course, whether in medicine or in the classroom. Recent news items and a recent book on the problem of the second opinion in medicine suggest that this much-vaunted strategy for ensuring one's health and safety is more problematic than an idealizing medical mythology suggests. At the same time, the problem of medical errors and the deaths and injuries apparently caused by them each year has also received both media and political attention (as well as attention from doctors and hospitals themselves), and the explicit public support for seeking out a second opinion has grown. In the classroom, of course, a certain "quantity" of material is always presented as mere fact, and the tyrannical teacher who is not really interested in students' opinions appears regularly in the compilations of teacher evaluations published at Brown. On the other hand, there can be no such thing as disciplinarity without the cultivation of differences of opinion; the practice of classroom "discussion" is one of its institutional forms.

6. This is true even of "private" schools at all levels and of trade or technical schools. Part of the apparent stalling of the "privatize" education movement the spectacle of financial losses in the "privatized" health care industry, both in the hospital and the HMO sectors. But there also seem to be inherent difficulties. Despite the sums of money involved, the increasingly explicit polemic for education as job training, and the absolute reign of marketing and advertising ideologies over the presentation of schools of every kind to their potential "consumers," the paradigm of education

resists complete assimilation to any business model currently available. One area that is particularly vulnerable, however, to corporate models (and corporate "investment") is research funding, especially in bio-medical and computing fields. See Mary Poovey and Richard Daniels for two recent analyses of the current situation.

7. In the United States, the National Labor Relations Board ruled in 2000 that teaching assistants at private universities are employees with a protected right to organize. A segment of the teaching assistants at Brown University have recently voted on the question of affiliating with the UAW for the purposes of collective bargaining. The ballots have been impounded while the University appeals the NLRB decision that authorized the election. The Modern Language Association newsletter of 2001 reports the members' approval of a resolution supporting unionization for university employees. Nurses have long been unionized in many U.S. hospitals, and physicians may not be far behind.

8. The figure whose work may be of most interest in this respect would be Pierre Bourdieu; despite its tendency to regress towards a straightforwardly economistic conception of class, the notion of cultural capital powerfully captures the tensions at work here.

9. See, for a range of examples, Althusser, Gallop, *Feminist Accused,* Gallop, ed. *Pedagogy*, and Johnson, ed.

10. If space permitted, I would here elaborate the difference between this claim and Habermas's view, in which the bourgeois public sphere "established the public as in principle inclusive" (37) and thus founded a genuinely critical practical discourse. Habermas celebrates the historical and social process through which "the issues discussed became 'general' not merely in their significance, but also in their accessibility: everyone had to *be able* to participate" (37); this is the basis, in his view, for the bourgeois public sphere's *principle* of universality, its ideal of transcending social hierarchies in the name of "communication and understanding between people in their common quality as human beings and nothing more than human beings" (34). Many scholars have criticized this analysis, both as history and as political theory, but most have not taken the additional step of arguing that exclusion itself founds critical practice precisely by locating and orienting it in a field of subjects, none of whom can hope to embody "'human being' *per se*" (29). This is an argument I pursue elsewhere.

11. From this point of view, homeschooling is an oxymoron, a contradiction in terms precisely because the intimacy of the private home is too intense, even in the coldest domestic scene, for the critical relation privileged as the form of the semiprivate.

12. Last month, law and economics polemicist and Federal Appeals Court Judge Richard Posner entered the conversation, in a manner of speaking, by publishing *Public Intellectuals: A Study in Decline.* The book's main contribution to the discussion, beyond its list of the one hundred most important public intellectuals in the United States (Posner is number seventy-seven), may be to have definitively discredited empirical methods of disclosing the impact of any intellectual's work in the public sphere. A number of the public intellectuals on Posner's list are dead.

13. See, among the legion of possibilities in both polemical and more historical idioms, Seyla Benhabib, Craig Calhoun, Michael Bérubé, Stanley Fish, Nancy Fraser, Henry Louis Gates, Jr., Jürgen Habermas, Stuart Hall, Bruce Robbins, Edward

Said, Gayatri Spivak, and Cornel West; the 1998 MLA Presidential Forum on "Nice Work: Going Public" (Elaine Showalter); the entire gestalt of cultural studies, from Birmingham to Illinois; and feminist work of virtually every stripe.

14. The contemporary discussion in the U.S. that takes up the category of the private or the private/public distinction is astonishingly wide-ranging and touches upon all facets of life, from the mapping of the genome to popular culture (*Big Brother, Survivor,* and *Temptation Island,* of course, but also *The Truman Show* and *Pleasantville*), from political life—or perhaps I should say, politicians' lives (Monica Lewinsky, the spate of revelations concerning members of Congress, the model marriages of the presidential candidates in 2000)—to Internet security, webcasts of all kinds, privacy law and, always, abortion rights, homosexual rights, the separation of church and state. A recent work intended for a popular audience is Jeffrey Rosen's *The Unwanted Gaze: The Destruction of Privacy in America.* The current project of mounting a homeland defense has intensified these arguments in light of facial recognition technology, ethnic profiling, and domestic surveillance, though the "argument" has been rather one-sided thus far.

15. Lorraine Daston argues, "The structure of our own world map of knowledge [is] clearly dominated by the disciplines, and the moral economy of scholarly life [is] equally dominated by the disciplines" (68).

16. The current political climate, in which the Attorney General of the United States flatly accuses even his mildest Congressional critics of giving aid and comfort to terrorists plotting attacks on the country and many accept the premise that war requires the suspension of normal partisan debate on a whole range of issues, illustrates the most extreme form of pluralist universalism. Even those conflicts that have historically been the most openly acknowledged (and institutionalized) are now ruled out of order. That such a capitulation would in itself amount to a concession to terrorism ("the terrorists will have won") is a perspective that seems to be gaining adherents.

17. See feminist film theory by Laura Mulvey and Mary Ann Doane; the entire range of feminist scholars who have appropriated Althusser's paradigm of interpellation; critical work on the problematics of race and class by Kimberlé Crenshaw, Cherríe Moraga, Saidiya Hartman, and Wahneema Lubiano; and recent books by Judith Butler, Jane Gallop, Barbara Johnson, Gayatri Spivak, Patricia Williams, and essays by Ann duCille, Deborah McDowell, and Chela Sandoval, among others.

18. For the paradigmatic investigation of this impossible question, see Spivak.

19. In the manuscript from which this article is drawn, I look closely at the problematic of "personal criticism," a discourse that has developed within feminist literary and cultural studies. I analyze its frequent tendency to fall short of the "impersonal intimacy" that I am here attributing to other feminist work. Space does not permit a full discussion of this point here, but I would stress that "personal" subject matter does not necessarily indicate that "personal criticism" is at hand; it is the explicit privileging of the category of experience and a persistent unwillingness to take the personal as a text (a non-authoritative example) that distinguishes personal criticism and opposes it to the figure of the semiprivate as I am seeking to elaborate it. The semiprivate and its operation of address cannot be assimilated to the workings of personal criticism or, for that matter, to the logic of identity politics, both of which

have prominent feminist avatars; indeed, the discontinuities among these related problematics are of critical interest.

20. Fleming qualifies here by distinguishing between two types of constitutive exclusions—not very convincingly in my view.

Works Cited

Alcoff, Linda. "The Problem of Speaking for Others." *Cultural Critique,* no. 20 (Winter 1991–92): 5–32.

Althusser, Louis. "Ideology and Ideological State Apparatuses." In *Lenin and Philosophy and Other Essays,* 127–86. New York: Monthly Review Press, 1971.

Bourdieu, Pierre. *Distinction: A Social Critique of the Judgment of Pure Taste.* Cambridge: Harvard University Press, 1979.

Calhoun, Craig, ed. *Habermas and the Public Sphere.* Cambridge: MIT Press, 1997.

Daniels, Richard, with Lisa Blasch and Peter Caster. "Resisting the Corporatization of the University." In Geoffry White and Flannery C. Hauck, *Campus, Inc.: Corporate Power in the Ivory Tower,* 61–84. Amherst: Prometheus, 2000.

Daston, Lorraine. "The Academies and the Unity of Knowledge: The Disciplining of the Disciplines." *differences. A Journal of Feminist Cultural Studies* 10, no. 2 (1998): 67–86.

Derrida, Jacques. *The Ear of the Other: Otobiography, Transference, Translation.* New York: Schocken, 1985.

Fish, Stanley. *Professional Correctness: Literary Studies and Political Change.* New York: Oxford University Press, 1995.

Foucault, Michel. *The Birth of the Clinic.* Trans. A. M. Sheridan Smith. New York: Vintage Books, 1994.

Fraser, Nancy. *Unruly Practices: Power, Discourse and Gender in Contemporary Social Theory.* Minneapolis: University of Minnesota Press, 1989.

Gallop, Jane. *Feminist Accused of Sexual Harassment.* Durham: Duke University Press, 1997.

———, ed. *Pedagogy: The Question of Impersonation.* Bloomington: Indiana University Press, 1995.

Habermas, Jürgen. *The Structural Transformation of the Public Sphere: An Inquiry into a Category of Bourgeois Society.* Cambridge: MIT Press, 1989.

Johnson, Barbara, ed. *The Pedagogical Imperative.* Special issue of *Yale French Studies* 63 (1982).

Landes, Joan, ed. *Feminism, the Public and the Private.* New York: Oxford University Press, 1998.

MacKinnon, Catherine. "Feminism, Marxism, Method and the State: Toward Feminist Jurisprudence." *Signs* 8, no. 4 (1983): 635–58.

McCarthy, Thomas. "Practical Discourse: On the Relation of Morality to Politics." In *Habermas and the Public Sphere.* Ed. Craig Calhoun, 51–72. Cambridge: MIT Press, 1997.

Meehan, Johanna, ed. "Introduction." In *Feminists Read Habermas: Gendering the Subject of Discourse.* Ed. Meehan. New York: Routledge, 1995.

Negt, Oskar, and Alexander Kluge. *Public Sphere and Experience: Toward an Analysis of the Bourgeois and Proletarian Public Sphere.* Minneapolis: University of Minnesota Press, 1993.

Nikolchina, Miglena. "The Seminar: *Mode d'emploi:* Impure Spaces in the Light of Late Totalitarianism." *differences: A Journal of Feminist Cultural Studies* 13, no. 1 (2002): 96–127.

Poovey, Mary. "The Twenty-First Century University and the Market: What Price Economic Viability?" *differences: A Journal of Feminist Cultural Studies* 12, no. 1 (2000): 1–16.

Posner, Richard. *Public Intellectuals: A Study in Decline.* Cambridge: Harvard University Press, 2002.

Riley, Denise. "'The Right to Be Lonely.'" *differences: A Journal of Feminist Cultural Studies* 13, no. 1 (2002): 1–13.

Robbins, Bruce. *The Phantom Public Sphere.* Minneapolis: University of Minnesota Press, 1993.

Roof, Judith, and Robyn Wiegman, eds. *Who Can Speak? Authority and Critical Identity.* Urbana: University of Illinois Press, 1995.

Rooney, Ellen. "Form and Contentment." *Modern Language Quarterly* 61, no. 1 (2000): 17–40.

———. *Seductive Reasoning: Pluralism as the Problematic of Contemporary Literary Theory.* Ithaca: Cornell University Press, 1989.

Rosen, Jeffrey. *The Unwanted Gaze: The Destruction of Privacy in America.* New York: Knopf, 2001.

Sinfield, Alan. *Faultlines: Cultural Materialism and the Politics of Dissident Reading.* Berkeley: University of California Press, 1992.

Spivak, Gayatri. "Can the Subaltern Speak?" In *Marxism and the Interpretation of Culture.* Ed. Cary Nelson and Lawrence Grossberg, 271–313. Urbana: University of Illinois Press, 1988.

Warner, Michael. "The Mass Public and the Mass Subject." In Robbins, Bruce. *The Phantom Public Sphere.* Ed. Bruce Robbins, 234–56. Minneapolis: University of Minnesota Press, 1993.

15 The Seminar: *Mode d'emploi,* Impure Spaces in the Light of Late Totalitarianism

MIGLENA NIKOLCHINA

To Stefan Marinov
In memoriam

I am Sybil and I tell you with brutality:
When something's talked about for too long,
It usually turns into reality.
—Stanev, "Predstavlenie i nakazanie"
(Performance and Punishment)

Theory and Terror

This essay will address the private/public division in the light of a phenomenon that emerged as a major feature of the last decade of the communist regime in Bulgaria and that came to be designated as "the seminar."

The seminar? In Bulgaria? More than ten years ago? Who would care about this? Yet over and beyond the nostalgia that drives the survivors into incessant squabbling over the fossils of the seminar, there is the major mystery that the seminar—from its restricted, elitist inception in the late 1970s to its spilling over from the bursting university auditoriums into street action and clashes with the police in the spring and summer of 1989—was produced as the dominant trajectory of the crumbling of totalitarian power.[1] Thus, if we cannot say that the seminar brought down the totalitarian regime—Although what did? There is no definitive answer yet—we can say for certain that the regime in Bulgaria brought along the seminar as the one major symptom of its demise. The seminar makes us face the enigma of an indomitable political, economic, and military machine disintegrated by discourse: by "glasnost," or—to put Gorbachev's unwittingly lethal term literally—by "voicing" (i.e., by the reverberation of sound in space).[2]

Immediately I have to add that there was something very specific about this reverberation so that even when, at its most lyrical, the seminar decided to sing, the result was the opera *Wittgenstein,* with Bertrand Russell and Ludwig Wittgenstein singing along with the native apparatchik sociologist Iribadjakov (all of them impersonated by seminar participants) and the chorus of "atomic facts" chanting "Where is the soup?" (The soup, as well as the freedom of speech, was never quite there.) The specificity, in short, of this deadly resonance, of this Jericho terror that brought the walls tumbling down, was that it was theoretical. The Bolshevik Revolution and its later East European editions was theory turned into terror. The glasnost extremism enacted the downfall of terror as theory. Through a curious move that reversed the actualization of theory into the terror of totalitarianism, the end of totalitarian terror took a theoretical turn.

What made it possible to bring about the demise of a regime by theory (if we assume that this is, indeed, what happened) was the very structuring of the regime as total discursive control. Discursive control secures the prerogative of a particular discourse to emanate reality. The surest way for a discourse to *be* reality is through enforcing itself as the only discourse there is. Through discursive control, the regime effected what it *said* to be equivalent to what *was.* The result was an ontological confusion where ideological statements took the form of factories and factories produced poems.[3]

This maneuver, however—the positing of a power as discursive monopoly—makes it very vulnerable to the proliferation of discourses, hence the status of intellectuals. Intellectuals were plentifully manufactured by the regime in order to, on the one hand, keep up its discursive monopoly through the constant maintenance of the master discourse. They were organized in paramilitary unions and were monitored closely by the secret police, with which they had to engage in discussions of neo-Hegelianism, for example. On the other hand, they had to exemplify the dangers of transgressing, if ever so little, the rules of the one language game that was allowed. The regime needed dissidents. The punishment of dissidents ensured the observance of a fundamental law: "Thou shalt speak as thou shalt speak."

Seen in this perspective, the seminar appears enmeshed in paradoxes because it inhabited the discursive machine it was trying to outwit—a predicament that is not a reason to deny its logic, that is, the logic of its illogicality, as demonstrated by Joan Scott's analysis of the paradoxes of French feminism trapped in the Rights of Man discourse (*Only Paradoxes*). The paradox with regard to the East European intellectuals was the following: The regime was bound to produce its subversion in order to sustain itself; the intellectuals were trying to subvert a power to which they owed their inflated subversive status. Ultimately, the seminar was possible because of the premises it shared with the regime it was undermining: belief in unassailable discursive power.

This statement raises, of course, questions about the relationship between language and power and about what has been described as the "collapsing of power into language [that] marked the invention of modern politics" and that opened, within democracies, the possibility for power to be "subverted by a linguistic act" (Goldsmith 139). Was the vulnerability of communism to linguistic dissidence a consequence of its deviation from or of its closeness to the democratic "collapsing of power into language"? Would such a vulnerability accompany any type of discursive monopoly, or did it betray the origins of communism as an aborted Enlightenment project? These questions seem to be especially pressing today because they highlight the fact that the discursive disintegration of communism happened from within and succeeded in being more or less peaceful (violence occurred in places where the regimes metamorphosed into other types of discursive monopoly, be it nationalist or religious). The nonviolent—discursive and theoretical—breakdown of the East European totalitarian regimes thus foregrounds the question of the role that theory will or will not continue to play in a world that is no longer haunted by the specter of communism but that is besieged by other specters. Does theory have a role to play in the context of religious discursive monopolies? Can it withstand the opaque power of the image through which the media operate in the "society of the spectacle"? These are large issues. I will try to limit my task by placing my discussion of the seminar in the perspective that marked most East/West feminist exchanges (and, frequently, confrontations) during the transition. In this perspective, questions of discourse were mediated by questions of public/private space. I will approach the seminar in and beyond the specific sense that "space" acquired through this debate.

In articulating all these neat questions and intentions, however, I do not want to raise overly high expectations. The seminar was a collective experience that, at least up to now, has remained incommunicable, partially because of the brutal change in the overall political and discursive framework, partially because of the seminar's inherent and unavoidably paradoxical antidiscursive drive. Insofar as the seminar was trying to destroy the discursive machine that structured it, it had to, somewhat inevitably, constitute itself as a discursive kamikaze. My questions will hence be corroded rather than answered by touching upon this exotic object.

Approaching the Seminar

"The seminar? Is it something about Lacan?" I was frequently asked when trying to introduce my topic. Lacan was a reference point, indeed, and an especially important figure in arguments concerning the morality of "method" and/or "shamanism" when trying to win over your seminar audience. And yet, Lacan was only one of the many illegitimate examples of the oral versus the written, examples that, with all due excuses in the direction of Derrida, ultimately took the seminar back to Plato and to his "unwritten doctrine."[4]

In its recourse to orality, to speaking rather than writing, to critical questioning as a "form of life," to the philosophical dialogue as an embodied experience, to collective inquiry through the art or the Eros, or, as it was finally formulated, the *ars erotica* of conversation, the seminar was a spontaneous indigenous growth to a large extent motivated by a censorship that could still control publishing but no longer controlled speaking. As Angel Angelov put it, "'Dialogue' was a humanitarian mind-set, normative and unattainable, that was cultivated in intellectual circles in the 1980s against the complacent and monological institutionalized discourse of the state. This mind-set presupposed the self-discipline of listening to the other while simultaneously neutralizing the noise of your internal authority. I wouldn't say that we were very successful and yet, to this very day, I can recognize the people who did not belong to the circles where dialogism was valued as a norm of behavior."

From the late 1970s on, this humanitarian "cultivation of dialogism" involved proliferating circles of people and events. The Sofia University Department of Philosophy was one of the centers and possibly the site of the seminar's beginning, but there were other centers, and with the years more and more events were organized in the framework of more and more academic institutions in and outside of Sofia. So far as I know, only one of the early seminars, the "Salon" of Nikolai Vassilev (one of four Sofia University professors who were later fired), took place in a private apartment. Most of the seminars, even at the early stages, chose at first to invade the smaller university offices and auditoriums and then gradually to move on to the larger ones. The attraction of official spaces was, apart from the drive to get into the open, one of sheer size. One of the most bizarre examples I can recall was a seminar on mathematical logic that took place in 1988 in the largest auditorium of Sofia University, with five hundred people listening carefully to the most obscure subject matter. A year later, a poetry reading held in the same auditorium drew a huge crowd that was trying to break into the central university building, with mounted police trying to stop it.

Although normally the seminars began in official buildings, the boundaries between the private and the public were blurred. When seminars took place in official buildings they needed, and got, official authorization. Yet much of what was going on could not fit into the temporal, spatial, and ideological limitations of institutions and expanded into private spaces. A paper or a number of papers would be presented—if it were a paper, indeed, since much of what went on was simply spoken. A discussion would follow that would naturally overflow into all-night talking, drinking, partying. There was a carnivalesque flavor to this aspect of the seminar. For example, the New Year's Eve of 1984 was celebrated as a rather wild "conference" on George Orwell, with portraits of Karl Marx dressed as Santa Claus hanging on the walls. There was a halo of other activities: exhibitions in private apartments, poetry readings, opera and theater productions. Something that might be called "disciplinary transvestism" was part of this carnivalization, with young philosophy professors singing in the "opera *Wittgenstein*" or a mathematical logician organizing a hugely popular "exhibition" of his "visual art." Some of the seminars took place within the regular curriculum but attracted growing audiences that needed neither grades nor credits. In most cases, seminars had an extracurricular status of one sort or another. Some of the seminars were run by a single individual; most of them were loosely organized and collective. Some were held once a year after careful planning and preparation; others would run for years on a monthly, weekly, or other regular or irregular basis. Some stuck to strict academic requirements and relied on the precise quotation, elegant reference, polite revision; others indulged in scandals and performative interventions (*vîzpalenie*—"inflammation," *iztsepka*—"cutting up") and looked for their precedents in Dada and Surrealism. The early seminars were usually focused on a single problem or author (be it Plato, Husserl, or Wittgenstein). They were exclusive and strictly professional in the hope of—among other things—keeping out informers. Yet the situation quickly changed, and the change was marked by the broadening of both the thematic and the disciplinary framework of the seminars.

An easy way to describe this change, which gave rise to a recurrent image of the library and of polyglottism (with or without reference to Borges's Babylonian Library), is to describe it as cumulative. People came with their individual research agendas and were incorporated into the seminar. The hermeneutic principle of "listening to all the witnesses" was implemented in an uncompromising manner. The number of discourses that thus accumulated was staggering and not very easy to place under the label of interdisciplinarity. There was a negative quality, an aspect of absence and emptiness, to this proliferation. It implied, in its totality, no schools, no authorities, no continuities, no allegiances, no demarcated "language game" communities. Inspired by the vision of the Total Book, this was a quest that knew the book would never be found. It roamed. It strayed. At the time I called this straying the "method of hovering among the bookshelves." Unaware that my "method" had a rather unique referent (i.e., the seminar), I claimed that it was a faithful description of some general condition, namely, the "postmodern library." "In its finished form," I asserted, the aimless "straying" and "hovering" among the bookshelves takes the form of a capsule moving with the speed of light. In it, the postmodern reader has all the books in the universe and an eternity to read them.[5]

Yet it was not as simple as that. Incommensurability was frequently discussed, yet everything was accepted as commensurable. No discourse was allowed to play the role of metadiscourse, but, on the other hand, no "*différend*" was allowed, no irreducible residue that could preclude further discussion. Communication, not the lonely capsule, was the rule. Neologisms sprang up, delineating a sort of linguistic *comme il faut.* There was snobbery; there were inner circles; there were fights among the different circles along methodological, ideological, or other lines of contention; and there were power games over who would be the star and who would be the "shaman." Through all this, the seminar had its ways of influencing the directions of individual endeavors. If it was felt at some point that a certain type of discourse was underrepresented, it could be commissioned as a sort of individual obligation to the group. This was how I was christened a feminist. I was asked to present feminism. I answered I could not do this with a clear conscience because I did not know enough. The answer was, "It doesn't matter. You *are* a feminist." So I made a presentation entitled "Feminism: Personification and Collage" in which I offered my physical presence as an exegesis of feminism. Ultimately, through its trust in a performative commensurability, the seminar posited itself as a unified field in which all actualized, possible, or, if need be, impossible discourses, whatever they were, were expected to operate as a concerted search.

This broadening was to a large extent intentional and accompanied by an effort to create a dialogue not simply among individuals but also across schools and disciplines. Some degree of self-reflexivity was probably inevitable. In an effort to ground itself in social reality, the seminar placed the discussion of communication, power, and everyday life among its ongoing preoccupations. Three wings were formed in the process. The "young Marxians" played an important role as a legitimizing buffer between the seminar and the regime. The "postmodernists" represented the poststructuralist and postmodern returns of "Eastern" formalism and structuralism that formed the traditional noncommunist theoretical background in Bulgarian academia.[6] The "classicists" or "medievalists" were united through their object rather than their method (which might vary from hermeneutics to semiotics and, more explicitly after the changes, to theology); they did, as a matter of fact, work on classical and medieval culture. Beyond this, there were the mathematicians, the poets, the playwrights. In the fall of 1987 one last attempt was made to create a somewhat more rigorous frame for developments that were clearly becoming unmanageable. This is how the Synthesis Seminar was created. It seems, however, that the seminar had already reached its limit. In the early summer of 1988, the seminar "Power and Identity" was having one of its sessions in the Faculty of Slavic Studies when we heard disturbing noises from outside and moved to another auditorium. Using the opportunity of a cultural event in the courtyard of the university, the poet Peter Manolov had driven the rain-soaked crowds into complete frenzy with a long poem consisting mostly of obscene abuse addressed to the party and government leaders. The end was coming. A year later the seminar was transformed and, in fact, dissolved into a political movement proper under the umbrella of Ecoglasnost, a small ecological club which by 1990 acquired a membership of 120,000 and played an important role in the political events of the 1990s.[7]

Parrhesia and Inakomislie

There is no doubt that the momentum for the seminar was political. If nothing else, its dramatic and immediate disintegration after the changes demonstrates this. However, the questions remain open as to the relationship between the seminar's highly theoretical, interdisciplinary functioning, on the one hand, and its actual role in the ensuing political events. How did belated modernist, postmodernist, feminist, Frankfurtian, young-Marxian, Heideggerian, neo-Kantian, classicist, hermeneutic, Christian Orthodox, Catholic scholars talk to each other? What discursive ingredient made the continuous cohabitation of such a wild variety of disciplines and methods possible? If bringing down the regime—a possibility never discussed that bluntly and until the last not quite believed in—was the unsaid that kept the dialogue going, does this mean that the seminar did, in fact, influence the bringing down of the regime? What mysterious force drove the rebellious crowds toward the *university building* as the locus from which freedom was expected to emerge?

In recent years key seminar figures have suggested two conceptual frameworks for addressing these questions.[8] The first is Alexander Kiossev's. Kiossev reconsiders Vaclav Havel, simultaneously via Foucault and opposed to

Foucault, as the paradigmatic "Eastern" versus the paradigmatic "Western" intellectual ("Golyamoto"). Kiossev regards Havel, who himself opposed the term *dissident*, as "parrhesiast" in the sense that Foucault brought forth in his 1983 lectures at Berkeley and in his 1984 lectures at the Collège de France. *Parrhesia*, a Greek term, is highlighted by Foucault as a specific usage of truth that relies on what might be described as the "incorporation" of truth.[9] The parrhesiastic game involves the rapport ("the harmonic relation") between truth and self, between "words" and "deeds," between "saying it all" and the biography of the person who says it. The persuasiveness of such truth—a truth of the type "the king is naked" that demands courage in the face of tyranny—does not belong to the order of discourse and does not draw its power from argument. Parrhesia is, in fact, frequently opposed to rhetoric and the rhetorical techniques of persuasion. The persuasiveness of parrhesia comes rather from "a kind of ontological harmony" between what one says and what one is, between logos and bios. It speaks of a truth that one guarantees with one's body and one's life. Havel's famous demand for "living within the truth" (Havel et al. 39), with all the ensuing risks that this demand cost him, is revealed, according to Kiossev, as a parrhesiastic act par excellence. Foucault's problematization of parrhesia, unfinished as it is, follows the shifts of meaning that it underwent from Euripides to Epictetus, emphasizing that throughout these shifts the Cartesian severance between what one believes to be true and what *is* true did not occur. Hence parrhesia, in this "naïve" Greek sense, according to Foucault, can no longer occur in the modern epistemological framework. In his analysis, Kiossev, who is concerned with the post-totalitarian 1990s, underscores precisely the risks of a return to presumptions that close off the division between "I say as I am" and "what I say is the truth." The problem seems to be that while parrhesia had a role to play in the face of totalitarian regimes, its usage in the context of new democracies leads to fundamentalist concepts of truth. Kiossev's Foucault/Havel juxtaposition is thus framed by two important presuppositions: that parrhesia has no place and is in fact dangerous in democratic societies because it involves a slippage from the correspondence between logos and bios to the claim for the possession of truth per se, and that, on the other hand, the parrhesiast is *the* type of intellectual who played a political role in opposing the communist regimes in Eastern Europe. The rest of us "were playing," Kiossev told me in conversation. In his early text on the Synthesis Seminar he envisions that the seminar generation would have been assimilated into the official communist structures of power (*Post-Theory* xvii).

Kiossev seems, therefore, to draw a dramatic division between totalitarian and democratic societies in terms of the usages of truth that they impose. Parrhesia makes sense in the face of tyranny but becomes a trap in the context of a democracy because it entails speaking about truth as a transcendent signified. The critical questioning of truth and the exposure of its multiple workings as normalizing power are consistent with democracies but too weak to resist totalitarian regimes. Against the grain of Foucault's own conceptualization of parrhesia as "care of the self," Kiossev is distrustful of "living in," of "incorporation," and of "I say as I am."

In contrast to this distrust and to the sharp disparity between "Eastern" and "Western" intellectual experience that it introduces, the second approach tends to see continuity rather than fracture. In this second approach, the gesture of the political dissident—"living within the truth"—is waived aside in favor of thinking through the concept of philosophical *inakomislie,* where *inakomislie* means literally "different thinking." Yet thinking itself in this usage has an aspect we might describe as parrhesiastic—as something like "living in difference," "living in/as thinking." "One cannot have philosophy without a philosophical form of life," Deyan Deyanov, the proponent of this view, told me. Or, as Foucault's cryptic remark from the Collège de France notes has it, "Shouldn't the true life be a life radically other?"

Socrates might be as important an emblem for this view as he was for Foucault's development of the figure of the parrhesiast—the Socrates for whom "thinking meant living. The animate word, the living word, the word that spreads on the occasion of and at the moment of meeting the other." This description of Socrates by Jean-Pierre Vernant is, in fact, his description of the Georgian-Russian philosopher Merab Mamardashvili who, like Socrates, "was not a man of the written word" (7). The fact that Mamardashvili wrote and that he reached the seminar in the 1980s in the form of smuggled manuscripts cannot change this constitutive orality that harmonized—a point to which I will return—with the seminar's obsession with the voice and the *phoné.* As Deyanov puts it, Mamardashvili is a difficult thinker because of "the layering of heterogeneous philosophemes . . . but also because of the oral form of his philosophizing, inseparable from his philosophical style. Not a spoken philosophy that could be written down but a spoken philosophy as opposed to the written one" ("Neklasicheskata" 6).

For Deyanov, it is important to emphasize that philosophical "thinking differently" survives the political exigencies that have mobilized it. "We all shared the belief in the need for a critique of modernity," he told me apropos the seminar. "Beyond the critique of the status quo, we always envisioned the critique of modernity." Deyanov's bringing forth of Mamardashvili as the emblematic East European intellectual from the last decades of the regime is carried out as part of this sustained critique. Once again, Foucault is evoked side by side with "Eastern" theory. Deyanov, however, reads Foucault via Mamardashvili's "nonclassical rationality" ("Neklasicheskata") and, conversely, Mamardashvili via Foucault in order, ultimately, to demonstrate the potential of philosophical *inakomislie* to counter normalization by creating "dialogic fields . . . where different interpretational strategies, genres and individual styles can meet. We insist on this because we believe that the thinking polyphony that opens dialogic fields for both the provocative explorations and the voices that counter them, is the condition that makes a new critical publicity possible" ("Neklasicheskata" 6).

An Aside with Some Questions

I believe that a split between political and philosophical dissidence as exemplified in the contrasting figures of Havel and Mamardashvili will not illuminate either the seminar or the circumstances that turned it into the symptom of—or, possibly, the illustration of—what brought about the regime's demise. Yet there is a mysterious point of convergence between Kiossev's and Deyanov's accounts that I have, somewhat clumsily, referred to as "incorporation." Did "incorporation" "matter" (with reference to Judith Butler's pun)? If incorporation did indeed matter, which type of it—the incorporation of "living within the "truth" or the incorporation of "living in/as thinking differently"—could and perhaps did matter more?

In asking these questions I introduce a speculative element that requires the displacement of the term *dissident,* a displacement exemplified by Havel's own resistance to this name. A "dissident" was the product of (external Western) media. "He was not a dissident," said a former colleague of Stefan Marinov, the man to whom my text is dedicated. "He simply wanted to say what he thought." A person who "simply wanted to say what s/he thought" and did not reach the Western media as "dissident" would, during communism, become a mental clinic patient, a prisoner, the victim of a car accident. By avoiding the term *dissident* and speaking in terms of parrhesia and inakomislie, of bios/logos harmony, and of embodied thinking differently, I will attempt—with all the risks that such an attempt entails—to look into ways that systems structured as total discursive control might be challenged from within. In this effort, my discussion of the seminar will leave aside as far as possible the role that the West as an "outside" played in bringing about the fall of communism, including its role, born of our isolation, as an intellectual (as opposed to consumerist) utopia.

The outside was nevertheless there and interested. There are discursive systems without an outside: the system of sexual difference, for example, or the system of a presumably globalized cyberspace world. My attempt to isolate the workings of the seminar from the various transactions with the outside is, from that point of view, an oblique attempt to approach the possible forms of resistance to such systems. The contemporaneous Western theories to which the seminar plentifully referred will hence be regarded as a steady drizzle of meteorites from outer space that sometimes burned while still in the stratosphere and sometimes reached the seminar ground in a more or less smelted form.

Spaces and Semispaces

It has often been argued that communism failed because it did not succeed in completely annihilating the private sphere as it intended to do (Raichev 198). After the changes, one of the continuations of this argument could be found in the East/West debate about feminism, or rather about the Eastern resistance to feminism.[10] This debate centered on a discussion of the public/private distinction (displacing, in most cases, the Habermasian terms that were supposed to provide its background), with Westerners frequently assailing and Easterners frequently defending the political importance that the private space acquired during the totalitarian regime. In the latter case, the family was conceptualized as a reserve of alternatives to the repressive political apparatus. According to this argument, the family was that private area where people could find refuge from the control of the state, and as such it was the locus of solidarity, rather than confrontation, of the sexes in their common resistance to the alienating political structure (Havelkova; Marody; Siklova, "Feminism"). As one commentator characteristically put it: "Political discussions were conducted around the kitchen table, the home represented the only place for open discussion like this; it was here rather than in any public sphere that the possibility for transcendence occurred" (Sharp 102).

This optimistic position, which is, perhaps, meant to demonstrate the readiness of the Central European middle-class family for European structures, ignores the somewhat more complicated history of gender manipulation that the different communist regimes implemented.[11] With this history taken into account it has been argued that, on the contrary, the duplicity resulting from a private life that was cynically distanced from the totalitarian public sphere in fact sustained the regime (Salecl 3). The family, with its sacrosanct private life, was part of the duplicity. Further, it could be argued that at least in some of the countries, the traditional structures of the family reproduced the conditions that made society as a whole susceptible to the charms of fundamentalist and totalitarian attitudes, be they communist, fascist, or nationalist. Still other accounts insist on the impossibility of reducing the problem of the sustainability of communism to the private/public dichotomy. The public space, to begin with, was not really public. It was an "as if" publicity and an "as if" space that has been described as "theatrical" or "make believe" (Bunzhulov), as spurious, ritualized, and flat. This quasi-public space of never-ending buffoonery could be approached through the distinction that Peggy Watson has recently introduced between understanding political space in "Newtonian terms" as a mere container, a void in which commensurable and autonomous agents move, and in "Einsteinian terms," where actors "constitute, as they are constituted by," a specific political space ("Rethinking"). Viewed in an "Einsteinian" perspective, the "as if" public space of "negative but equal citizenship" (Watson, "Civil" 25) that characterized the space of communism would appear as the product of a specific bifurcation of the political "gravitational field." This spurious space would be "constituted" by "negative citizens" who exert no gravity and have no mass or weight of their own. These citizens of spurious publicity would be equal in their weightlessness. Their commensurability would be the commensurability of shadows. As phantoms, they would partake of the equality in the land of the dead. They would be like the "dreams of a corpse" (Todorov, *Red* 4).[12] Their space would not simply be absolute in the terms of Newton and Einstein. It would be the space of Elysium.

On the other hand, there was the presumable locus where real discussion, real decisions, and real power were exercised: the dreaming corpse itself, the "mummacrum of power."[13] Behind the gravitationless space of phony publicity there was the "black hole" of utter opaqueness and absolute gravity. Havel described this still center of omnipresent control (the hidden source of discursive monopoly) as the place where "the center of power [was imposed as] identical with the center of truth" (25). The inscrutable folding in upon itself of this invisible space might be termed conspiratorial, and its genealogy might very well take us to the history of Russian terrorism and, beyond it, to the specific manipulation of representation that terrorism involves (Todorov, "Teror"). Suffice it to say at this point that what appeared as public space was the façade of a "privatization" of political representation by the party headquarters and involved a conspiratorial bifurcation of the "privatized" public domain into, on the one hand, the weightless, theatrical spuriousness and, on the other, the invisible black star emitting the ghostly show. If the quasi-publicity of communism presented such convolutions of space, it is hardly surprising that the so-called private space to which commentators tend to attribute the dual function of subverting and containing communism was no less ambiguous.[14]

Whatever this formation was to begin with, it did not stay put but grew into a sort of silent duplicate of the public-cum-conspiratorial space. The economic aspects of this shadowy area have been referred to as the "gray network." Beyond economy and the exigencies of overcoming deficits, however, there lay the further capacity of this quasi-private space to veritably duplicate both the "make-believe" and the conspiratorial roles, relations, and hierarchies with its own. Deficits would be overcome through "buddies"; dissidents would be saved by "uncles" and "aunties" who happened to operate one of the few state-controlled copy machines that would keep *samizdat* going. Because of its reduplicating power this pervasive formation was called the "second network" (Raichev). In its last stages, the regime was acutely aware of the danger and tried to counter it by identifying it as the "little truth" and opposing it to the great communist truth. The fear was well grounded because, unlike parrhesia, the "little truth" (which ultimately was the truth of survival) was silent, cautious, cunning, and ubiquitous. The second network offered no discourse; it was indifferent to discursive resistance.[15] This made it, in sharp contrast to parrhesia, practically immune to a persecution obsessed with discursive control.

The seminar might be seen as owing the very possibility of its existence to this particular failure of the system. Ensuring through the Dubcek-Gorbachev fallacy a sort of buffer in the conspiratorial structures (i.e., there were apparatchiks that supported the seminar because they wrongly believed the regime could coexist with freedom of speech), the seminar created its own network and thus struggled to create its own space. Dimitrina Petrova (a philosopher, one of the founders of Ecoglasnost) rightly noted in conversation with me that we had come to a point where having a prestigious standing in the seminar was widely considered more important than having an official career. The seminar disregarded not only the party hierarchies that were deemed more and more unacceptable but also the academic ones. Some of the participants had academic positions, others did not; selected students took part in the seminar on an equal basis. Key figures who ensured the seminar's functioning through their connections in the conspiratorial space were treated with open hostility and disdain, and yet they continued to attend the seminar and to take part in its discussions so that the very hostility they had to counter was articulated as part of the ongoing debates. Should one emigrate? Should one go underground? Should one make a party career and change things from within? The seminar opposed all these traditional options for Eastern intellectuals and insisted on opening its own "impure" space. Parrhesiasts appeared and flourished in this new environment. And yet parrhesia as exemplified by Havel was only one of the discursive games that the seminar nourished. Before I look into the topological operations that accompanied these games, one further aspect of communist space deserves to be mentioned.

Erotization: The Third Sex

What most accounts of space during communism omit, I believe, is the mystery of erotization. As a much more logical discursive machine than the French bourgeois revolution, communism resolved the paradox created for women by the "rights of man" discourse by giving women rights (spurious and theatrical as they were) insofar as they were men. There could be no "woman question" and no feminism if women were to have rights. In order to have rights, women had to not exist. More precisely, they had to be preserved only as a moment in an ever-increasing maleness according to the formula Men-Women-Men. Unlike Claude Lévi-Strauss's account of the exchange of women, here it is both men and women who take part in the circulation of exchange, where men, by analogy with Marx's formula of capitalism, Money-Commodity-Money, take the place of the forever-increasing capital and women are the commodity that mediates this increase (Popov). This is the *differencia specifica* of the new world of communism. Instead of capital, it produces the new man, Man. Man is, in fact, a new and third, sex that has reappropriated his rib (Todorov, *Red* 83) and whose genitals are symbolically represented by the intertwining of the hammer and the sickle (Popov 174).[16] Man is hence a self-sufficient creation that sustains itself in "a sort of intertwined, ejaculating but somehow permanent erection" best exemplified by Vera Mukhina's famous sculpture of the worker and the peasant (Popov 174). The creation of Man was dictated by a project to do away with sexuality altogether. As Andrei Platonov characteristically put it, "Having found the Good in the sexual feeling, people were petrified" (quoted in Todorov, *Red* 82). To combat this general petrification, communist regimes at their inception were very repressive of sex. Youthful folly was not tolerated, and adultery was punished through workers' collectives, frequently resulting in the blocking of professional and party careers. The trajectory that led from this repressiveness to the sexual laissez-faire of the later decades of communism still needs to be elucidated. I am not sure about the extent to which this trajectory was specific to Bulgaria. Aware as it was that the country had produced no serious challenges to the regime in the way Hungary, Czechoslovakia, and Poland had, the seminar offered an ironic view of the consecutive outbursts of sexual excess as the specific Bulgarian response to the dramatic political events in the other countries of the region (Ditchev, "Erotica" 156–57).

Whatever the reason, there was a clear overall tendency toward sexual liberalization. Moreover, it is clear that the workplace was the locus of the loosening of morals. In general, the workplace became a huge and blurry border between the various spaces already mentioned. It was heavily infiltrated with conspiratorial monitoring, and at the same time it sheltered a most amazing display of the pompous spuriousness of the public space in that it was expected to produce the working class as "leading metaphor of party ideology" rather than producing goods. Yet it was also a place continuously and systematically "appropriated" by the "gray" networks, which corrected, so far as possible, the deficits typical of the regime. The coded erotization participated in the privatization that positioned the workplace midway between work and leisure.[17]

The workplace thus became the locus of consumption and sexualization. Notoriously, during communism one went to work in order to chat, flirt, hear the latest political jokes, and do one's shopping through the gray networks. Work also occupied a hybrid position with respect to the conceptualization of gender. While the conspiratorial structures were almost entirely dominated by the male phratry[18] and the private sphere of the family was allowed to stick to its traditional patriarchal roles, work was the place where women were comparatively free from both the state and the family patriarchies. This was a mute tendency, however, that lacked any clear articulation. Thus, while the private sphere had its age-old articulation of roles (boys will be boys), and while the male conspiratorial structure emitted its make-believe third-sex messages (we are all equal because we are all Men), the workplace as the only place where practical redefinitions of gender happened was never—given the communist ban on any serious discussion—provided with a language for its gendered aspects. It operated through an indiscriminate mixture of the traditional and the official discourses and, since it was not easy to reconcile them, resolved the conflict in a sort of carnivalesque way. This multiple layering can be exemplified through the manner in which March 8 was celebrated. The state offered its repetitive tedious speeches on the equality it had granted to women in making them as good as men; husbands and lovers spent the day in endless lines to buy flowers (for even in cases like this the deficit was insurmountable); and workplaces, with or without the men in them, booked all restaurants or, even better, used their offices to organize veritable spring orgies in honor of the "day of the female colleague."

No matter how specific, the seminar was a workplace. It thus shared—and expanded—the hybridity that characterized the communist workplace. As already mentioned, the seminar indiscriminately occurred in institutional buildings with the consent of official authorities and then spilled over into private apartments that became the site of discussions, expositions, theater and opera performances. Sometimes all this seemed to be part of the educational system; sometimes it looked like a perennial party. Because the idea of working or office hours was lost in the process, the seminar amounted to round-the-clock cohabitation. The most brutal comment on this relentless eroticized togetherness is, perhaps, Ivaylo Ditchev's image of the Siamese twins joined forehead to forehead in a sort of perennial and inexorable cerebral copulation (Ditchev, "Literalisms"). The "promiscuous closeness" of the seminar functioned nevertheless as a verbal "exhausting of the drive" (both phrases are Vladislav Todorov's). Volumes of commentaries were produced on Plato's *Symposium,* on Marsilio Ficino's commentaries on the *Symposium,* and on eroticism throughout the ages and in any imaginable context. The philosophical Eros. The Eros of antiquity. The erotic world of the medieval person. An essay on the erotization of ethics. The *ars erotica* of conversation. Of reading. Of everyday existence. The erotic and communication. Rhetoric and the erotic. The Eros of communism. As a "knight of the prosthesis" (Todorov, "Eros" 219), Eros was an Eros of discourse—"Eros is the engine of conversation" (Katsarska 9)—and an Eros of distance, after all (Yanakiev 19). The verbal handling of the erotic gave rise, in its turn, to a series of essays on "writing and seduction" that brought into focus a select company of literary seducers notorious for their fear of sex (Damyanova; Stambolova). Krassimira Krushkova's pun on Wittgenstein's famous ending of *The Tractatus Logico-Philosophicus*—"whereof one cannot speak, thereof one must quote" (95)—turned the (men's) lips into "quotation marks" and provided an ironic summing up of the seminar's oral eroticism.

Hence, the seminar both shared and articulated, with various shades between sublimity and parody, the erotization that characterized the workplace. The result was that academic structures and, more important, the function that the regime ascribed to intellectuals were "privatized," and private life (whatever private life meant—during communism—sex, the family, or friendship) was expropriated and all but erased. In practice, the seminar left no time for private life and assimilated it into its perpetual activities. Friendships, coupling, and everyday concerns swam in this soup as little pieces of unstable vermicelli. An odd state of affairs, to be sure. And yet a certain type of hybridization (if hybridization is sufficient to denote this impure nexus) may be both unavoidable and constitutive of some specific places that have to allow for the appearance of the unfamiliar, the different, and the unforeseen.[19] Before being anything else, Eros is the *daimon* of the "impure," of the productive in between (Irigaray).

An Aside with Some Figures

The first big split in the communal and communicative ethos of the seminar occurred when in 1992 one of the young participants, Amelia Licheva, pointed out that the post-totalitarian accounts of the seminar systematically erased the participation of women.[20] The response that she received was, generally, that it was so because . . . it was so. Since it is highly unlikely that anyone will take the trouble of seriously reconstructing who attended seminars and how often, who spoke and how often, I decided to attempt to create some statistics based on the collections that, after the changes, were published from the seminar proceedings. The participating women turned out to be around 30 percent of the group—more than the women in the last communist parliament.[21] After the changes there was an attempt to revive the glorious past with a weekly seminar on "media and myths." Two collections came out of it, with women's participation dropping to between 4 and 5 percent, a figure much lower than the percentage of women in the Bulgarian post-totalitarian parliaments.

Out of the seminar proceedings, only men succeeded in publishing books and collections in other languages (English, German, Hungarian). The general impression is that they had less trouble becoming academically internationalized once the changes allowed this. Women from East European academia came under considerable pressure—both ideological and economical, for there was the question of sheer survival—to drop the dusty books and turn to the green tree of life (i.e., violence against women, sexual abuse, and sexual harassment).[22] The pressure of imposed priorities tended to treat East European women as empirical objects of anthropological enquiry and should be recognized as one of the (more or less) silent components of the East European resistance to feminism, with feminism being for the most part wrongly perceived as a monolithic doctrine of one sort or another rather than as a field of contention that cuts across any problem and debate.[23] After more than ten years the scene, insofar as gender is concerned, has changed beyond recognition. Peggy Watson is fully justified in noting that the masculinization of post-totalitarian societies had a logic of its own but that logic was also enhanced through structures imported, as Joan Scott points out, by sponsoring agencies that showed little sensitivity to the intellectual history of the region (Watson, "The Rise"; Scott, "Fictitious").

Elysium or Absolute Space

The man to whom this essay is dedicated was a parrhesiast. He went through all the hell of communist persecution (the interrogations, the mental clinic, the confiscation of his property, the harassment of his family after he left) because of (among other things) a protest letter he wrote in the late 1960s to Todor Zhivkov, the Bulgarian government and party leader for over thirty years. With the help of the "second network" and the international attention he succeeded in attracting, Marinov was eventually allowed to leave the country. His quarrel with communism, spectacular, ingenious, and full of mischievous invention as it was, came nevertheless accompanied by a *theory*—a theory of fundamental physics, as it happened. Stefan Marinov was a physicist who believed that Einstein was wrong. He was convinced that the speed of light was not the ultimate possible speed, that space was absolute and hence not curved by the mass of bodies, and that perpetual motion was conceivable and could be implemented.

After leaving the country Marinov became an active participant in clandestine anti-Einstein movements. He came to visit Bulgaria in the summer of 1997 at a time when the changes were apparently becoming irreversible. After the visit, he attended an international conference in Greece related to his scientific preoccupations. On returning to Graz, in Austria, where he had been living on welfare for many years, he wrote three lucid farewell letters explaining that he had lost all hope that he would live to see Einstein refuted and jumped to his death from the roof of the local library.

This death was Marinov's last demonstration of his uncanny parrhesiastic gift for leaving no space between thinking, speaking, and doing. Through it, Marinov offered a reading of the concurrence of his political and scientific defiance. If the fall of communism rendered Marinov's scientific agenda meaningless, it turns out that his theory of space was his form of resistance to communism. His subversive stance took on a theoretical cast. Through physics, Marinov was positing a topology of antitotalitarian subversion. With the space of communism collapsing, his theory of space lost sense—or at least so it seemed to him.

Through this parable, all too neat perhaps, I am trying to bring into focus my belief that it is not that easy to sort out parrhesia from thinking differently, Havel from Mamardashvili. In the perspective of the seminar, Marinov's absolute space—the space that might give room to weightless citizens and a perpetuum mobile to resistance—discloses a certain necessity.

The seminar would not exist without something that might be described as the ear of the absolute. A sort of librarian's or virtual Elysium, the seminar enacted the shadowy space of the dead. Walking through asphodel fields, it was absorbed in perennial discussions that would draw along anyone from Plato and Gaspara Stampa to Derrida. That the former were dead and the latter still living made no difference to the attentive cosmic ear in which the shadowy whispering finally coalesced. Like Dante in his dealings with the netherworld, the seminar felt no duty to distinguish between the living and the dead. It perceived its utterances as disembodied voices communicable through a vibrating medium that presented no obstacle. Its ethereal universe suspected no hierarchies, borders, or compartmentalized zones. It was a world of thorough transmittability. We could overhear anything and imagined ourselves overheard (in an unwitting positivization of paranoia) from any given point in the continuum. The seminar was a perpetuum mobile of entwined, spiraling voices that, having once reverberated, would resound forever. It was a panphonia that would never fade away but only get richer and fuller. And while linguistic and translation problems were debated in the minutest possible details, the idea of language never disturbed our conviction that, in writing and speaking Bulgarian, we inhabited the same dimension as the texts that we read (in whatever language) and passionately referred to. The seminar positioned itself under an absolute decoding machine that would allow no sign to remain unseen, unheard, and unread in the horizon of eternity.

Juri M. Lotman, the legendary semiotician from Tartu, provided us with an elaborate structure of this ultimate cosmic decoder, this apex where the multitudinous discursive witnesses attain their final hearing. Within and beyond the punctilious exploration of various sign systems, Lotman's work on what he defined as "semiosphere" is obsessed with the indestructibility of meaning. Meaning may be hidden, it may undergo changes and transformations (and we should study how they happen), it may get condensed and rarified, and it may acquire or lose dimensions through its interweaving with other meanings. Yet it never really disappears. Nonsense, noise, uproar, amnesia, the perfect eraser, or sheer stupidity (for it does exist after all) are of the order of illusion. Networks over networks of meaning intersect in an infinite horizon of actual or potential readers. Sooner or later, here or elsewhere, they will be read. Nothing will be forgotten. No one will be forgotten. It will all vibrate on atomic, subatomic, stellar, and nebular levels. It is built into the elements. Even dead, it will survive the monody of your one-tone message and, encoded, it will gush into the all-comprehending machine.

A Note on the Leap from the Library

The above description could serve as a description of the library or, alternatively, of cyberspace. The library, with or without reference to Borges, was one of the recurring themes of the seminar. That Marinov chose to kill himself by leaping from the roof of the library is a message I will choose to leave without comment here.

Logobiosis

Incorporation—the term through which I tried to designate the mysterious overlapping of Havel and Mamardashvili in what Foucault's discussion of parrhesia has unraveled as an "ontological harmony" between logos and bios—is an imperfect and rather misleading translation of one of the many neologisms of the seminar. This neologism, *obzhivyavam,* comes from the Bulgarian word for "live" and might be rendered as something like "to surround with life by being surrounded with the life of" or "to make something (a concept, a theory, a situation, a place, or whatever) part of my life, to assimilate it and introject it in my life by infiltrating it with and penetrating it with my life; to take part in the life of something by letting it take part in my life; to live in by letting be lived in." The root for "life" should not be taken too dramatically, however. The word does not imply some irrational overwhelming life force. Neither should the prefix, meaning something like "around" and "about," be taken too extremely. In regular cases when this prefix appears it usually adds the idea of a certain gliding motion that covers and traverses the space that the motion concerns without implying, however, the complete siege or capture of this space.

In fact, this neologism for "living about and around" was almost interchangeable with another neologism, *obgovaryam,* which attached the same prefix to the word for "speak." You surround something with your speaking, you speak around and about it, you gently embrace it on all sides with your words, and it thus becomes a part of your speech. Unlike other seminar neologisms that tended to emphasize extreme and excessive states and actions ("inflammation," abscess," "cutting up," or "engulfing"), "living around" and "speaking about" have a quiet aspect that suggests a touch, a gliding skin-to-skin, and a tender, although also thorough, movement from the unfamiliar to the familiar and from the distant toward the close. From that point of view, these terms might be regarded as antonyms of defamiliarization, of *ostranenie.* Could a combination between "lure" and "embrace"—not too tough and not too rough—indicate this movement? You enter a new house, and you lure it into your existence by embracing it with your life and your speech. You hear a new word, and you lure it into your thinking by embracing it with your life and your speech. You go to a foreign country, and you lure it into your biography by embracing it with your life and your speech. In all this, it is the strange that is being drawn closer; it is the unfamiliar that is being gently charmed in. Living as luring and speaking as embracing are hence inherently impure—they are the impurity of space per se.

These words turned out to be untraceable in terms of their origin. Some thought they invented them. Others thought they might be coming from terms in Alfred Schutz and his concerns with everyday life. Still others believed they might be existentialist terms of one sort or another, maybe from Heidegger. No one was sure of the definitions, and the suggestion was to go back to their uses in whatever seminar texts had been preserved. Vladislav Todorov, to whom I have frequently referred throughout this essay and who was the author of a great number of the seminar neologisms, thought there was no point in trying to track down the origin or, indeed, the meaning of these words. "The words that we were using then," he wrote to me, "had an erotic rather than a conceptual function. They were an object of desire rather than of knowledge; their value lay in pronouncing them and even ceremoniously shouting them, so that they caused somatic rather than semantic vibrations, something like inhabiting a secret, collective, sonorous ontos."

Todorov's injunction not to look for the meaning of the words comes, in fact, very close to what I believe the words mean. It evokes a cohabitation and a lived togetherness through the agency of the somatic and erotic reverberations of speaking. The indestructibility of meaning, of the meaning that is read by the absolute ear and that, via the wide arc of the political, the erotic, and the quasi-religious, enables the "thinking polyphony" turns out to be, in Todorov's description, an effect of reverberation. So are we back to the enigma of the *phoné,* of Bakhtin's polyphony not so much in the terms of some general dialogism but in terms of his idea of the "internal" proliferation of the "word" through the inscrutable agency of the "voice"? Bakhtin's "word" is an irreducible twist of reverberating multiplicity. Polyphony was his theory of the hope that the monological word of the master discourse will never be able to withstand the infraction of the *phoné,* of the indestructible explosive potential of voicing. Recalling that Gorbachev's terms that proved so lethal to the system were "glasnost," a term that echoes Bakhtin, and "perestroika," a term derived from Lotman, one might make a strong case in favor of the theoretical *logobiosis,* the symbiosis, that is, of living and thinking in the *phoné*. Logobiosis would thus name the luring of the unfamiliar and the new into the reverberating borders of multiple dialogic voices. I will stop short of this optimistic conclusion, however, in order to take heed of some further sounds and echoes.

Knock, Knock, Knock

One of the weirdest of the many weird texts that the seminar produced was Ivan Stanev's "farce" *Performance and Punishment,* which provided a rather dark and caustic comment on the seminar's preoccupations. The farce is written in the form of Old Greek tragedy, or rather cantata, for we are back to the very beginnings of drama here, with just a chorus and its leader on stage, a fitting dramaturgical description of the seminar situation. This hybrid between Samuel Beckett and Aeschylus stages (or at least claims to be staging) a paradigmatic nineteenth-century novel about agency, presenting the totalitarian metamorphosis of the utmost transgressive act. While in Dostoyevsky's novel *Crime and Punishment* murder is the crime, in Stanev's farce it is an obscene violation of language that verges on the imbecile.

In Dostoyevsky's novel, the protagonist Raskolnikov commits a senseless murder in order to prove his exceptionality and become Napoleon; he does not become Napoleon but is reborn as a moral individual, a "new man." *Crime and Punishment* is a classical rendition of the well-justified Russian anxieties concerning the road from theory to violence, following as it does the metamorphosis of "Western history" into "Eastern theory" and, beyond it, to terror. A later modernist reworking of this Russian obsession takes the murderer not to moral salvation but to the madhouse. Leonid Andreev's protagonist of *The Thought* has eventually to realize that he does not know whether he murdered to prove the impeccable power of his logic or whether his logic was the cunning of the madness that drove him to murder. Stanev's farce, however, corrodes any remnants of the grand drama of thinking and theory. With just the chorus and its leader playing all the parts, it does not become clear who (Raskolnikov? the Messiah? the playwright himself?) is murdering whom (Dostoyevsky's old usurer? a mysterious Sybil? an idea?) and whether the murder ever takes place in a final sort of way or is something repeated ad infinitum. At the very end, the only "persona" envisioned by the directions, the "Messiah," appears as a *deus ex machina,* turning the plot into a sort of slaughterhouse *Waiting for Godot* and repeating the "knock, knock, knock" that recurs throughout the play, with doors opened to murderers who sometimes seem to be entering and killing, sometimes not. The materialization of the Messiah does not help resolve the question of who has been knocking all along (the secret police? the dreaming corpse in Moscow? the end of history?). In fact, the Messiah's bloodthirsty "agency" looks like the half-witted excretion of "performance" itself. Thus while the somewhat obtuse chorus, a fairly unflattering representation of the collective intelligence of the seminar, is wondering whether the murder of some unspecified "idea" is not its own inadvertent doing, the play seems to "perform" the butchering of the "idea" through the very operation of its disintegrating language.

So much for the crime. What about the punishment? Is it in the turning of "what's been talked about for too long" into reality? In a last reference to the seminar's legitimate (and not that legitimate) uses of Foucault—and against my own promise to bracket the "outside"—I will invoke the description of the communist regime as "heterotopia" (Bunzhulov). Unlike utopias, which are imaginary spaces, heterotopias are, according to Foucault, "counter-sites, a kind of effectively enacted utopia in which the real sites, all the other real sites that can be found within the culture, are simultaneously represented, contested, and inverted" (24). For Foucault, the heterotopia is like a mirror, and Bunzhulov emphasizes precisely the function that the communist regime had of mirroring—by "representing, contesting, and inverting"—the structures of "normal societies." This mirroring, it is worth recalling, cannot be adequately studied along the lines of postcolonial othering (although, in trying to adjust to unyielding discursive frames, Eastern intellectuals have resorted willy-nilly to postcolonial "subject positions") but rather along the lines of what Nancy Fraser has defined as the "postsocialist" condition: "an absence of any credible overarching emancipatory project" (3). Fraser bewails this absence and joins the general grief over the fact that the East did not hold up the mirror properly and that, in addition, it let it drop. Between the widespread, admittedly premature, rejoicing over the end of history and the no less widespread and no less premature mourning over the end of overarching projects, the ultimate ear into which the impure heterotopic reverberations coalesced has turned out to be deaf after all.[24] *Sic transit* one of the most massive social experiments in history.

NOTES

I would like to thank Joan Scott, Dimitrina Petrova, Vladislav Todorov, Klaus Nellen, Wendy Brown, and Elizabeth Weed for their comments and support. I am grateful for the financial support of the Andrew W. Mellon Foundation, which allowed me to complete this essay as a fellow at the Institute for the Human Sciences in Vienna.

1. "After November 10 the fossils [of the seminar] were uncovered in the basement of the Sofia University" (Ilkov 11). Although many texts were written in the 1980s, few were published during this time, and the seminar was, for reasons of censorship, a mostly oral occurrence. Most of the publications and the controversies took place in book collections and in the press in the 1990s, with some major clashes occurring between "dark blue" and "light blue" opposition to communism, between "postmodernists" and "medievalists," and another one around feminism (no one proclaimed themselves antifeminist in this debate, but men systematically tended to forget about women in their account of events). Part of this already rather bulky writing spilled over into other languages (Kiossev, ed.; Stanev, *Lapsus;* Todorov, *Red*). These books exemplify both what the seminar produced at its most extreme and how it functioned. A tamer echo from the earlier years resulted from a somewhat consternating encounter between the seminar and the "West" that from a phantasmatic counterpart (a specific fruit of our isolation) materialized as a group of leading Foucault scholars who came to a conference in Sofia in 1993. There was a scandal or, to use Kiossev's phrase, a "big misunderstanding": political but also academic. Nevertheless, a collection did come out of it (Brossat et al.). The number of publications in Bulgarian that came directly out of the seminar's auditoriums is hard to estimate. The most extensive studies, both in Bulgarian and in other languages, focus on Ecoglasnost, that is, the final stage when the "seminar" was transformed into a political movement (Aumgartl). After the changes, two weekly magazines, *Literaturen vestnik* and *Kultura,* and the journal *kritika i humanism* provided a sort of continuation of the seminar, but they already reflected the new situation of stratified and fragmented aesthetic, theoretical, and political positions.

2. Gorbachev's term *glasnost* comes from the old Slavonic root for "voice" (*glas*), whose form and meaning have been preserved in Bulgarian. In Russian, the word has an archaic flavor and might take us to nineteenth-century resistance to tsarism or, as I will do toward the end of this essay, to Bakhtin's privileging of the irreducible multiplicity of the *phoné.*

3. "Factories are not built to produce commodities. . . . They are allegorical figures of industrialization. Industry represents the leading metaphor of party ideology and factories are the works of this ideology. They result in a deficit of goods, but an overproduction of symbolic meanings" (Todorov, *Red* 10).

4. The seminar era was marked by a number of seminars on Plato that problematized his "unwritten doctrine" and enacted the classical privileging of the oral over the written (Boiadjiev).

5. There was also a feminist method described in my text: the "method of flinging the book," with Martin Luther and Virginia Woolf as its venerable predecessors (they fling an ink pot at other things, but never mind). An indication that I had struck some communal seminar feeling was the fact that in 1989 I was invited to "tour" a number of different seminars with this text, and between 1990 and 1992 it was published three times (Nikolchina).

6. This tradition, the major Bulgarian proponents of which from the 1960s on have been Nikola Georgiev and Radosvet Kolarov, was related to the Russian formalists, the Prague linguistic circle, R. Jakobson, M. Bakhtin, and J. Lotman. The Sofia University graduates Tzvetan Todorov and Julia Kristeva, who in the 1960s in France acted as mediators for the Western reception of this tradition, became in the 1980s

emblematic figures for the reverse "traffic" of new developments in Western theory toward us.

7. This was a long year, though. Peter Manolov, for example, was forced, through threats concerning his son's life, to leave the country.

8. They are both "works in progress," as much as my own is, so I apologize in advance to the authors for possible misconceptions on my part.

9. Foucault's lectures from 1983–84 are unavailable in print but can be found on the Internet. See <http://Foucault.info./>.

10. "I Don't Know What Feminism Is, but I Say NO," "Why Is There No Feminism after Communism," and "Why I Am Not a Feminist" are titles that sum up the trend (Busheikin; Goldfarb; Marody). On the one hand, it was "we had enough of this emancipation crap during communism." On the other hand, feminism was perceived as on a par with McDonalds and Coca Cola (Siklova, "McDonalds"). The third type of response is not exactly one you can find in writing; it was summarized in private conversation by the daughter of an ad hoc activist as "I am your feminist, where is the money?" Or else, "You want us to be serious about feminism? We have bi-i-ig practice in being serious about Big Brothers (and Sisters)" (Muharska). The result has been that in the situation of the drastic impoverishment of Eastern academia, Western funding has consistently preferred the more compliant NGOs to an academy that remains critical to imposed priorities.

11. In "The Family: How to Use It" the Bulgarian theoretician Nicola Georgiev examines the consecutive ideological shifts in the treatment of gender differences (similar shifts were a common feature of many of the communist countries) in conjunction with the history of the family of Todor Zhivkov, who ruled Bulgaria for over thirty years. Far from either idealizing or underestimating the "uses" of the family, which was always the focus of new strategies of control, Georgiev lays bare the manipulative efforts exerted by the repressive ideological machine precisely in the arena of gender. The state-orchestrated shift from "revolutionary" to more traditional gender patterns is thus seen not as a simple and altogether benign softening of the regime, or, alternatively, as a popular victory that allowed age-old mores to reappear, but as a strategy that consolidated the power of the dictator by bringing into use his own family cum phallic mother, effaced wife, and daughter communicating with the powers that be.

12. Renata Salecl's insistence on the distinction between the "dead father" (empty space of authority) of democracy and the "obscene father" as the authoritarian leader can provide the basis for a distinction between the regime in former Yugoslavia (with its obscene fathers) and the regimes in the Soviet bloc proper where the dead and the obscene father collapsed into a corpse—Lenin's mummy (Salecl 99–101).

13. "Mummacrum" is the "mummy simulacrum." A reminder is perhaps necessary that the mummy of Lenin did take center stage in the quasi public space (Todorov, *Red* 135 and passim).

14. The ambiguity of private and public was a recurring preoccupation of the seminar (Nikolova, "Politanatomiya," *Smisîl i maitseubiistvo;* Subeva).

15. It had its language, of course, the language of cynical duplicity. This was the language that drivers of the comrades used while waiting, the language that journalists in big communist dailies used after work, the language that agents in the Sixth Department (the one dealing with intellectuals) used among themselves, the lan-

guage that everybody used in order to let off steam and go on living. This language survived the regime and played a disastrous role during the transition (Bogdanov; Deyanova).

16. As one of the last 1980s' jokes, the rather obscene collection on the "erotics of communism" where Popov's text appeared was published by the Sofia Institute for Children's Arts and Literature.

17. On the coded and normative "stylized" eroticism of the workplace in Russia (which, I believe, is applicable to other former communist countries) see Zdravomyslova.

18. There is a history to this, too, of course. It is a well-known but insufficiently explained fact that groups and movements that try to seize power readily include women and as readily exclude them when they get power.

19. For example, the classroom as discussed in chapter 14 by Ellen Rooney.

20. As Alexander Kiossev put it in one of the short-lived periodicals after the changes, "A spiritual community emerges only between two and only between men" (quoted in Licheva). After such a statement, the (possible) relegation of women's participation to the "spouses and friends" mentioned in Kiossev's introduction to *Post-Theory* (xvii) seems a positive development.

21. Women were much better represented in the "classicist" and "young Marxian" journals and collections than in the "postmodernist" ones. The exploration of this paradox would, I believe, ultimately take us to questions of time and genealogy. Women are perceived as a threat not in spatial terms but insofar as they disrupt male filiations. Postmodernist perspectives have been the only ones so far to present such disruption as a serious theoretical possibility, hence they are by far more wary of women's input. And yet, as Joan Scott has demonstrated in "Fantasy Echo," being a woman does not warrant a way out from this structural fix. I treat these issues in my book *Smisîl i maitseubiistvo* (Meaning and Matricide).

22. Renata Salecl touches upon this problem in her introduction (1–2).

23. The insightfulness that Joan Scott demonstrates in her paper "Vîobrazhaem: obshtnosti [Fictitious Unities]" is strikingly rare.

24. Globalism seems an overarching project to me. It has already produced and continues to produce its satrapic heterotopias of cultural difference.

Works Cited

Angelov, Angel. "Dialog i dialogizîm" (Dialogue and Dialogism). *Literaturen vestnik* 9 (April 1997): 9.

Bogdanov, Bogdan. "Dneven trud—edin prochit" (A Reading of Dneven Trud). In *Medii i prehod* (Media and Transition). Ed. Georgi Lozanov, Lilyana Deyanova, and Orlin Spasov, 328–41. Sofia: Center for Media Development, 2000.

Boiadjiev, Tzotcho. *"Nepisanoto uchenie" na Platon* (Plato's "Unwritten Doctrine"). Sofia: Nauka i izkustvo, 1984.

Brossat, Alain, et al. *Michel Foucault: Les jeux de la vérité et du pouvoir: Études transeuropéennes.* Nancy: Presses Universitaires de Nancy, 1994.

Bunzhulov, Andrei. "Modernoto obshtestvo i sotsialisticheskata heterotopia" (Modern Society and Socialist Heterotopia). *Kritika i humanism* 3 (1991): 207–23.

Busheikin, Laura. "I Don't Know What Feminism Is, but I Say NO!" In *Bodies of*

Bread and Butter: Reconfiguring Women's Lives in the Post-Communist Czech Republic. Ed. Susanna Trnka with Laura Busheikin, 6–13. Prague: Center for Gender Studies, 1993.

Damyanova, Jana. "Protsesît na samotniya prelîstitel ili stradanieto na pisatelya ot podzemieto" (The Process/Trial of the Solitary Seducer; or, The Suffering of the Writer from the Underground). In *Ars Erotic.* Ed. Orlin Spasov, 66–88. Sofia: Institute for Children's Literature and Art, 1992.

Deyanova, Lilyana. "Nevîzmozhnata kriticheska publichnost" (The Impossible Critical Publicity). In *Medii i prehod* (Media and Transition). Ed. Georgi Lozanov, Lilyana Deyanova, and Orlin Spasov, 240–56. Sofia: Center for Media Development, 2000.

Deyanov, Deyan. "Filosofskoto inakomislie na Mamardashvili" (The Philosophical Dissidence of Mamardashvili). *Kritika i humanism* 6 (1999): 17–38.

———. "Neklasicheskata ratsionalnost kato problemno pole" (Nonclassical Rationality as a Problem Field). *Kritika i humanism* 6 (1999): 5–6.

Ditchev, Ivaylo. "Erotika na komunizma" (The Erotic of Communism). In *Ars Erotica.* Ed. Orlin Spasov, 153–60. Sofia: Institute for Children's Literature and Art, 1992.

———. "Literalisms." In *Post-Theory, Games, and Discursive Resistance: The Bulgarian Case.* Ed. Alexander Kiossev, 3–9. Albany: SUNY Press, 1995.

Foucault, Michel. "Of Other Spaces." *diacritics* 16, no. 1 (1986): 22–27.

Fraser, Nancy. *Justice Interruptus. Critical Reflections on the "Postsocialist" Condition.* New York: Routledge, 1997.

Georgiev, Nikola. "Semeistvoto: nachin na upotreba" (The Family: How to Use It). In *Nova kniga za bîlgarskiya narod* (The New Book of the Bulgarian People), 7–49. Sofia: Sofia University Press, 1991.

Goldfarb, Jeffrey C. "Why Is There No Feminism after Communism?" *Social Research: An International Quarterly of the Social Sciences* 64, no. 2 (1997): 236–57.

Goldsmith, Steven. "The Textual Logic of Democracy: Theory and the Crisis of Representation." In *The Ends of Theory.* Ed. Jerry Herron, Dorothy Huson, Ross Pudaloff, and Robert Strozier, 135–45. Detroit: Wayne State University Press, 1996.

Havelkova, Hana. "Transitory and Persistent Differences: Feminism East and West." In *Transitions, Environments, Translations: Feminism in International Politics.* Ed. Joan W. Scott, Cora Kaplan, and Debra Keates, 56–62. New York: Routledge, 1997.

Havel, Vaclav et al. *The Power of the Powerless: Citizens against the State in Central-Eastern Europe.* New York: Sharpe, 1985.

Ilkov, Ani. *Izvorît na groznohubavite* (The Fountain of the Ugly Beauties). Sofia: Anubis, 1994.

Irigaray, Luce. "Sorcerer Love: A Reading of Plato, *Symposium,* Diotima's Speech." In Luce Irigaray, *An Ethics of Sexual Difference.* Trans. C. Burke and G. C. Gill, 20–33. Ithaca: Cornell University Press, 1993.

Katsarska, Boryana. "Dusha. Eros. Obshtnost" (Soul. Eros. Community). *Filosofski pregled* 2, no. 2 (1992): 3–14.

Kiossev, Alexander. "Golyamoto nedorazumenie. Zapad i iztok, paresiasti, filosofi, polititsi I medii v ikonomikata na istinata" (The Big Misunderstanding: West,

East, Parrhesiasts, Philosophers, Politicians and Media in the Economy of Truth). In *Medii i mitove* (Media and Myths). Ed. Georgi Lozanov and Orlin Spasov, 17–97. Sofia: Sofia University Press, 2000.

Kiossev, Alexander, ed. and intro. *Post-Theory, Games, and Discursive Resistance: The Bulgarian Case.* Albany: SUNY Press, 1995.

Krushkova, Krassimira. "Ustnite kato kavichki" (The Lips as Quotation Marks). In *Ars Erotica.* Ed. Orlin Spasov, 95–99. Sofia: Institute for Children's Literature and Art, 1992.

Licheva, Amelia. "Golyamoto mîzhko priyatelstvo ili ima li neshto obshto mezhdu Robinzon Kruzo, Herman Hese i Aleksandîr Kyosev?" (Sublime Male Bonding; or, What Does Alexander Kiossev Have in Common with Robinson Crusoe and Herman Hesse?). *Kultura,* July 10, 1992, 8.

Marody, Mira. "Why I Am Not a Feminist: Some Remarks on the Problem of Gender Identity in the United States and Poland." *Social Research: An International Quarterly of the Social Sciences* 60, no. 4 (1993): 853–64.

Muharska, Ralitsa. "Mîlchaniya i parodii. Feministkiyat dialog mezhdu iztoka i zapada. Kîde sme nie?" (Silences and Parodies: The Feminist Dialogue between East and West. Where Are We?). In *Maiki i dîshteri. Pokoleniya i posoki v bîlgarskiya feminizîm* (Mothers and Daughters: Generations and Directions in Bulgarian Feminism), 53–61. Sofia: Polis, 1999.

Nikolchina, Miglena. "Postmodernata biblioteka" (The Postmodern Library). In *I prochee* (Et cetera). Ed. M. Abigar, V. Miteva, and H. Todorov, 95–105. Sofia: Sofia University Press, 1990.

Nikolova, Nina. "Politanatomiya na moderniya chovek" (Political Anatomy of the Modern Human Being). *Kritika i humanism* 3 (1991): 91–109.

———. *Smisîl i maitseubiistvo. Prochit na Virdjinia Ulf prez Yulia Krîsteva* (Meaning and Matricide: Reading Woolf via Kristeva). Sofia: Sofia University Press, 1997.

Popov, Julian. "'Za nas kinoto e nai-vazhnoto izkustvo'" ("'For Us Cinema Is the Most Important Art'"). In *Ars Erotic.* Ed. Orlin Spasov, 172–76. Sofia: Institute for Children's Literature and Art, 1992.

Raichev, Andrei. "Migratsionnite obshtestva i vtorata mrezha" (The Migration Societies and the Second Network). *Kritika i humanism* 3 (1991): 195–204.

Salecl, Renata. *The Spoils of Freedom: Psychoanalysis and Feminism after the Fall of Socialism.* New York: Routledge, 1994.

Scott, Joan W. "Fantasy Echo: History and the Construction of Identity." *Critical Inquiry* 27 (2001): 284–304.

———. *Only Paradoxes to Offer: French Feminists and the Rights of Man.* Cambridge: Harvard University Press, 1996.

———. "Vîobrazhaem: obshtnosti—'pol,' 'iztok' i 'zapad'" (Fictitious Unities: "Gender," "East," and "West"). *Literaturen vestnik* 12 (March 2001): 7–9. A version of this article was presented in English at the Fourth Feminist Research Conference (Sept. 2000) in Bologna.

Sharp, Joanne P. "Gendering Nationhood: A Feminist Engagement with National Identity." In *BodySpace: Destabilizing Geographies of Gender and Sexuality.* Ed. Nancy Duncan, 97–108. New York: Routledge, 1996.

Siklova, Jirina. "Feminism and the Roots of Apathy in the Czech Republic." *Social Research: An International Quarterly of the Social Sciences* 64, no. 2 (1997): 258–80.

———. "McDonalds, Terminators, Coca Cola Ads and Feminism?" In *Bodies of Bread and Butter: Reconfiguring Women's Lives in the Post-Communist Czech Republic.* Ed. Susana Trnka with Laura Busheikin, 7–11. Prague: Center for Gender Studies, 1993.

Stambolova, Albena. "Pisane i prelîstyavane" (Writing and Seduction). In *Ars Erotica.* Ed. Orlin Spasov, 60–65. Sofia: Institute for Children's Literature and Art, 1992.

Stanev, Ivan. *Lapsus Linguae: Theaterstücke, Theoretische Lähmungen, Ontologische Gesänge* (Lapsus linguae: Plays, theoretical paralyses, ontological songs). Berlin: Autoren Kollegium, 1992.

———. "Predstavlenie i nakazanie" (Performance and Punishment). In *Izbitite obitateli: Poeziya, drama, teoriya: Iz tetradkite na edin zakîsnyal modernist* (The Slaughtered Tenants: Poetry, Drama, Theory: From the Notebooks of a Belated Modernist), 89–134. Sofia: Virga, 1994.

Subeva, Svetlana. "Kîm kriticheskata istoriya na modernata publichnost" (Towards the Critical History of Modern Publicity). *Kritika i humanism* 3 (1991): 111–22.

Todorov, Vladislav. "Eros, the Knight of the Prosthesis." In *Ars Erotica.* Ed. Orlin Spasov, 219–53. Sofia: Institute for Children's Literature and Art, 1992.

———. *Red Square/Black Square: Organon for Revolutionary Imagination.* Albany: SUNY Press, 1995.

———. "Teror i terorizîm" (Terror and Terrorism). In *Medii i mitove* (Media and Myths). Ed. Georgi Lozanov and Orlin Spasov, 250–59. Sofia: Sofia University Press, 2000.

Vernant, Jean-Pierre. "Mamardashvili, chovekît na slovoto" (Mamardashvili, the Man of the Word). *Kultura,* Dec. 1, 2000, 7.

Watson, Peggy. "Civil Society and the Politics of Difference in Eastern Europe." In *Transitions, Environments, Translations: Feminism in International Politics.* Ed. Joan W. Scott, Cora Kaplan, and Debra Keates, 21–29. New York: Routledge, 1997.

———. "Rethinking Transition: Globalism, Gender, and Class." *International Feminist Journal of Politics* 2, no. 2 (2000): 185–213.

———. "The Rise of Masculinism in Eastern Europe." *New Left Review* 198 (1993): 71–82.

Yanakiev, Kalin. "Vsekidnevniyat svyat na srednovekovniya chovek. Eros i distantsiya" (The Everyday Life of the Medieval Person. Eros and Distance). In *Ars Erotica.* Ed. Orlin Spasov, 19–33. Sofia: Institute for Children's Literature and Art, 1992.

Zdravomyslova, Elena, and Anna Temkina. "Social'noe konstruktirovanie gendera kak feministkaya teoriya" (The Social Construction of Gender as Feminist Theory). In *Zhenshchina, gender, kultura* (Woman, Gender, and Culture), 61–62. Moscow: MZGI, 1999.

CONTRIBUTORS

Rogaia Mustafa Abusharaf is a postdoctoral fellow at the Carr Center for Human Rights at the Kennedy School of Government, Harvard University, and an affiliated scholar at the Feinstein International Famine Center of Tufts University. She is author of *Wanderings: Sudanese Migrants and Exiles in North America.*

Wendy Brown is professor of political science and women's studies at the University of California, Berkeley. She is author of *Politics Out of History* and *States of Injury: Power and Freedom in Later Modernity.* With Janet Halley, she is the coeditor of *Left Legalism/Left Critique.*

Judith Butler, who holds the Maxine Elliott Chair at the University of California, Berkeley, is a professor of rhetoric and comparative literature. Her most recent publications include *Antigone's Claim: Kinship between Life and Death, The Psychic Life of Power: Theories in Subjection,* and *Excitable Speech: A Politics of the Performative.*

Eric Fassin teaches in the Department of Social Sciences at the École Normale Supérieure. His book *Same Sex, Different Politics: Comparative Politics of Gay Marriage* is in press in dual English and French editions.

Susan Gal is a professor of anthropology and linguistics at the University of Chicago. Her recent publications include *The Politics of Gender after Socialism,* coauthored with Gail Kligman; *Reproducing Gender: Politics, Publics and*

Everyday Life after Socialism, coedited with Gail Kligman; and *Languages and Publics: The Making of Authority,* coedited with Kathryn Woolard.

Faye Ginsburg is David B. Kriser Professor of Anthropology at New York University, where she is also the director of the Center for Media, Culture, and History. Her interest in cultural activism and feminist theory is long-standing; *Contested Lives: The Abortion Debate in an American Community,* her first book, is an award-winning study of abortion activism. She has worked with Rayna Rapp since the early 1990s, when they coedited *Conceiving the New World Order: The Global Politics of Reproduction.* "Enabling Disability" is the second article intended to launch a new joint research project on the production of the so-called epidemic in learning disabilities.

Gail Hershatter is a professor of history at the University of California, Santa Cruz, and co-director of the UCSC Center for Cultural Studies. Her publications include *Dangerous Pleasures: Prostitution and Modernity in Twentieth-Century Shanghai* and *A Guide to Women's Studies in China,* coedited with Emily Hoenig, Susan Mann, and Lisa Rofel. Her essay in this volume is part of a larger project entitled *The Gender of Memory: Rural Chinese Women and the 1950s.*

Rosalind C. Morris is an associate professor of anthropology and director of the Institute for Research on Women and Gender at Columbia University. She is also associate editor for the journal *connect: art, politics, culture, theory.* Her book *In the Place of Origins: Modernity and Its Mediums in Northern Thailand* was published in 2000.

Afsaneh Najmabadi is a professor of women's studies and history at Harvard Univerisity. Her English-language publications include *The Story of Daughters of Quchan: Gender and National Memory in Iranian History* and *Women's Autobiographies in Contemporary Iran.* She was also the editor of a special issue, "Wiles of Women—and Men: Literary and Historical Moments," of *Iranian Studies* in 1999–2000.

Miglena Nikolchina is an associate professor in the Department of Theory and History of Literature at Sofia University. She is the author of *Chovekît-Utopia* (The Uţopian Human Being), *Smisîl i maitseubiistvo: Prochit na Virdjinia Ulf prez Yulia Krîsteva* (Meaning and Matricide: Reading Woolf via Kristeva), and *Rodena ot glavata: Fabuli i syuzheti v zhenskata literaturna istoriya* (Born from the Head: Plots and Narratives in Women's Literary History). In English, her essays have appeared in *Semiotica, diacritics, Paragraph,* and *Tessera,* among others.

Zakia Pathak trained and worked for some years as a professional social worker before joining the Department of English at Miranda House, Delhi University, where she worked for twenty-two years. She has contributed essays to national and international publications on feminist pedagogy and the subjectification of women.

Rayna Rapp, a professor of anthropology at New York University, has edited or coedited works that include *Toward an Anthropology of Women, Promissory Notes, Articulating Hidden Histories* and *Conceiving the New World Order.* She is the author of *Testing Women, Testing the Fetus, the Social Impact of Amniocentesis in America.* Active in the reproductive rights movement and the movement to build women's studies in the United States, she considers the intersection of reproductive rights and disability consciousness to be a key site for her new and collaborative research.

Denise Riley's books include *War in the Nursery, Theories of the Child and Mother, "Am I That Name?" Feminism and the Category of "Women" in History,* and *The Words of Selves: Identification, Solidarity, Irony.* Her most recent collection is *Denise Riley: Selected Poems.* She is a reader in the School of English and American Studies at the University of East Anglia, U.K.

Ellen Rooney is an associate professor of modern culture and media and English at Brown University. She is the author of *Seductive Reasoning: Pluralism as the Problematic of Contemporary Literary Theory* and is at work on a book entitled *A Semiprivate Room.*

Joan W. Scott is Harold F. Linder Professor of the Social Sciences at the Instute for Advanced Study. Among her books are *Gender and the Politics of History* and *Only Paradoxes to Offer: French Feminism and the Rights of Man.*

Peggy Watson is a senior research associate at the Faculty of Social and Political Sciences, University of Cambridge, U.K. She has written widely on communism and postcommunism. Among her work is "Politics, Policy, Identity: EU Eastern Enlargement and East-West Differences" for the *Journal of European Public Policy* and essays in *Narrative, Generational Consciousness, and Politics,* edited by June Edmonds and Bryan S. Turner, and *Transitions, Environments, Translations: Feminisms in International Politics,* edited by Joan W. Scott, Cora Kaplan, and Debra Keates.

Melissa W. Wright is an assistant professor in the Department of Geography and Women's Studies at Pennsylvania State University. Her work has been published in journals, including *Cultural Anthropology, Social Text, Public Culture,* and *Environment and Planning.* She is coeditor, with Andrew Herod, of *Geographies of Power: Placing Scale.*

INDEX

The University of Illinois Press
is a founding member of the
Association of American University Presses.

Composed in 10.5/13 Adobe Minion
by Jim Proefrock
at the University of Illinois Press
Manufactured by Thomson-Shore, Inc.

University of Illinois Press
1325 South Oak Street
Champaign, IL 61820-6903
www.press.uillinois.edu